Real Estate "WHEEL OF FORTUNE"

VOLUME ONE

By The Best Selling Authors of
Formerly One Up On Trump **and**
Trickle "Up" Economics
show you how to be a syndication winner too
in Uncle Sam's $400 Billion
Real Estate "*WHEEL OF FORTUNE*"

Stephen J. Murphy **with Dr. Stanley Reyburn**

ACFH

Published by **American Capital Foundation for the Homeless, Inc.**
330 Washington Boulevard, Penthouse Suite
Marina Del Rey, California 90292

Library of Congress Cataloging-in-Publication Data

Murphy, Stephen J.
Real Estate "Wheel of Fortune"

By Stephen Murphy with Dr. Stanley Reyburn

Other books by Stephen Murphy:

Formerly One Up On Trump: How You Too Can Make $$$ Millions in Uncle Sam's $400 Billion Real Estate Firesale!

Financial Wizard R.E.O. OPOLY. . . What They Don't Teach You About Real Estate Finance in Business School.

Trickle "Up" Economics. . . What They Don't Teach You at U.C.L.A. Business School

ISBN: 1-883077-05-2

Printed in the United States of America

Cover design by: Catherine Herold Design
Inside design by: Neil Goldman and Catherine Herold Design

* * * * *

Special Announcement

(Tax Deductible, Charitable Donation to the Homeless)

100% OF THE EARNINGS FROM THE BOOK WILL FUND AND SUPPORT THE INITIATIVES OF THE PRIVATE, NON-PROFIT AMERICAN CAPITAL FOUNDATION FOR THE HOMELESS, A CALIFORNIA NON-PROFIT CORPORATION. YOUR PURCHASE OF THIS BOOK IS A 100% TAX DEDUCTIBLE, CHARITABLE DONATION TO THIS FOUNDATION. THIS ORGANIZATION IS COMMITTED TO PURCHASING REO HOMES AND APARTMENTS ACROSS AMERICA, TO PROVIDE HOMES AND NEW LIVING REHABILITATION PROGRAMS FOR THE MANY THOUSANDS OF AMERICANS WHO ARE OFTEN FORGOTTEN BY SOCIETY, AND OFTEN BESET BY THE DISEASE OF DRUG/ALCOHOL ABUSE. WE BELIEVE THAT THE BEST INVESTMENT THAT WE CAN MAKE IS IN OUR OWN PEOPLE. WE ARE HONORED AND PRIVILEGED TO HAVE THIS RESPONSIBILITY.

AMERICAN CAPITAL FOUNDATION FOR THE HOMELESS HAS ALREADY PURCHASED TWO HOMES AND AN APARTMENT BUILDING IN LOS ANGELES, CALIFORNIA AND NEW HAVEN, CONNECTICUT, AND HAS DONATED THE USE OF THEM TO HOMELESS VIETNAM VETERANS.

AMERICAN CAPITAL FOUNDATION FOR THE HOMELESS
330 WASHINGTON BOULEVARD, PENTHOUSE SUITE
MARINA DEL REY, CA 90292
(310) 822-0005

Praise for Stephen J. Murphy's *Formerly One Up On Trump, Financial Wizard R.E.O.OPOLY, What They Don't Teach You About Real Estate Finance. . .,* and *Trickle "Up" Economics.*

"The honesty, integrity and the in-your-face boldness of Mr. Murphy really manifests itself with every turn of the page. A truly enlightening source of financial know-how and, frankly, a whole lot of fun to read. Bravo, Mr. Murphy, on your book and on your amazing life."

—Johnny Nam

"Outstanding. This book is full of energy and knowledge. I can now put one foot forward in the right direction of financial success and freedom. Thank you, Stephen."

—Debora Wright

"Incredible book. Detailed and complete without being drudgery. I regard it as, quite simply, my blueprint to financial success. Thanks a million."

—Timothy L. Meck

"As an investment manager of real estate portfolios in excess of $300 million, I am happy to see Stephen Murphy's recognition of the market factors that affect real estate ownership. His synopsis of the political, stock market, and business cycles affecting the real estate market are both accurate and interesting. With the continued application of these principles coupled with his quantitative procedures, his portfolio and its returns should continue to grow."

—Shelby E. L. Pruett

"I found the book contains a lot of information helpful to me, a beginner. I hope to use the information in the future."

—Steve W. Gorzalski

"Thank you, Stephen Murphy, for showing the average investor how they can participate in real estate profit opportunities."

—Paul Ritkouski

"Great stuff!!!"

—Al Standish

"You think you know it all, then Steve comes around and writes a new chapter! Good stuff!!"

—Steve Murray

"A must read for any real estate professional. The most comprehensive due diligence how-to-book on the market."

—Walter F. Johnson

"Up to the minute, current and far-sighted outlook for real estate entrepreneurs."

—John S. Ray

"I've read a lot of books and listened to a lot of tapes and some have been good, but One Up On Trump *was great. It was everything I thought it would be. The cost was ten times worth the contents and cause!"*

—Alvino J. Enteria

"I have just received the book, but a quick perusal indicates it is an excellent publication."

—D. Hawley

"It's no wonder to understand why Stephen Murphy is where he is today. His book, "One Up On Trump" shows his methodical and least risk approach to how he made it. I have been influenced not only by his knowledge in real estate, but also in his character as a human being."

—Mike Lim

"Excellent, I feel very confident negotiating a residential or commercial piece of property. A must read if you are in the real estate industry. Do not forget this one for your library."

—Kelly J. Dube

"Stephen Murphy has the ability to convey what it really takes to be a success in real estate. He has the insight!"

—Kevin McClosky

"Packs an enormous wealth of information in a concise format. It's very useful for any real estate investor."

—Tim Lysgaaro

"Stephen Murphy's life story was absolutely inspirational! He discovered his purpose in life and after reading his book, so have I ... My future rests, or works with ACI."

—John C. Supp

"You don't need a Master's Degree in real estate to make money, just master this book."

—Eli Pan

"Fantastic "how to" book by someone with real experience. This should be required reading in business school, or at least for all commercial investment brokers! Thank you. "

—Dean Zander

"I learned a lot of information on buying real estate that I did not know before. I would recommend this book to anyone that would like to start buying real estate."

—Welba Keetch

"Stephen Murphy's book One Up On Trump *is a good how-to real estate book in that he provides you with many analytical examples in applying real estate transactions."*

—Michael G. Connors

"Reading this book One Up On Trump *was more exciting than the saga between Donald and Marla."*

—Reddy Kwan

"Best real estate investment book ever written."

—Roger Meneses

"One Up On Trump *is a concise and well-presented guide to benefiting from today's R.E.O. market. The chapters on due diligence and syndication are outstanding. In remarkable detail, Mr. Murphy illustrates how one can profit in this market."*

—Thomas Antic

"Wealth creation not wealth maintenance will save this country in the ninety's."

—Larry Hayes

"I've been involved in renovations of real property for over 12 years, but One Up On Trump *has given me new ideas and much valuable information not previously available to me. It's great!"*

—Joan H. Helch

"I enjoyed reading One Up On Trump *very much. It raised my curiosity of real estate as an investment, but the best part was the cost of the book that the proceeds go to help the homeless."*

—Matt Klepach

"A book every real estate student needs in his library."

—Lonnie Taylor

"The book was very interesting and informing the R.E.O. way of getting into real estate."

—Nathaniel P. Hayes III

"Steve Murphy shows step-by-step in simple English, how the 'average Joe' can go bottom fishing in the real estate market today and make money for the fainthearted he offers participation in A.C.I."

—Steve Nayampalli

"I have really enjoyed Mr. Murphy's book. It is really a Phd. course in making the most in the real estate market, further, I admire what Mr. Murphy's doing with his organization to help those who need a "hand-up." Thanks, Stephen from all of us who have benefited from your book and the example you have given us!"

—Charles Andes

"Having worked in an R.E.O. Department for a major California S & L, I was very impressed with Stephen Murphy's excellent grasp of what really happens in the R.E.O. process."

—Mark Reagan

"I have read all of Donald Trump's books and found them quite informative, but One Up On Trump *is truly the most educational and I feel great about having the proceeds go to a worthy cause."*

—Donna Campisi

"Sound advice that can't help but make you money, and avoid some costly mistakes."

—George Vercelli

"Your One Up On Trump *book gave me valuable information to help me pursue real estate investing in the 90s. Thanks for your information and for setting such a great example."*

—Alan Bercovitz

"I found the book a learning experience, and recommend it highly to anyone involved in real estate."

—Craig Lipton

"One Up On Trump *opened my eyes to opportunities I thought to be out of reach and made me eager to learn more. I applaud Steve's unique approach to helping the homeless...a very worthy and much neglected cause."*

—Rodger G. Caldwell

"The book is right for it's true. Stephen Murphy has applied the proper blend of real estate finance, economics and entrepreneurship to take advantage of the tremendous window of opportunity available in the real estate marketplace in the downturn."

—Douglas J. Graber, C.P.A.

"Unbelievable...the most comprehensive, easy to follow and informative book of its kind."

—Vincent Zito

"Stephen Murphy's research into the real estate market is eye-opening. He has dissected the business and is able to pinpoint a good investment while minimizing risk. One Up On Trump, *four stars ****.*

—John Schoenbeck

"Every real estate investor will benefit from reading the lessons in this book. Stephen Murphy's book puts success within reach of anyone willing to learn the rules and play by them.

—Harry Janoian

"A great book! Very timely."

—Clayton T. Fabeck

"I only wish Financial Wizard *had been available before my first forays into the R.E.O. market. In particular the chapters on case studies and property analysis have certainly helped define and plan any future acquisitions."*

—Dave Jackson

"Stephen Murphy's techniques have shown me how to recognize the different markets and cycles in real estate and how to capitalize on each for the greatest profit possible."

—Cris S. Duliga

"For beginner or expert this is a must for entry into the R.E.O. arena."

—R. Pierrre

"I found the Financial Wizard *to be of exceptional value for the first-time investor like myself. I will definitely recommend it to my friends."*

—Demesto Cedeno

Great book!! Must reading for any R.E.O. investor."

—E. Essick

"Don't take a course in real estate until you first read this book. Finally, a book that you can apply to the real world!"

—Joseph C. Newtz

"I found the book interesting and credible. Good luck to you!"

—Robert G. Fisher

"This book is an eye-opener indeed. I've learned so many facts and knowledge about the real estate market in this one book alone that I'll recommend this book to any serious investor."

—Tony Chen

"I find the book quite educating and beneficial in the real estate profession."

—Jugal Anand

"As a college student facing a rather uncertain job market, I have relied on Stephen J. Murphy to introduce me to the fundamentals of real estate. After studying his book One Up On Trump *I know that I am ready to graduate and succeed in the real estate market. Mr. Murphy, thank you!!"*

—Eric Young

"Very educational for the average real estate investor to get involved in commercial real estate."

—Anthony Brizic

"A 'must' read book for every real estate investor. His insight into the R.E.O. market is fantastic! We'll be investing with him as soon as possible. You should too."

—Carnell Shepard

"The book was terrific! I'm telling my friends , everyone: 'If you only had one option to learn about real estate investments and economics, One Up On Trump *is the option to choose.' It's like a text. I'm looking forward to* Financial Wizard R.E.O.Opoly. *Thanks, Stephen Murphy."*

—Michael Leighton

"Some day Steve Murphy's books will be used in every college as the basic courses in real estate—and analyzing-buying and owning property. Until that time, the man on the street can use it for his/her own benefit and become very well-off financially."

—Lucky Linton

"American Capital Investments, Inc. has with careful research, good judgment, and timeliness, purchased outstanding undervalued commercial Real Estate, resulting in excellent financial returns. A company in the right place at the right time."

—Betty Smay

"ACI has delivered on our investment. Stephen Murphy has done what he said he would. We recommend ACI to our friends for short term gains in the REO market. We're glad we had this opportunity."

—John and Linda Miller

"I invested in REOs with Steve Murphy and made 150% return. This was accomplished in a shorter period of time than any other investment I've made. His savvy insight and uncanny perception of timing and real estate opportunities has made me a much wiser are richer investor."

—Marc Tanner

"Stephen Murphy has increased my investment as quickly as he promised. Small investors should join the American Capital Investments team!"

—G. A. Tobey

". . . Since I have been invested with American Capital Investments, I have been involved in two of their projects, one of which paid 135% profit . . . and the other pays 16% annualized, paid monthly. If you're looking for investments or a place to roll over your IRA — give these guys a try."

—Larry Finan

"Investing with Stephen Murphy and his American Capital Investments, Inc. renews our faith in the American dream. Not only has it proved to be a profitable experience, it is good for the soul. Murphy does not forget from whence he came, and his American Capital Foundation for the Homeless, which benefits from many of his projects is an example for all of corporate America to follow."

—Sheryl Feuerstein

"I was very impressed by the performance of my initial investment with American Capital in the Orlando project. To make 50% in 3 months is almost unheard of with any investment vehicle, and they showed me it was possible with their REO projects."

—Nick Di Paolo

"This is my first year investing with American Capital Investments, Inc. I have found the projects well described, payments promptly distributed and a rate of return that is very good. This appears to be an aggressive organization, well managed, and should yield high profits."

—Robert A. Anderson

"Although I am a very small investor with ACI, they have been very good about keeping me informed about happenings in the world. Their personnel are excellent and knowledgeable."

—Lila L. Fernyhough

"Building for my future was made much easier by affiliating with American Capital Investments, Inc. Stephen Murphy, with his dedicated professionals, has shown perceptive financial skill in bestowing a risk/reward factor very comfortable to live with. To be at the right place at the right time helps. American Capital Investments, Inc. is, and so was I!"

—Richard Van Note

"As investors in American Capital, we highly recommend it to others. Expecting only a 50% return on our first investment, we were pleased with an initial 135% return, enjoy 16% annual interest, and expect additional gains."

—John and Elaine Rohr

"I find R.E.O.opoly *to be filled with creative ideas, a real God-send, to and for the common man."*

—David E. Reeder

"Steve Murphy's commitment to the homeless is exemplary and his knowledge of the R.E.O. marketplace is invaluable. I am a former active duty Marine who really appreciates Stephen's accomplishments."

—Greg Moore

"Stephen Murphy's book, One Up On Trump, *presents an opportunity for the average investor to take advantage of real estate ventures once only available to the wealthy. This book is for anyone interested in exploiting the fabulous real estate opportunities available in today's market."*

—J.T. Leslie

"As a novice real estate investor aspiring to take advantage of the present financial mess in Southern California and the country, I am fired up by Murphy's insights. Thanks for making the complex simple, and the unattainable appear within reach. I now truly believe that fortunes can be made by even the "little guys," like me."

— Leif Olson

"This is an excellent book. I recommend it to anybody who wants to really understand and make money in real estate."

—Meier Dorf

"A lot of information in a short book. Well-written and easy to read. It is a must for anyone who is seriously considering a real estate investment in the near future."

—Bill Crawford

"This book was very well put together and researched. It is also very beneficial and informative. I would highly recommend this book to anyone who needs knowledge on real estate finance."

—Jeff Silvers

"If you ever wanted to learn all there is to know about the real estate business, this book is a must! The information it provides will excite you and keep your dreams alive!"

—David M. Rosalez

"One of the best books in the real estate industry!"

—Homi Farah

"For anyone contemplating an active approach to real estate investing, Mr. Murphy's book in invaluable for understanding the financing aspect from the lenders' point-of-view. Without an understanding of mortgage financing, an investor is at the mercy of mortgage brokers, trust-deed sharks and bankers trying to make up for non-performing loans."

—Ralph Wallace

"One Up On Trump *helped me get to where the money is...'Real Estate.' Thank you, Steve."*

—Kenneth S. Crawford

The book One Up On Trump is exciting and has a lot of information. I, Thomas Landacre swear by this book and it's worth its weight in gold."

—Thomas J. Landacre

"I purchased One Up On Trump *and I just got excited about the potential ACI provides the investor. I'm working on a business plan with other investors. Steve, you'll be hearing from me real soon. God Bless."*

—Patrick Ching

"One Up On Trump *is one of the most fabulous real estate books ever. It helped me to focus on my goals and realize the potential that already lives within each and every one of us."*

—David Thompson

"Stephen Murphy and Stanley Reyburn have a remarkable book in One Up On Trump. *It is a valuable learning experience and will enable both the novice and the experienced investor to develop sure-fire strategies to venture into the R.E.O. market."*

—Robert McLellan

"I believe that your book One Up On Trump *is a very good roadmap to follow and I agree with your views on acquiring real estate in a down market."*

—Ricardo Fornos

"I have read many books on making money in real estate, but none have covered the methods and details of hands-on, how-to as you have in your book, What They Don't Teach You About Real Estate Finance In Business School. *Many thank you's for such great money-making methods and ideas."*

—Lee Barker

"This is the most complete real estate book on the inside workings of the complete transaction from start to finish. Very well written and well thought out. I found your book very easy to understand."

—Danny C. Pollock

"This book has really enhanced my knowledge of the real estate market. And, for a successful investor such as Stephen Murphy to give something back to help the homeless makes him an exceptional humanitarian. I recommend anyone who is interested in real estate investment to purchase this book... Pronto!"

—Steve Thomas

"Not only was Steve Murphy's book One Up On Trump *an incredibly informative book, but it has also helped me re-evaluate my investment objectives. And, I was able to help the homeless at the same time."*

—Drew Zingone

"This is one of the best books I have read on real estate finance. The subject matter covered in this book is very extensive and well-rounded."

—Henry Uy Tong

"I highly endorse this book to anyone seeking information on how to invest in the '90s. The author provides both timely and sophisticated insights on how to succeed in today's marketplace."

— Harold Unruh

"Besides providing a unique lender's perspective Financial Wizard R.E.O. Opoly *carries exacting detail, documentation and dedication to and actual value. A rare show of talent and fair play. Moreover, your books are well produced, no sloppy editing, etc. Great work."*

—Robert Bailey

"Just the concise information I have been looking for."

—Robert S. Young

"Excellent book, very explanatory. Anyone interested in possessing real estate should have this book."

—Robert Irvine

"The book was fabulous! I couldn't put it down until finished. Look forward to getting my hands on more of Stephen Murphy's strategies!"

—Eric K. Aulbach

"I just thought I knew everything about buying R.E.O. properties. These books showed me how little I really knew. An absolute must in any R.E.O. investor's library."

—David A. Rogers

"As a novice real estate investor, I found One Up On Trump *an excellent premier. It introduces a complex world in simple, easy terms that makes the book read like a novel. Don't miss this one, it's worth the read--it is an investment."*

—James R. Dwyer

"A must book to read. Informative, inspirational, and very motivational. Keep up the good work Steve and God Bless you."

—Joseph Pitak

"I was impressed by the completeness of information provided by Mr. Murphy. His honesty and integrity shine though on every page. For a beginning novice investor, this book gives you all the information necessary to negotiate a deal. Mr. Murphy is a "visionary" who is not afraid to share his knowledge with others!"

—Joel Pierre

"Valuable information in What They Don't Teach You About Real Estate Finance In Business School *which we are currently using to prepare an offer on a $2.5m apartment complex. Thanks for your help."*

—John F. Lowe

"I just finished reading Stephen Murphy's book, One Up On Trump for the third time. It is, by far, the best book written to date on real estate, and it can be easily understood by the layman as well."

—Charles Houston

"Great book! A definite guide to the new style of real estate investing. In simple, uncluttered terms, Stephen Murphy explains, how fortunes are made in today's commercial property market. Once again, a must read!"

—Nuldan Supp

"What more needs to be said? Stephen Murphy is a genius. Unfortunately, I bought when the market was up and am now paying for it. With the help of Murphy's One Up On Trump, *I'll never make that mistake again."*

—Doug Wroan

"As a former HUD employee and a Real Estate teacher in the community colleges, both books One Up On Trump *and* Financial Wizard R.E.O. Opoly, *I would recommend all students in real estate and urban planning to read."*

—John Clark Fortson

"Thank you for a fine summary of the true inner workings of real estate finance. I really enjoyed this book."

—Dr. Stan Blair

"We are very pleased with Financial Wizard R.E.O. Opoly *and are using it as a training/reference manual. I have ordered a copy for an associate who also is a construction/commercial real estate loan broker."*

—Jack Doetzel

"There will be more housing for homeless thanks to Mr. Murphy. Political figureheads should stop worrying about notoriety and bureaucratic gratuities and be productive for the needy who unfortunately are the majority."

—Mini Brokerage

"One Up On Trump *is the best book on real estate investing I've seen. It's loaded with insightful, historical trends and up-to-date current events which will influence future investments. It's a great book for a great price and the money goes to a great cause!"*

—Sheldon Gott

"I thought the book gave great insight to the mechanism of real estate to finance. I feel that I gained more knowledge about property financing than I learned in any of my business classes. I want to get all of Mr. Murphy's books."

—Michael S. Barry

"As a Regional Manager for a major brokerage firm I see hundreds of transactions per year. Stephen's method and insights are timely, accurate and cutting edge. His book is a "must" read for experienced and novice (future millionaires) alike."

—Adam J. Petriella

"This book Financial Wizard R.E.O. Opoly *certainly covers the subject very nicely and should help me in future purchases. One Up On Trump... Excellent choice of material and illustrations. It is well written and understandable. It should help me in making a success in real estate."*

—Harry Gerstein

"As a decorated Vietnam vet myself, I found Mr. Murphy's methods for success enlightening."

—Michael P. Walsh

"What They Don't Teach You About Real Estate Finance In Business School *provides one with a wealth of information that would take months of time to research.*

—Marc P. Brenner

"I enjoyed your book What They Don't Teach You About Real Estate Finance In Business School. *Some of the subjects discussed in the book that were well-written, and give a lot of detailed information that a lender or investor would want to know, or financial analysis of existing residential income buildings, shopping centers, office buildings, medical buildings, and industrial warehouses. The subjects are approached from a lender's standpoint, and give a potential investor a lot of insight as to what a lender requires to finance that particular type of property. Special use commercial real estate properties, such as parking structures, mini-marts, bowling alleys, hotels and motels, and mobile home parks, are covered in more general terms. Congratulations Steve, on a well-written book, which will be helpful to many people; and on all the good work you are doing, helping veterans, and the homeless. Keep up the good work!"*

—John Laverne

"One Up On Trump *is a roadway is wise investing. It reveals with extraordinary details how to attain the towering 300% on your investment in just one year. It's wealthy in expertise and valuable information and makes the number one treasure for building your wealth."*

—Luiz Pires

"Wonderful, insightful. I've been in real estate business over 20 years and this book still taught me a lot. I'm very inspired by Stephen's story."

—Steven J. Exley

"I have read two books of Stephen Murphy and must admit that they were both very informative. I would like to pride myself on being knowledgeable in the real estate department for I have read many investors books, but they have never been this informative. I am very interested in helping the homeless and I now see myself doing so with the aid of your books. I am very anxious to read your next book."

—Reverend Stephen B. Perkins

"One Up On Trump *is without a doubt the most impressive book ever written on real estate. In it, Stephen Murphy presents the keys to success to all investors to enter the exciting new market of the R.E.O.s. Mucho kudos to Murphy and ACI!"*

—Robert McLellan

"As an experienced developer and investor I heavily recommend One Up On Trump. *A novice or experienced investor can gain valuable insight on the real estate market today!"*

—Alan Satterlee

"The book teaches us how to invest in real estate in the nineties and how to avoid the pitfalls of the eighties."

—Seng-Hong Jose Lim

"This book is very good. Well worth reading. I will not loan this book to anyone. Wish I had this information years ago!"

—Michael J. Mowles

"Complete, concise, and accurate information on what really works and not what they teach in real estate school a ton of immediately usable knowledge. A '10'."

—Adam P. Von Romer

"Excellent book!"

—M. Mahmood

"The evolution of the Southern California real estate market has created a myriad of challenges for both individuals and corporations. Stephen Murphy's books interpret relevant market cycles and provide the reader with a focused strategy."

—Joseph J. Yeyna

"Top notch. Captivating, hands-on, unique real estate finance manual. Very timely and relevant."

—Jim Mazzone

"One Up On Trump *is great. It is really giving me insight to this huge investment opportunity. It is a call to action for those with enough desire to succeed."*

—Mark Engel

"I have read One Up On Trump *and* Financial Wizard R.E.O. Opoly, *and would like to thank the author for writing these inspiring books! I have had adventurous thoughts about investing in R.E.O. Properties and hope to make a profitable investment this year."*

—Mr. & Mrs. Lou F. Olivieri

"The Financial Wizard R.E.O. Opoly *gave me the inside scoop on bank R.E.O.s. It is worth many, many times the donation."*

—Kevin Herzberg

"I have been ranting and raving about this book to every one of my colleagues in the mortgage industry. Truly horizon broadening!"

—David Winters

"Mr. Murphy's real estate finance book is very practical and to the point, not theory. I started using it the first day to get a commercial loan. He's been there, not just talked about it."

—Raymond D. Pendley

"I highly recommend One Up On Trump *for the small investor or for the first time investor. I particularly liked the comparison between the stock market and real estate cycles."*

—Tom Gian Frisco

"I bought One Up On Trump *about two months ago and read it in two days. It was very interesting, insightful and concise. I have been interested in the REO market for a couple of years now, as the venue for major profit making situations. It just makes sense to me, given lenders' regulatory predicament, that killer deals will be made by investors who pursued the REO market. On that count, the first couple of chapters in your book were very satisfying. You managed to crystallize in an intelligible form, the hodge-podge of information I have picked up from*

seminars, the newspaper, and R/E professionals about why banks and S&Ls must sell, even at their own cost. The thing that surprised me in your book was the length to which you go in explaining the economics of R/E investing. Although, I think at times too much knowledge can be constricting, it was pleasing to find your economic insights were always relevant. As a R/E investor, this is information I can use short term and long term. I must say, I am very excited. There is a nice balance in your presentation here. I have read Trump's The Art of the Deal *and think it is a must read for any dealmaker and serious investor. I think any R/E investor worth their mettle should be investigating* One Up On Trump. *I thought it was great. I look forward to your next writing."*

—Benjamin Innes-Kar

"For the first time investor, it is important that one chooses a company he can trust. American Capital Investments, Inc., had made good on their word and are genuinely concerned about their clientele."

—John Armstrong

"ACI's formula for success is proven – buy undervalued commercial real estate, enhance the value though proper management, physical improvement, and inflationary appreciation, and sell high. In particular, Steve Murphy begins with a knowledge of the commerical REO marketplace, and uses his personal enthusiasm and commitment to success to structure what are clearly winning deals for investors looking for both current income and capital growth."

—Todd Eisenberg

". . . Mr. Murphy is the kind of guy that makes things happen. I had to cash in some of my investments to participate, but I have never looked back and have been kept apprised of the actions and potential for new investments."

—R. Al Morrison

"This was the quickest profit return I have experiences in all my years of attempted investing. A fifty percent return in less than a hundred days is what I call phenomenal. Thank you Steve Murphy."

—Ellen Gaslow

"Steve Murphy and American Capital Investments is the most incredible success story I've seen in 30 years in the Real Estate Investment business."

—Mike Stabach

"Investing in Real Estate never looked better—especially with the business expertise and personal attention shown to the investor, like myself, by Mr. Stephen Murphy, President of ACI, Inc. My retirement this year, from a financial standpoint, looks a helluva lot better than it did just six months ago. Thanks, Steve. 1993 — Here we come!"

—Bill Newman

"ACI is a hard working team that provides true leadership in seeking financial opportunities in today's commercial real estate market. They provide a realistic degree of capital and profit protection, incorporating a traditional environment of honesty and integrity."

—Wil Burkhart

"Since I met Steve Murphy, he has shown me how to make more money than I ever had imagined possible with REOs. He is truly today's MAVIN of Real Estate. He has shown a great concern for fellow mankind and is a real HAMISHAH MENTSCH. If not for his CHUTZPAH, his investors would have to settle for today's CD rates and not benefit from the WHOLESALE Real Estate purchases he's made. What he's done for his clients in an absolute MITZVAH. I would give him an honory membership in our TRIBE. He is an adept investor, great teacher and truly remarkable individual. I hope to be able to continue earning and learning with him in the years ahead."

—Alan Ramer

"Investors in Steve Murphy's American Capital benefit from his ability to find, negotiate, buy, manage — and ultimately sell — commercial real estate. As one of them myself, I recommend his talents as 'visionary,' and I rarely use that word. Some smart money is riding his coattails."

—Mike Geller

"As one of your fellow and smaller investors in the Orlando, Florida and San Diego, Sorrento Valley REO's over a short period of time, approximately three months, your professional marketing methods and strategies have me convinced that investing in REO's through American Capital Investments will certainly be rewarding to all investors regardless of the investment magnitude. I feel your marketing techniques and property management will reap great dividends to those investors who have the visibility, the courage and the financial ability to continue investing with the capital I expect will grow from my current and small investments. Being a veteran myself from WWII, I certainly respect and admire Mr. Stephen Murphy for his unselfish service and donations to and for disabled and impoverished war veterans. Keep up the good work Mr. Murphy."

—Edward Schultz, Jr.

"UNEQUALED EXCELLENCE!" Stephen Murphy has combined wit, talent, tenacity and a never say die attitude toward the pursuit of financial stardom. Relentless efforts have garnered admiration amongst his peers. The right deals just seem to be landing in his lap, and he knows just what to do with them. His genuine concern for his investors puts him a cut above the rest. And his heartwarming rise from adversity makes him truly one of a kind. If more people gave back to society what this man has, our world would be a much better place for all."

—Jeff Solomon

Acknowledgements

The efforts of many are required to produce any great achievement. I am especially indebted to the following person(s) for their own direct or indirect contributions to this book.

To Donald J. Trump, my mentor, a man I admire tremendously for his courage, determination, ambition, and character, for as Martin Luther King, Jr. so eloquently said, "The ultimate measure of any man is not where he stands in moments of comfort and convenience, but where he stands at the times of challenge and controversy."

To Harry Helmsley and Larry Wien, my mentors also, whose vision, persistence, and creativity accomplished for them in the '40s, '50s, and '60s, what American Capital is accomplishing today.

To my mom, Loretta, and dad, Arthur, who taught me the value of hard and careful work, and provided me a wonderful foundation of positive mental attitude and spiritual beliefs.

To my children, Michelle and Mai Ly, whose love for each other and for me has meant so very much.

To my colleagues at American Capital Investments, Inc., whose extra efforts have made American Capital's performance possible but who have received none of the favorable publicity.

To Jesus Christ for all the incredible blessings I have been given in my lifetime, and the spiritual guidance I continually receive.

To John Keaveney, whose spiritual presence and privileged friendship, is a genuine inspiration to me.

To my great friends and colleagues, Jeff Solomon, Major League Properties, real estate broker par excellence; and Cindy Watkins, the best attorney in the United States; without their assistance, American Capital's achievements and success would not have been as great.

To the friends and residents of New Directions, an organization that inspires me daily to care for and always lend a helping hand to the less fortunate.

To John Yzurdiaga, whose high standards of integrity and character served as a very positive influence on me at the crossroads of my life — Thanks.

To Brother Angelo, a great human being and a wonderful earthly spirit.

To the Boy Scouts of America, who provide a wonderful training environment for the next leaders of our country.

To Marty and Maureen Shaunnesy, whose spiritual guidance is a great inspiration.

To Cathy and Rick Herold, whose endless hours of work and dedication have contributed immensely to the production of my books.

To the staff of the Securities and Exchange Commission, the U.S. Treasury Department, the California Department of Corporations, the Internal Revenue Service, and the National Association of Securities Dealers for the documentation that appears in the Appendix. The incorporation of these documents in the Appendix does not in any way constitute an endorsement or approval of any portion of this text by any of the specific agencies mentioned.

And last, but not least, to the United States of America, the greatest democratic country in the world, that provides a free entrepreneurial atmosphere for all Americans to be the best that they can be.

Dedication

DEDICATED TO THE FORESIGHTEDNESS, CONVICTION AND COURAGE OF ALL MY MANY, MANY INVESTORS IN AMERICAN CAPITAL INVESTMENTS, INC., WHO HAVE ENTRUSTED THEIR SAVINGS TO ME AND WHO HAVE SENT HUNDREDS OF LETTERS AND MADE HUNDREDS OF CALLS COMPLIMENTING ME ON OUR HARD WORK AND VERY PROFITABLE RESULTS. GOD BLESS YOU.

Disclaimer

Although the authors have made conscientious attempts to adequately research the material presented in this work, no syndication procedures should be undertaken solely upon this text. Advice should be sought from competent legal and/or tax counsel with respect to any present or proposed syndication venture. The syndication process involves complexities far beyond the capability of most laymen and should only be undertaken with the assistance of expert advice. The information contained herein is merely for the purpose of providing some guidelines and pointing out the possibilities as well as the limitations of syndication.

FOREWORD

Uncle Sam's historic and biggest "Wheel of Fortune" is going on right now!! And whether you know it or not, you've already paid the entrance fee of $8,000 to $20,000 the personal liability tax every American has been forced to pay your share of the $400 Billion S&L Bailout tax bill.

But instead of just continuing to pay out for the inept mismanagement of America's economy, you can compensate yourself for this forced tax loss. You've already paid, so you might as well play!

Uncle Sam's $400 Billion Real Estate "Wheel of Fortune"

Uncle Sam's "Wheel of Fortune" is a "giveaway" program so colossal, so incomprehensible, it's truly unbelievable. Bank's and former S&L's are being forced by the R.T.C. to unload these liquidity-draining, repossessed R.E.O. (Real Estate Owned...the banking acronym for foreclosed real estate due to mortgage default) properties at garage sale prices.

Carrying billions of dollars of foreclosed properties on their books is costing banks and the RTC incredible sums of money every day and, usually without the specialization required to get R.E.O.'s back on their feet, they're desperate to dump them. In some cases, primarily major asset-bearing commercial properties, financial institutions are bending over backwards offering them for pennies on the dollar to any investor able to organize a down-payment of even a fraction of their former value. In other words. . . they want out !!

The long and short of tremendous investment returns

Today, in every real estate marketplace, highly motivated sellers set the stage for fabulous deals (for us, the buyers).

Investors snapping up the assets of these zapped insurance companies, savings and loans, banks and troubled Japanese speculators at prices far below their late 1980's highs recognize that certain areas of American real estate have tremendous and long-term potential.

Sensing opportunities to generate huge short-term profits, top Wall Street firms are also forming billion-dollar funds to buy distressed REO properties. Among them are GE Capital and Morgan Stanley.

However you look at it, Uncle Sam is giving away millions in a veritable real estate "WHEEL OF FORTUNE!"

Get in the fast lane on the road to riches

For any astute investor in this market, R.E.O. presently represents among the most undervalued assets for sale in America. Fortunes are literally being made every day. It's a very wise, excellent investment alternative to balance out a stock-laden portfolio.

Basically, there are two ways you can cash-in on Uncle Sam's $400 Billion real estate "Wheel of Fortune" and amply offset your personal S&L Bill:

1) Buy REO real estate yourself, using your own limited capital, time, and expertise, or

2) Carefully select and join a qualified group of investors, a proven syndication performer who has a track record demonstrating wise acquisitions, sound negotiating skills, excellent performing and very profitable properties, and outstanding property management skills.

My company, American Capital Investments, Inc, demonstrates in exemplary manner all these characteristics and more. . . with acquisitions of more than $50,000,000 at-cost prices (now worth substantially more), in a record time period of less than two years.

The definitive guide to successful syndication in the 90's

This Real Estate "WHEEL OF FORTUNE," a two-volume, 700+ page "bible to syndication investment" is the definitive work on syndication in the '90s.

Whether you do it yourself, or join a profitable syndication team, you'll find out how syndication really works, participant advantages, how to s-t-r-e-t-c-h your investment dollar, acquisition strategies, project selection, negotiation techniques, leveraging power, capital returns, investment trusts, formation considerations, legal requirements, creating equity, management and control, minding the store, allocating capital, due diligence, and maximizing return for the syndication.

A wealth of knowledge from the lessons of history

In many striking ways, the 1990s real estate investment environment mirrors the 1940s. Post-Depression era banks, insurance companies and investment houses, still smarting from the disastrous 1930s, wanted nothing to do with real estate. Even with an abundance of undervalued properties available nationwide, scarcity of financing availability kept buyers at a minimum. In very similar fashion to our 1990s open season on R.E.O. real estate, tremendous opportunities laid waiting for people with the money and acumen to buy.

Thus the stage was set for one of the most celebrated real estate investment syndication teams in history, that of Harry Helmsley and Larry Wien.

The classic case in the building of a syndication empire

The preeminent victory of the Helmsley/Wien syndicate was their acquisition of the Empire State Building, in 1961.

In 1951, the Crowns of Chicago had purchased the pinnacled symbol of the empire state from John J. Raskob's estate, for an unprecedented $51 million, the highest price ever paid for a building. Prudential Insurance purchased the underlying land on which the building stood, for $17 million. The tallest building in the world was also one of the most profitable. Modern technology enabled a bankroll of $10 Million a year in rent, a draw of $2 million from the observation tower, and at least $600,000 annually for allowing television and radio stations to use the antenna. After operating expenses and a million dollars each year to Prudential, the Crowns were still netting tremendous profits.

Harry Helmsley began courting the Crowns in 1957. Helmsley and Wein realized that in order to make this the deal of the century, the land would have to be included in the overall purchase. And as their strategy evolved, Wein designed the most complicated lease-sale-and leaseback syndication arrangement of all time.

The 102-story deal of the century

The Helmsley/Wein syndicate would buy the building from the Crowns for $65 million, and the land from Prudential for $17 million with Prudential loaning them $46 million of the overall purchase price. The syndicate would then sell everything back to Prudential for an artificially deflated price of $29 million. Finally, the Helmsley/Wein syndicate would then lease the married properties from Prudential for four successive terms of twenty-one years each at an annual rate of $3.2 million during the first term, giving Prudential a 1% increase on return, from 6% to 7%. And it was ultimately this extra 1% that persuaded Prudential to consent to the most complicated deal in the history of real estate.

Over than 3,000 syndication units, at $10,000 each, made up the required $36 million above Prudential's loan, which also covered $3 million in legal and brokerage fees. The syndicate's seductive prospectus promised investors $900 a year on each $10,000 unit.

The massive deal closed in December, 1961, involving over 150 people around the biggest conference table in the history of conference tables. One document was more than 400 pages long. The final signatures took over two hours.

The most profitable part of the Empire State Building accord was (are you surprised?) the operating lease. By restructuring property management and shrewdly reducing overhead expenses, Helmsley and Wein further boosted their profit margins, and return on investment for the syndicate's investors quickly went up.

New fortunes of opportunity in the 90's

This is just one example of a syndication's ultimate acquisitive dream. Yet, opportunities very much the same and equally exciting presently await today's astute and careful syndicator.

Within the over 700 pages of these two comprehensive volumes, you'll find the guidance and format to capitalize on the explosive opportunities that exist in today's real estate marketplace.

See you at the top,

Stephen J. Murphy

CONTENTS

VOLUME I

PREFACE 41

CHAPTER ONE - HOW IT ALL BEGINS 43
A. Syndication modules - defining terms 43
B. Choosing the project 46
C. Participant advantages 50

CHAPTER TWO - ORCHESTRATING 53
A. Role of the syndicator 53
B. Pros and cons of the syndication device 58

CHAPTER THREE - S-T-R-E-T-C-H-I-N-G THE INVESTMENT DOLLAR 61
A. Forming the investment team 61
1. Broker selection 61
2. Lawyer participation 62
3. Accountant 63
4. Project Analysts 63
5. Consultants 65
B. Analytical devices 66
C. Regulatory concerns 69

CHAPTER FOUR - PROJECT SELECTION 71
A. Economic factors 72
B. Political factors 75
C. Social factors 78
D. Financial Aspects 79

CHAPTER FIVE - ACQUISITION STRATEGY 83
A. Survey of available projects 83
B. Proposed construction 85
C. Existing construction 86

D. Negotiation techniques....87
E. Forming the purchase contract....88
F. Closing instructions - holding, sale and loan escrows....89

CHAPTER SIX - LEVERAGE POWER.... 133
A. Sources of funds....133
B. Uses of funds....138
C. Exposure of the syndicate....139

CHAPTER SEVEN - HOLDING TITLE.... 143
A. Corporations....143
B. Partnerships....175
1. General....175
2. Limited....176
C. Joint Ventures....177
D. Real Estate Investment Trusts....178
E. Land-owner based affiliations on proposed construction....180

CHAPTER EIGHT - SATISFYING THE IRS.... 183
A. Develop tax strategy....183
B. Impact of the Tax Reform Act of 1986....189
C. Selection of ownership entity....190
D. Documentation considerations....193
E. Tax treatment of transactions....193
F. Other taxing implications....194

CHAPTER NINE - PARTNERSHIPS — A PRINCIPAL SYNDICATION ENTITY....195
A. Formation considerations....195
B. Documentation drafting....201

CHAPTER TEN - THE PAPERWORK....253
A. Meeting legal requirements....253
B. The documentation sheath
1. Syndication offering circular....257
2. Acquisition instruments....258
3. Promotional devices....335
4. Entity formation....335
5. Setting syndication guidelines....336

CHAPTER ELEVEN - THE GENERAL PARTNER'S ROLE....337
A. Creating equity....337

B. Balancing risk and rewards 343

CHAPTER TWELVE - MANAGEMENT AND CONTROL 345
A. Minding the store 345
B. Problem solving 348
C. Regulator concerns 350

CHAPTER THIRTEEN - CREATING THE MARKET 353
A. Financing concerns 353
B. Marketing concerns 356
C. Legal considerations 358

CHAPTER FOURTEEN - MONEY — THE GREASE THAT MAKES IT ALL WORK 361
A. Acquiring capital 361
B. Allocating capital 364
C. Maximizing return to the syndicate 366

CHAPTER FIFTEEN - MAKING THE DREAM HAPPEN 369
A. The importance of coordination 369
B. Concern for due diligence 373
C. Concluding remarks 374

INDEX 377

VOLUME II

APPENDIX
A: Sample Prospectus for limited partnership offering 383
B: Sample limited partnership agreement 443
C: Selected S.E.C. documentation
C1: Rules 146, 240, and 242 479
C2i: Regulation A 507
C2ii: Form 1-A - Regulation A Offering Statement 515
C2iii: Form 2-1 - Report of sales and uses of proceeds pursuant of Rule 257 of Regulation A 561
C3i: Regulation D 565
C3ii: SEC Form D 577
C4: Industry Guides 585

D: Selected Department of Corporations documentation
D1: Limited Offering Exemption 615
D2: Application for Qualification by Coordination 631
D3: Application for Qualification by Permit 635
D4: Small Company Offering Registration Form (Form C-7) 641

E: NASAA Guidelines 665
F: S.E.C. Guide 5 711

BIBLOGRAPHY 737

ABOUT THE AUTHORS 739

PREFACE

John Heywood in his *Proverbs* published in 1546 noted: "Many hands make light work." The concept of syndication was created using this philosophy as its foundation.

Mankind has always been fascinated by the intrigue of real estate ownership. Countries have been invaded for it. Mankind has taken up arms to defend it. Fortunes have been accumulated by those who understand it. Fortunes have been lost through lack of attention to basics — yet the allure of real estate investment still spurs us on.

Syndication in the field of real estate may remain a mystery to many investors who consider themselves wise in the ways of other financial markets. The purpose of this work is to strip away some of the mystery that shrouds the syndication process, and allow the investor looking for portfolio diversity to discover a new avenue for directing capital which can provide tax benefits and returns which outpace other financial market segments in the process.

Do not be disillusioned that this form of investment is not without risk. The rewards are available simply because the element of risk exists. What the pages that follow will reveal are the methods whereby risk taking can be minimized through the vehicle of syndication while still managing to preserve better than average return for the investment dollar.

Investors may not realize it, but they are already part of the syndication process. If one has a deposit in a financial institution, pays premiums on a life insurance policy, or owns a share of stock in a corporation, they are already part of a syndication. In the case of financial institutions, the investors deposit is converted into loans and securities using the combined investment power of all depositors in the process while paying depositors "rent" in the form of interest on the money deposited. In the case of the insurance companies, who are major players in the real estate arena, policy premiums are reinvested in a variety of loans and investments designed to magnify the dollar power of the premiums through investment returns not available to the individual investor (unless they were in the billionaire class). Shareholders in a corporation are the penultimate example of syndication at work. Through the dollars provided by shareholders as the seed money to develop net worth, corporations perform their functions of providing goods and services to the public at large with the profits derived being allocated to the shareholders through increase in stock value, payment of dividends or a combination of both.

Real estate syndication is merely an extension of these principles which have been practiced by financial subsidiaries and corporate America for time immemorial.

The primary thrust of this tome will be to concentrate on the limited partnership form of syndication. It will study the primary risk taking role of the syndicator exploring the multifarious details involved in property selection, capital accumulation, due diligence and acting as custodian of the public's funds.

It's a fascinating journey. Won't you join us?

1
HOW IT ALL BEGINS

John Alois Schumpeter noted in *The Theory of Economic Development* in 1934, that ". . .Without development there is not profit, without profit no development. For the capital system it must be added further that without **profit** there can be no accumulation of **wealth**. . ."

SYNDICATE MODULES - DEFINING TERMS

Many in middle class America feel squeezed by the taxing process which seems to provide greater havens for those who have been fortunate enough to accumulate vast fortunes during their lifetime or through inheritance. The syndication device offers a new ray of opportunity for this beleaguered class of individuals. It serves as a means of **wealth accumulation** while attaining some of the tax benefits of the wealthy. Before venturing into the world of syndication it is important that the reader understand the terms involved in order that the material to follow can be absorbed at a higher comfort level.

Black's Law Dictionary defines the concept of syndicate for purposes of this text as ". . .An association of individuals formed for the purpose of conducting and carrying out some particular business transaction, ordinarily of a financial character, in which the members are mutually interested. . ."

In real estate there are a variety of devices used as a means of capital accumulation to acquire multi-million dollar investment-sized properties. Some of the more common vehicles are:

- Corporate - Through the sale of stock for seed capital, combined with a variety of financing strategies varying from bonded indebtedness, lines of credit, term financing and the like, assets are acquired as a means of providing profit distribution to shareholders. Many investors prefer this type of vehicle, since liability is normally limited to the amount of money invested in the initial stock purchase. It is extremely important to determine that the quality of management and support staff in an organization of this nature has the innate ability to generate profits with continued regularity.

- Partnerships

1) General - In this case a group of individuals form an association to conduct business for purposes that are specified in the partnership agreement. The ground rules for this form of organization are spelled out in the Uniform Partnership Code which has been adopted by many of the states including the state of California. In the case of California, the partnership entity is addressed in Section 15001, et. seq. of the Corporations Code. Usually when a general partnership is formed for the purpose of acquiring, developing and/or management of real property, it is designed along functional lines. A typical composition would be an attorney, a CPA, the "money person," possibly a building contractor and real estate/property manager type. Obviously the key to making the project work is the "money person," who provides the seed capital for the projects undertaken and serves as the pivotal force in obtaining additional leverage in the way of institutional financing for various partnership undertakings.

In this form of organization each of the general partners has joint and several liability for the acts of the partners, thus there is a larger possibility of risk in this type of organization.

2) Limited - This is the type of syndicate that will serve as one of the focal points for this work. Again, there is a Uniform Limited Partnership Act which has been adopted by a majority of the states, including California. It is codified in Sections 15501, et. seq. of the Corporations Code. The organization consists of one or more general partners serving as the risk takers for the organization who solicit limited partners as an investment accumulative source, and who are generally limited to the amount of contributed capital to the venture. Normally the partnership is formed with the objective of dealing with one particular project for purposes of acquisition, development, management and its eventual disposition and distribution of profits to the individual limited partners. It bears some of the aspects of a corporation, since limited partners (unless their interests are assessable) are normally

limited to the amount of their investment, insofar as liability is concerned, while the general partners bear the brunt of the risk. As far as the contribution of the general partner is concerned, it may be in the form of a cash contribution plus performance of services, or merely the latter, dependent upon the circumstances involved in a particular form of investment. One variation of this form of real estate investment device is for a landowner to form this type of organization with a syndicator contributing the land as the limited partnership offering while the syndicator performs the duties of developer and marketer of the property.

- Real Estate Investment Trust (REIT)- This was a form of quasi-corporate device that gained popularity during the early 1970s due to the fact that the trust incurred no tax liability if 90% of the profits were distributed to the shareholders who are designated as holders of beneficial interests in the trust. Initially the thrust of this type of syndication vehicle was to leverage the beneficial interests which served as the trust net worth through a variety of financing devices, including convertible subordinated debentures and similar financing devices devoted to real estate development. This strategy proved to be somewhat foolhardy, in many instances, since inexperienced low-paid personnel were chosen to supervise multi-million dollar projects. This caused ill-conceived developments that led to the demise of many of these organizations, just as the thrifts that fell by the wayside due to their unsafe and unsound lending practices of the 1980s. The one bright ray on the REIT horizon was the fact that a few of them chose to enter into the field of investing in real estate equities in income-producing properties. It is that handful of trusts that survived the stormy seas of developmental uncertainty that eroded the existence of those who trod those uncharted waters. Today, these equity-based trusts, on the whole, are surviving the treacherous swamp of commercial/industrial real estate investment satisfactorily with competent management.

- Tenancy in Common - Another somewhat questionable approach to the syndication problem was the "dimpled darling" of the 1970s. In this case, the syndicator would arrange his investment group in such a fashion as to create a percentage ownership in the fee or leasehold title obtained operating under a modified form of arrangement which placed the syndicator in charge of property management and distribution of earnings from the project for a fee. This was particularly popular in residential income property investments at the time. It was a very cumbersome way of investing in real property. Take a typical example of 50 investors each owning a one-fiftieth interest in an apartment building representing their individual contributions of $10,000 each. This $500,000 probably enabled these multifarious tenants in common to control a $2,500,000 property. One of the inhibitors in this type of investment is the fact that if, heaven forbid, their were deaths or incapacities on the part of the individual owners of undivided interests, the complexities in dealing with this type of device become onerous. A variation on this theme is being used today as a means of dealing with the Tax Revision Act of 1986 whereby individual limited partners initially obtain a percentage interest in the project which is immediately deeded to the limited partnership as a means of avoiding this more complex syndication methodology.

CHOOSING THE PROJECT

Not every form of real estate investment is an investor's cup of tea. It is important to understand that syndication usually has its specialists, just like other professions. Some syndicators are more comfortable dealing with residential properties and the property management problems attendant with this type of ownership, while others are more content to deal in the murkier waters of commercial/industrial properties which require a different type of expertise in their acquisition, management and control functions. One of the reasons for individual investors to choose the syndication route as an investment device is the fact that it represents efficient time management.

Hippocrates, more famous for his physician's oath noted in *Precepts* that, "Time is that wherein there is opportunity, and opportunity is that wherein there is no great time. . ." The importance of the judicious use of time in the due diligence process of seeking the ideal property for pursuit by the syndicate is where the syndicator fulfills the role of time devotion which might be considered a luxury on the part of the individual investors in the syndicate. The syndicator has the time and resources to devoted a full-time effort to providing the property which adequately fulfills the objectives of the syndicate with respect to appropriate return to the investor, tax advantage, plus the opportunity for appreciation in value as an added bonus to the investment. First, the types of property and their investment advantages/disadvantages should be noted.

- Residential income property

  Advantages - In particular this type of property can usually find a high occupancy level at some given rental rate, since shelter requirements are a basic need for the population. Obviously if large vacancy factors exist in apartments in the area indicating a supply of units far outstripping demand, it would appear that the price, in the form of rent would suffer accordingly. Since property owners usually apply leverage in one form or another to acquire these properties, debt service requirements may dictate not retreating below a certain level of rents in a given project. This makes continued ownership of the project somewhat in question. On the other hand, well located, properly managed properties can usually survive under the worst of economic situations.

  Disadvantages - If the ownership of residential income property is not dedicated to providing a high level of service and property management expertise to maximizing rents while minimizing expenses, occupancy levels will suffer accordingly. Anyone in the management side of this type of ownership must be attuned to tenant requirements having the people skills necessary to smooth out the wrinkles that develop in tenant relations.

- Shopping Centers

  Advantages - Shopping center ownership can be most rewarding for those with the unique skills needed to acquire retailers who appeal to the masses. The tendency today is toward "power centers" where the focal point is discounting. Operations like K-Mart and Wal-Mart are blazing trails in this form of merchandising that are drawing in the customers even during the bleakest of economic times. Due to the specialized area of this type of ownership, it should not be undertaken by investors who are not comfortable in the retailing world.

  Disadvantages - Financing availability and excessive vacancies have plagued the retail world during the early 1990s and will probably continue through the remainder of the decade until the supply of existing facilities finally gets into equilibrium with the demand for same. This does create a window of opportunity for the syndicator who can bid on centers with lower occupancies on the basis of a price that will service debt and provide a satisfactory investor-return based on these levels. Obviously the potential for appreciation through the use of efficient management techniques offers the possibility of considerable appreciation in value as occupancies increase.

- Office Buildings

Advantages - Many ill-conceived developments of this type of structure were attempted during the 1980s. The principal culprit in this scenario is the fact that there was a mismatch between project costs and what realistic rentals could be achieved upon completion of the new office building developments that occurred during that period of time. This, however, creates a unique negotiation tool for syndicators who deal with financial institutions who lent money on the basis of physical cost not really understanding the economics of office building lending. This represents the thrifts which are now precluded under the Financial Institutions Reform, Recovery and Enforcement Act of 1989 (FIRREA) from being very active participants in this form of lending in the future. The thrifts have a considerable inventory of Real Estate Owned (REO) properties in this category which represent well-located structures that suffer from the replacement cost/rental capability gap that has been created from the economic atmosphere of the 1990s. Buildings are being purchased by syndicates at one third to one half of the replacement cost of the structures strictly based upon the **actual** income being derived from the structure, not what might be derived at some future time. Key to continued success in this type of ownership is identification of areas of economic growth which exist in the country, concentrating on well-located buildings within the identified geographic locations.

Disadvantages - Since this type of investment represents the highest form of risk due to extensive office vacancies evident throughout the country, there is always the possibility that occupancies could reach an even lower level in the future, thus diluting the value even more. A combative strategy is the placement of highly effective real estate property management personnel who aggressively market space while accommodating to the reasonable requirements of the existing tenancy, while maintaining rent scales at competitive levels.

- Industrial Buildings

Advantages - Industrial building ownership should only be attempted by those who are thoroughly familiar with the needs and requirements of this type of user. It is imperative that "safety valve" alternative tenancy strategy be developed as part of the ownership plan. An empty industrial building can stay in that mode for an extended time period with loan payments continuing to be due each month. On the upside of this type of investment is the fact that many of the tenants in this type of structure represent some of the more solid credits in our country, since a wide variety of industrial firms are either directly connected or are subsidiaries of major credit-worthy firms registered on national exchanges. To some extent, service-oriented firms are supplanting manufacturing and distribution uses that are being eroded by foreign competition.

Disadvantages - As previously noted, our foreign competition continues to cause our industrial sector to pull back their domestic operations seeking manufacturing outlets outside of the continental United States. This does not bode well for projected future occupancy. Alternative use allocation may be part of this solution. Since this is a very limited investment area for most syndicates with office, retail and residential income being the most prevalent types of investments, reduced activity is expected in this area in the immediate future. It is atypical for the ownership entity in many industrial firms to also be involved in the ownership of the real estate that they occupy. This is still another reason why investment opportunities are not as prevalent.

- Special Purpose Properties

Advantages - Since these properties which range from entertainment complexes to service stations to various types of franchise operations vary in nature and scope, only those with extensive experience in dealing with these very specialized uses should tackle this form of investment. Those who are experienced, particularly in the area of mobile home parks can find these investment niches quite rewarding.

Disadvantages - The lure of exotic property uses may be irresistible to some investors. Maybe its the intrigue of the unknown, but some continue to pursue elusive profits in this type of venture. One should not venture out in these shark infested waters without the insulation of knowledge. Ignorance can prove a handicap that is both foolhardy and expensive in nature.

PARTICIPANT ADVANTAGES

Why should one become an investor in a real estate syndication, no matter what the type of investment device? This is a legitimate question that must be faced by all who seek this investment alternative.

Some of the ways that investors can apply the principle of **magnification** to their accumulated capital is by combining it with the capital of others to command larger projects with the potential of higher returns on the invested dollar in the process. The sacrifice, on the investor's part, is the compensation to the syndicator who has provided the investment opportunity in the first place. The best way to underscore this advantage is through the use of an example of a typical investor who has $50,000 to devote to a particular investment. As a way of illustration, we will use an investment in a residential income property as the common denominator.

Consider the fact that individually this $50,000 will probably enable the individual investor to acquire an eight unit apartment building with modest rents. This type of investment brings up two very distinct disadvantages that will be obvious in the example used. The first disadvantage is the fact that just one vacant unit creates a twelve and one-half percent vacancy factor immediately. This is a tremendous reduction in income, percentage-wise. In addition, there are no economies of size in the expense reduction process, thus expenses represent a larger percentage of the effective income (that portion of the gross income after allowance for vacancy and maintenance).

To illustrate:

8 Units renting at an average of $400 per month generates potential gross income of $3,200 per month, converting to annual gross rentals of:	$38,400
Minimum vacancy allowance on this building would be 7 and 1/2%:	2,880
Thus, deriving an effective income of:	$35,520
Expenses will be in the 35% range, totalling:	12,432
Equating to a Net Operating Income (NOI) of:	$23,088

Considering that by applying a capitalization (risk) rate of 9% to this investment, an indicated value of $256,500 is applied to this property. On the basis of some shrewd negotiation (albeit time consuming) the investor is able to negotiate the purchase price of $250,000, financing the balance with a purchase money lien from a financial institution based upon a 9% rate 30/10 year terms, meaning that the loan will have a 30 year amortization with a balloon payment due at maturity in 10 years. Annual loan payments on the negotiated purchase obligation would be $17,860. This leaves cash flow after debt service at $5,228 deriving a 10.5% return on invested equity. On the surface, this appears to be quite satisfactory in an era where interest rates have not been this low since the 1960s, however, the vulnerability of occupancy for the low number of units controlled creates potential cash flow and return on investment problems in the future. Exacerbating this problem is that the individual will also have to invest valuable time in the areas of management and property maintenance, which will erode that seemingly attractive return on investment, since that time has not been accounted for.

Now, let us take the investor's same $50,000 and **magnify** it ten times through the miracle of syndication. Even with the price paid the syndicator to put this transaction together, the efficiencies of the syndication process and its impact on the purchasing power of the investment dollar become readily evident. Your syndicator has gleaned the real estate owned portfolios of hundreds of financial institutions throughout the country to find an apartment located in the midwest with similar rent levels to the building that our individual was going to purchase. In this case the $500,000 available has negotiating power to control the negotiated purchase of a 100 unit building, which is only 80% occupied. Due to the vacancy level, the syndicator is able to structure the following transaction:

Actual building rents -80 units averaging $400 per unit/month = annual rents of	$384,000
Vacancy allowance - Due to building's vacancy vulnerability, the syndicator will build into the transaction another 10% vacancy factor, or	38,400
Effective income then becomes:	$345,600
Expenses, somewhat reduced because of efficiencies of size, are:	95,600
Leaving net operating income of:	$250,000

Capitalization is based upon risk, so the high vacancy level warrants a 10% capitalization rate, which equates to a purchase price offer of

$2,500,000 with the balance of $2,000,000 being financed on the basis of 8% interest only for the first year converting to 8 and 1/2% on a 29 year amortization in the second through 30th years allowing the syndicator time to build up occupancy. The investor is now involved in a project 12 and one-half times the size of the original property where the risk of the investment is also reduced accordingly. Provided the syndicator applies the proper management techniques and actually increases the occupancy level during the first year, **immediate** appreciation in value occurs. To be on the conservative side, pretend that the project maintains the status quo during the first year. Under this assumption, the following potential return to the investor, without consideration for tax implications occurs: Annual debt service on $2,000,000, interest only at 8% for one year is: $160,000. This means that the combined equity of $500,000 yields $90,000 cash flow after debt service for 18% return. If the 10% vacancy allowance were added back in to increase this cash flow figure to $128,400, the return to the investors would be almost 26%! That is the value that the use of the syndication device brings to the table.

You, as the individual investor, not only maximize return on your investment, but, at the same time, have the advantage of a cadre of professional advisors assisting the syndicator in the syndicate's activities which can be supported due to the efficiencies of size that are brought to the forefront by seeking this form of investment vehicle.

In order to understand the pivotal role played by the syndicator in this ongoing process, our next chapter will be devoted to the services performed by the syndicator in the manner of due diligence, seeking counsel, negotiation, closing and management expertise which must be applied to each project under consideration.

2
ORCHESTRATING

Samuel Taylor Coleridge in his 1816 publication of *The Statesman's Manual* noted: "The imagination. . .that reconciling and mediatory power, which incorporating the reason in images of the sense and organizing (as it were) the flux of the senses by permanence and self-circling energies of the reason, gives birth to a system of symbols, harmonious in themselves, and substantial with the truths of which they are conducted. . ."

ROLE OF THE SYNDICATOR

The real estate syndicator is one who crystallizes Coleridge's imagination into a living, breathing entity in the form of an investment vehicle powered with the fuel of invested capital by the participants.

In order to reach the ultimate goal of a viable investment, the syndicator must possess inherent qualities allowing conversion of illusion into reality. Before devoting that hard-earned capital into a real estate syndication, it is important to understand the driving force behind the project. Since the syndicator plays this pivotal role, an examination of the traits necessary to properly discharge the duties of the position should be examined.

- Background - The syndicator (this encompasses the plural as well as the singular) usually possesses experience in the financial community in its broadest sense, either as a real estate professional, securities specialist, accountant, attorney, real estate developer, or some other real estate-allied activity. There must be a degree of assurance offered investors that this individual has the real estate expertise necessary to identify and assemble a viable project. Within this wide array of potential backgrounds that represent the typical syndicator profile, certain abilities must be present to provide assurance to the investing public that it passes the three investment goals:

1. Yield - The return offered on invested capital is commensurate with the risk undertaken. Investors in a real estate syndication will not be satisfied with a return that equates to that offered by a bank savings account. The return needs to be minimally double or triple that rate in addition to potential capital appreciation that might be realized upon sale.
2. Safety - This key investment ingredient is the function of the innate ability of the syndicator to identify viable projects which offer the greatest protection to the capital invested by the participants. Some investors fail to realize that there is a significant personal contribution of time, effort, and, in many cases, dollars, on the part of the investor prior to the time an offering is even presented to the public for consideration. By the time the offering is made, the property has already been identified and under the control of the syndicator.
3. Liquidity - In certain instances, limited partnership interests are already being marketed by the securities community. At the present, the market is fairly thin for sale of such interests to meet liquidity needs of individual investors, but some limited partnership arrangements provide for repurchase of limited partnership shares by the general partner. In fact, in many instances, the general partner also serves as a limited partner investor.

In addition to this varied background, the syndicator needs to possess the following essential elements either personally or within the syndication team:

- Organizational acumen - One must possess the faculties necessary to create the framework necessary to address the issues presented by the project in question. In the area of real estate, the issues vary based upon the type of property involved, its physical location, economic characteristics of the area, jurisdictional legal requirements, tax considerations, property management aspects, marketing challenges, negotiation strategies, feasibility, pro-forma preparation and the like. These individual aspects which must be considered on each project are indicative that this assemblage represents a team effort on the part of the syndicator. As an expansion to background, the syndicator must assume a variety of "hats" when addressing a project.

- Real Estate Sense - Although not found in any textbook, the principle of real estate sense is well founded. A real estate person can be placed on a plane for any destination in this country, given a rental car at the destination, and within an abbreviated period will be able to identify the real estate potential of the area. This does not mean that further investigation would not be required prior to the investment, but this innate ability to identify opportunity sets the person with **real estate sense** apart from other practitioners. The main point is that the syndicator must understand the nuances of the real estate market and the opportunities it offers in a given situation.
- Econometrics - The syndicator must be attuned to the myriad of statistical data that is generated by private and governmental sources to interpret the real world meaning of this data. Mere increases in population does not necessarily represent economic opportunity. One has to study demographics to fully interpret this statistic. Obviously employment trends, income levels and the like together with the vulnerability of the study area economically all go into the investment formula prior to committing on any project.
- Appreciation of the appraisal process - Appraising is not a black and white type of profession. There are many shades of gray and nuances which tend to affect valuation conclusions. The syndicator must take a hard-nosed approach to value and look at each income-producing parcel from the perspective of a worst-case scenario. Appraising represents a melding of economic principles into a conclusion as to value based upon the present value of future income streams actually being realized by the project in the case of existing construction. An income-producing property only has the worth of its productivity of net operating revenue after taking into consideration vacancy, expense factors and debt service requirements. Thus, the appraisal report must be viewed under that very constrictive perspective.
- Feasibility - The syndicator must be able to apply economic and appraisal principles when studying the community and neighborhood factors that highlight the elements required to assure investors of well-located real estate which possesses sustained earning potential. In this era of consumer concern for ecological matters, the issue of environmental hazards also presents itself. This is particularly evident in the case of commercial and

industrial properties where dumping of hazardous materials in the past may preclude investment due to the enormous clean-up costs required by various superfund legislative edicts.

- Hucksterism - Although some may take this attribute in a negative fashion, it is imperative that the syndicator have the ability to tell the story of the project to the investing public. It is not a simple process, since, in most cases, an offering circular for the project has to be created under strict guidelines as a means of investor protection. This means that the syndicator must use other media avenues to seek investors in order to just be in the position to send them an offering circular to consider the investment. Just as the expression goes, "You can lead a horse to water, but you can't make him drink," the same principles apply to investors. Thus, the syndicator has to be an effective salesman in addition to all other qualities essential for individual success in this form of endeavor.
- Appreciation of legal restraints - In any form of organization where the public's monies are entrusted to another, a series of safeguards have been put in place as a means of protection. These safeguards will be discussed later, but suffice it to say that legal advice is required by the syndicator, even though the syndicator may be an attorney, due to the specialized body of law that applies to the field. The syndicator must not only be aware of the essence of the law, but seek appropriate advice in the formation and marketing fazes of the project. Additionally the unique documentation requirements of the area where the property is located must be considered as well as the manner in which potential investors may be solicited must be taken into consideration. For example, the western part of the United States generally closes transactions using escrow, while the eastern part of the country is used to using attorneys with round table closings.
- Accounting and tax matters - It is essential that the financial structuring of the project be done in such a manner to attract investment capital through noting the tax advantages of the project in question. This implies that the reporting function concerning the operating results of the project as well as an explanation of the tax consequences of the investment be clearly stated to all potential investors. For this reason, accounting specialists in this area, totally familiar with the nuances of the Tax Reform Act of 1986 need to be employed in the formation of the investment.
- Analytical sense - Once the feasibility, valuation, legal and accounting matters have been resolved, project viability from an

investment sense must be addressed. Here the syndicator must have the ability to assemble a project pro-forma operating statement to determine its attraction as an appropriate investment. Within this analysis, several scenarios should be produced in order that alternative negotiation strategies can be developed with sellers. Obviously a key factor in this analysis is the use of leverage as a means of increasing the yield potential from the project. Financing alternatives have to be factored in to this analysis in order to discover all viable alternatives to making the investment a reality. This is a strong argument for considering real estate owned from financial institutions where negotiation leverage is on the side of the purchaser due to regulatory pressure on the institution to aggressively market these properties and get them "off the books."

- Negotiation - Considerable time will be spent on this subject later in this work. Suffice it to say that the syndicator either "makes" or "breaks" the project during this phase. How the project is structured during the negotiation stage will determine its future investment potential. This calls for flexibility, sound judgment, a facile mind and a flair for the give and take of the process. One of the principal objectives in this process is that the syndicator have the ability to tie up the process while completing the due diligence investigation needed for analysis.

- Management acumen - In addition to being an excellent organizer, the syndicator must also be able to extend to the full spectrum of management in dealing with staff and consultants. This means direction, coordination, follow-up and the like with the very human qualities needed in developing a well-meshed compatible staff working toward the common goal of the organization. Within this framework, there should be a mission statement given which exemplifies the corporate thrust of the organization. A typical mission statement might be:

> "It is the objective of this organization to provide the highest level of service to its clients consistent with the professional standards of our industry. It will be our corporate mission to implement this objective through proper staff development retaining ethical procedures consistent with this objective."

Management objectives must be pursued not only within the organization, but through the use of any consultants, such as real estate brokers, attorneys, accountants, appraisers and the like which might be employed. A primary management duty, once the project has been acquired, other than accounting for operating results, is the management of the project itself. The property management duties will vary with the type of property involved. More intense management applications would be required in residential properties as opposed to commercial/industrial properties, since consumers are involved in the former, while business people are involved in the latter.

It can be seen by the foregoing that the talent "bank" either possessed by the syndicator personally or by osmosis through the use of consultants is as multifarious as the shades of a rainbow. Investment in a syndication is not necessarily idyllic for everyone, irrespective of how much capital one has available to invest. Whether this represents the investor's "cup of tea" or not eventually depends upon whether this type of risk is in mesh with individual investment philosophy. The choice is a very personal one.

PROS AND CONS OF THE SYNDICATION DEVICE

Why would an individual investor seek the device of syndication as a means of alternative utilization of capital? The answer to this question lies in how the services of the syndicator are perceived to render value to the project. The arguments "for" seeking this type of investment arrangement are:

- Time management - Investors who have extensive earning capacity do not want to devote the time necessary to perform the duties undertaken by the investor noted above. Their earning capacity at their chosen profession (in many cases these same people are medical professionals, attorneys and accountants themselves) would be diminished performing the due diligence process required to identify an appropriate individual investment. The filtering process has already been performed by the syndicator and reduced to a paperwork level which requires a "go" or "no go" decision making process.
- Capital efficiency - The invested capital has the impact of a howitzer, as compared to a B. B. gun. In other words, the investor gets more "bang" out of each dollar devoted to a larger project than one could afford on an individual basis.

- Yield - Yields on larger projects, particularly real estate owned in financial institutions or regulatory liquidators, tend to be higher than smaller projects due to the efficiencies of size as well as the financing terms available. Leverage can increase yields by several hundred basis points.
- Appreciation potential - If an acquired project is only 70% leased with the negotiations creating a purchase price predicated upon the project's current cash flow, appreciation in value through applied property management expertise can enhance the value over time. In many instances, residential income, commercial and industrial real estate owned is being acquired for a fraction of its replacement cost. This aspect of the transaction can create a doubling or tripling of the initial investment, dependent upon the circumstances.
- Potential Opportunities as a Syndicator - In some instances, investors have enhanced their capital position to the point that operating as a syndicator becomes an alternative. This is particularly true in the area of real estate development where returns are high, but the risks equate due to the vulnerability of these projects to acceptance by the marketplace. It is suggested that one who wishes to assume the role of syndicator look to an existing structure as the initial venture.

Not all is idyllic in the area of syndication. There are a thousand horror stories of projects that have gone awry, syndicators that have provided a negative image for this type of endeavor and the like. This is why it is so important to deal with a syndicator who has a track record of performance. If this project represents a syndicator's initial effort in this field, potential success of the venture may be tempered somewhat. With this admonishment, it must be noted that there is a down side to syndication that must also be considered by those who seek participation in this type of endeavor:

- Economic factors - The ill wind of adversity has struck many of us at one time or another. A plant closing that represents the majority of jobs in a given location, change in government policy, such as military base closings in areas highly dependent upon this activity, and the like all give one pause for considering investment. Understanding the economic components of the area where the project is located is of prime importance prior to the dedication of funds to its purchase. Urban areas with a wide degree of economic diversity lessen the risk in this activity.

- Performance factors - Even though a building may be acquired that only has 70% occupancy and the price negotiated was appropriate for that level, the possibility of **reduced occupancy** is a possibility. Sometimes it is a function of poor property management, while in others, it is merely supply and demand factors at work. When acquiring any project, it is important to understand the competition and react to it. Competition not only exists in the form of existing property, but the potential development sites for similar projects in the area.
- Safety - If one desires that an investment be totally secure, the investment device would be U.S. Treasury bonds, not real estate. No syndicator can assure you that the investment is 100% safe and secure. All the syndicator can do is try to **reduce the risk to an acceptable level for investment purposes.**
- Liquidity - Investors should not seek out a syndication if they are not committing funds to the long haul in the project. It is not a simple device to sell shares in a closely held corporation, a real estate investment trust, a general partnership interest, or a limited partnership interest when the principal investment of this endeavor is income producing real estate where its performance is incontrovertibly connected to its physical location and the peculiarities attendant thereto. If one desires liquidity, deposits in financial institutions or government obligations provide a safer haven for investment capital. It should be noted, that high yields can only be attained by investors if they have the willingness to **accept the risk that goes with the investment.**
- Integrity of the syndicator - It is important that investors understand that the capital invested is only as secure as the one who acts as custodian for this capital. It is important that one deal with a person who has proven honesty and integrity of purpose. The experience of the 1980s in the real estate market has taught investors that not all syndicators operate ethically or professionally. It is essential that one feel comfortable that the syndicator utilized as custodian for the funds adheres to professional and ethical standards providing an accurate accounting of the syndicate's activities.

It can be seen that the syndication of income-producing real estate provides both challenge and opportunity to the sophisticated investment professional. How the syndicate is formulated from inception to disposition will be reflected in the chapters to follow.

3

S-T-R-E-T-C-H-I-N-G THE INVESTMENT DOLLAR

Milton Friedman noted in *Capitalism and Freedom* that: "Fundamentally there are only two ways of coordinating the economic activities of millions. One is central direction involving the use of coercion — the technique of the army and of the modern totalitarian state. The other is voluntary cooperation of individuals — the technique of the marketplace. . ."

FORMING THE INVESTMENT TEAM

The syndicator has been previously described as a person who must possess an array of multifaceted talents to apply to the project at hand. This is not to say that the person orchestrating the enterprise does not have a supporting cast. A variety of specialized skills are needed to properly establish an appropriate atmosphere for a successful syndication offering that will appeal to investors. This, as Friedman's observation of the marketplace would indicate, requires the cooperative effort of a variety of individuals to put it all together. Some of the aspects requiring outside assistance are listed below.

- Broker Selection - Some syndicators prefer to stick to their own back yard and only deal in properties within a fair degree of proximity to their home base. Thus a syndicator in Los Angeles would only seek Southern California locations as the focal point for syndication efforts. Others, driven by the whims and caprices of economic concerns may seek pockets of economic opportunity, such as the Orlando, Florida area or Houston, Texas in a search for income-producing properties with potential for upscale appreciation in addition to positive cash flow based upon acquisition price. In cases such as this, the services of a real estate professional well versed in a particular locality is a necessity. The expertise combined with intimate knowledge of the marketplace aids the syndicator in identifying the appropriate investment opportunity within this special economic enclave. The selection process for identifying the proper broker to use in a given area is performed on a results basis. One tries to seek a commercial/industrial broker that is a member of the Society of Industrial Realtors, which is an indication of dedication to professionalism, who generates the maximum amount of activity on the results side in the study area. One should not stop there, however. It is incumbent upon the syndicator to personally interview the broker to understand whether the broker's perception of the syndicator's needs is in mesh with the syndicator. One must understand that the venture is a cooperative effort and if the parties are like two horsemen trying to direct the horse in two different directions, no mutually acceptable result will occur. One needs to find a broker who has the ability to **identify acceptable opportunities within the market which fit the specifications outlined by the client**.

Once an appropriate property has been located, then the due diligence process is undertaken. This usually consists of conducting a formal or informal feasibility analysis, preparing a proforma operating statement for the project, possibly obtaining an appraisal report and then outlining a negotiation strategy for dealing with the seller. The real estate broker engaged by the syndicator may provide assistance in many or all of the areas mentioned. Usually at this point in time, other members of the team are engaged in the process.

- **Lawyer Participation** - Every state has its own particular legal parlance, particularly the state of Louisiana, where the legal process is totally different from the rest of the country, and it is important that one engage legal assistance from one who is familiar with the particular legal nuances of the area. As one ventures further eastward in the United States, lawyer involvement in real estate transactions becomes more extensive, particularly in the closing process. In the western part of the country where escrow is more prevalent the participation of lawyers is less evident in closings. It is imperative that outside legal assistance be sought, unless the syndicator happens to be an attorney familiar with forming syndications. The mountains of paperwork essential in the negotiation process from the basic sales contract to closing instructions, to the offering circular, organizational formation documents and the like require legal expertise from one totally familiar with the process. Another reason for seeking this type of assistance stems from the various regulatory requirements entailed in syndication offerings which must be complied with in order to avoid enforcement actions imposed by regulatory authorities. The assistance required does not normally end with just legal advice, however, since other areas in forming the syndication must be considered.

- **Accountant** - Since real estate investment is a vehicle powered by the vicissitudes of our tax laws, the income tax aspects of the transaction from a federal and state viewpoint need to be considered by a professional. The transaction must be structured with due regard for the implications of the Tax Revision Act of 1986 on a federal level and the various state tax laws which might impact the project under study. One of the more interesting state laws involves the California version of the Foreign Investors Reporting Tax Act, better known as Cal FIRPTA. Where the federal equivalent of the state law merely affects the sale of real estate owned by nonresident aliens, California law is imposed on the basis of property sale by anyone who is **not a resident of California!** The talents of legalese and accountancy must work in tandem, since they are intermeshed in the proper formation of the syndication. This is the reason why there are many attorneys who are jointly qualified as CPAs as well in order to properly structure a transaction. The accountant is intimately involved not only in the syndication structure, but in the preparation of pro-forma statements and structuring distributions to the investor participants as well. In addition to the duties outlined, all of the reporting to investors and filing of appropriate tax returns would also be performed by the project accountant.

- **Project Analysts** - Usually this is the area of expertise of the syndicator, but sometimes outside assistance may be required. There are activities, such as the preparation of a feasibility study, a rental survey, due diligence in a property development process, appraisals, environmental impact reports and the like which may require outside assistance. The extent and scope involved in project analysis is a function of the size, nature and scope of the project itself. A totally different strategy is required for proposed construction than that which would be involved in analyzing an existing building. The type of property involved would also have a bearing on the nature of the study. One has to compare apples with apples. In the case of an office building, comparable competitive structures in the area would have to be analyzed not only to consider their affects on the performance of the building under study, but to determine if the rent levels being attained by subject were realistic. Sometimes it can be discovered that a building that is only 50% occupied is that way because the rent schedule is $2.25 per square foot/month in a $1.75 market. This is valuable information for any potential purchaser in that marketplace. With a few adjustments in rent levels, the occupancy rate could be increased significantly, thus enhancing the value of a building which is not producing cash flow at economically viable levels. By using this last example, one can note how a strategy could be developed to enhance the value of the 50% occupied building that is renting at $2.25 per square foot/month by comparing it to the competition renting at a lower level. For comparison, buildings with a net rentable square footage of 80,000 will be used. This might represent a five story structure. Also implicit in this example is the fact that the structures are located in an area where the economy is on the upswing and demand for office space is increasing. Our analysis, then, is as follows:

Consider the competitive building is 90% occupied at $1.75 per square foot/month, thus the valuation formula becomes:

80,000 x $1.75 x 12 =	$1,680,000
Vacancy allowance - actual - 10%	168,000
Effective income	$1,512,000
Expenses - 25%	378,000
Net Operating Income (NOI)	$1,134,000

Capitalizing this figure at 9% (dividing by .09), the indicated economic value of this structure is $12,600,000. Taking the same building with a 50% occupancy renting at $2.25 per square foot/month, negotiation for purchase would be on this basis:

40,000 square feet (actual occupancy) x $2.25 x 12 =	$1,080,000
Vacancy allowance - still 10% due to potential loss to competition -	108,000
Effective income	$ 972,000
Expenses have increased to 35% due to the smaller incomebase to offset them equating to:	340,200
Deriving a NOI of:	$ 631,800

Using the same capitalization formula of 9%, the economic value of the building under these conditions becomes $7,020,000, thus setting the purchase price criteria under these market conditions.

After acquisition if the purchaser through proper marketing and efficient property management is able to adjust rental levels to meet competition, reduce operating expenses and, in the process, increase building occupancy to 80%, the results of these efforts are shown as follows:

64,000 square feet (80% occupancy) x $1.75 x 12 =	$1,344,000
Again, to be on the safe side, 10% vacancy allowance	134,400
Effective income becomes:	$1,209,600
Expenses, through reduction techniques become 30%, or:	362,880
Generating a NOI of:	$ 846,720

Capitalizing this figure at 9%, the new valuation becomes $9,408,000! Just this one little strategy has created a 34% appreciation in value!

- **Other Consultants** - Again, dependent on the project, environmental engineers, geologists, subdivision consultants, property management specialists (which may also be the broker used in the project) and the like may be required on an as-needed basis. The list is continuous and exhaustive in the process of providing a project to the investing public that represents a viable dedication of capital, while minimizing the risk in an area where returns can equate the risk factor involved possibly exceeding the expectations of all parties. This is particularly true when the property represents real estate owned controlled by a financial institution or regulatory source, such as the Resolution Trust Corporation. Each source is under mandate to dispose of the properties under their control in an expeditious manner, thus allowing considerable latitude for purchasers in the negotiation process including attractive leverage arrangements.

ANALYTICAL DEVICES

A variety of tools are used by the negotiator to arrive at the conclusion that the property under study meets the investment criteria which has been established by the syndicator. In order to understand the type of analysis required, it is essential to point out the fact that the syndication is driven by four forces:

1) **Appreciation** - The possibility that the investment under study has the innate qualities that can contribute to upward mobility in value. For this reason alone, 100% occupied buildings rented at the upper end of the rental echelon in a given marketplace have little investment attraction, since there is little prospect for upward movement in value. The factor of appreciation, dramatically illustrated in the example above, is a strong motivator for participation in a well structured syndication.

2) **Income** - Particularly with the inception of the Tax Revision Act of 1986, the fact that the project has the ability to either break even, from a tax reporting standpoint, or possibly even generate some after tax revenue serves as a considerable attraction to investors who may have negative passive income situations in other projects. The principal motivator would be the return on capital which would appropriately reflect the risk involved in the investment. Since the investment in income property, particularly in the 1990s, represents a higher than average risk, investors would normally expect low double digit returns on their investment.

3) **Tax Shelter** - Naturally the investor desires that a large share of the return realized from invested capital remain free of taxation through the pass-through benefits of depreciation, a non-cash item, proper tax structuring of the syndicate is of prime importance. The syndicator must serve as an effective communicator of the tax benefits that can be derived from the project.

4) **Amortization** - Although there may be some advantage to the syndicate to negotiate and interest only loan during the early stages of ownership, amortized loans are a method of creating

equity build-up, thus increasing the value of the investment. Since this does not represent an additional devotion of capital on the part of the investor, amortization represents an addition to capital just as much as the process of appreciation.

With this framework as a guideline, the syndicator needs to structure a two-pronged analysis. The first phase is a thorough investigation of the property to properly judge its potential to meet the four criteria essential to marketing a successful syndication, and then to create the documentation necessary to bring this about within the regulatory framework that applies to a given transaction. It is important for the syndicator to remember not to hog these benefits nor to allocate tax benefits to the investors that will not survive an IRS audit. There has to be equilibrium brought to the forefront that not only provides an appropriate reward to the syndicator for structuring the project, but to the investor participant as well.

With this as a backdrop for analysis, it appears that minimally, the following forms of analysis would be appropriate after accumulation of all consultation services in this coordinated effort to form a syndicate:

- Testing pro-forma operating statements - After reviewing feasibility reports, seeking advice from real estate professionals, consulting rental surveys and the like, the syndicator must now determine if the figures in the pro-forma are valid and reliable. The one cardinal rule that should be followed by **all** syndicators is that a personal physical inspection of the premises should be conducted. When considerable devotion of dollars to a particular project is involved, it is imperative that a thorough examination of the building and its environs be conducted. No figures on paper will ever replace inspection of the situs and its surroundings. This can provide data far surpassing mere figures on paper. It is the acid test for investment purposes. In the process, the syndicator needs to paint a word picture for potential investors which will place the investor in the shoes of the syndicator as the syndicator views the subject in the community where it is located.

- Legal and accounting review - The reason for seeking this type of expertise is to determine that the project is viable from both a legal and financial standpoint. The syndicator must be the final decision maker in the process and be able to ferret out any of the glitches that might appear to be roadblocks in the acquisition process. This also will serve as a guide to determine how the property will be controlled by the syndicator. Acquisition methods vary from lease-option to straight option to outright purchase in nature.

- Environmental and valuation review - There may be information derived either from feasibility studies, appraisal reports or environmental data which might impact the investment decision. This may dictate the structuring of the offer, particularly in the environmental area, where some form of indemnification might be required from the seller if particular environmental concerns exist. Appraisals might also indicate potential environmental problems such as earthquake activity, Federal Emergency Management Agency flood zone data and the like.

- Future use application review - In the case of developmental real estate, highest and best use analysis can be mitigated by checking with local zoning and planning personnel concerning how the intended use fits in the master plan for the community and the political atmosphere of the area concerning receptivity to the proposed project. If the proposal involves a considerable addition of new jobs to a community during the early 1990s, it probably stands a better chance than one which may have some controversial aspects to it, such as a shopping center which involves considerable increase in traffic in a residential area.

- Negotiation strategy - Once the acquisition decision has been made, the syndicator must then develop the offer to present the seller. In order to increase the probability of acceptance of any offer, alternative strategies must be developed in consideration of any counter-offer that might be presented by the seller. For example, if a syndicator offered $7,020,000 with 25% down for our office building with the $2.25 rents, the seller might counter with a pricing of $8,000,000. Knowing the potential of this building, the syndicator might be willing to accept the counter by using leverage as a means of increasing cash flow. The counter might be made on the basis of interest only at a below market interest rate for the first year allowing the syndicator to make the necessary property management adjustments necessary to increase occupancy and also to reduce the down payment requirement to 20% on the higher price. In this fashion, the required down payment has been lowered to $1,600,000 from $1,755,000 offering the potential of higher yield to the investment group due to the lower equity requirement.

REGULATORY CONCERNS

There are three basic categories involved in the syndication process:

- The sponsor's (syndicator's) organizational and operating activities.
- The offering circular combined with issuance of interests in the syndicate.
- Agents or principals offering sale of interests in the syndicate.

Within this framework, several regulatory agencies have some form of jurisdictional aegis over the syndication process. Some of these regulators are:

Real Estate Commissioner of the State in which the property is located - Either through the licensing process or through issuance of permits to solicit real estate securities, this entity may be involved from a regulatory standpoint.

National Association of Securities Dealers - Special licensing requirements may be necessary for those persons who solicit real estate securities interests. Legal advice may be required by the syndicator in this regard.

State Corporations Commissioner - In the case where corporate securities are involved, such as a real estate investment trust, permission may be required from this source.

Internal Revenue Service and State Taxing Agencies - The method of distribution of profits to the syndicator and individual investors is of vital concern at both the state and federal levels.

Securities and Exchange Commission - Various federal laws impact the sale of securities to the public. Depending upon the size and scope of the project, federal securities laws may apply.

Local Authorities - The process of government extends its long arm from the legislative halls of Washington, D.C. to the locality in which the property may be located. Local ordinances, zoning regulations, retrofit requirements and the like may impact the way that property may be used and also have some implications concerning permits required, local revenue assessments and the like. For example, in the city of Los Angeles, there is not only rent control on existing apartments, the city clerk also imposes a tax based upon the revenue derived from the building on an annual basis, considering such operation in the form of a business permit.

Regulation plays a large part in the selection of an appropriate project, since the nature of regulation may impact cash flow, thus having a direct bearing on value. This emphasizes the need for due diligence prior to commitment. The next chapter will devote attention to this process in more detail.

4
PROJECT SELECTION

Alfred Marshall provided a pragmatic insight into the process of selectivity in his 1890 publication of *Principles of Economics,* when he observed: "We might as reasonably dispute whether it is the upper or under blade of a pair of scissors that cuts a piece of paper, as whether value is governed by utility or the cost of production. . ."

In this era of monetary sophistication, the battle of value seems to find utility as the victor. When dealing with income-producing property in this threshold to the 21st century, the cost of reproducing existing improvements falls far down on the priority pecking order when negotiating the purchase of the property. The only thing that governs price, or value if you prefer, is the productivity of the improvements in the fashion of cash flow generated from its occupancy. This is the true representation of utility in a world where over-production has created sharp value contrasts to past perceptions of cost playing a large role in determination of pricing.

An important priority on the syndicator's agenda is the identification of opportunity to create a viable project to whet the commitment appetites represented by the elusive investment dollar bombarded by a wide array of opportunities presented as financial products for consideration. This signifies, by implication, that the syndicator has to do the homework necessary to identify properties which will supply an unfilled nest in a variety of investment portfolios while providing adequate return to the one who is creating the opportunity - the syndicator. In order for any project to become a reality, a certain regimen has to be applied in order to determine whether the project and its location meet the litmus test of feasibility in the sense that an appropriate return can be derived commensurate with the risk undertaken. Obviously if the group were syndicating U. S. Government guaranteed securities, as some mutual funds and money market accounts undertake, the return would be considerably less than investment in an office structure where many marketplace forces can impact that fragile factor of value.

ECONOMIC FACTORS

If there were such a thing as a syndicator check list when assessing any project, gauging the atmosphere of the economic climate would be at the top of the list. As noted in *Formerly One Up On Trump*, a variety of investment "pockets of opportunity" are scattered throughout the country which represent special situations existing in an economy staggering toward the next century in a state of disequilibrium. Especially vulnerable to this aberrative wobble of the economic pendulum is the state of California. As *Formerly One Up On Trump* notes, not all of the glitter has disappeared from the Golden State.

From a pragmatic point of view, the syndicator must make an in-depth investigation of the factors which impact economic activity in a specific location that either provides indications of future growth or shrinkage.

In the example of California, it is well documented that major industries, particularly aerospace, a large segment of that state's economic viability, have been downsizing, relocating to other areas and generally impacting the vitality of business activity in general. Even with this sizable economic upheaval, long term potential for California still exists simply due to the infrastructure which is already in place providing a certain economic edge merely due to its location. As the Clinton administration prepares for a number of closings of military installations in California, these closings should not necessarily be viewed as negatively impacting business. A more positive observation would be the consideration of some of the surplus properties now available for private development in some prime locations throughout the state. California is just one isolated example of where opportunity may lurk irrespective of the blinders placed upon the public by the media's negative connotations of what is happening in the state.

If history is any indicator of where the general population desires to locate, a good indicator would be "follow the sun" When one traces the development of states in the far south and southwest in the so-called "sun belt," the movement of population into these areas which has progressed significantly since the end of World War II, is a definite indicator that these areas offer opportunities not available in the far north and northeast of our country. Additionally, the vast midwest is now experiencing a renaissance of business relocations strictly based upon the fact that the cost of housing is less expensive than other areas. The cost of housing will continue to drive business decisions relative to relocation for some time to come. One of the other reasons for this ideology is the fact that business is striving to downsize and reduce costs, particularly in the personnel area. A popular method of cost reduction is to rely more heavily on the less expensive labor pool of part-time workers who are afforded no benefits. By the elimination of benefits packages for a large segment of the work force, businesses are able to reduce personnel costs by 20 to 30%. The syndicator must understand these economic trends that are underway in the marketplace in order to see how this affects average wage levels which translate into **purchasing power**.

If office space, industrial sites or retail establishments are under study by the syndicator, an economic profile of the area must be accumulated to determine its state of health. Areas which would be especially attractive for investment purposes are those where their exports exceed their imports. For example, Orlando, Florida, which is geared to tourism and the entertainment industry has become an economic mecca that appeals to the investment dollar. Major hotels, the movie and cable television industry have found this area to be ideal for their business. Leading examples are Epcot Center and Universal Studios in that regard. Some of the ways that one feels the economic "pulse" of an area is to review trends developing which indicate the thrust of future economic activity. Some of the items that warrant study are:

- Population - Not only increases numerically in the area, but the demographics of the numbers become quite important. In California, for example, one in every four citizens has a hispanic surname - that's a significant statistic and has considerable implications with respect to business marketing strategy, submarkets that can be explored, etc. Trends in the area of net-inmigration (the surplus of those seeking residence in the state over those that have left the state) can also have a bearing on the area's economic future. It is possible, for the first time, that California will have more people leaving the state than entering the state in 1993. The "warp and woof" of population statistics represented by demographics (a fancy word for studying the composition of the population) provides a strong indication of what the future holds for business in a given area. If the nature of the population that is leaving the area indicates that people are leaving who are middle class taxpayers, while the ones entering the state tend to be of the type who would be tax users, such as welfare and medicaid recipients, there are dire implications relative to the future economic viability of the area.
- Wage levels - Trending in median family income, average weekly hours, hourly earnings and weekly earnings give a clear picture of business trends in a given area. As the number of weekly hours

and earnings increase, purchasing power and the ability to save increases along with them.

- Professional work force - Medical professionals, financial consultants, educators, lawyers and accountants are drawn to areas that possess physical and cultural amenities suited to their tastes which tend to embody this elusive trait referred to as "job satisfaction." Abraham Harold Maslow found when establishing his "hierarchy of needs" that remuneration was actually far down in the pecking order in the priorities of things for ones who sought a satisfactory employment environment. In his *Motivation and Personality,* Maslow notes: "A musician must make music, an artist must paint, a poet must write, if he (sic) is to be ultimately at peace with himself. What a man can be, he must be." Stated simply, to engage in the activity one is trained for in tandem with an aspiration to perform in this area serves as the ultimate job satisfaction. Thus, the syndicator needs to consider the level of professional activity in the area as one indicator of upward mobility financially.

- Receptivity of the area to business - Is the area one, such as the state of Kentucky, which actively solicits business on an aggressive basis, or does it entertain anti-business philosophies which discourage retailers, industrialists and the like from locating their facilities in the area. If the entrepreneur is welcomed with open arms, this also spells opportunity for the syndicator.

- Trends in service industries - As our country continues to experience the metamorphosis of conversion from an industrial-based to a service-based economy, it is important for the syndicator to note whether the area under study is keeping up with the trend or is it relying upon a sole manufacturing concern which survives using obsolete equipment and a shrinking market share to survive. Local chambers of commerce are invaluable sources for a variety of data concerning everything from retail sales to the total spectrum of area features which they perceive to be attractive for businesses desiring to locate there. It can also provide valuable data concerning the industrial base of the region. In this latter area, it can be determined if the area possesses the diversity necessary to weather any economic storm clouds on the horizon. California possesses an eclectic jumble of diverse industries within its confines. It is still the premiere state in the country in agricultural diversity presenting one of the strongest arguments that the state will shrug off its current economic woes in the long run. On the other hand, California's woes become opportunities for Arizona, Texas and states east of the Colorado River with new opportunities represented by the influx of California's professionals relocated there either through job transfer or by personal choice.

- Affordability Index - One of the measurements of housing demand is the affordability index. As the cost of financing reduces in the form of easier money at lower interest rates, the ability of the average family to afford the median priced home in the area increases commensurately. Ability does not necessarily represent **action**. Even though a family may be able to afford a new home or resale housing, that does not necessarily translate to a commitment to purchase. Another factor comes into the decision making process. This factor economists refer to as the index of consumer confidence where the perception of the economic future on the consumer level is reduced to a statistic. At the time of President Clinton's election, this index increased just based upon the change of administration. In 1993 when the general public has had a chance to view the problems that the new administration has to face, the economic realities of the situation has caused the perception of the public to be reduced somewhat. Even though this is a very rough economic indicator, it does provide the syndicator with an idea of what future consumer strategy may be.

POLITICAL FACTORS

Whether engaged at a local, state or federal level, political factors can play a large role in business decisions. When the pressure of voters extends to the political process many strange things can happen. Some of the political actions which have an impact on property acquisition are the following:

- Rent control ordinances - This type of local legislation is a indirect means of controlling value. It has an extremely negative impact for investment purposes.
- Slow growth legislation - In areas where the citizens are of the slow-growth or no-growth mentality, this can actually work to the advantage of syndicators, since competitive properties are unlikely to affect rent levels with only existing competition to contend with in the process. If new projects are approved, adequate time is

provided to adjust to this competition and rent levels can probably be offered at a much lower rate than new construction.

- Planning and zoning - Most urban areas in this country have developed a master plan for community development. Within the master plan zones are established identifying suitable locations for residential, commercial and industrial activities. Actual requirements in the form of building standards are established to assure the public health and safety. Some of the special requirements include elimination of environmental hazards, seismic standards, flood control, sewage disposal, energy efficiencies and the like. All of the safeguards required have a dollar value attached to them including the hidden construction costs represented by an array of permit and inspection fees involved in the property development phase. New construction syndications can be most rewarding, but caution need be taken in order that expensive cost overruns are kept to a minimum. Even when acquiring an existing building, there may be retrofit requirements, such as shatterproof glass on outside sliding doors, water conservation devices, installation of fire sprinklers, earthquake reinforcement, etc. that may be required to bring the structure "up to code" These retrofit requirements vary by community, but they need to be investigated.

- Environmental legislation - This area represents an economic, social and political concern since prior business activity has created a negative attitude on the part of the consuming public relative to how they perceive corporate citizenship in the 1990s. If one notes the institutional advertising campaigns by large firms, such as Chevron, U.S.A., for example, it will be noted that they stress what the company is doing to improve the environment and preserving precious ecological balance. This type of advertising was woefully absent during the prior decades. With the advent of Three Mile Island, Love Canal, Exxon Valdez and a variety of other ecologically impacting disasters, corporate attitudes are gradually changing. When studying a site, environmental laws play a large part in determining its viability. For example, if the syndicator is of the type contemplating developing a commercial or industrial parcel, an Environmental Phase I report is now a necessity. Even municipalities can be deluded by not properly investigating before they invest. For example, the city of Palm Springs acquired a parcel for a $1,000,000 investment with the objective of developing an auto mall as a means of stimulating business tax revenue for the area. **After the property had been**

acquired, test borings were made to determine whether the soil had bearing capacity, etc. It was soon discovered that drums containing hazardous material had been buried on the site which was formerly a military air field during World War II. The grandiose plans for this auto mall have since been scrapped and the city ponders their $1 million Excedrin™ headache.

- Political interface - The syndicator must have a sense of the political structure of the community together with the ability to interface with the political process, particularly if the thrust of the syndication effort is land development. In this consumer-driven political arena, public relations acumen is an **absolute necessity**. The public in general must be convinced that the proposed project fulfills their needs, not just the developer's desire to obtain profits. Syndicators who restrict their acquisition efforts to existing construction only are not exempt from the political process. This is particularly true where a project is acquired which contains excess land which can be developed in the future. This places the syndicate in the same position as one that is development-driven in nature. The group's representative (i. e., the syndicator) has to state the case for the group in order that further development of the parcel can be achieved. No matter what any highest and best use analysis may indicate, if the project cannot be approved by local planning authorities, it diminishes in value as an investment vehicle.

- Measuring political atmosphere - As the political climate changes, atypical of the early 1990s, it is important that the syndicator realizes the nuances that appear, impacting value of income-producing real estate. When vast segments of the industrial sector continue to downsize, vast amounts of vacancies are likely to occur in industrial properties. The financial services industries continue to consolidate, thus making office space vulnerable to increased vacancy ratios, the shopping center glut of the 1980s has created vulnerability in this area as well. This retail trend is further exacerbated by major market players of the department store variety entertaining a group of strategies designed to offset the aggressive competition of the discounters. This represents a social and political trend which has been encouraged by communities eager to avail themselves of the sales tax revenues that discounter locations represent. Keeping attuned to national, state and local trends helps the syndicator reinforce the motivation behind the ultimate commitment decision.

If the economic and political climate does not appear viable, there is no basis for investment in the community and opportunities must be sought elsewhere. If it appears to offer promise, a property is identified to undertake the next aspect of investigation.

SOCIAL FACTORS

Webster defines social as ". . .of or having to do with human beings living together as a group in a situation in which their dealing with one another affect their common welfare. . ." As one can cogently observe, common welfare and its perception can gradually change over time. Man was perfectly content at one time for the horse to serve as a means of transportation. Now jets may be supplanted with rockets for interplanetary transportation, miniaturization of electronics devices have gone beyond the wildest dreams of Buck Rogers and we are quickly being thrust into a technologically driven era representing new challenges to the mores and folkways of our society today. Probably two of the most sensitive areas evolving create moral concerns as well as business issues to address. These areas involve artificial intelligence where science is on the doorstep of being able to reproduce human brain functions electronically and other forms of genetic engineering for the creation of artificial humans as well as creation of "perfect" Homo Sapiens.

Understanding the curious whims and changes of direction our society undergoes in searching for some sort of direction, the syndicator must learn to be a good student of human nature. What will be the taste of the American public in the future? How will this effect the use of office, retail and industrial space? Is the trend to home officing, just that, or a serious challenge to city builders on how one views not only how land use is to be allocated, but the types of improvements to meet the future needs of society? These are not easy questions to answer. One of the ways that consumers are brought into the overall picture is through the use of surveys which might be included within the framework of a feasibility study. The general purpose of such a study, which is undertaken by the syndicator either on an informal study basis, or through the use of professional consultants is to determine whether or not the purchase decision of a given parcel, improved or unimproved is justified. Due to the multifarious factors that must be considered which are really tailor made to the project in question, most of the Big 6 accounting firms provide feasibility consulting services in conjunction with real estate acquisitions involving the commitment of serious money. Some other accounting firms, such as Panell, Kerr, Foerster & Co. specialize in a given area of expertise. In the case of the latter firm, their area is hotel and motel acquisitions.

The feasibility study becomes a melange of economic, political and social factors that serve as the detailed "grist" supporting the recommendation "mill" representing the results of this examination of the project under study.

The ultimate decision is in the hands of the syndicator. If background investigation indicates that the decision to acquire has merit, then the number crunching aspect comes into play. There may be some preliminary data concerning the income-producing aspects of the property in question, as well as a survey of rental levels of competing projects. This all leads to the final segment of the selection process.

FINANCIAL ANALYSIS

It must be understood by the investing public that a syndicator will not normally undertake a profit where no personal gain can be realized by the undertaking. In the case of real estate brokers, earnings opportunities in the manner of commissions and fees are realized in addition to participation in the potential profits and appreciation in value that may be a corollary to this devotion of time, talent and capital. In the case of the general partnership form of syndicate, within the group there may be assembled all the talents necessary to perform the functions of the investment team required by the syndication itself. It is more common when dealing in the limited partnership, corporate, real estate investment trust and even lease participation forms to seek some form of outside counsel to create the syndication vehicle itself.

In any event, the financial analysis of the project represents the mechanism that will drive this vehicle into investment euphoria or the hallowed halls of Chapter 7 proceedings. Any venture of this type bears the element of risk. The first three phases of the project selection process are undertaken with the objective of risk reduction. This final, but most crucial, phase provides the acid test required to assure that the numbers are there to justify the effort expended. As a means of illustration, place yourself in the shoes of I. M. Committed, a sophisticated syndicator who has seen a variety of situations and is well versed in the skills of negotiation. He has expressed some interest in an office structure that was built in the late 1980s in an urban area in the Pacific Southwest that has been struggling to regain its flourishing economic identity of the past. The building is presently on the R. E. O. (real estate owned) portfolio of Seldom Used Savings Bank. I. M. Antsy, Vice President in charge of

Special Assets in that organization has provided you with a set up on the building in question.

The building is a class A (steel and concrete) office structure of curtain wall design with an exterior facade offering a pleasant aesthetic atmosphere to its well landscaped surroundings. The building site is located on two acres at the intersection of two major arterials which provide public transportation from the suburbs to its city center location.

This ten story structure contains a gross building area of 250,000 square feet with net rentable space, fully tenant improved, of 212,500 square feet. At the inception of Seldom Used Saving's loan, the building was 90% occupied with an average monthly rental factor of $1.60 per square foot on a gross basis. Recently, a two floor tenant filed bankruptcy causing the loss of income from 42,500 square feet, or 20 percent of the structure, leaving the occupancy level at 70%. Due to the fact that a concession had been made to the bankrupt tenant, current rent levels have now increased to $1.70 per square foot/month on the 70% of the net rentable area still under lease with an average of 10 years remaining.

With this basic information armed with the amalgamation of economic, political and social factors of the area produced by the feasibility study, physical examination of the site under study should have already been undertaken by the syndicator as a means of creating an understanding of the site and its environment. Now it is a question of not only determining profit potential, but financing alternatives available to make it a reality along with tax consequences of the organization structure contemplated. The reason that financial analysis is so critical is that it provides a basis for establishing **an upper limit on price**. With this background information on the project, the syndicator will then perform a massage of the figures sans the usual quarter you devote to the "magic fingers" vibrator attachment found on a motel bed. This is a real life situation where real life factors have to be considered. Not only must the quantity of the income be studied, but the vulnerability of the remaining tenants to the vicissitudes of the current economic situation of the area. Do the remaining tenants have the potential of completing their lease obligation? Do they have the financial wherewithal to survive? If these questions have a positive response, then the next question to be answered is - Does this building have the potential for upward mobility in occupancy? What are the advantages of this building over competitive structures? Possibly some of this may be answered by the feasibility study or an appraisal report. These are serious and long-term impacting questions that need to be answered in a reasonably well-informed fashion. Then the analysis begins. Here is one form of approach to the process.

The Problem: What should be the range of offering prices that the syndicate would be willing to present to the present owner to acquire this property? To answer this question, the syndicator would analyze the income of the building based upon its present performance, not the "what might be" of the future. With this thought thoroughly implanted, the analysis would look something like this:

Current Rent levels of $1.70 p.s.f on 148,750 square feet of net rentable space annualized =	$3,034,500
Since there is a vulnerability to tenant loss with new ownership, a 10% vacancy allowance is attributable to the structure, or:	303,450
Yielding an effective rents level of:	$2,731,050
Deferred maintenance by the current owner has increased the level of expenses and replacement reserves required to rehabilitate the premises causing the initial year's expenses to be 38%, or:	1,037,800
Leaving a net operating income figure for analytical purposes of:	$1,693,250

Since the building has a higher than normal investment risk, capitalization of net income would be at the rate of 9 and 1/2%, deriving an economic valuation and price discussion mode in the area of: $17,500,000. Upper limits of price negotiation would probably be in the $19,000,000 to $20,000,000 range, dependent upon how the vacancy and expense factors might be addressed. The physical replacement value of this building is probably in excess of $30 million. **This has no bearing on the price proposed to be offered on this project. The principal criteria for negotiation is the income productivity of the building - period!**

The next step in the process is to factor in the effect of leverage. Say, for example, that current interest rate levels for structures of this size and condition in the institutional financing market are in the 9 and 1/2% range with ten year call on a 30 year amortization basis. The syndicator knows that considerable regulatory pressure has been applied on Seldom Used Savings to dispose of the property and replace it with an earning asset. Since loans serve as an earning asset, financing would serve as part of the negotiation package. In the area of "loans to facilitate," which means those loans negotiated by lenders as a means of disposing real estate owned, there is a high degree of latitude in the manner of terms that can be offered to purchasers. The syndicator will try to work this advantage to the maximum. Obviously a loan for 100% of the purchase price, interest only deferred for one year at 2% would fulfill the wildest dreams of any investor. The syndicator must be realistic in the approach to leverage. Probably the normal down payment of 25% can be shaved downward to 20%, that's possible. As far as the rate is concerned, possibly the lender will offer interest only for one year at a rate of interest 150 basis points (one and one-half percent) below the prevailing market, with amortization kicking in after one year. Predicated upon a purchase price of $18 million with an 80% of purchase price obligation with a rate of 8%, interest only, for the first year, the analysis would look something like this:

Annualized rents (actual)		$3,034,500
Vacancy allowance (normal)	- 5%	151,725
Effective rent - new analysis		$2,882,775
Expenses, based upon efficiencies and purchasing power can be reduced to 30%, or		864,800
NOI under revised analysis is:		$2,017,975
Interest on $14,400,000 at 8% for one year =		1,152,000
Net income available to the syndicate **after** debt service		$ 865,975

The return on the down payment requirement of $3,600,000 would then be calculated to be $865,975 divided by the above number for a rate to the investor based upon the first year's leverage of 24%! By this criteria, it would appear that the transaction would not only be viable, but desirable. If the risk factor assigned to the investors' after debt service net was 10%, the $8,660,000 value (rounded) derived would provide a total project value of the $14,400,000 loan plus the latter figure creating a project value in excess of $23,000,000 based upon the leverage package alone. In addition if, after the first year, the amortized rate is still 8%, the small sacrifice in additional payments would be more than made up by the advantage of equity build up. Each of these factors has to be considered by the syndicator who also serves as a marketer of investment units in the project. If the marketing aspect of the process is not properly addressed, the entire effort will fail due to lack of inertia on the part of the promotor.

In going through the process of project selection, a slight intervention may have occurred with the next chapter. This intervention was intentional as a means of creating a foundation for the material to be presented as a body to create the acquisition strategy so critical to the success of any project.

5
ACQUISITION STRATEGY

John Fitzgerald Kennedy put it succinctly when he said: "Let us never fear to negotiate out of fear, but let us never fear to negotiate. . ."

In the formulation of any transaction involving the upside potential of considerable return on the investment, the element of greed will surely present itself in the process. For this reason and this reason alone, the syndicator walks that perilous tightrope which separates a successful acquisition to a busted bubble of the illusion that "might have been." For this reason, if no other, the syndicator can not play the acquisition hand too aggressively or face the potential of ending with an empty deck. The first order of priority, once an area of opportunity has been identified, is to comb that location for projects, existing or proposed, that fit the objectives outlined for the proposed investment vehicle.

SURVEY OF EXISTING PROJECTS

From the concrete canyons of the "Big Apple" to the rural atmosphere of Appalachia, syndicators seek that financial plum which will lure the investment dollar. In an effort to create some "order out of chaos," a systematized search of available opportunities must be created. It goes beyond the placement of a few phone calls. Syndicators who operate on a nationwide basis are much more apt to seek the expertise of local real estate talent than take on this extensive search alone. The tendency on the part of some syndicators is to specialize in a specific area concentrating on what they know best. This is the history of the Tishman family, architects of significant real estate holdings in New York along with the Bings, Urises, Minskoffs, Paternos, Campagnas and Roths who launched towering projects designed to meet the needs of 20th century America in modern metropolises. Many of these individuals took lease participation into the classification as an art form in its use as a syndication device. In New York there are skyscrapers representing considerable leverage, yet having no real estate debt. The lease became the ultimate leverage device for the more modern titans, such as Harry Helmsley and Donald Trump. It is like comparing the cap pistol with an atomic bomb in the fiscal impact one can have on a project which flourishes through a lease syndication device. The flexibility in this device almost defies description when structuring a transaction. First, from the vast array of merchandise, the suitable property that fits portfolio requirements needs refinement in order to create the swan out of an ugly duckling. Incidentally, this is the way that many have increased their personal fortunes in real estate through the simple application of the economic principle of **value added.** Using this philosophy, one would not take on what investors would classify as a "flagship property." Some illustrations of this type of property would be the World Trade Towers, Chrysler Tower and Empire State Buildings in New York; The Prudential Tower in Chicago; The Transamerica Tower in San Francisco; The Bank of America/Arco Towers in Los Angeles; etc. These properties will probably out-price their utility and not serve as an appropriate investment vehicle. This is not to say that location will not play a part in selecting the appropriate acquisition parcel. It will play a very large part in the scenario. Locational factors vary with the type of property chosen for investment.

Residential income property requires a different regimen of investigative tactics than those applied to commercial and industrial parcels. While residential income is concerned primarily with locational attributes which lend themselves to identifying with a desirable neighborhood for living, commercial and industrial property searches are much more intent and complex in nature. This is why Ernie Hahn specialized in shopping centers; R. B. Management specializes in apartments with a slight detour into industrial properties, thanks to Los Angeles' rent control ordinances; Jim Kilroy specializes in office/industrial structures; and the list goes on just as it does throughout the country.

One person who can be of great assistance is a real estate professional, preferably affiliated with the Society of Industrial Realtors. Having a professional C.C.I.M. designation does not hurt, but that should not serve as an ultimate criteria in the selection process. Selection should be based upon an interview process by the syndicator which can extract the "real estate sense" of the broker about the community. He needs to be questioned about what physical and natural divisions create transitional areas, what linkages have developed in recent years to create suburbs and the thrust of growth patterns in the area. Brokers are usually proud of their domain and will give the syndicator a grand tour of the merchandise enabling a personal inspection as confirmation of the observations given within the oakened confines of a real estate office. The true test of a professional is the degree of sensitivity to the merchandise and the factors that can affect value.

Even though one may not be able to wrest control of what is considered the "flagship" location in town, accessibility to its citizens in the form of adequate transportation access, job opportunities, police and fire protection, infrastructure adequacy, educational and recreational resources, houses of worship, shopping facilities, and the like, offer locational advantages which help to preserve long term value for existing or proposed projects.

Once the list of the desired type of property has been formed, it then becomes incumbent upon the syndicator to sift through the various prospects, whether it be an apartment, commercial or industrial site, in order to ascertain one that is of a size and scope that fulfills investment criteria. In the case of an office facility, usually low-rise one or two story structures in an area where land costs are extensive will not prove to be economically feasible. In high land cost areas, such as urban California, New York, Chicago, Philadelphia, etc., only investment in high-rise structures would seem feasible due to inadequate returns just on the basis of size and the percentage impact that just one vacancy would create.

Choice of a particular property or group of properties is dependent upon whether or not the syndicator can prove investment in the property would not only meet the criteria of investors within the syndicate, but that there was that little plus of upward mobility in value due to undercapacity of the improvements caused by vacancies. The ultimate choice criteria also varies as to whether the project is existing or proposed construction.

PROPOSED CONSTRUCTION

Development parcels tend to be much more complex than existing properties, since the planning process, subdivision procedures and building permits are required as part of the overall analysis. In addition, there is no instant income immediately available from the project. There is even a likelihood that the project may never reach fruition out of the planning process. For this reason it is important to tie up the land prior to purchase through any combination of lease/option or option agreement. Some syndicators even use long-term escrows as a means of tying up the land for an extended period while the due diligence process to determine feasibility takes place. One of the stumbling blocks in going forward with any developmental proposal is the fact that local planners have a way of bartering square footage for infrastructure in such a manner that the project may lose all feasibility. They also have another device called downzoning, which could be disastrous. When you are planning to build a ten story office building in the City of Beverly Hills that now only allows five stories of office in addition to parking structure allowance, this impacts the economic viability of development.

Developmental syndication, many times done in partnership with landowners, can prove to be hazardous to the investor's health due to the unseen road blocks which prevent elimination of the two risks involved in any development:

- Risk of completion - Getting the project up and running is a high risk venture in itself.
- Risk of the marketplace - Even if the project is complete, it has to be occupied by paying tenants in order for appropriate rental income to be generated to service debt and provide a proper return for the investors.

EXISTING CONSTRUCTION

In the case of an existing building, whether it be an office, retail center, industrial building or apartment, never look for the "cream puff." The seller will expect purchasers to pay a pride of ownership premium which does wonders for the ego, while deflating the pocket book. In the case of real estate owned, many times the property is managed in a haphazard fashion with little attention to service or proper property maintenance as a means of reducing the cost of handling the property while arranging for its sale. This is the lender's bad luck in preparing a property for purchase and the buyer's stroke of good fortune, since the buyer is immediately in the driver's seat due to the poor maintenance program that has been followed by the lender. By the development of an effective property management routing, syndicators can create instant value to a property after acquisition just by paying attention to the existing tenants' requirements.

Through the judicious use of a little tender loving care combined with effective property management, value can be significantly enhanced. Preventive maintenance is an investment in future return using present dollars. The value added principle applies. If a building has a leaky roof and there is interior damage, the roof replacement is a far less expensive approach, usually, than repairing extensive interior water damage.

NEGOTIATION TECHNIQUES

Bob Woolf in *Friendly Persuasion* provides a systematic approach to the negotiation methodology. Probably the true value of his work lies in the remarks made by radio and television host Larry King in the Foreword to the book. To paraphrase, King describes Woolf as not the "main factor," rather "There are larger things. Things like integrity, truth, fairness and consideration, a friendly shoulder, an 'always there' approach"

Investors must feel similarly toward the syndication group where they plunk down cold hard cash with the expectation to a satisfactory return for the risk undertaken. This means they want to deal with an "up front" individual who does not pull punches about the potential success or failure of a given project. Although Woolf deals mainly with media moguls, his techniques are applicable to any negotiation process.

One of the main ingredients in any negotiation is that the parties involved establish a relationship of trust between them. Nobody feels comfortable dealing from a position of distrust. The main advantage of using a syndicator as a negotiator is the fact that the elusive scamp of purchase price is bandied between the seller on one side and the negotiator on the other side, like an imaginary tennis match which constantly keeps ending up with a deuce score. Strong arguments have to be presented by the syndicator to substantiate the offering price and terms in order to drop over that lob shot which will win the set and the match from the seller. This means that the syndicator has done a thorough investigative process not only on the attributes (or lack of them) in the project as well as what motivates the seller to dispose of the property. The motivation on the part of the seller can change the entire negotiation strategy. If the seller is negotiating from a point of weakness (i.e., pending foreclosure, relocation requirements, whatever) the techniques applied can be much more aggressive than a seller who is not highly motivated to move on price. In the case of real estate owned properties they involve somewhat unique circumstances where the sellers usually have someone else in the form of regulatory authorities who are "calling the shots" concerning the pressing need of the institution to dispose of this property. In these cases, unusual leverage arrangements can be introduced as part of the negotiation package. The syndicator should always be prepared to have supportive ammunition defending the offer presented. There should always be an understanding and appreciation of the negative aspects of this transaction vis a vis the seller.

At this point in time, the words of President Kennedy serve as an appropriate backdrop of guidance in conducting the negotiation process. If the seller knows that the potential purchaser is running scared, he'll go for the jugular and not let go. If the buyer provides an indication that it is essential that this property be acquired, the sales price is likely to go right through the roof. Play tight fisted with a closed deck in dealing with sellers. Don't give away your hand. To some extent, syndicators might give the impression that the seller can either "take it or leave it." This strategy should only be followed where buying positions are strong. Deal always with plans B, C, and D in readiness to supplant plan A. There is no more frustrating remark in a negotiation process where a buyer will say to a seller, or vice versa, that "I'll have to go back and check with my people." Be sure you are dealing with the one who has decision making authority. To do less is a waste of time and completely frustrating. If one has ever dealt with Japanese corporations this is one of the more frustrating features of negotiating with them, since it is not easy to identify who the decision maker is in the room. It may not be the person who is directly handling the transaction. It may be another who sits unobtrusively in the corner orchestrating the transaction from the sidelines or possibly one who is not present. The dealing party never quite knows the results of negotiation even after leaving the negotiation table.

The negotiation arena should be preferably on the syndicator's turf or neutral ground, never in the seller's office, since this places the advantage in the seller's corner. **Never be vindictive in any negotiation process because you might want to deal with the same person again. It's the equivalent of "burning your bridges," and not appropriate business practice.** One should have the field of combat available for another day and another transaction. Even though the results of an individual transaction may be distasteful, the opportunity of future satisfactory relations should not be ruled out. If negotiations are successful, the next stage of the process gets underway.

FORMING THE PURCHASE CONTRACT

The contract of purchase represents the culmination of purchase negotiations. It memorializes the agreement of the principles concerning the disposition of the transaction ranging from purchase price, down payment and financing requirements to the due diligence process on the part of the buyer which must be undertaken prior to acquisition. Obviously, in the case of property for development, there may be an extended process before a deed is ever given by the seller to place the property in the buyer's name. As a matter of form, the syndicator should indicate the name of the buyer as being Irving Partnerformer, a single man or nominee. In this fashion, control of appointing the actual ownership entity remains in the control of the purchaser and the syndicator can then go through the process required to form the acquisition entity, sell shares of participation and prepare the necessary legal documentation required to consummate the transaction. A typical purchase agreement (sometimes referred to as a deposit receipt) is shown as Illustration 5-1.

CLOSING INSTRUCTIONS

In the case of capital accumulation, usually a holding escrow for subscriptions to the project is formed as a means to accept investor deposits contributed toward the closing of the project. Once the subscription is complete, this amount is then transferred over to the sale escrow to consummate purchase. In addition there may be a separate loan escrow involving the purchasing entity to deal with the financial details of leverage negotiated in the project. A sample sale agreement is shown as Illustration 5-2.

Since financing represents another aspect of the negotiating process, separate consideration must be given to its impact. Our next chapter will cover the types of consideration that must be given to leverage. In this examination, suitable examples will be provided to graphically illustrate the impact of leverage upon investment return as well as showing how appreciation can be built up in the transaction simply through the use of leverage.

Illustration 5-1

PURCHASE AND SALE AGREEMENT
AND JOINT ESCROW INSTRUCTIONS

THIS PURCHASE AND SALE AGREEMENT AND JOINT ESCROW INSTRUCTIONS (the "**Agreement**") is dated, for reference purposes only, January 11, 1993, and is executed on the dates set opposite the signatures below, by and among PACIFIC CENTRE, a California general partnership (the "**SELLER**") and AMERICAN CAPITAL INVESTMENTS, INC., a California corporation (the "**BUYER**").

R E C I T A L S

A. SELLER owns certain property consisting of a retail/office center located in the City of Solana Beach (the "**City**"), County of San Diego, State of California, which is commonly known as "**Pacific Centre**" (the "**Property**"). The Property is more specifically described as follows:

(i) All of SELLER's right, title and interest in and to that certain real property located in the County of San Diego, State of California, as more particularly described in **Exhibit "A"** attached hereto (the "**Land**"), together with all rights of way, privileges and appurtenances pertaining thereto, including any right, title and interest of SELLER in and to any street adjoining any portion of the Land.

(ii) All of SELLER's right, title and interest in and to all structures, buildings, compressors, appliances, engines, electrical, plumbing, heating, ventilating and air conditioning machinery and property of every kind, character and description appurtenant to the Land (the "**Improvements**").

(iii) All of SELLER's right, title and interest in and to all equipment and articles of personal property, tangible or intangible, which are attached, appurtenant to, installed or placed in or upon, or used for the maintenance, occupancy or operation of the Property (the "**Personal Property**").

(iv) All of SELLER's right, title and interest in, to and under the Service Contracts (as hereinafter defined) to the extent assignable, the Leases (as hereinafter defined) and all security deposits and other deposits held or received in connection with the Leases.

(v) All of SELLER's right, title and interest in and to all licenses and permits, if any, issued by any federal, state or municipal authority relating to the use, maintenance or operation of the Property and in favor of the Property to the extent that any of the foregoing are assignable by SELLER.

Illustration 5-1 (cont.)

(vi) All of SELLER's right, title and interest in and to the use of the name **"Pacific Centre"**.

B. BUYER desires to purchase the Property and SELLER is willing to sell the Property in accordance with the terms and conditions set forth in this Agreement.

NOW, THEREFORE, for good and valuable consideration, the receipt and adequacy of which is hereby acknowledged, SELLER agrees to sell the Property to BUYER, and BUYER agrees to purchase the Property from SELLER, upon the terms and conditions set forth below.

ARTICLE I

PURCHASE PRICE

1.1 **Purchase Price**. The purchase price (the **"Purchase Price"**) for the Property shall be Five Million Two Hundred Fifty Thousand Dollars ($5,250,000.00).

1.2 **Payment of the Purchase Price**. The Purchase Price shall be paid by BUYER as follows:

(a) BUYER has previously delivered to SELLER outside of Escrow (as defined below), and SELLER hereby acknowledges its receipt of, the sum of Fifty Thousand Dollars ($50,000.00) (the **"First Deposit"**). The First Deposit constitutes separate consideration for SELLER agreeing to consider the selling the Property to BUYER and for SELLER's time, effort and expense in connection with the negotiation and preparation of this Agreement, and is fully-earned and shall be non-refundable to BUYER for any reason or in any event whatsoever (including, without limitation, SELLER's breach hereunder, BUYER's disapproval of the Property pursuant to Section 3.1(b) below, SELLER's failure to obtain the approvals required pursuant to Section 3.2 below for any reason whatsoever, or the failure of this transaction to close for any other reason whatsoever). BUYER expressly acknowledges and agrees that the First Deposit was a material inducement to SELLER to consider entering into this Agreement and to expend its time, effort and funds in connection with the negotiation and preparation of this Agreement, and SELLER would not have considered entering into this Agreement (and would not have entered into this Agreement) or expended its time, effort or funds in connection herewith without BUYER's payment of the First Deposit to SELLER upon the terms described above. If BUYER approves the Property pursuant to Section 3.1(b) below, then BUYER shall deposit with Escrow Holder (as defined below) the additional sum of One Hundred Fifty Thousand Dollars ($150,000.00) (the **"Second Deposit"**) not later

Illustration 5-1 (cont.)

than the end of the Inspection Period (as defined below) in accordance with Section 3.1(b) below. The First Deposit and the Second Deposit are sometimes collectively referred to hereinafter as the **"Deposit."** The Second Deposit shall be placed by Escrow Holder in an interest-bearing account at a federally-insured financial institution selected by BUYER for the benefit of BUYER, unless BUYER is in default under this Agreement, in which event the Deposit, together with all interest accrued thereon, shall be paid to SELLER as liquidated damages pursuant to Section 7.2 below. Upon the Close of Escrow (as defined below) the Deposit, plus all interest which accrues on the Second Deposit while held by Escrow Holder, shall be applied to the Down Payment (as defined below).

(b) BUYER shall pay to SELLER upon the Close of Escrow a total cash payment (the **"Down Payment"**) in a sum equal to One Million Two Hundred Fifty Thousand Dollars ($1,250,000.00) (including the Deposit plus all interest which accrues on the Second Deposit while held by Escrow Holder).

(c) The balance of the Purchase Price shall be represented by the purchase money loan described in the financing addendum attached hereto as **Exhibit "B"** (the **"Financing Addendum"**) and this Section 1.2(c) below, provided that BUYER expressly acknowledges and agrees that the purchase money financing contemplated by the Financing Addendum and this Section 1.2(c) below shall be subject to, and contingent upon, the satisfaction of all of the terms and conditions contained herein and in the Financing Addendum. In addition to the other requirements contained in the Financing Addendum and the Loan Application (as defined in the Financing Addendum), BUYER shall execute and deliver to SELLER upon the Close of Escrow a note in the form set forth in **Exhibit "B-1"** attached hereto (the **"Note"**) in the principal amount of Four Million Dollars ($4,000,000.00), and upon the other terms and conditions described in the Note. Without limiting the generality of the foregoing, (i) the principal sum of the Note shall bear interest at the rate of eight and one-half percent (8.5%) per annum and shall be amortized over a period of thirty (30) years, (ii) BUYER shall pay to SELLER installments of principal and interest on the first day of each calendar month after the Close of Escrow, and (iii) all principal, accrued but unpaid interest and all other fees, charges and other amounts due but unpaid under the Note shall be due and payable by BUYER seven (7) years after the Close of Escrow. The Note shall be dated as of the date of the Close of Escrow. The Note shall be secured by a first lien deed of trust, assignment of rents, security agreement and fixture filing in the form set forth in **Exhibit "B-1"** attached hereto (the **"Trust Deed"**), an assignment of leases, rents and profits in the form set forth in **Exhibit "B-1"** attached hereto (the **"Assignment of Rents and Leases"**), a Form UCC-1 Financing Statement in

Illustration 5-1 (cont.)

SELLER's standard form (the **"Financing Statement"**) and such other security instruments as may be required pursuant to the Financing Addendum (collectively, the **"Security Documents"**). The Trust Deed and the Assignment of Rents and Leases shall be executed, acknowledged and delivered by BUYER in favor of SELLER, shall encumber the Property as security for the Note and shall be recorded in the Official Records of San Diego County, State of California (the **"Official Records"**) at the Close of Escrow. Conformed copies of the Trust Deed and the Assignment of Rents and Leases showing the recording information shall be immediately delivered to BUYER and SELLER at the Close of Escrow, and the original of the Trust Deed and the Assignment of Rents and Leases shall be delivered to SELLER promptly following recordation. The Financing Statement shall be executed and delivered by BUYER in favor of SELLER and shall be filed with the Office of the Secretary of State of California immediately upon the Close of Escrow.

ARTICLE II

CONDITION OF TITLE

2.1 Permitted Exceptions. BUYER agrees to accept title to the Property subject to the following matters (collectively, the **"Permitted Exceptions"**):

(a) Liens for current real property taxes and any general or special assessments or bonds that are not delinquent as of the Close of Escrow.

(b) Leases and tenancies (**"Leases"**) and all other contracts or agreements (**"Service Contracts"**) affecting the Property.

(c) The Security Documents and any matters created by BUYER.

(d) Any matters disclosed in that certain Preliminary Report, Order No. 1008292-11, dated as of August 20, 1992 issued by Escrow Holder, a copy of which Preliminary Report has been previously received and reviewed by BUYER.

(e) Any other matters that may hereafter be disclosed by Escrow Holder.

2.2 Title Policies. Either a CLTA or ALTA Owner's Title Insurance Policy (the **"Buyer's Title Policy"**) shall be issued to BUYER by the Escrow Holder, or its underwriter, at the Close of Escrow. Such policy shall be a CLTA Owner's Title Insurance policy unless BUYER elects, by appropriate escrow instructions to

Illustration 5-1 (cont.)

the Escrow Holder, to cause the Escrow Holder or its underwriter to issue an ALTA Owner's Title Insurance Policy in place of the CLTA Title Policy; provided, however, the issuance of an ALTA Policy shall not be a condition to BUYER's obligations under this Agreement. If BUYER elects to have an ALTA Policy issued, BUYER shall pay all costs associated with, and the premium for, said ALTA Policy in excess of the costs and premium that would have been incurred for a CLTA policy. The Buyer's Title Policy shall be in the amount of the Purchase Price for the protection of BUYER as the fee owner of the Property, subject to the Permitted Exceptions. In addition, the "Mortgagee's Title Policy" contemplated by Paragraph 21 of the Financing Addendum insuring the lien of the Trust Deed (the "**Mortgagee's Title Policy**") shall be issued to SELLER by Escrow Holder, or its underwriter, at the Close of Escrow in accordance with the terms and conditions contained in the Financing Addendum. In connection therewith, BUYER shall obtain and deliver to SELLER and Escrow Holder not later than five (5) days prior to the Closing Date, at BUYER's sole cost and expense, the survey required in connection with the Mortgagee's Title Policy, as more particularly described in the Financing Addendum.

2.3 **No General Title Warranty**. Nothing in this Agreement (including, without limitation, the Recitals above) shall be construed as a warranty or representation by SELLER concerning SELLER's title to the Property, and SELLER makes no such warranty or representation. BUYER is relying solely upon: (a) the Buyer's Title Policy, and (b) BUYER's own investigations respecting SELLER's title to the Property.

ARTICLE III

APPROVALS AND CONDITIONS

3.1 **BUYER's Conditions**. The obligations of BUYER under this Agreement shall be subject to and contingent upon satisfaction of the following conditions, which conditions, if not satisfied or waived by BUYER within the applicable time periods described herein, shall entitle BUYER to terminate this Agreement as provided below, in which event Sections 3.3(a) and (c) below shall apply:

(a) **Approval of Purchase Money Loan**. The purchase money loan contemplated under Section 1.2(c) above shall be approved in accordance with Sections 3.2 and 5.4 below.

(b) **Inspection of Property**. From and after the full execution of this Agreement by SELLER and BUYER until 5:00 p.m. on January 15, 1993 (the "**Inspection Period**"), BUYER may, at BUYER's sole cost and risk and subject to Section 5.1 below,

Illustration 5-1 (cont.)

inspect the physical condition and operations of the Property and investigate the zoning, building and other requirements governing the Property. If BUYER, in its sole and absolute discretion, approves the Property, then BUYER shall deliver the Second Deposit to Escrow Holder not later than the end of the Inspection Period. BUYER's delivery of the Second Deposit to Escrow Holder as aforesaid shall constitute BUYER's unconditional and irrevocable approval of the Property and the satisfaction of this condition, and BUYER's purchase of the Property shall be on an "AS-IS" basis in accordance with Section 4.1 below. If by the end of the Inspection Period BUYER has not delivered the Second Deposit to Escrow Holder, then BUYER shall be deemed to have disapproved the Property, in which event this Agreement shall terminate and Sections 3.3(a) and (c) below shall apply.

3.2 **SELLER's Conditions.** The obligations of SELLER under this Agreement shall be subject to and contingent upon satisfaction of the following conditions prior to the Closing Date, which if not satisfied, shall entitle SELLER to terminate this Agreement, in which event Sections 3.3(a) and (c) below shall apply:

(a) **RTC Approval.** The transaction set forth in this Agreement, including, without limitation, the purchase money loan contemplated by Section 1.2 above, shall be approved by the Resolution Trust Corporation (the "RTC"), as receiver for San Jacinto Savings Association, F.A. ("San Jacinto"), the ultimate shareholder of SELLER's general partners.

(b) **SELLER's Approvals.** The transaction set forth in this Agreement shall be approved by the Boards of Directors of each of SELLER's general partners, SoPac Properties, Inc., a Delaware corporation, and SoPac Kohala Corp., a California corporation.

Not later than three (3) business days after the execution of this Agreement by SELLER and BUYER, BUYER shall complete, execute and deliver to SELLER, the Loan Application, all supporting exhibits, documentation and information required to be submitted in connection with the Loan Application, the non-refundable Application Fee and the non-refundable Underwriting Fee (as such terms are described in the Loan Application). Further, not later than three (3) business days after request therefor, BUYER shall deliver to SELLER and/or the RTC in form and substance reasonably satisfactory to SELLER and/or the RTC any other documents and information reasonably required by SELLER and/or the RTC to satisfy all applicable regulatory requirements (federal and state) in connection with obtaining the foregoing approvals. SELLER shall, in good faith, promptly attempt to obtain such approvals but SELLER cannot guaranty such approvals and nothing contained in this Agreement shall be construed as such a

Illustration 5-1 (cont.)

guaranty. SELLER shall promptly notify BUYER and Escrow Holder in writing of SELLER's receipt of the foregoing approvals from, or the disapproval of this transaction by, the entities from whom approval is required pursuant to this Section 3.2. If SELLER has not received notice of the approval of this transaction as required pursuant to this Section 3.2 on or before the Closing Date or if this transaction is disapproved by any of the entities from whom approval is required pursuant to this Section 3.2, then this Agreement shall terminate and Sections 3.3(a) and (c) below shall apply.

3.3 Consequences of Termination of This Agreement.

(a) Non-Default. If this Agreement is terminated by either party for any reason other than a default hereunder by the other party (which reasons shall include, but not be limited to, SELLER's failure to obtain any of the approvals required pursuant to Section 3.2 above), then the following shall occur: (i) the Second Deposit, deposited by BUYER with Escrow Holder pursuant to Section 1.2(a) above, together with all interest accrued thereon while held by Escrow Holder, and any other monies deposited by BUYER into the Escrow shall be refunded to BUYER; (ii) any documents deposited with Escrow Holder by either party shall be returned to the party depositing the same; (iii) BUYER shall promptly return to SELLER all documents delivered by SELLER to BUYER pursuant to this Agreement; (iv) BUYER and SELLER shall split equally any cancellation and other fees of Escrow Holder, and (v) SELLER shall retain the non-refundable First Deposit in accordance with Section 1.2(a) above. Upon completion of all of the foregoing, this Agreement shall be deemed terminated and, subject to Section 3.3(c) below, neither party shall have any further rights against or obligations to the other hereunder or in connection herewith.

(b) Default. If this Agreement is terminated by either party due to a default hereunder by the other party, then: (i) the defaulting party shall be solely responsible for all cancellation and other fees of Escrow Holder, and (ii) Sections 7.1 and 7.2 below, as the case may be, shall apply.

(c) Technical Data. Promptly after any termination of this Agreement for any reason other than a breach by SELLER hereunder or the failure of SELLER's conditions as described in Section 3.2 above, BUYER shall deliver to SELLER, at no cost to SELLER, all technical data prepared or obtained by BUYER and/or BUYER's Representatives in connection with the Property, including, but not limited to, land plans, maps, engineering studies, soils studies, geological studies and other engineering information in BUYER's or BUYER's Representatives' possession or under BUYER's or BUYER's Representatives' control, all of which shall become the property of SELLER.

Illustration 5-1 (cont.)

ARTICLE IV

WARRANTIES

4.1 **Sale "As-Is"**. Except as specifically set forth in Section 4.3 below, the parties acknowledge that SELLER does not hereby make, and has not made, any warranties or representations, either expressed or implied, as to the Property's legal, physical and/or financial condition now or in the future, including but not limited to compliance with any laws, codes, ordinances, rules, regulations, or requirements regarding the Property, or in connection with the purchase, ownership, development, subdivision, maintenance, leasing, sale, zoning, land use, and/or utility and infrastructure availability, including, without limitation, water, sewer, electricity and other utilities, with respect to the Property. BUYER hereby expressly acknowledges that no such representations or warranties have been made, except as specifically set forth in Section 4.3 below. In addition, SELLER shall not be liable or bound in any manner for any verbal or written statements, representations, real estate brokers' "set-ups" or any other information pertaining to the Property furnished by any real estate broker, agent, employee, representative, officer, director or other person or entity. BUYER hereby acknowledges that it is buying the Property in an "AS-IS" AND "WITH ALL FAULTS" condition and is relying solely upon its own inspections, studies and investigations, and, if circumstances, conditions or facts turn out differently than BUYER believed, then SELLER shall have no liabilities or obligations whatsoever in connection therewith and BUYER shall not be relieved of any obligations under this Agreement, which obligations shall remain in full force and effect.

4.2 **Representations and Warranties of BUYER**. BUYER represents and warrants as follows:

(a) **Organization**. BUYER is a corporation duly organized, validly existing and in good standing under the laws of the State of California, with full power to enter into this Agreement, and BUYER is duly qualified to transact business in California.

(b) **Authority**. The execution and delivery of this Agreement has been duly authorized and approved by all requisite action and the consummation of the transactions contemplated hereby has been authorized and approved by all requisite action of BUYER, and no other authorizations or approvals, whether of governmental bodies or otherwise, are or will be necessary in order to enable BUYER to enter into or to perform its obligations under the terms of this Agreement.

Illustration 5-1 (cont.)

(c) **Binding Effect of Documents**. This Agreement and the other documents to be executed by BUYER hereunder, upon execution and delivery thereof by BUYER, will have been duly entered into by BUYER, and will constitute legal, valid and binding obligations of BUYER. Neither this Agreement nor anything provided to be done under this Agreement violates or shall violate any contract, document, understanding, agreement or instrument to which BUYER is a party or by which it is bound.

4.3 **Representations and Warranties of SELLER**. Subject to the satisfaction of the conditions set forth in Section 3.2 above in the case of Sections 4.3(a), (b) and (c) below, SELLER represents and warrants as follows:

(a) **Organization**. SELLER is a partnership duly organized, validly existing and in good standing under the laws of the State of California with full power to enter into this Agreement, and SELLER is duly qualified to transact business in California.

(b) **Authority**. The execution and delivery of this Agreement has been duly authorized and approved by all requisite action and the consummation of the transactions contemplated hereby will be duly authorized and approved by all requisite action of SELLER, and no other authorizations or approvals, whether of governmental bodies or otherwise, will be necessary in order to enable SELLER to enter into or to comply with the terms of this Agreement.

(c) **Binding Effect of Documents**. This Agreement and the other documents to be executed by SELLER hereunder, upon execution and delivery thereof by SELLER, will have been duly entered into by SELLER, and will constitute legal, valid and binding obligations of SELLER. Neither this Agreement nor anything provided to be done under this Agreement violates or shall violate any contract, document, understanding, agreement or instrument to which SELLER is a party or by which it is bound.

(d) **Leases**. There are no leases, subleases, occupancies or tenancies in effect pertaining to the Property except for the Leases (true, correct and complete copies of which have been previously delivered to BUYER), and SELLER is not aware of any oral agreements with respect to the occupancy of any portion of the Property. The Leases have not been amended, supplemented or extended, in writing or otherwise, and no concessions, abatements or adjustments have been granted to any tenants thereunder, except as described in the Leases.

BUYER expressly acknowledges and agrees that the representation and warranty of SELLER set forth in Section 4.3(d) above is based solely on the actual present knowledge of Ronald B. Coleman,

Illustration 5-1 (cont.)

without any investigation or duty to investigate whatsoever, and that the knowledge of any other person or entity shall not be imputed to Mr. Coleman or SELLER for purposes of this Section 4.3 or otherwise.

ARTICLE V

ADDITIONAL AGREEMENTS OF BUYER AND SELLER

5.1 **Right of Entry**. BUYER and its representatives, employees, contractors, agents and designees ("BUYER's Representatives") shall have the right to enter upon the Property, at BUYER's sole cost and expense, in order to inspect and investigate the Property and to conduct any and all surveys, tests and studies BUYER deems necessary or convenient, provided that BUYER shall promptly restore any damage done to the Property as a result of any such entry, inspections, tests, surveys or studies. All such entries shall be made only after reasonable advance written notice to SELLER by BUYER and at times reasonably acceptable to SELLER. BUYER shall indemnify, defend and hold harmless SELLER, SELLER's Affiliates (as defined below) and the Property from and against any and all Damages (as defined below) arising out of any such entry by BUYER or BUYER's Representatives. Any inspections of the Property conducted by BUYER and/or BUYER's Representatives shall be subject to the terms of this Section 5.1. As a condition precedent to BUYER's and/or any of BUYER's Representatives' right of entry hereunder, BUYER and/or BUYER's Representatives, as the case may be, shall obtain and keep in force until Close of Escrow comprehensive public liability insurance insuring BUYER, BUYER's Representatives and SELLER against any liability arising out of such entry on the Property. Such insurance shall be in an amount of not less than One Million Dollars ($1,000,000) for injury or death of any number of persons in any one accident or occurrence. Insurance required hereunder shall be in companies with a policy holder rating of "A" or better and a financial size category of "V" or better in "Best's Insurance Guide." BUYER shall provide SELLER with a certificate of insurance evidencing compliance with the foregoing insurance requirements prior to any entry upon the Property by BUYER or BUYER's Representatives. As used in this Agreement: (i) the term "Damages" shall mean any and all losses, debts, obligations, liabilities, claims (whether formal or informal, including, without limitation, any and all foreseeable and unforeseeable damages, fees, costs, losses and expenses, including, without limitation, any and all experts', consultants' and attorneys' fees and costs, directly or indirectly arising therefrom, and including, without limitation, any fines and penalties assessed, levied or asserted, and including, without limitation, any and all claims for contribution or indemnity, whether arising at law, in equity or otherwise), charges,

Illustration 5-1 (cont.)

damages, actions, causes of action, suits or proceedings (whether pending, threatened or completed), administrative orders, costs, expenses and fees (including, but not limited to attorneys' fees, including said fees on appeal) of any kind or nature whatsoever, whether matured or unmatured, whether known or unknown, whether suspected or unsuspected, or whether contingent or absolute, and (ii) the term **"SELLER's Affiliates"** shall mean each of SELLER's past, present and future partners, predecessors, successors, parents, divisions, assigns, subsidiaries and affiliates and each past, present and future officer, director, shareholder, employee, representative, heir, attorney, principal or agent of SELLER or of any such partners, predecessors, successors, parents, divisions, assigns, subsidiaries or affiliates.

5.2 **Approval of Subsequent Leases and Service Contracts and Modifications Thereto**. After BUYER has approved the Property pursuant to Section 3.1(b) above, (i) BUYER shall have the right to approve any new Leases or Service Contracts SELLER proposes to execute if such new Lease or Service Contract will survive the Close of Escrow, which approval shall not be unreasonably withheld, and (ii) SELLER shall not materially amend, modify, revise or adjust or terminate any Lease or Service Contract if such Lease or Service Contract will survive the Close of Escrow without BUYER's approval, which approval shall not be unreasonably withheld. BUYER shall approve or disapprove of any such new Leases or Service Contracts or amendments, modifications, revisions, adjustments or terminations of any then existing Leases or Service Contracts by written notice to SELLER within three (3) business days of the delivery of such new Lease or Service Contract or proposed amendment, modification, revision, adjustment or termination by SELLER to BUYER. BUYER's failure to notify SELLER in writing of its disapproval thereof (and reasons therefor) within said time period shall be deemed to be BUYER's approval of the same.

5.3 **Water Intrusion Problems**. BUYER acknowledges that the Property has suffered water damage as a result of water intrusion problems affecting the Improvements. In connection therewith, SELLER has received a report from J.R. Bardin Company (**"Bardin"**) containing proposed solutions concerning the water intrusion problems, a copy of which report (the **"Bardin Report"**) has been previously delivered to BUYER. BUYER hereby acknowledges its receipt of a copy of the Bardin Report and represents to SELLER that Buyer has reviewed the Bardin Report and is aware of the water intrusion problems described therein. BUYER also acknowledges that SELLER has engaged Bardin to perform the remediation work (the **"Remediation Work"**) contemplated by the Bardin Report. Buyer further acknowledges that Bardin has commenced the Remediation Work, and that SELLER intends to cause Bardin to complete the Remediation Work substantially in accordance with the Bardin Report, and agrees that SELLER shall

Illustration 5-1 (cont.)

have the right, in its sole and absolute discretion, to change the scope of, or terminate, the **Remediation Work** at any time and from time to time. BUYER hereby expressly acknowledges and agrees that, subject to BUYER's approval rights pursuant to Section 3.1(b) above, BUYER shall have no right whatsoever to approve or disapprove the Remediation Work and that it is purchasing the Property in an "AS-IS" condition in accordance with Section 4.1 above. If the Escrow closes, then, effective as of the Close of Escrow: (i) SELLER shall indemnify, defend and hold harmless BUYER from and against any and all Damages incurred by any tenant or former tenant of the Improvements as a result of any water intrusion problems which occurred prior to the Close of Escrow, (ii) BUYER shall indemnify, defend and hold harmless SELLER and SELLER's Affiliates from and against any and all Damages arising out of any water intrusion problems and/or the Remediation Work which occur on or after the Close of Escrow, and (iii) except for SELLER's obligations under Section 5.3(i) above and the payment of any and all sums due and owing Bardin (or any successor contractor) in connection with the Remediation Work, BUYER, for itself and its officers, directors, shareholders, affiliates, partners, limited partners, parent and subsidiary corporations, legal representatives, agents, successors and assigns (the **"Releasing Parties"**), completely and unconditionally waives, releases, acquits and forever discharges SELLER and SELLER's Affiliates (collectively, the **"Released Parties"**) from any Damages which any of the Releasing Parties ever had, now has, or may, shall or can hereafter have or acquire, arising out of, due to or in respect of any water intrusion problems occurring at the Property and/or in connection with the Remediation Work, it being the express understanding and agreement of the parties that if the Escrow closes, then SELLER shall have no further liabilities or obligations in connection with such matters from and after the Close of Escrow (except for SELLER's obligations under Section 5.3(i) above and the payment of any and all sums due and owing Bardin (or any successor contractor) in connection with the Remediation Work). At the request of any of the Released Parties, Releasing Parties shall prepare, execute, acknowledge (if necessary) and deliver to such Released Parties such other documents as may be reasonably required by such Released Parties to evidence the release contained in this Section 5.3. Releasing Parties further agree that all rights under Section 1542 of the California Civil Code and any similar laws are hereby expressly waived with respect to the matters specifically released by this Section 5.3 above. Said Civil Code section reads as follows:

> "A general release does not extend to claims which the creditor does not know or suspect to exist in his favor at the time of executing the release, which if known by him

Illustration 5-1 (cont.)

must have materially affected his settlement with the debtor."

BUYER expressly acknowledges that BUYER has received the advise of its counsel prior to signing this Agreement. BUYER executes the waiver and release provided in this Agreement, knowingly and voluntarily, with full knowledge of its significance, and with the express intention of affecting the legal consequences provided by a waiver of California Civil Code Section 1542. Notwithstanding anything to the contrary contained in this Agreement, SELLER shall retain, as its sole and separate property, any and all claims (including, without limitation, all claims for damages of any kind or nature whatsoever), choses in action, causes of action, rights and remedies which it may now have or hereafter acquire against any third parties (including, without limitation, any contractor or architect) in connection with the water intrusion problems described above, and BUYER agrees to allow SELLER and SELLER's Affiliates access to the Property upon reasonable advance notice to BUYER and at times reasonably acceptable to BUYER, and to otherwise cooperate with SELLER and SELLER's Affiliates (at no cost to BUYER), in connection with SELLER's and/or SELLER's Affiliates pursuit of any such claims, choses in action, causes of action, rights and/or remedies after the Close of Escrow. SELLER and SELLER's Affiliates shall indemnify, defend and hold harmless BUYER and the Property from and against all Damages arising out of any such entry by SELLER or SELLER's Affiliates after the Close of Escrow.

5.4 <u>Purchase Money Loan</u>. BUYER shall comply, in a timely manner, with all of the terms, conditions and requirements set forth in the Financing Addendum and the Loan Application (including, without limitation, the delivery to SELLER through the Close of Escrow of the "Opinion of Borrower's Counsel", the "BUYER's Certification" and the "Conditional Assignment of Management Agreement" in their respective forms set forth in Exhibit "B-1" attached hereto) in order to allow BUYER to obtain the purchase money loan contemplated by Section 1.2 above. BUYER's failure to comply with all of the terms, conditions and requirements set forth in, and to timely perform all of its obligations under, the Financing Addendum and the Loan Application shall constitute a material breach by BUYER under this Agreement, in which event SELLER shall have the right to terminate this Agreement and to retain the Deposit (plus all interest accrued thereon), the Application Fee and the Underwriting Fee in accordance with Section 7.2 below and the Loan Application, respectively.

Illustration 5-1 (cont.)

ARTICLE VI

CLOSING

6.1 **Escrow**. The purchase of the Property shall be consummated by means of an escrow (the "Escrow") established at First American Title Insurance Company, 411 Ivy Street, San Diego, California 92101, Attention: Tricia Erickson, Escrow Officer (the "Escrow Holder"). The parties shall deliver to Escrow Holder a fully executed original of this Agreement within two (2) business days after the mutual execution hereof. The parties shall close the Escrow on or before February 28, 1993 (the "Closing Date"). Although the parties have agreed and are bound to said Closing Date, the term "Close of Escrow" as used herein shall mean that date when the grant deed conveying the Property to BUYER is recorded in the Official Records.

6.2 **Escrow Instructions**. SELLER and BUYER agree that this document shall also constitute instructions to Escrow Holder. In addition, the parties agree to execute and deliver to the Escrow Holder such reasonable and customary escrow instructions in the usual form of Escrow Holder for the purpose of consummating the sale contemplated by this Agreement; provided, however, that standard extension provisions in such escrow instructions shall not apply and in the event there are any conflicts or inconsistencies between the terms and conditions set forth in such escrow instructions and those contained in this Agreement, then the terms and conditions set forth herein shall control. Escrow Holder shall perform all customary functions of an escrow holder to consummate this transaction, including, among other duties of Escrow Holder, preparation and recordation of the deed to be executed by SELLER and calculation of the prorations and closing costs (as described in Section 6.6 below) required by this Agreement, as well as serving as depository for all funds, instruments and documents needed for the Close of Escrow. The Escrow Holder shall also be instructed to issue at the Close of Escrow the Buyer's Title Policy provided for in Section 2.2 above showing title to the Property vested in BUYER, subject only to the Permitted Exceptions, and the Mortgagee's Title Policy provided for in Section 2.2 above in the amount of the Note for the protection of SELLER as the beneficiary under the Trust Deed.

6.3 **BUYER's Obligations**. On or before the Closing Date as provided below, BUYER shall deliver to Escrow Holder all of the following:

(a) The Down Payment in immediately available funds shall be deposited not later than twenty-four (24) hours prior to the Close of Escrow;

Illustration 5-1 (cont.)

(b) The executed and, where appropriate, acknowledged Note, Trust Deed, Assignment of Rents and Leases and Financing Statement;

(c) The BUYER's Certification;

(d) The Conditional Assignment of Management Agreement;

(e) All sums, certifications, surveys, insurance and other documents required by the Financing Addendum and the Loan Application;

(f) A copy of the resolution of the Board of Directors of BUYER authorizing the execution, delivery and performance by BUYER of this Agreement and designating one or more officers to execute documents in BUYER's name in connection herewith, certified as correct and complete by a secretary or an assistant secretary of BUYER, together with an incumbency certificate for each person executing documents on behalf of BUYER;

(g) A Bill of Sale and Assignment and Assumption of Leases, Warranties and Service Contracts in the form attached hereto as Exhibit "C" (the "Bill of Sale"), executed by BUYER;

(h) All costs and fees required to be paid by BUYER pursuant to Section 6.5 and 6.6(b) below; and

(i) Such other documents and instruments as may be reasonably requested by SELLER or by the Escrow Holder in order to consummate this transaction and to issue the Mortgagee's Title Policy.

6.4 <u>SELLER's Obligations</u>. On or before the Closing Date, SELLER shall deliver to Escrow Holder all of the following:

(a) A fully executed and acknowledged grant deed conveying the Property to BUYER;

(b) A copy of the partnership authorization of SELLER authorizing the execution, delivery and performance by SELLER of this Agreement and designating one or more partners to execute documents in SELLER's name in connection herewith;

(c) Originals or copies (if originals are not available) of the Leases and Service Contracts;

(d) The Bill of Sale, executed by SELLER;

(e) A certificate of Non-Foreign Status with respect to SELLER;

Illustration 5-1 (cont.)

(f) All costs and fees required to be paid by SELLER pursuant to Sections 6.5 and 6.6(a) below; and

(g) Such other documents and instruments as may be required herein or by the Escrow Holder in order to consummate this transaction and issue the Buyer's Title Policy.

6.5 **Prorations and Adjustments.** SELLER shall be responsible for and pay all accrued expenses with respect to the Property accruing up to 11:59 P.M. on the day prior to the Closing Date (the **"Adjustment Date"**) and shall be entitled to receive and retain all revenue from the Property accruing up to such time.

(a) **Prorations at Closing.** On the Closing Date, the following adjustments and apportionments shall be made in cash as of the Adjustment Date:

(i) Rents for the month in which the Closing Date occurs (the **"Closing Month"**) as and when collected. If past due rents are owing by tenants for the Closing Month and/or any months prior to the Closing Month (the **"Rent Arrearages"**), BUYER shall include in its rental bills to such tenants, an amount attributable to such Rent Arrearages and shall use its best commercially reasonable efforts to collect all Rent Arrearages, and SELLER shall be entitled to any funds received from such tenants by BUYER after the Closing Date which are in excess of amounts then owing to BUYER from such tenants for months including or after the Closing Month. In determining the amounts required to be paid to SELLER pursuant to the immediately preceding sentence, (A) BUYER shall not be permitted to accept any rentals or amounts owing to BUYER under any Leases in advance of the due dates therefor, and (B) the amount owing to BUYER for the Closing Month shall reflect the proration of such amounts as provided above. BUYER shall compute and bill all tenants for all "additional rent" and other amounts required to be paid under each tenant's lease, including, without limitation, common area maintenance, real estate tax and operating expense pass-throughs (collectively, the **"Additional Rents"**) as the same become due after the Closing Date under the terms of each tenant's lease. BUYER shall use its best commercially reasonable efforts to collect all Rent Arrearages and Additional Rents. Notwithstanding anything to the contrary contained herein, BUYER shall have no obligation to commence any litigation (including, without limitation, an unlawful detainer action) with respect to any Rent Arrearages and/or any Additional Rents. If, as and when the BUYER collects payments from a tenant on account of Additional Rents or Rent Arrearages, BUYER shall hold such funds as trustee for SELLER to the extent SELLER is entitled

Illustration 5-1 (cont.)

to any portion of such funds pursuant to this subsection and BUYER shall pay SELLER an amount equal to the Rent Arrearages or SELLER's pro rata share of such Additional Rents within five (5) days after BUYER or its agent receives each such payment. If a tenant's lease provides for any Additional Rents to be paid more frequently than annually and provides for an annual adjustment to reflect the actual operating expense or real estate tax figures for a twelve-month period, then BUYER shall debit or credit (as the case may be) the SELLER with SELLER's pro rata share of such adjustment. SELLER shall have the continuing right after the Close of Escrow to collect any Rent Arrearages and/or Additional Rents to which it is entitled hereunder by any lawful means available to SELLER. SELLER shall also have the right, upon reasonable advance notice and during normal business hours at BUYER's office, to review and audit the BUYER's records with respect to Additional Rent and the Rent Arrearages payable to or collected by BUYER. The Trust Deed shall provide that it secures BUYER's obligations under this Section 6.5(a)(i) and that BUYER's failure to pay the amounts when due under this Section 6.5(a)(i) or otherwise perform its obligations under this Section 6.5(a)(i) shall be deemed an Event of Default under the Trust Deed. BUYER shall deliver to SELLER two (2) semi-annual collection reports showing the sum, if any, paid by each tenant at the Property and the unpaid balance owed by such tenant pursuant to its lease through the end of each such six (6) month period; the first such collection report shall be delivered to SELLER within ten (10) days after the last day of the sixth (6th) calendar month after the Close of Escrow and the next such collection report shall be delivered to SELLER within ten (10) days after the last day of the twelfth (12th) calendar month after the Close of Escrow.

(ii) Real property taxes.

(iii) Any and all installments currently due on assessments or bonds encumbering the Property, provided BUYER shall assume all future obligations on any such assessments or bonds.

(iv) Charges under Service Contracts affecting the Property on the Closing Date, utility charges and deposits, including without limitation electricity, gas, water, and sewer charges, if any, and any other operating expenses affecting the Property.

(v) Income from vending machines and tenant services, if any.

Illustration 5-1 (cont.)

(b) **Security Deposits.** At the Close of Escrow, SELLER shall credit the Purchase Price by an amount equal to all unapplied security deposits payable to tenants under Leases in effect on the Closing Date (to the extent such security deposits are payable to the tenants under such Leases pursuant to the terms thereof or applicable law) against BUYER's receipt and indemnification therefor. Upon making such credit, BUYER will be deemed to have received all such security deposits and shall be fully responsible for the same as if a cash amount equal to such security deposits were actually delivered to BUYER. Prior to the Closing, SELLER reserves the right to apply all security deposits as provided under the respective Leases; provided, however, if SELLER has so applied any security deposit under any Lease which has not been terminated and SELLER is entitled, pursuant to the terms of such Lease, to require the tenant under such Lease to redeposit with SELLER the amount of such deposit, then SELLER agrees to use its reasonable efforts (without any cost to SELLER and without any resort to litigation) to cause such tenant to redeposit with SELLER the amount of such deposit (to the extent applied).

6.6 Closing Costs.

(a) SELLER shall pay:

(i) The premium for a standard CLTA Owner's Policy of Title Insurance.

(ii) One-half (1/2) of Escrow Holder's escrow fee.

(iii) Documentary transfer taxes.

(iv) The cost of recording the grant deed.

(v) The cost of any of SELLER's other obligations under this Agreement.

(b) BUYER shall pay:

(i) Any additional premium for an ALTA Owner's Policy of Title Insurance (if BUYER elects to receive same pursuant to Section 2.2 above), the cost of any title endorsements desired by BUYER, the premium for the Mortgagee's Title Policy (including the cost of any endorsements required by SELLER).

(ii) One-half (1/2) of Escrow Holder's escrow fee.

(iii) The cost of recording and filing, as the case may be, the Security Documents.

Illustration 5-1 (cont.)

(iv) The cost of any of BUYER's other obligations under this Agreement.

Any other closing costs or expenses of the Escrow shall be borne by the parties in accordance with customary practice in San Diego County, California.

ARTICLE VII

REMEDIES

7.1 **Remedies.** If SELLER defaults under this Agreement, and BUYER is ready, willing and able to perform all of its obligations under this Agreement, and is not in default hereunder, then BUYER may, at BUYER's option, bring an action to terminate this Agreement and the Escrow or pursue any other rights or remedies that BUYER may have at law or in equity; provided, however, prior to BUYER's exercise of any remedy of specific performance, including the filing of a Lis Pendens against the Property, BUYER shall: (i) deposit into Escrow all of the items listed in Section 6.3 above necessary to close the Escrow established hereunder, including, without limitation, the entire Down Payment in cash without any offset of any amounts (except for a credit in the amount of the First Deposit) or modification of any documents, and (ii) authorize the release of such items upon SELLER's compliance with Section 6.4 in order to effectuate the Close of Escrow. If Escrow does not close within forty-five (45) days after BUYER's so depositing such items because of SELLER's failure to deposit the items listed in Section 6.4 above and authorize the release of such items upon BUYER's compliance with Section 6.3 in order to effectuate the Close of Escrow, then Escrow Holder shall automatically, and without any further instructions from either SELLER or BUYER, deliver to BUYER all sums deposited by BUYER into Escrow and BUYER may, subject to the satisfaction of any requirements which may otherwise be applicable to a specific performance action, thereafter continue with the enforcement of its remedy of specific performance. If BUYER exercises any such remedy of specific performance without first complying with the foregoing requirements, then BUYER shall be deemed to have waived its right to specific performance (including the filing of a Lis Pendens against the Property) and BUYER's sole and exclusive remedy hereunder shall be a monetary remedy for damages. If BUYER defaults under this Agreement, SELLER's sole and exclusive remedy shall be to terminate this Agreement and to retain the First Deposit in accordance with Section 1.2(a) above, the Second Deposit (and all interest accrued thereon) in accordance with Section 7.2 below and the Underwriting Fee and the Application Fee in accordance with the Loan Application; provided, however,

Illustration 5-1 (cont.)

SELLER's right to retain the First Deposit, the Underwriting Fee and the Application Fee shall also be governed by Section 1.2(a) above and the Loan Application, respectively, and shall not be limited by this Section 7.1 or by Section 7.2 below.

7.2 **Liquidated Damages**. BUYER AND SELLER ACKNOWLEDGE AND AGREE THAT: (1) IT WOULD BE IMPRACTICAL OR EXTREMELY DIFFICULT TO DETERMINE SELLER'S ACTUAL DAMAGES IN THE EVENT OF BUYER'S DEFAULT UNDER THIS AGREEMENT, AND (2) TAKING INTO ACCOUNT ALL OF THE CIRCUMSTANCES EXISTING ON THE DATE OF THIS AGREEMENT, THE SUM OF THE FIRST DEPOSIT, THE SECOND DEPOSIT, THE UNDERWRITING FEE AND THE APPLICATION FEE, TOGETHER WITH ALL INTEREST ACCRUED THEREON, IS A REASONABLE ESTIMATE OF SELLER'S ACTUAL DAMAGES IN SUCH EVENT. CONSEQUENTLY, IN THE EVENT OF BUYER'S DEFAULT UNDER THIS AGREEMENT, SELLER'S SOLE AND EXCLUSIVE REMEDY SHALL BE TO TERMINATE THIS AGREEMENT AND TO RETAIN THE FIRST DEPOSIT, THE SECOND DEPOSIT, THE UNDERWRITING FEE AND THE APPLICATION FEE, AND ALL INTEREST ACCRUED THEREON, PROVIDED THAT, IF SELLER IS REQUIRED TO ENFORCE THIS LIQUIDATED DAMAGES PROVISION AND PREVAILS, THEN SELLER SHALL ALSO BE ENTITLED TO RECOVER ALL COSTS OF ENFORCEMENT, INCLUDING, BUT NOT LIMITED TO, ATTORNEYS' FEES AND COSTS IN ACCORDANCE WITH SECTION 9.4 BELOW.

________________ BUYER   ________________ SELLER

ARTICLE VIII

MANAGEMENT PENDING CLOSING; DAMAGE TO PROPERTY; EMINENT DOMAIN

8.1 **Management Pending Closing**. SELLER agrees to maintain its present policies of fire insurance on the Property in full force and effect from the date of this Agreement through and including the Close of Escrow. Further, until the Close of Escrow, SELLER shall operate the Property in accordance with reasonable and prudent business procedures and standards (but in no event shall a higher standard of care than currently followed by SELLER be required) and, at the Close of Escrow, the Property shall be in substantially the same condition as it is in as of the date hereof, reasonable wear and tear excepted.

8.2 **Election to Terminate**. If on or before the Close of Escrow either (a) all or a substantial part of the Property is damaged or destroyed by fire or the elements or by any other cause, or (b) any part of the Property is taken by condemnation or other power of eminent domain, the BUYER may, by written notice given to SELLER within ten (10) days after BUYER shall have notice of the occurrence or the taking (but in no event

Illustration 5-1 (cont.)

later than one (1) day prior to the Closing Date), elect to terminate this Agreement. For the purposes hereof, with respect to damage or destruction resulting from a casualty, a "substantial part" of the Property shall be deemed to mean a portion of the Property having a value of One Hundred Thousand Dollars ($100,000) or more or which would require expenditure of One Hundred Thousand Dollars ($100,000) or more for repair or restoration, as determined by a general contractor and reasonably acceptable to SELLER and BUYER.

8.3 Election Not to Terminate.

(a) Damage or Destruction. If on or before the Close of Escrow: (i) all or a substantial part of the Property is damaged or destroyed but this Agreement is not canceled pursuant to Section 8.2 above, or (ii) an insubstantial part of the Property is damaged or destroyed, then: (A) if such damage or destruction is adequately covered by insurance, then BUYER shall take the Property as diminished by such damage or destruction and, on the Close of Escrow, SELLER shall credit the Purchase Price with an amount equal to any sums of money collected by SELLER under its policies of insurance or renewals thereof insuring against the loss in question, after deducting (1) any actual and documented expenses incurred by SELLER in collecting such insurance (including, but not limited to, reasonable attorneys' fees) and (2) any amount that SELLER shall have paid, agreed to pay, or shall have been obligated to pay, for repairs or restoration of the damage, and in addition, SELLER shall assign, transfer and set over to BUYER all of SELLER's right, title and interest in and to said policies with respect to the Property and any further sums payable under said policies, or (B) if such damage or destruction is not adequately covered by insurance, then BUYER shall take the Property as diminished by such damage or destruction and the Purchase Price shall be reduced by an amount equal to the cost of repairing such damage or destruction, as determined by a general contractor reasonably acceptable to BUYER and SELLER.

(b) Condemnation. If on or before the Close of Escrow any part of the Property is taken by condemnation or other power of eminent domain but this Agreement is not canceled pursuant to Section 8.2 above, then the Purchase Price shall be reduced by an amount equal to the amount, if any, that was paid to SELLER for such taking (after deducting any actual and documented expenses incurred by SELLER in collecting such amount, including, but not limited to, reasonable attorneys' fees) and SELLER shall assign, transfer and set over to BUYER all of SELLER's right, title and interest in and to any awards that may in the future be made for such taking.

Illustration 5-1 (cont.)

ARTICLE IX

MISCELLANEOUS PROVISIONS

9.1 Brokerage Commissions. SELLER hereby represents and warrants to BUYER that SELLER has made no statement or representation to nor entered into any agreement with a broker, salesman or finder in connection with the transaction contemplated by this Agreement, except with Sperry Van Ness. BUYER hereby represents and warrants to SELLER that BUYER has made no statement or representation to nor entered into any agreement with a broker, salesman or finder in connection with the transaction contemplated by this Agreement, except with Major League Properties. If, and only if, the Escrow closes, then SELLER shall pay: (a) to Sperry Van Ness through the Close of Escrow from the proceeds due SELLER hereunder a total sum equal to two percent (2%) of the Purchase Price paid by BUYER hereunder, pursuant to separate instructions from Sperry Van Ness, and (b) to Major League Properties through the Close of Escrow from the proceeds due SELLER hereunder a total sum equal to two percent (2%) of the Purchase Price paid by BUYER hereunder, pursuant to separate instructions from Major League Properties. If the Escrow fails to close for any reason whatsoever (including, without limitation, a default by BUYER or SELLER hereunder), then SELLER shall have no obligation whatsoever to pay any commission, fee or other compensation or amounts to Sperry Van Ness and/or Major League Properties. Subject to the foregoing, in the event of a claim for any brokers' or finders' fees or commissions in connection with the negotiation or execution of this Agreement or the transaction contemplated hereby, SELLER shall indemnify, hold harmless and defend BUYER from and against such claim and any Damages arising out of such claim if such claim shall be based upon any statement or representation or agreement alleged to have been made by SELLER and BUYER shall indemnify, hold harmless and defend SELLER and SELLER's Affiliates from and against such claim and any Damages arising out of such claim if such claim shall be based upon any statement, representation or agreement alleged to have been made by BUYER.

9.2 Notice. Any notice, demand, approval, consent, or other communication required or desired to be given under this

Illustration 5-1 (cont.)

Agreement in writing shall be directed to the party involved at the address indicated below:

SELLER: Pacific Centre
c/o SoPac Real Estate Group
2 North Lake Avenue, Suite 800
Pasadena, California 91101
Attention: Mr. Paul J. Giuntini
Mr. Ronald B. Coleman
Telephone No.: (818) 577-1130
Telecopier No.: (213) 684-2391

with a copy to:

Morgan, Lewis & Bockius
4675 MacArthur Court, Suite 740
Newport Beach, California 92660
Attention: Keith E. Thomas, Esq.
Telephone No.: (714) 851-6333
Telecopier No.: (714) 851-1624

BUYER: American Capital Investments, Inc.
330 Washington Boulevard, Penthouse Suite
Marina Del Rey, California 90292
Attention: Mr. Stephen Murphy, President
Telephone No.: (310) 822-0005
Telecopier No.: ____________

with a copy to:

____
____
____
____
Telephone No.: ____________
Telecopier No.: ____________

Any notice, demand, approval, consent or other communication may be given by personal service, fax (with hard copy to follow immediately), recognized overnight air courier or by mail. Any notice, demand, approval, consent or other communication given (a) personally shall be deemed delivered upon receipt, (b) by fax shall be deemed delivered upon being transmitted and received on the facsimile machine of the addressee, provided a "hard copy" has been deposited in the U.S. mail, (c) by recognized air courier, freight prepaid, shall be deemed delivered on the next business day, and (d) by mail shall be deemed to have been given when three (3) business days have elapsed from the date it was deposited in the United States mail, certified and postage prepaid, addressed to the party to be served at said address or

Illustration 5-1 (cont.)

at such other address of which that party may have given notice under the provisions of this Section 9.2.

9.3 **Modification.** This Agreement may not be modified or amended except by a written agreement executed by SELLER and BUYER, and only to the extent set forth therein.

9.4 **Attorneys' Fees.** If any party to this Agreement shall bring any action or proceeding for any relief against the other, declaratory or otherwise, arising out of this Agreement, the losing party shall pay to the prevailing party a reasonable sum for attorneys' fees and costs incurred by said prevailing party in bringing or defending such action or proceeding and/or enforcing any judgment granted therein, all of which shall be deemed to have accrued upon the commencement of such action or proceeding and shall be paid whether or not such action or proceeding is prosecuted to final judgment. Any judgment or order entered in such action or proceeding shall contain a specific provision providing for the recovery of attorneys' fees and costs, separate from the judgment, incurred in enforcing such judgment. The prevailing party shall be determined by the trier of fact based upon an assessment of which party's major arguments or positions taken in the proceedings could fairly be said to have prevailed over the other party's major arguments or positions on major disputed issues. For the purposes of this Section 9.4, attorneys' fees shall include, without limitation, fees incurred in the following: (a) post-judgment motions; (b) contempt proceedings; (c) garnishment, levy, and debtor and third-party examinations; (d) discovery; and (e) bankruptcy litigation. This Section 9.4 is intended to be expressly severable from the other provisions of this Agreement, is intended to survive any judgment and is not to be deemed merged into the judgment.

9.5 **Form of Documents.** All instruments and documents to be executed and delivered under this Agreement by any party to any other party shall be in form satisfactory to the other party.

9.6 **Successors and Assigns.** This Agreement shall be binding upon, and shall inure to the benefit of, the successors and assigns of the parties. BUYER may not assign its rights or duties under this Agreement without SELLER's prior written consent, which may be withheld in its sole and absolute discretion. In addition, during the term of this Agreement, there may not be any transfer of any legal or beneficial interest in BUYER without SELLER's prior written consent, which may be withheld in its sole and absolute discretion, and any attempt to transfer any such interest shall constitute a material breach by BUYER of this Agreement. Any attempted assignment of this Agreement by BUYER which is not in strict compliance with this

Illustration 5-1 (cont.)

Section 9.6 shall be null and void and shall constitute a material breach by BUYER of this Agreement.

9.7 **Duplicate Counterparts.** This Agreement may be executed in duplicate counterparts, all of which together shall constitute a single instrument, and each of which shall be deemed an original of this Agreement for all purposes, notwithstanding that less than all signatures appear on any one counterpart.

9.8 **Section Headings.** The various section headings in this Agreement are inserted for convenience of reference only, and shall not affect the meaning or interpretation of this Agreement or any provision hereof.

9.9 **Survival of Covenants, Etc.** All agreements, conditions, acknowledgements, representations, warranties and other obligations set forth in this Agreement shall survive the Close of Escrow, and any doctrine that would hold that performance is deemed completed upon the closing shall not apply to this Agreement because many obligations under this Agreement are to be performed after the Close of Escrow.

9.10 **Holidays.** When performance of an obligation or satisfaction of a condition set forth in this Agreement is required on or by a date that is a Saturday, Sunday, or legal holiday, such performance or satisfaction shall instead be required on or by the next business day following that Saturday, Sunday, or holiday, notwithstanding any other provisions of this Agreement.

9.11 **No Recorded Memorandum.** Prior to Close of Escrow, neither this Agreement nor any memorandum hereof or reference hereto, shall be filed in any place of public record. Failure of BUYER to comply with this Section 9.11 shall be a material default by BUYER under this Agreement and, at the election of SELLER shall automatically and immediately terminate all of BUYER's rights under this Agreement, and thereafter BUYER shall not have any right, title, or interest in or to the Property whatsoever.

9.12 **Exhibits.** All Exhibits attached to, and to which reference is made in, this Agreement are incorporated into, and shall be deemed a part of, this Agreement.

9.13 **Entire Agreement.** This Agreement is the entire agreement of SELLER and BUYER with respect to the Property, containing all of the terms and conditions to which SELLER and BUYER have agreed. This Agreement supersedes and replaces entirely all previous oral and written understandings of SELLER and BUYER respecting the Property, including, without limitation, any such undertakings contained in that certain Letter of Intent

Illustration 5-1 (cont.)

dated January 8, 1993, by and between SELLER and BUYER with respect to the Property.

9.14 Time. Time is of the essence in this Agreement and each and every provision of this Agreement.

9.15 Offer to Buy. Execution of this Agreement by BUYER constitutes an offer to buy the Property from SELLER on the terms and conditions set forth herein. Under no circumstances whatsoever, including, without limitation, any oral representations or statements, shall this Agreement be deemed an offer by SELLER to sell the Property or be binding upon SELLER until executed by a duly authorized officer of SELLER.

9.16 Severability. If any term, provision, covenant or condition of this Agreement is found by a court of competent jurisdiction to be invalid, void, or unenforceable, the remainder of this Agreement shall continue in full force and effect and shall in no way be affected, impaired or invalidated.

9.17 Governing Law. This Agreement shall be governed by the laws of the State of California.

9.18 Confidentiality. BUYER and SELLER each agree that all of the provisions of, and all transactions contemplated, by, this Agreement, except to the extent otherwise mutually agreed in writing by BUYER AND SELLER, shall remain confidential until the Close of Escrow. If this Agreement terminates for any reason without BUYER purchasing the Property, BUYER and SELLER shall each return to the other any documents and other materials received from the other and shall keep the provisions of, and all transactions contemplated by, this Agreement confidential. BUYER hereby agrees that any and all information pertaining to SELLER or the Property disclosed to BUYER by SELLER (the "Confidential Information"), whether directly or indirectly, either before or after the date hereof, will be kept by BUYER in strict confidence and not disclosed to any person other than BUYER's internal personnel and outside consultants, lenders/investors, attorneys and other parties necessary to BUYER's investigation of the Property, without the prior written consent of SELLER. BUYER shall provide to each such party such information only to the extent necessary to allow such party to perform its job for BUYER and BUYER shall use its reasonable efforts to ensure that its internal personnel, outside consultants, lenders/investors, attorneys and other parties necessary to BUYER's investigation of the Property do not disclose any Confidential Information. BUYER shall not use, or permit to be used, the Confidential Information or any other information regarding SELLER or the Property disclosed by SELLER to BUYER at any time in any manner detrimental to SELLER, any of SELLER's Affiliates or the Property. Notwithstanding the foregoing, nothing contained in

Illustration 5-1 (cont.)

this Section 9.18 shall prevent either party from disclosing any Confidential Information where such disclosure is compelled by legal process or required by law or is necessary or appropriate in any legal administrative hearing relating to this Agreement and/or the transaction contemplated hereby.

9.19 __**Representation by Counsel**__. All parties hereto acknowledge that they have each been represented by independent counsel of their own choice throughout all of the negotiations which preceded the execution of this Agreement. This Agreement shall be construed fairly as to all parties and not in favor of or against any of the parties, regardless of which of the parties prepared this Agreement, and the parties hereby waive California Civil Code Section 1654.

IN WITNESS WHEREOF, this Agreement is executed by the parties on the dates set opposite their signatures below, but shall be deemed dated for reference purposes as of the date first above written.

"SELLER"

PACIFIC CENTRE, a California general partnership

By: SoPac Properties, Inc., a Delaware corporation, its General Partner

Dated: ____________________ By: ____________________
Name:
Its:

By: SoPac Kohala Corp., a California corporation, its General Partner

Dated: ____________________ By: ____________________
Name:
Its:

"BUYER"

AMERICAN CAPITAL INVESTMENTS, INC. a California corporation

Dated: ____________________ By: ____________________
Stephen Murphy, President

Illustration 5-2

AGREEMENT OF PURCHASE AND SALE

AND JOINT ESCROW INSTRUCTIONS

THIS AGREEMENT OF PURCHASE AND SALE AND JOINT ESCROW INSTRUCTIONS ("**Agreement**") dated as of March 10, 1993, is by and between AMERICAN CAPITAL INVESTMENTS, INC., a California Corporation ("Seller"), and SANDERSON J. RAY DEVELOPMENT ("Buyer").

FOR VALUABLE CONSIDERATION, the receipt and sufficiency of which are hereby acknowledged, Seller and Buyer agree, and establish these escrow instructions, as follows:

1. **Purchase and Sale**. Seller agrees to sell to Buyer, and Buyer agrees to purchase from Seller, subject to and upon the terms and conditions set forth in this Agreement, Seller's entire right, title and interest in and to the following (collectively, "**Property**"): (a) that certain real property located in the City of Westminster, in the County of Orange ("**County**"), State of California ("**State**"), more particularly described in Exhibit "A" attached hereto ("**Real Property**"); (b) all buildings, fixtures, structures, parking areas, landscaping and other improvements constructed or situated on the Real Property and owned by Seller ("**Improvements**"), but excluding any such items owned by any and all persons or entities now or hereafter leasing, renting or occupying space on the Real Property pursuant to written or oral agreements ("**Tenants**") or owned by any public or private utilities or contractors under contract; (c) any and all furniture, fixtures, carpeting, draperies, appliances, machinery, equipment, stock in trade, merchandise and other tangible, personal property owned by Seller and attached to or appurtenant to the Real Property ("**Personal Property**"), which shall be quitclaimed to Buyer without warranty; and (d) those certain written or oral rental agreements described on Exhibit "B" attached hereto ("**Tenant Leases**").

2. **Purchase Price**. The purchase price for the Property shall be One Million, Six Hundred Sixty-Eight Thousand Dollars ($1,668,000.00) ("**Purchase Price**").

3. **Payment of Purchase Price.**

3.1 **Deposit**. Buyer shall deposit with Beverly West Escrow, 433 North Camden Drive, Suite 1010, Beverly Hills, California 90210, Escrow No. 5555-CC, Attention: Ms. Kathy Corrado ("**Escrow Holder**") a deposit in the aggregate sum of Ten Thousand Dollars ($10,000.00) ("**Deposit**"). Within two (2) business days following the Contingency Date, Buyer shall deposit an additional Forty Thousand Dollars ($40,000.00) to Escrow Holder in cash or cash equivalency (which for purposes of this Agreement shall mean a wire transfer of immediately available funds or a bank cashier's check of immediately available funds drawn on a reputable bank or savings and loan association licensed to do business in the State and acceptable to Seller).

3.2 **Balance**.

3.2.1 **Cash Payment**. On or before (1) business day prior to the Close of Escrow, Buyer shall deposit into Escrow (as defined in Paragraph 5 of this Agreement), in cash or cash equivalent, One Million, Six Hundred and Eighteen Thousand Dollars ($1,618,000.00) representing the balance of the Purchase Price, subject to Buyer's share of prorations and adjustments, closing costs and any other obligations of Buyer hereunder, and minus those funds actually paid by Buyer to the Escrow Holder together with interest thereon (collectively, "**Cash Payment**").

Illustration 5-2 (cont.)

4. Condition of Title and Deed. At the Close of Escrow, Seller shall convey to Buyer by a grant deed in the form attached hereto as Exhibit "C" ("**Deed**") fee simple title to the Real Property, subject only to the following matters (collectively, "**Approved Title Conditions**"): (a) real property general and special taxes and assessments not delinquent and the lien of supplemental assessments; (b) the exceptions to the title set forth on Exhibit "D" ("**Title Exceptions**") attached hereto which are approved by Buyer pursuant to Paragraph 6.1.1, (c) matters affecting the condition of title to the Property created by or with the written consent of Buyer; and (d) such other matters as may appear of record and be approved or waived by Buyer.

5. Escrow. An escrow ("**Escrow**") shall be opened with Escrow Holder for the consummation of the transactions contemplated herein upon the delivery into Escrow of this Agreement following its execution by Buyer and Seller ("**Opening of Escrow**"). Escrow shall close ("**Close of Escrow**") on a date ("**Closing Date**") no later than May 31, 1993. Should the Closing Date fall on a Saturday, Sunday or national, state or local holiday, or a holiday recognized by Seller, the Closing Date shall occur on the first following business day that is not a national, state or local holiday, or a holiday recognized by Seller. To the extent any general escrow provisions which are furnished by the Escrow Holder conflict with any provisions of this Agreement, this Agreement shall control.

6. Conditions.

6.1 Conditions Precedent to the Contingency Date. Buyer's obligations to purchase the Property are subject to the satisfaction, not later than April 23, 1993 ("**Contingency Date**") of each of the following conditions. These conditions shall be either approved or disapproved in writing by Buyer on or before the Contingency Date set forth herein or shall be deemed approved conclusively if no written disapproval has been submitted by Buyer to Escrow Holder and Seller as of the Contingency Date. Buyer's approval of any of these conditions shall not be unreasonably withheld.

6.1.1 Title. Seller shall use its reasonable efforts to cause to be delivered to Buyer prior to the Contingency Date a standard preliminary title report relating to the Real Property ("**Title Report**") and copies of all recorded documents relating to the exceptions shown ("**Title Documents**"). Buyer shall have until the Contingency Date to deliver to Seller and Escrow Holder written notice of Buyer's approval or disapproval of the matters of title shown in the Title Documents ("**Buyer's Title Notice**)". Buyer's Title Notice shall specify the grounds of any disapproval.

6.1.1.1 If Buyer properly disapproves any such items, Seller shall then have the right, but not the obligation, in Seller's sole discretion, to attempt to cure or remove the objection. Seller shall exercise its right to attempt to cure or remove the objection by depositing notice in Escrow with a copy to Buyer within five (5) business days after Seller's receipt of Buyer's Title Notice. Failure or refusal of Seller to deposit such notice electing to attempt to cure or remove Buyer's objections shall be deemed an election by Seller not to attempt to so cure or remove the objections.

6.1.1.2 If Seller elects to cure or remove Buyer's objections, then Seller shall have until the Close of Escrow to cure or remove said objections. Seller shall be deemed to have cured Buyer's objections if Title Company commits to provide insurance coverage within Buyer's

Illustration 5-2 (cont.)

Title Policy (as defined in Paragraph 9 of this Agreement) against loss sustained by reason of the matters objected to by Buyer.

6.1.1.3 If Title Company requires a survey or physical inspection of the Property in connection with the issuance of a title insurance policy, the deadlines for the following items shall be extended to accommodate said survey or inspection for a period not to exceed five (5) business days: (a) the insurance of the Title Report; and (b) Buyer's Title Notice. This paragraph shall not extend the Contingency Date with respect to any other rights or obligations, nor shall it extend the Closing Date.

6.1.2 <u>Operating Documents</u>. Prior to the Contingency Date, Buyer at Buyer's sole cost shall have the right to secure, review and approve the following documents and materials respecting the Property and its operation, but only to the extent available and in the possession and control of Seller: (i) Tenant Leases for current Tenants, if any; (ii) copies of income and expense statements for the Property since the date the Property was acquired by Seller; (iii) copies of the most recent bills issued for the real property taxes and assessments against the Real Property; (iv) copies of all service contracts and agreements relating to the operation of the Property ("**Service Contracts**") in effect and copies of all applicable warranties affecting the Property. Seller shall use its reasonable efforts to provide Buyer with such documents and materials as set forth below prior to the Contingency Date.

6.1.3 <u>Inspection of Property</u>.

6.1.3.1 On or before the Contingency Date, Buyer shall have completed and approved or disapproved the results of any and all inspections, investigations, tests and studies, with respect to the Property as Buyer may at Buyer's reasonable discretion elect to make or obtain (including, without limitation, investigations with regard to the environmental condition, zoning, building codes and other governmental regulations, architectural and/or structural inspections, mechanical, engineering tests, economic feasibility studies and soils, seismic, geologic and environmental reports). The cost of any such inspections, tests, reviews, reports and studies shall be borne exclusively by Buyer. Buyer and its representatives, agents, consultants and designees shall have the right upon reasonable advance notice to Seller and during business hours to enter upon the Property to make such reasonable inspections, investigations and tests as Buyer may elect to make or obtain, subject to such reasonable restrictions as Seller may elect to impose, to the provisions of this Agreement, to the rights of Tenants, occupants, guests and customers, and to any restrictions imposed upon Seller and its property manager. Notwithstanding anything stated above, Buyer shall not engage in any destructive testing or cause any physical damage to the Property without Seller's prior written consent. Buyer shall indemnify and hold Seller, its property manager and the Property free of and harmless from any and all claims (including mechanics' liens), liabilities, losses, damages, costs and expenses, including,without limitation, attorneys' fees and costs caused by or arising out of the activities of Buyer and its agents, employees, consultants and designees on or about the Property, whether pursuant to the terms hereof or otherwise. Notwithstanding any contrary provisions hereof, this indemnification shall survive the termination of this Agreement, the cancellation of Escrow or the Close of Escrow.

6.1.3.2 In the event that Buyer reasonably disapproves of the condition of the Property as provided herein, Buyer shall deposit with Escrow Holder prior to

Illustration 5-2 (cont.)

the Contingency Date, with a copy to Seller, a writing identifying the items disapproved and specifying the reasons for the disapproval, along with a copy of any reports, test results or other documents verifying the disapproved conditions.

6.1.3.3 If Buyer disapproves any such items, Seller shall then have the right, but not the obligation, in Seller's sole discretion, to attempt to cure or remove the objection. Seller shall exercise its right to attempt to cure or remove the objection by depositing notice in Escrow with a copy to Buyer within five (5) business days after Seller's receipt of Buyer's notice. Failure or refusal of Seller to deposit such notice electing to attempt to cure or remove Buyer's objections shall be deemed an election by Seller not to attempt to so cure or remove the objections. If Seller elects to cure or remove Buyer's objections, then Seller shall have until the Close of Escrow to cure or remove said objections.

6.1.3.4 The environmental site assessment, dated August 20, 1991, Project No.1C2889AA001, as prepared by Diagnostic Engineering, Inc., in favor of Seller ("**Environmental Report**") attached hereto as Exhibit "E" is being provided by Seller to Buyer for information purposes only, without representation or warranty, express or implied, of any kind or nature. Buyer agrees to hold the Environmental Report and its contents and findings in the strictest of confidence and agrees not to distribute, disclose, disseminate, copy or reproduce, directly or indirectly, or in any other manner, the Environmental Report, its findings or contents to any individual, firm, proprietorship, association, trust, partnership, corporation or any other entity; provided, however, that Buyer may provide a copy of the Environmental Report to its legal counsel of record on the condition that such person agrees in writing to hold such Environmental Report subject to the same restrictions as set forth herein. The obligations to safeguard the confidentiality of said Environmental Report shall survive and continue after the termination of this Agreement, the cancellation of Escrow or the Close of Escrow. Buyer acknowledges, understands, represents and agrees that: (1) Buyer is purchasing the Property in an "**AS-IS CONDITION**" "**WITH ALL FAULTS**"; (2) Buyer is not relying upon and shall not rely upon the Environmental Report in purchasing the Property; and (3) Buyer shall conduct or cause to be conducted, in its sole discretion, an independent investigation, inspection, survey and analysis as it deems necessary, to determine the threat or presence of any Hazardous Substance (as defined in Paragraph 17.2 of this Agreement) at, on, under, about, above, from or adjacent to the Property and its surroundings.

6.1.4 <u>**Disclosure Statement**</u> On or before the Contingency Date, Buyer shall have approved the documents and the disclosures listed in Exhibit "F" ("<u>**Disclosure Statement**</u>"). Buyer shall be deemed to have approved the documents and disclosures listed in the Disclosure Statement unless Buyer notifies Seller of its disapproval, in writing, on or before the Contingency Date. Seller is providing the Disclosure Statement for the purpose of disclosure only. Seller makes no representations or warranties whatsoever regarding the accuracy or completeness of the Disclosure Statement. Buyer shall not rely upon the Disclosure Statement in any way, shape or form. Buyer agrees to, and represents that it will, make an independent investigation of each and every aspect of the condition of the Property without reliance on the Disclosure Statement, or assume all risk of not conducting an independent investigation.

6.2 <u>**Failure of Conditions Precedent to the Contingency Date**</u>. Except as otherwise provided, Buyer may

Illustration 5-2 (cont.)

terminate this Agreement and cancel Escrow by reason of Buyer's disapproval prior to the Contingency Date of any of the items set forth in Paragraphs 6.1.1, 6.1.2 and 6.1.3, which Seller elects not to cure or remove as provided, in which case the Initial Deposit and interest thereon shall be returned to Buyer and the cancellation charges required to be paid to Escrow Holder shall be divided equally between Buyer and Seller, and all other charges shall be borne by the party that incurred the charge.

6.3 <u>Conditions Precedent to Seller's Obligation to Close</u>. Seller's obligations under this Agreement are subject to the satisfaction, no later than the Closing Date, of the following conditions precedent: (i) Buyer shall have delivered to Escrow Holder, for disbursement as herein set forth, the Cash Payment; (ii) Buyer shall have delivered to Escrow Holder the documents described in Paragraph 7.2 below, duly executed and acknowledged as provided therein, (iii) Buyer's representations, warranties and covenants set forth in Paragraph 13 shall be true and correct in all material respects as of the Closing Date; (iv) Buyer shall not have represented itself as the owner or lessee of the Property for any purpose, including, without limitation, for marketing the Property, pursuing any lease commitment or negotiating any lease, sale or development at or affecting the Property, nor shall Buyer have taken any action that would adversely affect or impact the occupancy, operation and/or marketing of the Property.

6.4 <u>Mutual Conditions Precedent to Close of Escrow</u>. The Close of Escrow and the obligations of both Buyer and Seller under this Agreement are subject to the satisfaction, no later than the Closing Date, of the following conditions precedent: (i) all conditions precedent to the Close of Escrow as provided for in this Agreement shall be fully performed and satisfied; and (ii) as of the Closing Date, Title Company shall have issued, or shall have committed to issue, Buyer's Title Policy (as defined in Paragraph 9 of this Agreement) to Buyer.

6.5 <u>Failure of Conditions Precedent to Close of Escrow</u>.

6.5.1 <u>Title and Condition of Property</u>. In the event that Buyer's Title Policy is not in conformity with the matters approved by Buyer as provided in Paragraph 4 as of the Closing Date or Buyer has reasonably disapproved of the condition of the Property pursuant to Paragraph 6.1.3, and Seller has elected not to attempt to remedy or cure the defects or objections, or is unable to do so, then Buyer either shall terminate this Agreement and cancel Escrow or waive the objections and purchase the Property without such objections being so remedied and with no reduction in the Purchase Price, and such election shall be Buyer's sole remedy.

6.5.2 <u>Other Conditions Precedent.</u> In the event any of the conditions set forth in Paragraph 6.3 or 6.4 are not timely satisfied or waived: (i) this Agreement shall terminate, the rights, obligations and liabilities of Buyer and Seller shall terminate, and Escrow shall be canceled, except as otherwise provided herein; (ii) Escrow Holder shall promptly return to Seller and Buyer all funds (except as provided in Paragraph 6.5.2 (iii) hereinbelow) and documents respectively deposited by them into Escrow which are held by Escrow Holder on the date of said termination and cancellation less the amount of any cancellation charges required to be paid by such party under Paragraph 6.6; and (iii) if any

Illustration 5-2 (cont.)

condition set forth in Paragraph 6.3 (i) through (iv), inclusively, was not timely satisfied or waived, Seller shall retain or receive from Escrow Holder the Deposit and the Deposit Interest. However, if the unsatisfied, unwaived conditions relate exclusively to Paragraph 6.4 (ii), Seller shall return to Buyer the funds actually delivered by the Buyer to Escrow Holder, with interest thereon.

6.6 **Cancellation Fees and Expenses**. Except as otherwise set forth herein, in the event this Agreement terminates and Escrow is canceled because of: (i) the non-satisfaction of any condition set forth in Paragraph 6.3 (i) through (iv), inclusively, the cancellation charges required to be paid to Escrow Holder shall be borne by Buyer, and all other charges shall be borne by the party that incurred the charge; (ii) the non-satisfaction of any condition set forth in Paragraph 6.4 (ii), the cancellation charges required to be paid by and to Escrow Holder shall be equally divided between Buyer and Seller, and all other charges shall be borne by the party that incurred the charge; (iii) any default by Buyer or Seller, the cancellation charges required to be paid by and to Escrow Holder shall be borne by the defaulting party; and (iv) the mutual agreement of Buyer and Seller, Escrow Holder's fees and all other costs shall be divided equally between Buyer and Seller.

6.7 **Back-Up Offer**. Until the Closing of Escrow, Seller shall have the right to continue to present the Property for sale and accept "back-up" offers, contingent upon Buyer's failure to perform under the terms, covenants and conditions of this Agreement.

7. **Deliveries to Escrow Holder.**

7.1 **Deliveries by Seller**. Seller shall deliver to Escrow on or prior to the Closing Date, duly executed and acknowledged as required, each of the following: (i) the Original Deed; (ii) the original quitclaim bill of sale in the form attached as Exhibit "G" ("**Bill of Sale**"); (iii) the original Assignment of Leases and Contracts, in the form attached as Exhibit "H" ("**General Assignment**"); (iv) an affidavit certifying that Seller is not a "foreign person" under the Federal Investment in Real Property Transfer Act, in the form attached as Exhibit "I" ("**FIRPTA Affidavit**"); (v) the most current rent roll, for the Property as of the Closing Date and a schedule of the Service Contracts; (vi) corporate resolutions or certificates in form and substance satisfactory to Title Company; and (vii) a closing statement as prepared by Escrow Holder.

7.2 **Deliveries by Buyer**. Buyer shall deliver, duly executed and acknowledged as required, each of the following: (i) the original General Assignment, countersigned by Buyer; (ii) the original Bill of Sale, countersigned by Buyer; (iii) such proof of Buyer's authority and authorization to enter into this Agreement and the transactions contemplated hereby, and such proof of the power and authority of the individuals executing and/or delivering any instruments, documents or certificates on behalf of the Buyer to act for and bind Buyer as reasonably may be required by Title Company, Lender or Seller; (iv) the Cash Payment; and (v) a closing statement as prepared by Escrow Holder.

8. **Deliveries to Buyer Upon Close of Escrow**. To the extent available and within the possession or control of Seller, Seller shall deliver to Buyer, on or before the Closing Date, the following items, the delivery of which shall not be a condition to the Close of Escrow: (i) originals of all of the Tenant Leases, or, to the extent an original is unavailable, a copy thereof, if available; (ii) keys to all building entrances

Illustration 5-2 (cont.)

and keys to all locks located on the Property; and (iii) any Service Contracts, to the extent continuing in effect.

9. **Title Insurance.** At the Close of Escrow, Buyer and Seller shall cause Title Company to issue to Buyer a standard coverage CLTA owner's title insurance policy showing fee title to the Real Property vested in Buyer, and with coverage in the amount of the Purchase Price ("**Buyer's Title Policy**"), subject only to Title Company's standard printed exceptions, and to the Approved Title Conditions. Buyer may request an extended-coverage CLTA owner's policy or an ALTA owner's policy, provided that Buyer pays the difference between the cost of the standard policy and the more expensive policy, and that Buyer shall be responsible for obtaining and paying the cost of any survey requested by Title Company.

10. **Costs and Expenses.** Buyer and Seller shall divide equally any documentary transfer taxes, or equivalent or like taxes, and all Escrow, recording and filing fees. Seller shall pay the entire cost of the standard-coverage premium for Buyer's Title Policy. Each party shall be responsible for its own attorney's fees incurred in connection with the review, negotiation and preparation of this Agreement, the Exhibits attached to this Agreement and any other agreement, instrument or document prepared by Buyer's or Seller's legal counsel in connection with this transaction.

11. **Prorations and Adjustments.**

11.1 **General.** All rents, revenues and other income and the expenses from and of the Property, including delinquent rents, prepaid rents, real estate taxes and operating expenses shall be prorated as of 11:59 P.M. on the day preceding the Close of Escrow in accordance with the provisions set forth below. Any apportionments and prorations which are not expressly provided for below shall be made in accordance with customary practice in the County.

11.2 **Schedule.** Buyer and Seller agree to prepare a schedule of tentative adjustments prior to the Closing Date. Such adjustments, if and to the extent known and agreed upon as of the Close of Escrow, shall be paid by Buyer to Seller (if the prorations result in a net credit to the Seller) or by Seller to Buyer (if the prorations result in a net credit to the Buyer) by increasing or reducing the Cash Payment to be paid by Buyer at the Close of Escrow. Any such adjustments not determined or not agreed upon as of the Close of Escrow shall be paid by Buyer to Seller, or by Seller to Buyer, as the case may be, in cash or cash equivalent as soon as practicable following the Close of Escrow but in any event not later than sixty (60) calendar days after the Closing Date. A copy of the schedule of adjustments as agreed upon by Buyer and Seller shall be delivered to Escrow Holder at least two (2) business days prior to the Closing Date.

11.3 **Tenant Deposits.** Buyer shall be credited and Seller shall be debited with an amount equal to all Tenant security deposits collected or otherwise held by Seller in connection with currently-existing Tenant Leases, but only to the extent that the respective Tenant remains entitled to any reimbursement or credit. Such credit shall be an adjustment to the Cash Payment.

Illustration 5-2 (cont.)

11.4 Capital Improvements. Any capital improvements made by Seller after the execution of this Agreement shall be prorated under the provisions of this Paragraph 11 based upon an amortization period determined by generally accepted accounting principles. Seller shall make no capital improvements in the Property in an amount greater than Five Thousand Dollars ($5,000) except in an emergency or with the prior written consent of Buyer, which consent shall not be unreasonably withheld.

12. Closing: Recording and Disbursements. On or before the Closing Date and when all conditions precedent have been satisfied, Escrow Holder shall close Escrow by proceeding as follows: (i) cause the Deed, and any other documents which the parties mutually designate to be recorded or filed in the Official Records or the appropriate State Office, as the case may be, and obtain conformed copies thereof for distribution to Buyer and Seller (the Deed shall state that after recording, the document is to be returned to Buyer; (ii) disburse all funds deposited with Escrow Holder by Buyer in payment of the Purchase Price and any other obligations hereunder as follows: (a) deduct from the account of Seller all items chargeable to Seller under this Agreement, including any amounts due under Paragraphs 10 and 19, and under Paragraph 11 if the prorations result in a debit to Seller's account; (iii) credit to the account of Seller all items due to Seller under this Agreement, including any amounts due under Paragraph 11 if the prorations result in a credit to Seller's account; (iv) disburse to Seller by wire transfer promptly upon the Close of Escrow the remaining amount due to Seller; and (v) any funds remaining after deducting Buyer's share of the closing costs and expenses, Buyer's share of the prorations and adjustments, if any, and all other amounts chargeable to Buyer under this Agreement, shall be returned to Buyer by Escrow Holder's check (vi) direct the Title Company to issue Buyer's Title Policy to Buyer; (vii) disburse to Buyer the fully executed original of the Bill of Sale, the General Assignment and the FIRPTA Affidavit together with a conformed copy of the Deed, the Disclosure Statement, the Closing statement, Borrower's Certification, and any other documents deposited into Escrow by Seller pursuant hereto; (viii) disburse to Seller the original Disclosure Statement, a conformed copy of the deed, and a copy of the Bill of Sale, General Assignment, the FIRPTA Affidavit, the Closing Statement as executed by both Buyer and Seller and any other documents deposited into Escrow by Buyer pursuant hereto.

13. Buyer's Representations and Warranties. In addition to any express agreements of Buyer contained herein, the following constitute representations and warranties of Buyer and shall be true and correct as of the Closing Date, and shall survive the recordation of the Deed and the Close of Escrow.

13.1 Power. Buyer has the legal power, right and authority to enter into this Agreement and the instruments referenced herein, and to consummate the transaction contemplated hereby.

13.2 Requisite Action. All requisite action (corporate, trust, partnership or otherwise) has been taken by Buyer in connection with the entering into this Agreement and the instruments referenced herein and the consummation of the transaction contemplated hereby. No further consent of any shareholder, creditor, investor, judicial or administrative body, governmental authority or other party is required.

Illustration 5-2 (cont.)

13.3 **Authority.** The individuals executing this Agreement on behalf of Buyer represent and warrant that they have the legal power, right and actual authority to bind Buyer to the terms and conditions hereof.

13.4 **Validity.** This Agreement and all documents required hereby to be executed by Buyer are and shall be valid, legally binding obligations of, and enforceable against, Buyer in accordance with their terms, subject to bankruptcy, insolvency and other limitations on creditors' rights.

13.5 **Conflicts.** Neither the execution and delivery of this Agreement and the documents referenced herein, nor the incurring of the obligations set forth herein, nor the consummation of the transaction contemplated herein, nor compliance with the terms of this Agreement and the documents referenced herein, conflicts with or results in the material breach of any terms, conditions or provisions of, or constitute a default under, any bond, note or other evidence of indebtedness or any contract, indenture, mortgage, deed of trust, loan partnership agreement, lease or other agreement or instrument to which Buyer is a party.

14. **As-Is Purchase.** Buyer has made, or will by Close of Escrow have made, an on-site inspection of the Property, including all Improvements and Personal Property, the books and records relating to the operation of the property, and/or has otherwise investigated the Property, its operations, zoning, title matters, environmental condition and the like to Buyer's satisfaction. Except as specifically provided to the contrary in this Agreement, Seller is fully and completely released from all responsibility and liability regarding the condition, fitness, suitability, valuation and/or utility of the Property. Buyer expressly acknowledges that Buyer is buying the Property in an "AS IS" condition and Buyer has not relied on any warranties, promises, understandings or representations, express or implied, of Seller or any agent of Seller relating to the Property and all aspects thereof. Buyer acknowledges that the Environmental Report and any and all leasing information, feasibility, marketing or environmental reports, or other information of any type that Buyer has received or may receive from Seller or Seller's agents is furnished on the express condition that Buyer shall or would make an independent verification of the accuracy of any or all such information, all such information being furnished without any warranty whatsoever (express or implied), except as otherwise specifically provided in this Agreement. Buyer agrees that it will not attempt to assert any liability against Seller, the Related Persons (as defined in Paragraph 16 of this Agreement) and any other third parties for furnishing such information, and Buyer agrees to indemnify and hold Seller, the Related Persons and any other third parties free of and harmless from any and all such claims of liability. This indemnity shall survive the Close of Escrow or the termination of this Agreement.

14.1 **Confidentiality.** The Disclosure Statement is Seller's confidential information. Buyer agrees not to disclose the existence or contents of the Disclosure Statement to any person or entity not a party to this Agreement. Buyer's obligation to safeguard the confidentiality of the Disclosure Statement shall survive the termination or cancellation of this Agreement.

Illustration 5-2 (cont.)

15. __Condemnation and Destruction__.

15.1 __Uniform Act__. This Agreement shall be governed by the Uniform Vendor and Purchaser Risk Act as set forth in Section 1662 of the California Civil Code ("Act") as supplemented by this Paragraph 15. For purposes of the Act, (a) a taking by eminent domain of the portion of the Property shall be deemed to affect a "material part" of the Property if the estimated value of the portion of the Property taken exceeds twenty percent (20%) of the Purchase Price, (b) the destruction of a "**material part**" of the Property shall be deemed to mean an insured or uninsured casualty to the Property following Buyer's inspection of the Property and prior to the Close of Escrow having an estimated cost of repair which equals or exceeds twenty percent (20%) of the Purchase Price.

15.2 __Definitions__. For purposes of this Paragraph 15, (a) the phrase "**estimated value**" shall mean an estimate obtained from a reputable M.A.I. appraiser selected by Seller and approved by Buyer, and (b) the phrase "**estimated cost of repair**" shall mean an estimate obtained from an independent contractor selected by Seller and approved by Buyer. Buyer shall not unreasonably withhold or delay its approval under this Paragraph.

15.3 __Notice; Credit to Buyer__. Buyer shall have the right to terminate this Agreement in the event all or a material part of the Property is destroyed without fault of Buyer or a material part of the Property is taken by eminent domain. Buyer shall give written notice of its election to terminate this Agreement under the Act within five (5) business days after Buyer first has knowledge of any damage to or condemnation of the Property which entitles Buyer to terminate this Agreement. If Buyer does not give such notice, then this Agreement shall remain in full force and effect and there shall be no reduction in the Purchase Price, but Seller shall, at the Close of Escrow, assign to Buyer (a) any insurance proceeds payable with respect to such damage, or (b) the entire award payable with respect to such condemnation proceeding, whichever is applicable.

16. __Indemnification__. Seller hereby agrees to indemnify Buyer and its employees, directors, officers, agents and affiliates against, and to hold such parties harmless from all claims, demands, liabilities, losses, damages, costs and expenses, including without limitation, attorney's fees and costs, incurred by such parties in connection with the Property and arising from the acts or omissions of Seller occurring during Seller's ownership of the Property and prior to the Close of Escrow. Buyer hereby agrees to indemnify Seller, any past, present or future Parent Company ("Parent Company") of Seller, any past, present or future affiliate or subsidiary company of Seller or Parent Company, including the employees, agents, representatives, directors, officers, shareholders, attorneys, accountants, successors and assigns, of any of them (collectively, the "**Related Persons**") against, and to hold such parties harmless from all claims, demands, liabilities, losses, damages, costs and expenses, including, without limitation, attorneys' fees and costs, incurred by such parties in connection with the Property and arising from acts or omissions of Buyer occurring on or after the Close of Escrow and from any and all claims, demands, liabilities, damages, costs and expenses, including, without limitation, attorneys' fees and costs, of whatever kind or nature resulting from or in any way connected with the environmental condition of the Property, on or after the Close of Escrow.

Illustration 5-2 (cont.)

17. **Release**. Buyer hereby waives and releases any claims against Seller and the Related Persons pertaining to the existence, release or threatened existence or release of Hazardous Substances (as defined in Paragraph 17.2 of this Agreement) at, on, under, about, above, or adjacent to the Property or the environmental condition of the property, including, without limitation, claims arising under one or more Environmental Laws (as defined in Paragraph 17.1 of this Agreement).

17.1 **Environmental Laws**. Environmental Laws shall mean any and all federal, state, municipal and local laws, statutes, ordinances, rules, regulations, orders and decrees, whether statutory or common law, as amended from time to time, now or hereafter enacted, or promulgated, pertaining to the environment, public health and safety and industrial hygiene, including the use, generation, manufacture, production, storage, release, discharge, disposal, handling treatment, removal, decontamination, clean-up, transportation or regulation of any Hazardous Substance as defined in Paragraph 17.2 of this Agreement. Environmental Laws shall include, without limitation, the Comprehensive Environmental Response Compensation Liability Act of 1980 ("CERCLA"), as amended, 42 U.S.C. Sections 9601, et seq., the Hazardous Materials Transportation Act, 49 U.S.C. Section 1801 et seq. and the California Health and Safety Code Section 25100, et seq., as amended from time to time. This definition shall not be construed or interpreted to limit or restrict any definition or provision of any Exhibit to this Agreement.

17.2 **Hazardous Substance**. Hazardous Substance shall mean any hazardous substance, hazardous waste or hazardous material as defined in one or more Environmental Laws, petroleum hydrocarbons including crude oil or any fraction thereof, asbestos, polychlorinated biphenyls, any noxious, toxic, flammable explosive or radioactive substance, waste, material, or matter, and any other substance, material, waste or matter now or hereafter regulated by one or more Environmental Laws. This definition shall not be construed or interpreted to limit or restrict any definition or provision of any Exhibit to this Agreement.

18. **Notices**. All notices or other communications required or permitted hereunder shall be in writing, and shall be personally delivered (including by means of professional messenger service) or sent by registered or certified mail, postage prepaid, return receipt requested or by recognized overnight air courier (e.g., Federal Express) and shall be deemed received upon the date of receipt thereof and addressed as follows:

Buyer: Sanderson J. Ray Development
2699 White Road, Suite 150
Irvine, CA 92714

With a Copy to: ______________________

____

____

Seller: American Capital Investments, Inc.
a California corporation
330 Washington Blvd., Penthouse Suite
Los Angeles, CA 90292

Illustration 5-2 (cont.)

With a Copy
to: Cindy Watkins, Esq.
30 Powder Horn Hill Road
Wilton, CT 06897

Escrow
Holder: Beverly West Escrow
Attn: Cathy Corrado
433 North Camden Drive, Suite 1010
Beverly Hills, CA 90210

Notice of change of address shall be given by written notice in the manner detailed in this paragraph.

19. **Broker**. Seller represents and warrants to Buyer that, except for Major League Properties, Inc. ("Seller's Broker"), no broker or finder has been engaged by Seller in connection with the transaction contemplated by this Agreement, or to its knowledge is in any way connected with such transaction. Buyer represents and warrants to Seller that, except for CB Commercial Real Estate Group ("**Buyer's Broker**"), no broker or finder has been engaged by Buyer in connection with the transaction contemplated by this Agreement, or to its knowledge is in any way connected with such transaction. Except for the brokerage commission payable as expressly provided herein, in the event of any claim for brokers' or finders' fees or commissions in connection with the negotiation, execution or consummation of this Agreement, Buyer shall indemnify, save and hold harmless and defend Seller and the Related Persons from and against such claims if they shall be based upon any statement, representation or agreement by Buyer, and Seller shall indemnify, save and hold harmless and defend Buyer if such claims shall be based upon any statement, representation or agreement made by Seller. This indemnification clause shall survive the Close of Escrow, the termination of this Agreement or the cancellation of Escrow. Upon Close of Escrow, Seller shall pay, or cause to be paid from Escrow, a brokerage fee in the amount of Forty One Thousand Seven Hundred Dollars ($41,700.00) to Seller's Broker and Forty One Thousand Seven Hundred Dollars ($41,700.00) to Buyer's Broker (collectively), "**Brokerage Fee**"), which Brokerage Fee represents five percent (5%) of the Purchase Price. The Brokerage Fee is due and payable only upon consummation by Buyer of the purchase of the Property, the payment of the Purchase Price, and the recording of the Deed at the Close of Escrow.

20. **Further Assurances**. Buyer and Seller agree to execute all such instruments and documents and to take all actions pursuant to the provisions hereof to consummate the purchase and sale herein contemplated and shall use their reasonable efforts to accomplish the Close of Escrow in accordance with the provisions hereof.

21. **Legal and Equitable Enforcement of this Agreement**.

21.1 **Default by Seller**. EXCEPT AS PROVIDED HEREIN, IN THE EVENT THE CLOSE OF ESCROW AND THE CONSUMMATION OF THE TRANSACTION CONTEMPLATED HEREIN DO NOT OCCUR BY REASON OF ANY DEFAULT BY SELLER, AND PROVIDED BUYER SHALL NOT BE IN DEFAULT UNDER THIS AGREEMENT, BUYER'S SOLE AND EXCLUSIVE REMEDY SHALL BE THE RETURN OF ALL FUNDS PAID BY BUYER TO ESCROW HOLDER TOGETHER WITH INTEREST THEREON, THE PAYMENT BY SELLER OF ANY CHARGES REQUIRED TO BE PAID BY OR TO ESCROW HOLDER OR TITLE COMPANY, AND THE REIMBURSEMENT BY SELLER FOR BUYER'S ACTUAL OUT-OF-POCKET EXPENSES ARISING FROM SELLER'S BREACH AS SHOWN BY

Illustration 5-2 (cont.)

INVOICES AND OTHER EVIDENCE SATISFACTORY TO SELLER. THIS REMEDY IS IN LIEU OF ALL OTHER REMEDIES BUYER MAY HAVE AT LAW OR IN EQUITY, INCLUDING THE SPECIFIC PERFORMANCE OF THIS AGREEMENT AND BENEFIT-OF-THE-BARGAIN MONEY DAMAGES.

__________________ __________________

Buyer's Initials Seller's Initials

21.2 **Default by Buyer**. IN THE EVENT THE CLOSE OF ESCROW DOES NOT OCCUR AS PROVIDED BY REASON OF ANY DEFAULT OF BUYER, BUYER AND SELLER AGREE THAT IT WOULD BE IMPRACTICAL AND EXTREMELY DIFFICULT TO ESTIMATE THE DAMAGES WHICH SELLER MAY SUFFER. THEREFORE BUYER AND SELLER HEREBY AGREE THAT A REASONABLE ESTIMATE OF THE TOTAL NET DETRIMENT SELLER WOULD SUFFER IN THE EVENT BUYER DEFAULTS AND FAILS TO COMPLETE THE PURCHASE OF THE PROPERTY HEREUNDER IS AND SHALL BE, AS SELLER'S SOLE AND EXCLUSIVE REMEDY, WHETHER AT LAW OR IN EQUITY, AN AMOUNT EQUAL TO THE DEPOSIT PLUS ACCRUED INTEREST THEREON SAID AMOUNT SHALL BE THE FULL, AGREED AND LIQUIDATED DAMAGES FOR THE BREACH OF THIS AGREEMENT BY BUYER, ALL OTHER CLAIMS TO DAMAGES OR OTHER REMEDIES BEING HEREIN EXPRESSLY WAIVED BY SELLER. UPON DEFAULT BY BUYER AND UPON SELLER'S ELECTION, THIS AGREEMENT SHALL BE TERMINATED AND NEITHER PARTY SHALL HAVE ANY FURTHER RIGHTS OR OBLIGATIONS HEREUNDER, EACH TO THE OTHER, EXCEPT FOR THE RIGHT OF SELLER TO COLLECT SUCH LIQUIDATED DAMAGES FROM BUYER AND ESCROW HOLER AS HEREIN PROVIDED.

__________________ __________________

Buyer's Initials Seller's Initials

22. **Assignment**. Buyer shall not assign, transfer or convey any of Buyer's rights and obligations under this Agreement without the prior written consent of Seller, which consent Seller may withhold in its sole and absolute discretion. Should Seller consent to the assignment, transfer, or conveyance of Buyer's rights and obligations under this Agreement, the party or entity to whom such rights and obligations are assigned, transferred or conveyed shall agree to accept the rights and assume the obligations of this Agreement. Notwithstanding the foregoing, no such assignment, transfer or conveyance shall relieve the Buyer from its liabilities and obligations under this Agreement. Buyer shall not assign the right to acquire the Property, or any portion thereof, or nominate another party to acquire title to the Property, or any portion thereof, or resell the Property, or any portion thereof, through a Double Escrow without Seller's prior written consent, which consent may be withheld at Seller's sole and absolute discretion.

23. **Leasing**. Until the Close of Escrow, Seller shall be authorized to continue to execute new rental agreements and lease modifications in the ordinary course of leasing, operation and management of the Property.

24. **General Provisions**.

24.1 **Partial Invalidity**. If any term or provision of this Agreement or the application thereof to any person or circumstance shall, to any extent, be invalid or unenforceable, the remainder of this Agreement, shall not be affected thereby, and each such other term and provision of this Agreement shall be valid and be enforced to the fullest extent permitted by law.

24.2 **Waivers**. No waiver of any breach of any covenant or provision herein contained shall be deemed a waiver of any preceding or succeeding breach thereof, or of any other covenant or provision herein contained. No extension of

Illustration 5-2 (cont.)

time for performance of any obligation or act shall be deemed an extension of the time for performance of any other obligation or act.

24.3 Survival of Representations. Except as otherwise provided, the covenants, agreements, representations and warranties made herein shall survive the Close of Escrow and shall not merge into the Deed.

24.4 Successors and Assigns. This Agreement shall be binding upon and shall inure to the benefit of the heirs, devisees, legatees, personal representatives, administrators, executors and the successors and assigns of the parties hereto.

24.5 Professional Fees. In the event of the bringing of any action or suit by a party hereto against another party hereunder by reason of any breach of, or to enforce, any of the covenants, agreements or provisions on the part of the other party arising out of this Agreement, then in that event the prevailing party shall be entitled to have and recover of and from the other party all costs and expenses of the action or suit, including reasonable attorneys' fees, accounting and engineering fees, and any other professional fees resulting therefrom.

24.6 Entire Agreement. This Agreement (including all exhibits attached hereto) is the final expression of, and contains the entire agreement between, the parties with respect to the subject matter hereof and supersedes all prior understandings with respect thereto, including all prior letters of intent. This Agreement may not be modified, changed or supplemented, except by written instrument signed by the party to be charged or by its agent duly authorized in writing or as otherwise expressly permitted herein. The parties do not intend to confer any benefit hereunder on any person, firm or corporation other than the parties hereto.

24.7 Time of Essence. Time is strictly of the essence with respect to each and every term, condition, obligation and provision hereof. Failure to timely perform any of the terms, conditions, obligations or provisions hereof by either party shall constitute a material breach of a non-curable (but waivable) default under this Agreement by the party so failing to perform.

24.8 Construction. Headings at the beginning of each paragraph and subparagraph are solely for the convenience of the parties and are not a part of this Agreement. Whenever required by the context of this Agreement, the singular shall include the plural and the masculine shall include the feminine and vice versa. This Agreement shall not be construed as if it had been prepared by one of the parties, but rather as if both parties had prepared the same. Unless otherwise indicated, all references to paragraphs and subparagraphs are to this Agreement. All exhibits referred to in this Agreement and attached hereto are incorporated herein by this reference.

24.9 Counterparts. This Agreement may be executed in one or more counterparts, each of which shall be an original, but all of which shall constitute one.

24.10 Governing Law. This Agreement shall be governed by, interpreted under, and construed and enforced in accordance with the laws of the State of California.

Illustration 5-2 (cont.)

IN WITNESS WHEREOF, Seller and Buyer hereto have executed this Agreement.

BUYER

SANDERSON J. RAY DEVELOPMENT,
A______________________

By:______________________

Name:______________________

Title:______________________

SELLER

AMERICAN CAPITAL INVESTMENTS, INC.
A CALIFORNIA CORPORATION

By:______________________

Name: Stephen Murphy

Title: President

BUYER'S BROKER

By:______________________

Name:______________________

Title:______________________

SELLER'S BROKER

By:______________________

Name:______________________

Title:______________________

ESCROW HOLDER

By:______________________

Name:______________________

Title:______________________

Illustration 5-2 (cont.)

Exhibits Attached:

Exhibit A - Legal Description
Exhibit B - Tenant Lease
Exhibit C - Deed
Exhibit D - Title Exceptions
Exhibit E - Environmental Report
Exhibit F - Disclosure Statement
Exhibit G - Bill of Sale
Exhibit H - General Assignment
Exhibit I - FIRPTA Affidavit

6
LEVERAGE POWER

In his classic, *Of Human Bondage,* Somerset Maugham noted: "Money is like a sixth sense, without which you cannot make a complete use of the other five. . ."

Money sense, in the world of syndication separates the achievers from the also-rans. Proper utilization of leverage magnifies the value of the investment. This chapter will outline some examples of where leverage can provide the difference between a healthy yield and a so-so return on invested capital. In order to explore this fascinating avenue toward increase in personal worth, it's important to note the variety of money sources available to the syndicate in addition to its participants.

SOURCES OF FUNDS

In the helter-skelter economic shock waves of the early 1990s, acquisition opportunities for investment sized properties (generally $5mm and above) abound for a variety of reasons explored in previous American Capital Foundation for the Homeless works. This opens up a flood gate of unique financing sources not normally available to the investor. In particular, the real estate owned portfolios of financial institutions and their regulators provide interesting financing alternatives under unconventional terms.

First, an examination of the traditional real estate finance sources is in order:

- Commercial banks - In order to maintain their commercial lending base of business clients, the commercial banking community, almost by default, is also a source of financing to accommodate the real estate financing needs of their clients. Typical advances would not normally exceed 75% of economic value of the property involved. Rates and fees would be adjusted to market conditions.

Variable rate financing does not accommodate well to the needs of the borrowing public when it comes to income-producing property, thus fixed rate terms are normally offered, but the maturities may be shorter than the amortization schedule in order that the lender does not get locked in to a fixed rate that is in juxtaposition to the general level of interest rates in the market place. Thus, it is not unusual to see 30 year amortization with a five, seven or ten year call provision as a hedge against rising interest rates. This is merely a variation on the theme of the "Canadian rollover" type of loan prevalent with our neighbors to the North where the interest rate on their loans is renegotiated each five years. Banks obtain lendable funds from deposits, portfolio income, and sale of real estate loans to the secondary market.

- Thrifts - The income-producing property financing "wings" of this category have effectively been "clipped" by FIRREA. The principal area where savings and loans still maintain a fairly active posture is in connection with the financing of apartments, since their principal concentration from the inception of the industry has been in residential financing. A calamitous exploration of commercial and industrial lending by this industry couple with disastrous investments in junk bonds brought the industry to its knees by the end of the decade. This fragile circumstance also makes this particular lender a prime candidate for dealing in real estate owned on particularly attractive terms with no concern for replacement value of the improvements - only cash flow being the determinant in the negotiations. Funds for new applications come from repayments from the secondary market, since normally thrifts would sell fixed rate loans and retain the variable rate loans, income from investments, and deposits.
- Mutual Savings Banks - Typically located in the Northeastern section of the country, this institution is roughly equivalent to the thrifts. Through a combined entity of Residential Funding Corporation their lending activities are expanded in the secondary market. Again, their concentration is in the residential and residential income field.
- Life Insurance Companies - Once this industry was the major player in the field of income property financing as well as formulating a variety of sale-leaseback situations with various grade A credit national companies financing their real estate acquisitions. As the New Jersey based Mutual Benefit Life Insurance Company's precarious position came to light with respect to excessive defaults in their investment portfolio, the

fallout from the rest of the industry has been significant. Mainly life companies concentrate their lending activities on newer properties with existing project financing for purposes of purchase or refinance having secondary position to their principal thrust. Each company follows the loan to value guidelines of the Insurance Commissioner of their state of domicile. For example, Prudential Insurance would follow the dictates of the state of New Jersey, while its rival behemoth, Metropolitan Life Insurance follows the dictates of the state of New York. Their loan to value advances tend to follow the same percentage of advance as the commercial banks. During the uncertain economic times of the early '90s, however, this percentage of advance is normally lowered significantly to provide the equity protection felt necessary under the individual company's underwriting (the ground rules substantiating the business decision to make the loan) guidelines. In the case of leasehold financing, where the borrower merely has the right to the use of land for a specified time period, percentage of advance is normally limited to no more than two-thirds of the economic productivity of the improvements. To illustrate, take the example of a lessee/borrower who owns a building that generates an annual net operating income, before leasehold payments of $1,200,000. Annual leasehold payments of $450,000 reduce this income figure to $750,000. If the capitalization rate of 10% were applied to the latter figure, the value of the leasehold estate for lending purposes thus becomes $7,500,000 with a maximum loan advance of $5,000,000. Today any submission to an insurance company for commitment would be under the condition of a minimum acceptable occupancy ratio at a given level of rents prior to funding. Insurance company investable funds are obtained through policy premiums combined with the substantial earnings from their investment portfolios. Since actuarial science has allowed an orderly investment agenda for life companies, as opposed to the tempestuous sea surrounding their casualty neighbors, they are able to program their investments several years in advance. This is another reason why they prefer newer properties, as they can issue a commitment that will not be taken down for two or three years from the date of issuance which involves the period of construction on the particular project that has been committed.

- Securitization - Securitization occurs in a variety of fashions. If one becomes a syndicate investor, one holds a form of security in the form of a share of stock in a corporation, a beneficial interest in a real estate investment trust, a percentage share of a leasehold estate, a tenancy in common percentage interest in direct property ownership, a general or limited partnership interest in a partnership entity, or a co-venture position in a joint venture. The list of possibilities is almost endless, since assets are securitized in a variety of fashions. In the case of income-producing property, securitization for the purpose of financing properties in the $10mm range and above may be in the form of the securitization of the debt and sale of such securities through an underwriter, such as the St. Louis based A. G. Edwards & Sons, who is active in this emerging field. The securities firm, after underwriting, sells these securities to their customers. In the case of the other entities, individuals use savings and/or leverage to take positions in these various investment vehicles.

- Seller-based financing - With the emergence of problem properties that has surfaced throughout the country, financial institutions find themselves in the uncomfortable position of being owners, rather than lenders. This places them in a form of double jeopardy, since they are not well equipped to handle the property management aspects of this unique situation, they also are subjected to considerable regulatory pressure to dispose of the property. Herein lies one of the significant areas of opportunity for real estate investment. Individual sellers usually cannot go below the balance of existing financing when offering a property for sale. In the case of institutions, they may be willing to sell a property **below the balance of their foreclosed loan** as a matter of expedience to cut their losses. Thus some properties may be obtained at one-third to one-half of their replacement cost in the process. The key to a really successful negotiation with this source is the ability to arrange a financing package in conjunction with the property acquisition.
- Commercial finance companies - With increasing frequency, General Electric Credit, Westinghouse Credit and a variety of other players in this field are looking at real estate financing as a means of expanding their credit horizons. This is particularly true in the income-producing property area, where large loan amounts are available at fairly attractive yields. Since their funds source is usually the issuance of short-term commercial paper, they are more of an interest-sensitive type of lender than the rest of their institutional brethren.
- Mortgage Bankers - This very eclectic lending category may include institutional lenders performing this function as well as

corporations who exclusively originate, sell and service mortgage loans as a business. The traditional mortgage banker is able to borrow on a line of credit from a commercial bank on the basis of a geometric proportion of their net worth, sometimes 10 to 20 times, to fund loans which are earmarked for their investors. Mortgage bankers not only do the traditional FHA, VA and conventional financing packaged for resale to the secondary market or other investors such as pension funds, insurance companies, institutional and private sources generally located outside of their service area. Certain mortgage bankers also specialize in the financing of income-producing property further segmented by specialization in certain areas, such as industrial projects, shopping centers, office buildings and the like. Most of the major life insurance companies in the country have mortgage loan correspondents (mortgage bankers) appointed as part of their loan origination network. Some mortgage bankers also perform other services, such as interim financing for construction lending, real estate brokerage activities, insurance sales and other collateral activities tied to their lending function.

- Mortgage Brokers and "Hard Money" lenders - Generally this origination source does not have the capability of funding real estate loans. The hard money segment of loan brokerage does usually perform the servicing function of collecting payments, handling delinquencies and the like. Mortgage brokers may exclusively represent one lender or submit packages to a group of lenders, dependent upon their individual business arrangements. The principal function that this origination segment performs for the institutional lending fraternity is the preparation of the loan package and the supporting documentation required to make an intelligent underwriting decision on residential and income-producing properties. Most hard money sources are strictly oriented to loan to value ratios with little regard to whether or not the property or the borrower has the ability to service debt. They are geared to property acquisition at below market prices through the foreclosure process.

- Various government programs - The list is exhaustive, some on a direct basis, such as Cal-Vet and other state veterans programs designed for home and farm purchase. The Department of Housing and Urban Development has a variety of direct and indirect (through mutual mortgage insurance) financing programs for residential as well as income producing property, the Veterans Administration also has home and farm loan guaranty programs, and state and local agency lending programs are available on a regional basis. Each of these programs may have direct or indirect support through the taxpayers.

With the close to three trillion dollars of mortgage debt in this country, the source of funds to acquire and/or refinance properties is continuous and exhaustive. When it comes to a particular type of property, things start to take a different perspective.

USES OF FUNDS

Especially in the area of income-producing properties, the list of lenders interested in pursuing this type of credit extension starts to shorten. The thrifts eliminate themselves from every category except for multiple units (five or more). Commercial banks tend to follow the route of their customer base. If a bank specializes in business banking, there will be a lot of loans secured by industrial properties. If a bank tends to specialize in retail banking, credit cards, residential real estate, auto and personal loans are high on the agenda. Insurance companies are still trying to recover from the early 1990s "shell shock" of non-performing real estate that has tainted their pristine portfolios. Their conservative nature causes retrenchment, to a certain degree, after the first shock wave appears. Life insurance companies, when they are in the marketplace, tend to find their own particular niches. The New York-headquartered companies are geared to office building financing and feel comfortable with this type of credit. When you get out to the tall corn state of Iowa, small industrial buildings seem to fit into many of the Iowa-based firms. Hartford firms seem to go for large shopping centers, and the list goes on. For example, one can become very specialized as one St. Louis-based company who seems to take a liking to a rental form of mobile home park. It takes a certain amount of mobility within the marketplace to find the source that would be most inclined to finance a certain property. It is important to go through the filtering process in order to find the particular lender who has the most potential as a viable source of funds for the project in question. One of the harder categories of income properties to finance involves any commercial and industrial parcel where the loan request is less than $2 million. Generally the only source for monies of this type are commercial banks, sellers or the hard money people.

It is extremely important, especially when dealing with insurance companies, who have a tendency to do whereases and wherefors to the maximum, to not only read the language of the loan commitment letter, but the supporting documentation as well.

EXPOSURE OF THE SYNDICATE

Dependent upon the form of organization of the syndicate, a certain degree of exposure can be experienced by the syndicate members, even if they are only limited partners in a partnership or shareholders in a REIT or corporate entity. This exposure can result from any fraudulent activity on the part of the borrowing entity to entice lenders into a potential exposure which, had it not been for the applicant, they would have never experienced. It is **extremely important** that syndicate members be satisfied with the honesty and integrity of the syndicating group.

Even more hazardous is the situation where a loosely formed syndicate is involved to perform property management and marketing functions where each of the members hold title as tenants in common with an undivided interest in the real property. Each member of the syndicate has the potential exposure based upon actions of other syndicate members over which they have no control. This is a strong argument for the limited partnership/REIT/corporate forms for that very reason. The New York approach of selling interests in master leases is just another form of tenancy in common, only involving a lesser than fee type of ownership.

Maximum leverage at a time of depressed market conditions may prove to be precarious giving potential of property loss through foreclosure and thus a total loss of principal to the investor. This represents a strong argument for dealing in properties with a lot of upside potential as well as having the present ability to service debt. It further supports the argument of not pursuing those properties that have the glow of pride of ownership and are fully leased. There is only one way to go in that type of property - down!

Maintaining a healthy balance between equity contributed and the leverage used to complete the purchase price of a given parcel is essential. Each situation should be examined on the basis of checking out the return on invested capital when compared to an all cash sale vs. one that is leveraged. Equity can also buy down interest rates in certain instances, as well. Let us illustrate this point. Take into consideration an office structure that is presently 80% occupied in its 300,000 square feet of net rentable space. The average gross monthly rental including parking rights is $1.50 per square foot/month. Tenancy has remained steady at this level for the past three years and the average remaining term on the existing leases is seven years. Armed with this data, an analysis of the income stream might be something like this:

240,000 (current rented square feet) x $1.50 x 12 = annual rent of	$4,320,000
Vacancy allowance - 5%, or	216,000
Effective rent	$4,104,000
Expenses - 29%, or	1,190,160
Net operating income before debt service =	$2,913,840

In analyzing the building, capitalization rates would be applied on the basis of negotiation. An investor may have formed a syndicate offering $29,000,000 cash based upon a 10% capitalization rate. Obviously, since cash was paid for the property, the return on the cash flow, sans any tax considerations is 10%.

Taking a look at the same building through the use of leverage, a totally different picture can be obtained. If, for example, the lender assigned a 9 and 1/2% capitalization rate as the risk for this building, a value of $30,700,000 is attached to the parcel. Say the syndicate offers $30mm for the property and is able to negotiate a 8%, interest only loan for the first year, converting to 8 and 1/2% for the remaining 29 years with a 7 year call. The lender may offer two lending programs, based upon the down payment that can be offered by the syndicate. They are willing to do the terms outlined above at 25% down. If the syndicate provides 30% down, interest during the first year and remaining years is reduced by 1%. Our analysis then becomes:

25% down

NOI	$2,913,840
Annual debt service - first year on 75% financing of $22,500,000 @8%	1,800,000
Net income **after** debt service =	1,113,840

Return on down payment =
1,113,840 divided by $7,500,000 = 14.85%.

30% down

NOI	$2,913,840
Annual debt service - first year on $21,000,000 at 7% =	1,470,000
Net income **after** debt service =	$1,443,840

Return on down payment =
1,443,840 divided by $9,000,000 = 16.04%!

In the negotiation process, arrangement of financing is critical because it is something that the syndicate must live with for an extended period of time. Equity is a means of gaining yield advantage on the part of the investment group. The advantage of a syndicate as a source of equity funds, is the volume of equity that the syndicate can create to extract the most attractive financing arrangements in the process. The actual entity used in forming the syndicate can also provide a specified regimen of documentation which must be accumulated for the mutual protection of the syndicator and the investment group that forms the syndicate as well. This process will be explored in the ensuing chapters.

7
HOLDING TITLE

John Kenneth Galbraith, noted economic guru, observed in his 1967 publication of *The New Industrial State* that: "The imperatives of technology and organization, not the images of ideology, are what determine the shape of economic society. . ."

Organization plays an integral part in the formation of any syndicate. The form which this entity may take forms the subject matter of this chapter. There are many choices of ownership entity with certain ground rules which apply. The nuances of each will be covered in detail.

CORPORATIONS

Black's Law Dictionary defines corporation as, "An artificial person or legal entity created by or under the authority of the laws of a state. An association of persons created by statute as a legal entity. . ."

Within this broad definition of an entity which can hold title to property, is composed of an ownership consisting of shareholders, and can sue and be sued, lies a variety of categories which represent, more or less, some form of corporate existence. One of the critical factors in organizing a corporation is the choice of a state of incorporation. Certain states, such as Delaware, due to favorable laws of incorporation, are preferential to larger firms, even though the bulk of their enterprise may be conducted in other areas of the country. Some of the terms used to describe corporate organizations are:

- Acquired corporation - This is a common term for one which evaporates as the result of merger or acquisition, common during the 1980s.
- Acquiring corporation - This doesn't mean the one that is acquiring title to property, it merely means one who is offering a

merger or acquisition, atypical of the T. Boone Pickens, Kirk Kerkorians, et. al.

- Aggressor corporation - This is the type reminiscent of "green mail," where a hostile takeover bid of another corporation through tender offer or exchange of stock. Sometimes this process is just a means of obtaining a quick profit on taking a position in the stock, by reselling it to the company in exchange for giving up the attempt to wrest control.
- Business corporation - This would be the type that would be involved in real estate investments, since this form of entity, as opposed to a not-for-profit corporation, has a profit motive with the objective of obtaining a satisfactory return on the investment of shareholders.
- Closely held corporation - Many business corporations, particularly those dealing in real estate, may have only a few stockholders and the shares are not freely traded. Normally these stocks would not be listed on an exchange, unless there was a later decision to "go public," which would involve a stock offering sponsored by a securities brokerage.
- Brother-sister and controlled corporations - In the former, common shareholder interests tie two or more corporations together, usually within the control of one key person as majority stockholder.
- Collapsible corporation - This is similar in structure to the joint venture, where the enterprise is established for the purpose of one project, such as the development, rental and sale of an apartment building. Upon completion of the sale, the corporation is dissolved, having completed the corporate objective.
- Subchapter S corporation - This type of entity represents an election by the shareholders for income tax purposes. In this instance, there are a limited number of shareholders, many times only a single shareholder, who elect, for income tax purposes to have the corporate income taxed to the shareholders at regular income tax rates. This has some of the features of a limited partnership—a popular form of syndication vehicle—in the tax impacts of earnings from real estate ventures.
- Other categories - Special situations exist, such as the not-for-profit corporation, usually organized for charitable purposes, which receives special tax treatment. A unique form of not-for-profit corporation is the Corporation Sole, usually signifying an individual, such as a Catholic Bishop or Archbishop

overseeing an Archdiocese, whose successor becomes the corporation upon death or resignation. Certain corporations, such as cities, who are municipal corporations, are non-stock corporations in nature with the citizens serving in judgment over those who would serve to head the entity, such as mayor, city council, etc. Shell corporations represent entities that are reserved for future use containing few assets, but maintaining required filings to preserve corporate existence.

No matter where the state of incorporation, if a corporate entity wishes to do business in a state other than its state of incorporation, it must comply with the requirements for doing business in that state. If, for example, a corporation was organized under the state laws of Delaware and desired to do business in California, it must comply with the provisions of the state of California's Corporations Code with respect to qualifications of foreign corporations to do business in that state. Some of the legal requirements for doing business by a foreign corporation would be to:

- File a copy of the articles of incorporation with the Secretary of State of the state in question. See Illustration 7-1 as a typical example.
- Appoint an agent for purpose of process serving.
- Pay license fees.
- Designate and maintain an office in the state.
- Keep books and records.
- Deposit bonds or securities with the state treasurer for purposes of protecting any individual who might suffer loss by reason of the corporation's conduct.

If a foreign corporation does not qualify to do business in another state, it cannot legally conduct business in that state. If it conducts business without compliance, it is referred to as a **de facto** corporation, as opposed to a **de jure** corporation, which signifies one that has complied with state statute.

The corporate process begins with an application for charter by usually not less than three individuals who are United States citizens. In this application, the following information is usually required:

Illustration 7-1

1816441

ENDORSED
FILED
In the office of the Secretary of State
of the State of California

MAR 3 1992

MARCH FONG EU, Secretary of State

ARTICLES OF INCORPORATION

OF

AMERICAN CAPITAL INVESTMENTS, INC.

I

The name of this corporation shall be American Capital Investments, Inc.

II

The purpose of this corporation is to engage in any lawful act or activity for which a corporation may be organized under the General Corporation Law of California other than the banking business, the trust company business or the practice of a profession permitted to be incorporated by the California Corporations Code.

III

The name and address in the State of California of this corporation's initial agent for service of process is:

STEPHEN MURPHY
2554 Lincoln Boulevard, Suite 675
Marina del Rey, California 90291

IV

The corporation is authorized to issue only one class of shares of stock and the total number of shares which this corporation is authorized to issue is 100,000.

V

The liability of the directors of the corporation for monetary damages shall be eliminated to the fullest extent permissible under California law. The corporation is authorized to provide for full indemnification of its agents (as defined in Section 317 of the California Corporations Code) for breach of duty to the corporation and its shareholders, through its bylaws, by agreement or otherwise, in excess of the indemnification otherwise permitted by Section 317 of the California Corporations Code, subject to the limits on such excess indemnification set forth in Section 204 of the California Corporations Code.

DATED: March 2, 1992

Cindy Casteel Watkins
CINDY CASTEEL WATKINS

Illustration 7-1 (cont.)

1816441

State of California
OFFICE OF THE SECRETARY OF STATE

CORPORATION DIVISION

I, *MARCH FONG EU*, Secretary of State of the State of California, hereby certify:

That the annexed transcript has been compared with the corporate record on file in this office, of which it purports to be a copy, and that same is full, true and correct.

IN WITNESS WHEREOF, I execute this certificate and affix the Great Seal of the State of California this

MAR - 4 1992

March Fong Eu
Secretary of State

STATE FORM CE-107

Cindy Casteel Watkins
CINDY CASTEEL WATKINS

Illustration 7-1 (cont.)

State of California

OFFICE OF THE SECRETARY OF STATE

CERTIFICATE OF STATUS
DOMESTIC CORPORATION

I, MARCH FONG EU, *Secretary of State of the State of California, hereby certify:*

That on the 3rd *day of* March, *19* 92,

AMERICAN CAPITAL INVESTMENTS, INC.

became incorporated under the laws of the State of California by filing its Articles of Incorporation in this office; and

That no record exists in this office of a certificate of dissolution of said corporation nor of a court order declaring dissolution thereof, nor of a merger or consolidation which terminated its existence; and

That said corporation's corporate powers, rights and privileges are not suspended on the records of this office; and

That according to the records of this office, the said corporation is authorized to exercise all its corporate powers, rights and privileges and is in good legal standing in the State of California; and

That no information is available in this office on the financial condition, business activity or practices of this corporation.

IN WITNESS WHEREOF, I execute this certificate and affix the Great Seal of the State of California this 9th *day of* December, 1992

March Fong Eu

Secretary of State

- Names and addresses of incorporators
- Name of the corporation
- The object for which the corporation is formed
- Duration of corporate life - This is in the case of a collapsible corporation, since corporate life can be theoretically perpetual
- Location of the principal office of the corporation
- The total authorized capital stock, preferred or common and the number of shares in each category
- The names and addresses of the subscribers to the stock together with the amount subscribed and paid in by such subscribers. Usually a further requirement of the immediate issuance of stock along with the method of payment by subscribers in either property or cash is noted.

Upon approval of the application for charter, it is registered with the secretary of state, an incorporation meeting is held where by-laws (See Illustration 7-2) are prepared and officers and directors elected.

State laws vary with respect to procedural matters including amendments to the original charter by the corporation. This form of entity may be used for the acquisition of the property as a corporate asset, or temporarily while forming a limited partnership where the corporation will serve as general partner, or possibly as a tenant-in-common owner or percentage owner of a master lease. The ownership entity possibility using this form of ownership is continuous and exhaustive. The key to the method of ownership deals with the tax implications involved in the use of the ownership entity.

In the case of corporations, the firm itself is subject to taxation as a corporation in addition to the various qualification fees required in the states where they do business along with various business taxes that may be imposed upon them by local jurisdictions. In addition, shareholders are taxed individually on the dividends received from the corporation distributed out of earnings. Depending upon the dispersion of ownership, trading of shares may be easily accomplished if there are a large number of shares outstanding and a broad-based market for trading in these shares. In the case of closely held firms, disposition of stock becomes a bit more difficult, with the possibility that only the sale of the corporation will allow a stockholder to recoup the invested capital.

Illustration 7-2

BY-LAWS
OF

AMERICAN CAPITAL INVESTMENTS, INC.
a California corporation

ARTICLE I

OFFICES

Section 1. PRINCIPAL EXECUTIVE OFFICE. The principal executive office of the corporation is hereby fixed and located at 330 Washington Street, 9th Floor, Marina del Rey, California 90292. The Board of Directors is hereby granted full power and authority to change said principal executive office from one location to another. The location of the principal executive office of the corporation need not be in the State of California.

Section 2. OTHER OFFICES. Branch or subordinate offices may at any time be established by the Board of Directors at any place or places.

ARTICLE II

MEETINGS OF SHAREHOLDERS

Section 1. PLACE OF MEETINGS. All meetings of shareholders shall be held either at the principal executive office or at any other place within or without the State of California which may be designated either by the Board of Directors pursuant to authority hereinafter granted to said Board, or by written consent of all shareholders entitled to vote thereat, given either before or after the meeting, filed with the Secretary of the corporation.

Section 2. ANNUAL MEETINGS. The annual meetings of shareholders, commencing with the meeting to be held in June, shall be held at 10:00 o'clock a.m. on the second Tuesday of the month, if not a legal holiday, and, if a legal holiday, then on the next business day following which is not a legal holiday, or at such other time and date as may be designated by the Board of Directors. At such meeting the shareholders shall elect a Board of Directors in accordance with the provisions of Article II, Section 6 of the By-Laws, and transact such other business as may properly be brought before the meeting.

Illustration 7-2 (cont.)

Written notice of each annual meeting shall be given to each shareholder entitled to vote thereat, either personally or by mail or other means of written communication, charges prepaid, addressed to such shareholder at his or her address appearing on the books of the corporation or given by him or her to the corporation for the purpose of notice. If any notice or report addressed to the shareholder at the address of such shareholder appearing on the books of the corporation is returned to the corporation by the United States Postal Service marked to indicate that the United States Postal Service is unable to deliver the notice or report to the shareholder at such address, all future notices or reports shall be deemed to have been duly given without further mailing if the same shall be available to the shareholder upon written demand of the shareholder at the principal executive office of the corporation for a period of one year from the date of the giving of the notice or report to all other shareholders. If a shareholder gives no address, notice shall be deemed to have been given him or her if sent by mail or other means of written communication addressed to the place where the principal executive office of the corporation is situated, or if published at least once in some newspaper of general circulation in the county in which said office is located.

All such notices shall be given to each shareholder entitled thereto not less than ten (10) days nor more than sixty (60) days before each annual meeting. Any such notice shall be deemed to have been given at the time when delivered personally or deposited in the mail or sent by other means of written communication.

Such notices shall specify:

(a) the place, the date, and the hour of such meeting;

(b) those matters which the Board, at the time of the mailing of the notice, intends to present for action by the shareholders;

(c) if Directors are to be elected, the names of nominees intended at the time of the notice to be presented by management for election;

(d) the general nature of a proposal, if any, to take action with respect to approval of: (i) a contract or other transaction with an interested Director, (ii) amendment of the Articles of Incorporation, (iii) a reorganization of the corporation as defined in Section 181 of the California General Corporations Law, (iv) voluntary dissolution of the corporation, or (v) a distribution in dissolution other than in accordance with the rights of outstanding preferred shares, if any; and

Illustration 7-2 (cont.)

(e) such other matters, if any, as may be expressly required by statute.

Section 3. SPECIAL MEETINGS. Special meetings of the shareholders, for any purpose or purposes whatsoever, may be called at any time by the Chairman of the Board or the President, or by the Board of Directors, or by holders of shares entitled to cast not less than ten percent (10%) of the votes at the meeting. Upon request in writing directed to the Chairman of the Board, President, Vice President or Secretary by any person (other than the Board) entitled to call a special meeting of shareholders, such officer forthwith shall cause notice to be given to shareholders entitled to vote that a meeting will be held at a time requested by the person or persons calling the meeting, not less than thirty-five (35) nor more than sixty (60) days after receipt of the request. If the notice is not given within twenty (20) days after receipt of the request, the persons entitled to call the meeting may give the notice. Except in cases where other express provision is made by statute, notice of such special meeting shall be given in the same manner as required for annual meetings of shareholders. In addition to the matters required by items (a) and, if applicable, (c) of Section 2 above, notice of any special meeting shall specify the general nature of the business to be transacted, and no other business may be transacted at such meeting.

Section 4. ADJOURNED MEETINGS AND NOTICE THEREOF. Any shareholders meeting, annual or special, whether or not a quorum is present, may be adjourned from time to time by vote of a majority of the shares, the holders of which are either present in person or by proxy thereat, but in the absence of a quorum (except as provided in Section 7 below), no other business may be transacted at any such meeting.

When any shareholders meeting, either annual or special, is adjourned for forty-five (45) days or more, or if after adjournment a new record date is fixed for the adjourned meeting, notice of the adjourned meeting shall be given as in the case of an original meeting. Except as provided above, it shall not be necessary to give any notice of the time and place of the adjourned meeting or of the business to be transacted thereat, other than by announcement of the time and place thereof at the meeting at which such adjournment is taken.

Section 5. AFFIDAVIT OF MAILING. Whenever any shareholder entitled to vote has been absent from any meeting of shareholders, whether annual or special, an entry in the minutes to the effect that notice has been duly given shall be sufficient evidence that due notice of such meeting was given to such shareholder as required by law and the By-Laws of the corporation.

Illustration 7-2 (cont.)

Section 6. VOTING.

(a) Generally: The shareholders entitled to notice of any meeting or to vote at any such meeting shall be only persons in whose name shares stand on the stock records of the corporation on the record date determined in accordance with Section 1 of ARTICLE VI.

(b) Ballots: Such vote may be viva voce or by ballot; provided, however, upon demand made by a shareholder at any election and before the voting begins, all elections for Directors must be by ballot.

(c) Action by Majority: If a quorum is present except with respect to election of Directors, the affirmative vote of the majority of the shares represented at the meeting and entitled to vote on any matter shall be the act of the shareholders, unless the vote of a greater number or voting by classes is required by the California General Corporation Law or the Articles of Incorporation.

(d) Cumulative Voting: Subject to the requirements hereinbelow provided, every shareholder entitled to vote at any election for Directors shall have the right to cumulate such shareholder's votes and give one candidate a number of votes equal to the number of Directors to be elected multiplied by the number of votes to which the shareholder's shares are entitled, or to distribute the shareholder's votes on the same principle among as many candidates as he shall think fit. No shareholder shall be entitled to cumulate votes unless the name of the candidate or candidates for whom such votes would be cast has been placed in nomination prior to the voting and the shareholder has given notice at the meeting, prior to the voting, of the shareholder's intention to cumulate the shareholder's votes. If any one shareholder has given such notice, all shareholders may cumulate their votes for candidates in nomination. The candidates receiving the highest number of votes of shares entitled to be voted for them, up to the number of Directors to be elected, shall be elected.

Section 7. QUORUM. The presence in person or by proxy of the holders of a majority of the shares entitled to vote at any meeting shall constitute a quorum for the transaction of business. The shareholders present at a duly called or held meeting at which a quorum is present may continue to do business until adjournment, notwithstanding the withdrawal of enough shareholders to leave less than a quorum, if any action taken (other than adjournment) is approved by at least a majority of the shares required to constitute a quorum.

Illustration 7-2 (cont.)

Section 8. CONSENT OF ABSENTEES. The transactions of any meeting of shareholders, either annual or special, however called and noticed, shall be as valid as though had at a meeting duly held after regular call and notice if a quorum is present either in person or by proxy, and if, either before or after the meeting, each of the persons entitled to vote, not present in person or by proxy, or who, though present, has, at the beginning of the meeting, properly objected to the transaction of any business because the meeting was not lawfully called or convened, or to particular matters of business legally required to be included in the notice, but not so included, signs a written waiver of notice, or a consent to the holding of such meeting, or an approval of the minutes thereof. Except as provided in Sections 601(e) and 601(f) of the California General Corporation Law, the business transacted at the meeting need not be specified in a written waiver of notice by a shareholder, in a consent to the holding of the meeting by a shareholder or in an approval of the minutes of the meeting by a shareholder. All such waivers, consents or approvals shall be filed with the corporate records or made a part of the minutes of the meeting.

Section 9. ACTION WITHOUT MEETING.

(a) <u>Election of Directors by Written Consent</u>: Directors may be elected without a meeting by a consent in writing, setting forth the actions so taken, signed by all the persons who would be entitled to vote for the election of Directors. A Director may be elected at any time to fill a vacancy not filled by the Directors by the written consent of persons holding a majority of the outstanding shares entitled to vote for the election of Directors.

(b) <u>Other Actions by Written Consent</u>: Any other action which under any provision of the California General Corporation Law may be taken at a meeting of the shareholders may be taken without a meeting and without notice, except as hereinafter set forth, if a consent in writing, setting forth the action so taken, is signed by the holders of outstanding shares having not less than the minimum number of votes that would be necessary to authorize or take such action at a meeting at which all shares entitled to vote thereon were present and voted.

(c) <u>Notice of Action by Written Consent</u>: If the consents of all shareholders entitled to vote have not been solicited in writing, and if the unanimous written consent of all such shareholders shall not have been received, the Secretary shall give prompt notice of the corporate action approved by the shareholders without a meeting. This notice shall be given in the manner specified in Section 2 of this ARTICLE II. In the case of approval of (i) contracts or transactions in which a Director has a direct or indirect

Illustration 7-2 (cont.)

financial interest, pursuant to Section 310 of the Corporations Code of California, (ii) indemnification of agents of the corporation, pursuant to Section 317 of that Code, (iii) a reorganization of the corporation, pursuant to Section 1201 of that Code, and (iv) a distribution in dissolution other than in accordance with the rights of outstanding preferred shares, pursuant to Section 2007 of that Code, the notice shall be given at least ten (10) days before the consummation of any action authorized by that approval.

(d) Record Date: Unless, as provided in Section 1 of Article VI of these By-Laws, the Board of Directors has fixed a record date for the determination of shareholders entitled to notice of and to give such written consent, the record date for such determination shall be the day on which the first written consent is given. All such written consents shall be filed with the Secretary of the corporation.

(e) Revocation of Written Consent: Any shareholder giving a written consent, or the shareholder's proxy holders, or a transferee of the shares or a personal representative of the shareholder or their respective proxy holders, may revoke the consent by a writing received by the corporation prior to the time that written consents of the number of shares required to authorize the proposed action has been filed with the Secretary of the corporation, but may not do so thereafter. Such revocation is effective upon its receipt by the Secretary of the corporation.

(f) Form of Written Consent: The form of written consent shall be governed by the provisions of Section 604 of the California General Corporation Law where applicable.

Section 10. PROXIES. Every person entitled to vote or execute consents shall have the right to do so either in person or by one or more agents authorized by a written proxy executed by such person or his duly authorized agent and filed with the Secretary of the corporation. Any proxy duly executed is not revoked and continues in full force and effect until: (i) an instrument revoking it or a duly executed proxy bearing a later date is filed with the Secretary of the corporation prior to the vote pursuant thereto, (ii) a subsequent proxy is executed by the person executing the prior proxy and is presented to the meeting, (iii) the person executing the proxy attends the meeting and votes in person, or (iv) written notice of the death or incapacity of the maker of such proxy is received by the corporation before the vote pursuant thereto is counted; provided that no such proxy shall be valid after the expiration of eleven (11) months from the date of its execution, unless the person executing it specifies therein the length of time for which such

Illustration 7-2 (cont.)

proxy is to continue in force. Notwithstanding the foregoing, a proxy may be made irrevocable pursuant to the provisions of Section 705(e) of the California General Corporation Law. The form of proxy shall be governed by the provisions of Section 604 of the California General Corporation Law, where applicable.

Section 11. INSPECTORS OF ELECTION. In advance of any meeting of shareholders, the Board of Directors may appoint any persons other than nominees for office as inspectors of election to act at such meeting or any adjournment thereof. If inspectors of election are not so appointed, the Chairman of any such meeting may, and on the request of any shareholder or his proxy shall, make such appointment at the meeting. The number of inspectors shall be either one (1) or three (3). If appointed at a meeting on the request of one or more shareholders or proxies, the majority of shares represented in person or by proxy shall determine whether one (1) or three (3) inspectors are to be appointed. In case any person appointed as inspector fails to appear or fails or refuses to act, the vacancy may, and on the request of any shareholder or a shareholder's proxy shall, be filled by appointment by the Board of Directors in advance of the meeting, or at the meeting by the Chairman of the meeting.

The duties of such inspectors shall be as prescribed in Section 707(b) of the California General Corporation Law and shall include: determining the number of shares outstanding and the voting power of each, the shares represented at the meeting, the existence of a quorum, the authenticity, validity and effect of proxies; receiving votes, ballots or consents; hearing and determining all challenges and questions in any way arising in connection with the right to vote; counting and tabulating all votes or consents; determining when the polls shall close; determining the result; and such acts as may be proper to conduct the election or vote with fairness to all shareholders. In the determination of the validity and effect of proxies, the dates contained on the forms of proxies shall presumptively determine the order of execution of the proxies, regardless of the postmarked dates on the envelopes in which they are mailed.

The inspectors of election shall perform their duties impartially, in good faith, to the best of their ability and as expeditiously as is practical. If there are three (3) inspectors of election, the decision, act or certificate of a majority is effective in all respects as the decision, act or certificate of all. Any report or certificate made by the inspectors of election is prima facie evidence of the facts stated herein.

Illustration 7-2 (cont.)

ARTICLE III

DIRECTORS

Section 1. POWERS. Subject to any limitations in the Articles of Incorporation and the California General Corporation Law relating to action requiring shareholder approval, the business and affairs of the corporation shall be managed and all corporate powers shall be exercised by or under the direction of the Board of Directors. The Board of Directors may delegate the management of the day-to-day operation of the business of the corporation to a management company or other person, provided that the business and affairs of the corporation shall be managed and all corporate powers shall be exercised under the ultimate direction of the Board of Directors. Without prejudice to such general powers, but subject to the same limitations, it is hereby expressly declared that the Board shall have the following powers in addition to the other powers enumerated in these By-Laws:

(a) To select and remove all the other officers, agents, and employees of the corporation, prescribe the powers and duties for them as may not be inconsistent with law, or with the Articles or these By-Laws, fix their compensation, and require from them security for faithful service.

(b) To conduct, manage, and control the affairs and business of the corporation and to make such rules and regulations therefor not inconsistent with law, or with the Articles or these By-Laws, as they may deem best.

(c) To adopt, make, and use a corporate seal, and to prescribe the forms of certificates of stock, and to alter the form of such seal and of such certificates from time to time as in their judgment they may deem best.

(d) To authorize the issuance of shares of stock of the corporation from time to time, upon such terms and for such consideration as may be lawful.

(e) To borrow money and incur indebtedness for the purposes of the corporation, and to cause to be executed and delivered therefor, in the corporate name, promissory notes, bonds, debentures, deeds of trust, mortgages, pledges, hypothecations, or other evidences of debt and securities therefor.

Section 2. NUMBER AND QUALIFICATIONS OF DIRECTORS. The authorized number of Directors of the corporation shall be one (1) until changed by the shareholders either by amendment of the Articles of Incorporation or by an amendment of the By-Laws.

Illustration 7-2 (cont.)

If no shares have been issued, this section may be amended by a By-Law duly adopted by the Directors.

Section 3. ELECTION AND TERM OF OFFICE. The Directors shall be elected at each annual meeting of the shareholders, but if any such annual meeting is not held, or the Directors are not elected thereat, the Directors may be elected at any special meeting of the shareholders held for that purpose. All Directors shall hold office at the pleasure of the shareholders or until their respective successors are elected. The shareholders may at any time, either at a regular or special meeting, remove any Director and elect his or her successor.

Section 4. RESIGNATION AND REMOVAL OF DIRECTORS.

(a) Resignation: Any Director may resign effective upon giving written notice to the Chairman of the Board, the President, Secretary or the Board of Directors of the corporation, unless the notice specifies a later time for the effectiveness of such resignation, in which case such resignation shall be effective at the time specified.

(b) Unsound Mind; Felony: The Board of Directors may declare vacant the office of a Director who has been declared of unsound mind by an order of Court or convicted of a felony.

(c) Removal Without Cause by Shareholders: Any or all of the Directors may be removed without cause if such removal is approved by the affirmative vote of a majority of the outstanding shares entitled to vote, provided that no Director may be removed (unless the entire board is removed) when the votes cast against removal, or not consenting in writing to such removal, would be sufficient to elect such Director if voted cumulatively at an election at which the same total number of votes were cast (or, if such action is taken by written consent, all shares entitled to vote were voted) and the entire number of Directors authorized at the time of the Director's most recent election were then being elected.

(d) Reduction of Authorized Number of Directors: No reduction of the authorized number of Directors shall have the affect of removing any Director before his term of office expires.

Section 5. VACANCIES.

(a) Vacancy Defined: A vacancy in the Board of Directors shall be deemed to exist in the case of the death, resignation or removal of any Director, if a Director has been declared of unsound mind by order of Court or convicted

Illustration 7-2 (cont.)

of a felony, if the authorized number of Directors is increased, or if the shareholders fail at any annual or special meeting of shareholders at which any Director or Directors are elected to elect the full authorized number of Directors to be voted for at that meeting.

(b) Action by Board of Directors: Vacancies in the Board of Directors, except for a vacancy created by the removal of a Director, may be filled by a majority of the remaining Directors, although less than a quorum, or by a sole remaining Director, and each Director so elected shall hold office until a successor is elected at an annual or a special meeting of the shareholders. A vacancy in the Board of Directors created by the removal of a Director may be filled only by the vote of majority of the shares represented and voting at a duly held meeting at which a quorum is present, or by the written consent of the holders of a majority of the outstanding shares.

(c) Action by Shareholders: The shareholders may elect a Director or Directors at any time to fill any vacancy or vacancies not filled by the Directors. Any such election by written consent other than to fill a vacancy created by removal shall require the consent of holders of a majority of the outstanding shares entitled to vote.

Section 6. PLACE OF MEETING. Regular and special meetings of the Board of Directors shall be held at any place within or without the State which has been designated in the notice of the meeting, or, if not stated in the notice or there is no notice, designated by resolution of the Board of Directors or, either before or after the meeting, consented to in writing by members of the Board pursuant to the provisions of ARTICLE III, Section 10 of these By-Laws. If the place of a regular or special meeting is not designated in the notice or fixed by a resolution of the Board or consented to in writing by all members of the Board, it shall be held at the corporation's principal executive office.

Section 7. ORGANIZATION MEETING. Immediately following each annual meeting of shareholders, the Board of Directors shall hold a regular meeting for the purpose of organization, election of officers, and the transaction of other business. Notice of such meeting is hereby dispensed with.

Section 8. SPECIAL MEETINGS. Special meetings of the Board of Directors for any purpose may be called at any time by the Chairman of the Board or the President or any Vice President or the Secretary or any Assistant Secretary, or any two Directors. Notice of the time of special meetings shall be delivered personally or by telephone or telegraph or sent to the Directors by mail. In case notice is given by mail, or telegram,

Illustration 7-2 (cont.)

it shall be sent, charges prepaid, addressed to him or her at his or her address as it is shown on the records of the corporation, or if it is not on these records or is not readily ascertainable, at the place where the regular Board meetings are held. If notice is delivered personally or given by telephone or telegraph, it shall be given or delivered to the telegraph office at least twenty-four (24) hours before the meeting. If notice is mailed, it shall be deposited in the United States mail at least forty-eight (48) hours before the meeting.

A notice, or waiver of notice, need not specify the purpose of the meeting of the Board of Directors.

Section 9. ACTION WITHOUT MEETING. Any action required or permitted to be taken by the Board of Directors by law, according to the Articles of Incorporation or according to these By-Laws may be taken without a meeting, if all members of the Board shall individually or collectively consent in writing to such action. Such written consent or consents shall be filed with the minutes of the proceedings of the Board, and shall have the same force and effect as a unanimous vote of such Directors.

Section 10. BY CONFERENCE TELEPHONE. Members of the Board of Directors may participate in a meeting through use of conference telephone or similar communications equipment, so long as all members participating in such a meeting can hear and speak to one another. Participation by a Director in a meeting in the manner provided in this Section shall constitute presence in person by such Director at such meeting.

Section 11. ACTION AT MEETING: QUORUM AND REQUIRED VOTE. Presence of a majority of the authorized number of Directors at a meeting of the Board of Directors constitutes a quorum for the transaction of business, except as hereinafter provided. Every act or decision done or made by a majority of the Directors present at a meeting duly held at which a quorum is present is the act of the Board of Directors, unless a greater number, or the same number after disqualifying one or more Directors from voting, is required by law, the Articles of Incorporation or these By-Laws. A meeting at which a quorum is initially present may continue to transact business notwithstanding the withdrawal of one or more Directors, provided that any action taken is approved by at least a majority of the required quorum for such meeting.

Section 12. WAIVER OF NOTICE. The transactions of any meeting of the Board of Directors, however called and noticed or wherever held, shall be as valid as though had at a meeting duly held after regular call and notice, if a quorum be present, and if, either before or after the meeting, each of the Directors not present or who, though present, has prior to the meeting or at its commencement, protested the lack of proper notice to him,

Illustration 7-2 (cont.)

signs a written waiver of notice or a consent to holding such meeting or in approval of the minutes thereof. A waiver of notice need not specify the purpose of any regular or special meeting of the Board of Directors. All such waivers, consents or approvals shall be filed with the corporate records or made a part of the minutes of the meeting.

Section 13. ADJOURNMENT. A majority of the Directors present, whether or not a quorum is present, may adjourn any meeting to another time and place. If the meeting is adjourned for more than twenty-four (24) hours, notice of the adjournment to another time or place shall be given prior to the time of the adjourned meeting to the Directors who are not present at the time of the adjournment.

Section 14. FEES AND COMPENSATION. Directors shall not receive any stated salary for their services as Directors, but, by resolution of the board, a fixed fee, with or without expenses of attending, may be allowed for attendance at each meeting. Nothing herein contained shall be construed to preclude any Director from serving the corporation in any other capacity as an officer, agent, employee, or otherwise, and receiving compensation therefor.

ARTICLE IV

OFFICERS

Section 1. OFFICERS. The officers of the corporation shall be:

a. President

b. Secretary

c. Chief Financial Officer

The corporation may also have, at the discretion of the Board of Directors, a Chairman of the Board, one or more Vice-Presidents, one or more Assistant Secretaries, one or more Assistant Financial Officers, and such other offices as may be appointed by the Board of Directors. Officers other than the Chairman of the Board need not be Directors. One person may hold two or more offices.

Section 2. ELECTIONS. The officers of the corporation designated in the preceding section of this Article, except such officers as may be elected or appointed in accordance with Section 3 or Section 5 of this Article, shall be chosen annually by the Board of Directors, and each shall hold his or her office

Illustration 7-2 (cont.)

at the pleasure of the Board of Directors, who may, either at a regular or special meeting, remove any such officer and appoint his or her successor.

Section 3. SUBORDINATE OFFICERS, ETC. The Board of Directors may appoint such other officers as the business of the corporation may require, each of whom shall hold office for such period, have such authority and perform such duties as are provided in the By-Laws or as the Board of Directors may from time to time determine.

Section 4. REMOVAL AND RESIGNATION. Any officer may be removed, either with or without cause, by the Board of Directors at that time in office, at a regular or special meeting of the Board, or, except in case of an officer chosen by the Board of Directors, by any officer upon whom such power or removal may be conferred by the Board of Directors, subject, in each case, to the rights, if any, of an officer under any contract of employment.

Any officer may resign at any time by giving written notice to the Board of Directors or to the President, or to the Secretary of the corporation without prejudice, however, to the rights, if any, of the corporation under any contract to which such officer is a party. Any such resignation shall take effect at the date of the receipt of such notice or at any later time specified therein; and unless otherwise specified therein, the acceptance of such resignation shall not be necessary to make it effective.

Section 5. VACANCIES. A vacancy in any office because of death, resignation, removal, disqualification or any other cause shall be filled in the manner prescribed in the By-Laws for regular appointments to such office.

Section 6. CHAIRMAN OF THE BOARD. The Chairman of the Board, if there shall be such an officer, shall, if present, preside at all meetings of the Board of Directors, and exercise and perform such other powers and duties as may be from time to time assigned to him or her by the Board of Directors as prescribed by the By-Laws.

Section 7. PRESIDENT. Subject to such supervisory powers, if any, as may be given by the Board of Directors to the Chairman of the Board, if there be such an officer, the President shall be the Chief Executive Officer of the corporation and shall, subject to the control of the Board of Directors, have general supervision, direction and control of the business and affairs of the corporation. He shall preside at all meetings of the shareholders, and in the absence of the Chairman of the Board, or if there be none, at all meetings of the Board of Directors. He shall be ex officio a member of all the standing

Illustration 7-2 (cont.)

committees, including the executive committee, if any, and shall have the general powers and duties of management usually vested in the office of President of a corporation, and shall have such other powers and duties as may be prescribed by the Board of Directors or the By-Laws.

Section 8. VICE-PRESIDENT. In the absence or disability of the President, the Vice-Presidents in order of their rank as designated by the Board of Directors, if there shall be such officers, shall perform all the duties of the President, and when so acting shall have all the powers of, and be subject to all the restrictions upon, the President. The Vice-President shall have such other powers and perform such other duties as from time to time may be prescribed for them respectively by the Board of Directors or the By-Laws.

Section 9. SECRETARY. The Secretary shall record, or cause to be recorded, and shall keep a book of minutes at the principal executive office, or such other place as the Board of Directors may order, actions taken at all meetings of the Board of Directors and its committees, and at all meetings of shareholders, with the time and place of holding, whether regular or special and, if special, how authorized, the notice thereof given, the names of those Directors and shareholders present, the number of shares present or represented at shareholders meetings, and the proceedings thereof.

The Secretary shall keep, or cause to be kept, at the principal executive office or at the office of the corporation's transfer agent, a share register, or a duplicate share register, showing the names of the shareholders and their addresses; the number and classes of shares held by each; the number and date of certificates issued for the same; the number and date of cancellation of every certificate surrendered for cancellation.

The Secretary shall give, or cause to be given, notice of all meetings of shareholders and of the Board of Directors, as required by law or these By-Laws to be given, and shall have such other powers and perform such other duties as may be prescribed by the Board of Directors or the By-Laws.

Section 10. CHIEF FINANCIAL OFFICER. The Chief Financial Officer of the corporation shall keep and maintain, or cause to be kept and maintained, adequate and correct accounts of the properties and business transactions of the corporation, including accounts of its assets, liabilities, receipts, disbursements, gains, losses, capital, surplus, surplus shares and shall send or cause to be sent to the shareholders of the Corporation such financial statements and reports as are by law or these By-Laws required to be sent to them. Any surplus, including earned surplus, paid in surplus and surplus arising from a reduction of stated capital, shall be classified according

Illustration 7-2 (cont.)

to source and shown in a separate account. The books of account shall at all times be open for inspection by any Director.

The Chief Financial Officer shall deposit all monies and other valuables in the name and to the credit of the corporation with such depositories as may be designated by the Board of Directors. He or she shall disburse the funds of the corporation as may be ordered by the Board of Directors and shall render to the President and Directors, when they request it, an account of all of his or her transactions as Chief Financial Officer and of the financial condition of the corporation, and shall have such other powers and perform such other duties as may be prescribed by the Board of Directors or these By-Laws.

ARTICLE V

EXECUTIVE AND OTHER COMMITTEES

The Board may appoint one or more committees, each consisting of two or more Directors, and delegate to such committees any of the authority of the Board except with respect to:

(a) the approval of any action for which the California General Corporation Law also requires shareholders' approval or approval of the outstanding shares;

(b) the filling of vacancies on the Board or on any committee;

(c) the fixing of compensation of the Directors for serving on the Board or on any committee;

(d) the amendment or repeal of By-Laws or the adoption of new By-Laws;

(e) the amendment or repeal of any resolution of the Board which by its express terms is not so amendable or repealable;

(f) a distribution to the shareholders of the corporation except at a rate or in a periodic amount or within a price range determined by the Board;

(g) the appointment of other committees of the Board or the members thereof.

Any such committee must be appointed by resolution adopted by a majority of the authorized number of Directors and may be designated an Executive Committee or by such other name as

Illustration 7-2 (cont.)

the Board shall specify. The Board shall have the power to prescribe the manner in which proceedings of any such committee shall be conducted. In the absence of any such prescription, such committee shall have the power to prescribe the manner in which its proceedings shall be conducted. Unless the Board or such committee shall otherwise provide, the regular and special meetings and other actions of any such committee shall be governed by the provisions of this Article applicable to meetings and actions of the Board. Minutes shall be kept of each meeting of each committee.

ARTICLE VI

CORPORATE RECORDS AND REPORTS -- INSPECTION

MISCELLANEOUS

Section 1. RECORD DATE. The Board of Directors may fix a time in the future as a record date for the determination of the shareholders entitled to notice of and to vote at any meeting of shareholders or entitled to give consent to corporate action in writing without a meeting, to receive any report, to receive any dividend or distribution, or any allotment of rights, or to exercise rights in respect to any change, conversion, or exchange of shares. The record date so fixed shall not be more than sixty (60) days nor less than ten (10) days prior to the date of any meeting, not more than sixty (60) days prior to any other event for the purposes of which it is fixed. When a record date is so fixed, only shareholders of record on that date are entitled to notice of and to vote at any such meeting, to give consent without a meeting, to receive any report, to receive a dividend, distribution, or allotment of rights, or to exercise the rights, as the case may be, notwithstanding any transfer of any shares on the books of the corporation after the record date, except as otherwise provided in the Articles of Incorporation or By-Laws.

If no record date is fixed by the Board, the record date for determining shareholders entitled to notice of or to vote at a meeting of shareholders shall be at the close of business on the business day next preceding the day on which notice is given or, if notice is waived, at the close of business on the business day next preceding the day on which the meeting is held. The record date for determining shareholders entitled to give consent to corporate action in writing without a meeting, when no prior action by the Board is necessary, shall be the day on which the first consent is given.

Illustration 7-2 (cont.)

The record date for determining shareholders for any other purpose shall be at the close of business on the day on which the Board adopts the resolution relating thereto, or the 60th day prior to the date of such other action whichever is later.

Section 2. INSPECTION OF CORPORATE RECORDS. The accounting books and records, the record of shareholders, and minutes of proceedings of the shareholders and the Board and committees of the Board of this corporation and any subsidiary of this corporation shall be open to inspection upon the written demand on the corporation of any shareholder or holder of a voting trust certificate at any reasonable time during usual business hours, for a purpose reasonably related to such holder's interests as a shareholder or as the holder of such voting trust certificate. Such inspection by a shareholder or holder of a voting trust certificate may be made in person or by agent or attorney, and the right of inspection includes the right to copy and make extracts.

A shareholder or shareholders holding at least five (5) percent in the aggregate of the outstanding voting shares of the corporation or who hold at least one (1) percent of such voting shares and have filed a Schedule 14B with the United States Securities and Exchange Commission relating to the election of Directors of the corporation shall have (in person, or by agent or attorney) the right to inspect and copy the record of shareholders' names and addresses and shareholdings during usual business hours upon five (5) business days' prior written demand upon the corporation and to obtain from the transfer agent for the corporation, upon written demand and upon the tender of its usual charges, a list of the shareholders' names and addresses, who are entitled to vote for the election of Directors, and their shareholdings, as of the most recent record date for which it has been compiled or as of a date specified by the shareholder subsequent to the date of demand. The list shall be made available on or before the later of five (5) business days after the demand is received or the date specified therein as the date as of which the list is to be compiled.

Every Director shall have the absolute right at any reasonable time to inspect and copy all books, records and documents of every kind and to inspect the physical properties of the corporation. Such inspection by a Director may be made in person or by agent or attorney and the right of inspection includes the right to copy and make extracts.

Section 3. CERTIFICATION AND INSPECTION OF BYLAWS. The original or a copy of these By-Laws, as amended or otherwise altered to date, certified by the Secretary, shall be open to inspection by the shareholders at all reasonable times during office hours. If the principal executive office of the

Illustration 7-2 (cont.)

corporation is outside the State of California and the corporation has no principal business office in such state, it shall upon the written notice of any shareholder furnish to such shareholder a copy of these By-Laws as amended to date.

Section 4. CHECKS, DRAFTS, ETC. All checks, drafts or other orders for payment of money, notes or other evidences of indebtedness, issued in the name of or payable to the corporation, shall be signed or endorsed by such person or persons and in such manner as shall be determined from time to time by resolution of the Board of Directors.

Section 5. CONTRACTS, ETC. -- HOW EXECUTED. The Board of Directors, except as the By-Laws otherwise provide, may authorize any officer or officers, agent or agents, to enter into any contract or execute any instrument in the name of and on behalf of the corporation. Such authority may be general or confined to specific instances.

Section 6. ANNUAL AND OTHER REPORTS. The annual report to shareholders referred to in Section 1501 of the California General Corporation Law is expressly waived, but nothing herein shall be interpreted as prohibiting the Board from issuing annual or other periodic reports to shareholders.

Section 7. REPRESENTATION OF SHARES OF OTHER CORPORATIONS. The President or any Vice-President and the Secretary or Assistant Secretary of this corporation are authorized to vote, represent and exercise on behalf of this corporation all rights incident to any and all shares of any other corporation or corporations standing in the name of this corporation. The authority herein granted to said officers to vote or represent on behalf of this corporation any and all shares held by this corporation in any other corporation or corporations may be exercised either by such officers in person or by a person authorized so to do by proxy or power of attorney duly executed by said officers.

Section 8. CONSTRUCTION AND DEFINITIONS. Unless the context otherwise requires, the general provisions, rules of construction and definitions contained in the California General Corporation Law shall govern the construction of these By-Laws. Without limiting the generality of the foregoing, the masculine gender includes the feminine and neuter, the singular number includes the plural and the plural number includes the singular, and the term "person" includes a corporation as well as a natural person.

Illustration 7-2 (cont.)

ARTICLE VII

CERTIFICATES AND TRANSFER OF SHARES

Section 1. CERTIFICATE FOR SHARES. Every holder of shares in the corporation shall be entitled to have a certificate signed in the name of the corporation by the Chairman or Vice-Chairman of the Board or the President or a Vice-President and by the Chief Financial Officer or an Assistant-Treasurer or the Secretary or any Assistant Secretary, certifying the number of shares and the class or series of shares owned by the shareholder. Any of the signatures on the certificate may be facsimile, provided that in such event at least one signature, including that of either officer or the corporation's registrar or transfer agent, if any, shall be manually signed. In any case any officer, transfer agent or registrar who has signed or whose facsimile signature has been placed upon a certificate shall have ceased to be such officer, transfer agent or registrar before such certificate is issued, it may be issued by the corporation with the same effect as if such person were an officer, transfer agent or registrar at the date of issue.

Any such certificate shall also contain such legend or other statement as may be required by Section 418 of the General Corporation Law, the Corporate Securities Law of 1968, the federal securities laws, and any agreement between the corporation and the issue thereof.

Certificates for shares may be issued prior to full payment under such restrictions and for such purposes as the Board of Directors or the By-Laws may provide; provided, however, that any such certificate so issued prior to full payment shall state on the face thereof the amount remaining unpaid and the terms of payment thereof.

No new certificate for shares shall be issued in lieu of an old certificate unless the latter is surrendered and canceled at the same time; provided, however, that a new certificate will be issued without the surrender and cancellation of the old certificate if (1) the old certificate is lost, apparently destroyed or wrongfully taken; (2) the request for the issuance of the new certificate is made within a reasonable time after the owner of the old certificate has notice of its loss, destruction, or theft; (3) the request for the issuance of a new certificate is made prior to the receipt of notice by the corporation that the old certificate has been acquired by a bona fide purchaser; (4) the owner of the old certificate files a sufficient indemnity bond with or provides other adequate security to the corporation; and (5) the owner satisfies any other reasonable requirements imposed by the corporation. In the event of the issuance of a new certificate, the rights and

Illustration 7-2 (cont.)

liabilities of the corporation, and of the holders of the old and new certificates, shall be governed by the provisions of Section 8104 and 8405 of the California Commercial Code.

Section 2. TRANSFER ON THE BOOKS. Upon surrender to the Secretary or transfer agent of the corporation by proper evidence of succession, assignment or authority to transfer, it shall be the duty of the corporation to issue a new certificate to the person entitled thereto, cancel the old certificate and record the transaction upon its books.

Section 3. LOST OR DESTROYED CERTIFICATES. Any person claiming a certificate of stock to be lost or destroyed shall make an affidavit or affirmation of that fact and advertise the same in such manner as the Board of Directors may require, and shall if the Directors so require give the corporation a bond of indemnity, in form with one or more sureties satisfactory to the Board, in at least double the value of the stock represented by said certificate, whereupon a new certificate may be issued of the same tenor and for the same number of shares as the one alleged to be lost or destroyed.

Section 4. TRANSFER AGENTS AND REGISTRARS. The Board of Directors may appoint one or more transfer agents or transfer clerks, and one or more registrars, which shall be an incorporated bank or trust company -- either domestic or foreign, who shall be appointed at such times and places as the requirements of the corporation may necessitate and the Board of Directors may designate.

Section 5. RECORD DATE AND CLOSING BOOKS. The Board of Directors may fix a time in the future as a record date for the determination of the shareholders entitled to give consent to corporate action in writing without a meeting to receive any report, dividends or distribution, or any allotment of rights, or to exercise rights in respect to any change, conversion or exchange of shares. The record date so fixed shall be not more than sixty (60) days prior to any other event for the purposes of which it is fixed. When a record date is so fixed, only shareholders of record on that date are entitled to notice of, and to vote at any such meeting, to give consent without a meeting, to receive any report, to receive a dividend, distribution, or allotment of rights, or to exercise the rights, as the case may be, notwithstanding any transfer of any shares on the books of the corporation after the record date, except as otherwise provided in the Articles of Incorporation or By-Laws.

The Board of Directors may close the books of the corporation against transfers of shares during the whole or any part of a period of not more than sixty (60) days prior to the date of a shareholders' meeting, the date when the right to any

Illustration 7-2 (cont.)

dividend, distribution, or allotment of rights vests, or the effective date of any change, conversion, or exchange of shares.

ARTICLE VIII

INDEMNIFICATION

Section 1. DEFINITIONS. For purposes of this Article, "agent" means any person who is or was a director, officer, employee or other agent of the corporation, or is or was serving at the request of the corporation as a director, officer, employee or agent of another foreign or domestic corporation, partnership, joint venture, trust or other enterprise, or was a director, officer, employee or agent of a foreign or domestic corporation which was a predecessor corporation of the corporation or of another enterprise at the request of such predecessor corporation; and "proceeding" means any threatened, pending, or completed action or proceeding, whether civil, criminal, administrative or investigative.

Section 2. INDEMNIFICATION OF DIRECTORS AND OFFICERS. The corporation shall indemnify, in the manner and to the full extent permitted by law (including, without limitation, the indemnification authorized by Article V of the Articles of Incorporation), any person (or the estate of any person) who was or is a party, or is threatened to be made a party, to any proceeding by reason of the fact that such person (1) is or was a director or officer of the corporation or a predecessor corporation, or (2) is or was an agent other than a director or officer of the corporation or a predecessor corporation who, at the time, is or was also serving as a director or officer of the corporation or a predecessor corporation. Where required by law, the indemnification provided for in this Section shall be made only as authorized in the specific case upon a determination, in the manner provided by law, that indemnification is proper under the circumstances.

To the full extent permitted by law, the indemnification provided for in this Section shall include expenses (including attorneys' fees and expenses of establishing a right to indemnification under this Section) in any proceeding or in connection with any appeal therein, judgments, fines, and amounts paid in settlement. In the manner and to the full extent permitted by law, any such expenses shall be paid by the corporation in advance of the final disposition of such proceeding. The provisions of this Paragraph are subject to the provisions of Section 3 of this Article.

Illustration 7-2 (cont.)

Section 3. NOTIFICATION AND DEFENSE OF CLAIM.

A. A person's right to indemnification and advancement of expenses under the provisions of Section 2 of this Article (hereinafter referred to in this Section as "Indemnification Provisions") is conditioned upon his having promptly given the corporation written notice after learning of his involvement in a proceeding; however, a person's failure to give such notice promptly shall not relieve the corporation of any liability it may have to the person (1) under the Indemnification Provisions unless the corporation is materially prejudiced by such failure or (2) otherwise than under the Indemnification Provisions.

B. With respect to any proceeding of which the corporation has been given the notice required by Paragraph A of this Section, the corporation shall have the right to participate in, and, to the extent that it may wish, jointly with any other indemnifying party similarly notified, to assume and control the defense thereof, with counsel chosen by the corporation but reasonably satisfactory to the person seeking indemnification (hereinafter referred to in this Section as "Indemnitee"); provided, however, that if the defendants in any such proceeding include both Indemnitee and the corporation, and counsel for the corporation shall have reasonably concluded that there is a conflict of interest that would prevent counsel for the corporation from also representing Indemnitee, then Indemnitee shall have the right to select separate counsel to participate in the defense of the proceeding on Indemnitee's behalf. After the corporation has notified Indemnitee of the corporation's election so to assume the defense of the proceeding, the corporation will not be liable to Indemnitee pursuant to the Indemnification Provisions for any legal or other expense subsequently incurred by Indemnitee in connection with the defense other than reasonable costs of investigation unless (1) Indemnitee shall have employed counsel pursuant to the provisions of this Paragraph as a result of a conflict of interest or (2) the corporation shall have authorized the employment of counsel for Indemnitee at the expense of the corporation. If the corporation elects to assume such defense, Indemnitee shall have the right, at his own expense and with counsel of his choice, to participate in such defense, and Indemnitee shall in all events cooperate fully with the corporation. Neither Indemnitee nor the corporation will compromise or settle any proceeding without the prior written consent of the other, provided that in the event that the corporation proposes a monetary settlement the acceptance of which would release Indemnitee from all claims asserted in such proceeding and if Indemnitee withholds his consent to such settlement, then the liability of the corporation shall be limited to the total sum representing the amount of the proposed compromise or settlement and the amount of reasonable

Illustration 7-2 (cont.)

attorneys' fees incurred by Indemnitee up to the time such approval is withheld.

Section 4. INDEMNIFICATION OF OTHER AGENTS. The corporation may provide indemnification and may advance expenses, in the same manner and to the same extent required in Section 2 of this Article for those agents specified therein, to any person (or the estate of any person) who was or is a party, or is threatened to be made a party, to any proceeding by reason of the fact that such person is or was an agent other than an agent specified in Section 2 of this Article.

Section 5. SUCCESSFUL DEFENSE. To the extent that any agent has been successful on the merits in defense of any claim, issue or matter therein, the agent shall be indemnified against expenses (including attorney's fees) actually and reasonably incurred by the agent in connection therewith.

Section 6. OTHER INDEMNIFICATION PERMITTED. The indemnification provided by this Article shall not be deemed exclusive of any other rights to which those seeking indemnification may be entitled under any bylaw, agreement, vote of shareholders or disinterested directors or otherwise, both as to action in an official capacity and as to action in another capacity while holding such office. Nothing contained in this Article shall affect any right to indemnification to which any person may be entitled in another capacity, by contract or otherwise.

Section 7. INSURANCE. The corporation may, in the manner and to the full extent permitted by law, purchase and maintain insurance on behalf of any agent of the corporation against any liability which may be asserted against him.

Section 8. PRESUMPTIONS. The termination of any proceeding by judgment, order, settlement or conviction or upon a plea of nolo contendere or its equivalent shall not of itself create a presumption that any standard has not been satisfied that by law must be satisfied for indemnification to be proper under the circumstances.

Section 9. SUBSEQUENT AMENDMENT. No amendment, termination or repeal of this Article, Article V of the Articles of Incorporation, or relevant provisions of the California Corporations Code or any other applicable law shall affect or diminish in any way the rights to indemnification under the provisions of this Article with respect to any proceeding arising out of, or relating to, any actions, transactions or facts occurring prior to the final adoption of such amendment, termination or repeal.

Illustration 7-2 (cont.)

Section 10. MERGER, CONSOLIDATION, ETC. If the corporation is merged into or consolidated with another corporation and the corporation is not the surviving corporation, or if substantially all of the assets or stock of the corporation are acquired by any other corporation, or in the event of any other similar reorganization involving the corporation, the Board of Directors of the corporation or the board of directors of any corporation assuming the obligations of the corporation shall assume the obligations of the corporation under this Article with respect to any proceeding arising out of or relating to any actions, transactions or facts occurring before to the date of such merger, consolidation, acquisition or reorganization.

Section 11. SEVERABILITY. If any part of this Article shall be found in any proceeding or appeal therefrom or in any other circumstances or as to any particular agent to be unenforceable, ineffective or invalid for any reason, the enforceability, effect and validity of the remaining parts or of such parts in other circumstances shall not be affected, except as otherwise required by applicable law.

ARTICLE IX

CORPORATE SEAL

The corporate seal shall be circular in form, and shall have inscribed thereon the name of the corporation, the date of its incorporation, and the word "California."

ARTICLE X

AMENDMENTS TO BY-LAWS

Section 1. BY SHAREHOLDERS. New By-Laws may be adopted or these By-Laws may be repealed or amended at their annual meeting, or at any other meeting of the shareholders called for that purpose, by a vote of shareholders entitled to exercise a majority of the voting power of the corporation, or by written assent of such shareholders, except as otherwise provided by law, the Articles of Incorporation, or Section 2 of this Article X.

Section 2. POWER OF DIRECTORS. Subject to the right of shareholders as provided in Section 1 of this Article X to adopt, amend, or repeal By-Laws, other than a By-Law or amendment thereof changing the authorized number of Directors, these By-Laws may be adopted, amended or repealed by the Board of Directors; provided, however, that if no shares have been issued, the Board of Directors may adopt a By-Law or amendment thereof changing the authorized number of Directors.

Illustration 7-2 (cont.)

CERTIFICATE OF SECRETARY

I, the undersigned, hereby certify:

1. That I am the duly elected, qualified and acting Secretary of American Capital Investments, Inc., a California corporation.

2. That the foregoing By-Laws of said corporation were duly adopted as the By-Laws thereof by an Action Taken by Unanimous Written Consent of the Board of Directors of said corporation on March 16, 1992 and that the same do now constitute the By-Laws of said corporation.

Executed on March 16, 1992.

Stephen Murphy
Secretary

PARTNERSHIP

Black's defines a partnership as: ". . .A business owned by two or more personas not organized as a corporation. Voluntary contract between two or more competent persons to place their money, effects, labor and skill, or some or all of them, in lawful commerce or business, with the understanding that there shall be a proportional sharing of the profits and losses between them. . ."

Within this broad ownership entity definition lies one of the principal structures used for the purpose of acquiring income producing property used as an investment organization for the purpose of ownership, management and distribution of earnings from the venture. It is important to differentiate between the two types of partnership form, since there are legal ownership consequences in each.

- **GENERAL PARTNERSHIP**

  In this partnership form, the management, profits and losses are shared equally by the partners. Capital contributions can be on an equal or unequal basis.

  In most states, the general partnership is under the aegis of the Uniform General Partnership Act, which has been adopted by a majority of the states. In California, the codified portion of this legislation will be found in Section 15501, et. seq. of the Corporations Code.

  In accordance with the code, a partnership certificate is filed in the county clerk's office where the partnership's principal place of business is located. The certificate will contain the following information:

  - The name of the partnership
  - The character of the business
  - The location of the principal place of business
  - The name and residence of the general partners
  - The term for which the partnership is to exist
  - Other housekeeping items, dependent upon the state of business location's laws

A partnership is really a form of cotenancy which has been recognized as a legal unit for title insurance purposes and thus takes on the appearance of a legal entity. The certificate of fictitious name identifying the partnership and its partners is required to be published in an approved legal publication located within the judicial district where the partnership's principal business office is located. Since a partnership is a form of cotenancy, title may be acquired in the names of the partners without specifically mentioning the business name. It is a matter of intent upon the individual partners themselves as to the effect of this ownership, whether it be as individuals or as partners. Another version of this type of ownership is the informal arrangement, popular during the 1970s of creating percentage ownerships of individual investors in apartments held together with a loose property management arrangement usually under the supervision of a real estate licensee. There were considerable drawbacks in that form of real estate ownership due to the logistics involved.

The most popular reason for using partnerships revolves around situations where each of the individual members of the group supplies a particular talent to the group itself, as previously noted earlier. Information returns on the partnership are sent to federal and state taxing agencies with partnership earnings being reported by the individual partners as part of their annual tax reporting chores.

One of the principal drawbacks in general partnerships is the fact that each partner has joint an several liability for the acts of the partnership. Acts of individual partners on behalf of the partnership will bind the partnership.

- **LIMITED PARTNERSHIP**

The make-up and formation of this entity will be covered in detail in Chapter nine. This ownership entity represents one of the most popular forms of syndication ownership units, since investors can enjoy the shield of limited liability that their status of limited partner affords.

Black's depicts the limited partnership as a: "...type of partnership comprised of one or more general partners who manage business and who are personally liable for business debts, and one or more limited partners who contribute capital and share in profits but who take no part in running business and incur no liability with respect to partnership obligations beyond contribution. . ."

Armed with this definition, there are decided differences in the liability incurred by participants in this entity. Only the general partner or partners incur liability, while limited partners are generally limited to the extent of their personal investment in the venture. Similar to the general partnership, it takes two or more persons to form the limited partnership with the difference that there may be only one general partner plus one limited partner as the minimum legal requirement to form this association.

The limited partner used in real estate syndication is the investing entity which usually supplies a substantial portion of the equity capital required to acquire a given project. The governing law for formation of a limited partnership in most states is the Uniform Limited Partnership Act. In the state of California, this act is codified under Section 15502, et. seq. of the Corporations Code. The filing requirements are very similar to those required for the general partnership with additional requirements concerning the provision of the names of the limited partners, contributions, allocation of profits and changes in legal status that may occur along the way. The actual partnership agreement is an extensive document which will be examined in detail in Chapter nine.

JOINT VENTURES

The joint venture represents an association of persons in an enterprise for profit. The activities of joint ventures, or joint adventures as they are sometimes called, generally fall within the rules set forth for partnerships. Its objective is to form the association for one particular project. Upon completion of the project, the association is dissolved.

There are characteristics that differentiate this form of association from a partnership. Individual joint venturers cannot bind the joint venture. It must be a combined agreement of all of the participants. If individual venturers are married, spouse liability is incurred and spousal signature is required on all legal documents to bind the venture. A typical ownership vesting would be: A, B, and C as joint venturers doing business as Stonegate Apartments, a Joint Venture. This type of device is typically used by developers to construct an income-producing property for the purpose of resale to investors. One of the owners of the property may contribute equity as a means of joining this profit sharing association in the project.

REAL ESTATE INVESTMENT TRUSTS

Real estate investment trusts are designed to fill the need in the income producing real estate market that investment companies and mutual funds provide in the securities market. They provide a means of gaining financial leverage through the accumulation of capital contributed by a large investment base in the form of ownership in shares of beneficial interest.

Under California law, the REIT, as it is known, is defined as ". . .any unincorporated association or trust formed to engage in business and managed by, or under the direction of, one or more trustees for the benefit of the holders or owners of transferable shares of beneficial interest in the trust estate. . ."

In order to qualify for the special tax status that such organizations enjoy, this entity must pass one of two tests applied to their organization:

1) It must have received an order, permit, or qualification prior to 1976 from the Commissioner of Corporations finding that it was a REIT and for one or more of its three fiscal years prior to 1976, it must have complied with the federal requirements for REITS or in good faith have filed federal tax returns on the basis of these requirements. Note: this basically means that 95% of the earnings were passed through to the holders of beneficial interest, thus giving tax exempt status to the earnings that are "passed through" to such owners.

2) If it is formed for the purpose of engaging in business as a REIT under federal law, the sale of its shares has been qualified by the Commissioner of Corporations, and it has in good faith commence business as a REIT.

In the case of a REIT, their adjusted net worth prior to initial public offering must be no less than the lower of:

- Ten percent of the adjusted net worth upon completion of the public offering, or
- $200,000. The adjusted net worth of the trust must be not less than $1 million upon completion of the initial public offering.

This type of ownership on the part of the investor allows the following advantages:

1) Relatively small investments can be made, thus allowing the small investor to participate in trust activities.

2) Limited liability for investors under California law.

3) REITs have the capability of amassing large amounts of capital for investment.

4) The operation is cost effective due to an extensive portfolio being managed by a central staff.

5) If the REIT is publicly traded, shares are easily sold to provide liquidity.

6) REIT status election is optional.

7) REITs enjoy exemption from "Superfund" tax on corporations.

Disadvantages of REIT ownership entail the following:

1) Investments are limited in scope.

2) If the REIT fails to qualify, additional taxes may have to be paid due to prohibited investments undertaken or failure to distribute profits in accordance with tax regulations.

3) Income must be distributed in the year it is received, even though it may be a burden from a cash flow perspective for the trust.

4) There is usually a thin market for the shares of beneficial interest, since most REITs are not traded on a public exchange.

5) Even though the REIT may represent that they are willing to redeem shares of beneficial interest, they may not have that capability.

6) Contrary to tax treatment of corporations, a contribution of property in return for shares of beneficial interest is considered a taxable event for the shareholder.

Generally shares of beneficial interest in a REIT are considered securities and, as such, are subject to the securities laws of the state. This requires extensive documentation requirements and filings on the part of the REIT just to continue in business. This, in turn, adds to administrative costs thus reducing potential return to the holders of beneficial interest. This represents another disadvantage of this somewhat cumbersome investment vehicle. One of the largest single real estate transactions involving income property involved the Furman-Wolfson real estate trust. The syndicator that pulled off this amazing deal was Harry Helmsley, free wheeling New York based entrepreneur, who was able to pull off this amazing $165 million transaction in 1969 (which would be megabucks today) by strolling in to Chase Manhattan Bank, borrowing $78 million on his signature alone - unsecured debt for the purposes of acquiring real estate is unheard of these days - then combining with Irving Schneider to form a well subscribed syndication offering to raise the capital to close the deal. The syndication offering replaced the unsecured debt and Helmsley ended up as owner of thirty major buildings in New York, Chicago, Los Angeles, Des Moines and Newark. At least, temporarily, this put Harry Helmsley on the top of the real estate magnate heap in the "Big Apple." The man who was the pivotal part of an earlier acquisition of the Empire State Building now out shadowed his former partner, Larry Wien, who had been involved in a transaction with J. Myer Schine which went south due to some unfortunate pre-publicity causing Schine to up the ante on the price. Helmsley just got to be a harder and tougher negotiator after that fiasco. But not all syndications involve improved properties. For the brave at heart, property for development is their form of risk taking.

LAND OWNER BASED AFFILIATIONS ON PROPOSED CONSTRUCTION

Many syndicates are formed on the basis of contribution of talent and property. Never was it more true than in the real estate development process where it ranges from loose affiliations to formal arrangements in the form of partnerships or joint ventures. The developer's objective is to gain control of the parcel as a means of improving it. Some of these arrangements may involve the seller deeding to the developer and taking an unsecured note, or taking back a purchase money obligation with the understanding that it would be subordinated to construction financing, taking other property owned by the builder in a 1031 tax deferred exchange, or a variety of other arrangements which may vary from options to purchase to land leases in nature. The nature and configuration of the ownership vehicle can vary by type of transaction and circumstance.

Each of these methods of holding title share their advantages and disadvantages. Ultimately the overriding consideration in most real estate investment activity is the method by which the transaction may be structured to reduce the amount of tax obligation incurred by the investing public. Our next chapter will address the complexities of that issue.

8
SATISFYING THE IRS

Justice Holmes made the cogent observation in the case of Compania de Tabacos v. Collector in 1904: "Taxes are what we pay for a civilized society." This oft-quoted passage is just as valid today as it was at the turn of the century. Only the system of collection and allocation has become a bit more complex.

The taxation process occurs at more than just the federal level. As Illustrations 8-1 through 8-5 indicate, the impact of state and local government tax collections as a segment of the entire process is increasing at a rapid rate over the past decade. This means that investors not only have to cope with tax consequences on the federal level, principally represented in the provisions of the Tax Reform Act of 1986, they must also contend with taxation policy of their state of domicile.

DEVELOPING A TAX STRATEGY

Since the greatest impact on taxpayers who generate considerable personal cash flow is at the federal level, the syndicator concentrates on creating an entity which tends to reduce the impact of the Internal Revenue Service's portion of the return received in the form of payments from a given project.

The Tax Reform Act of 1986 has caused syndicators to rethink their strategy relative to setting up not only the organization form that represents the syndication vehicle, but how this can provide the maximum tax advantage to their investors.

Both Real Estate Investment Trusts and Partnerships have some pass-through advantages tax-wise to their shareholders and/or partners. In the case of the REIT there are corporate franchise taxes and corporate income taxes on a state level in many states, including California, where tax is imposed on the REIT's net income as defined in the Internal Revenue Code. Individual shareholders of REITs, just as partners in a

Illustration 8-1

State Government Tax Collections, by Type: 1970 and 1990

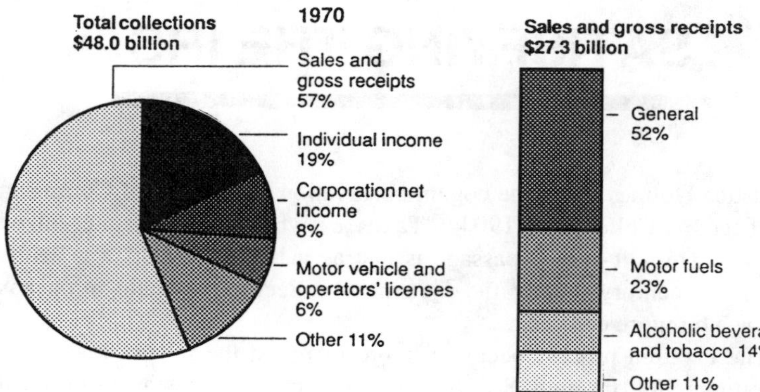

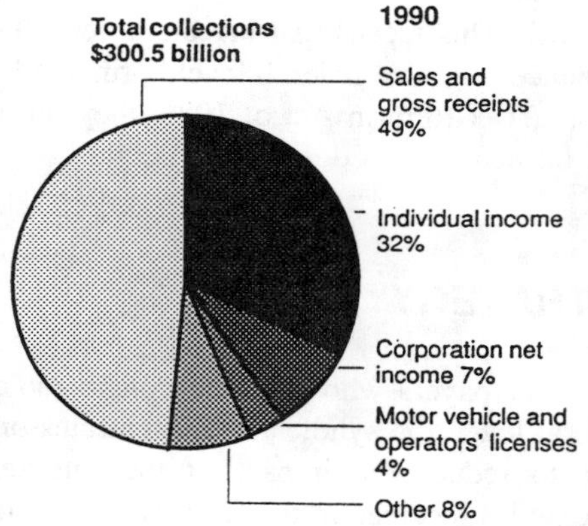

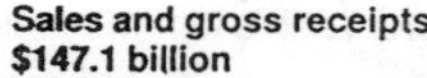

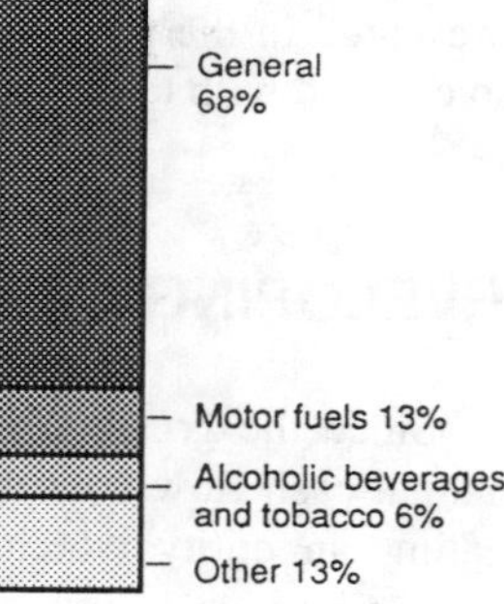

Source: Chart prepared by U.S. Bureau of the Census. For data, see table 463.

Number of Governmental Units, by Type of Government: 1942 to 1987

TYPE OF GOVERNMENT	1942	1952[1]	1957[1]	1962	1967	1972	1977	1982	1987
Total	**155,116**	**116,807**	**102,392**	**91,237**	**81,299**	**78,269**	**79,913**	**81,831**	**83,237**
U.S. Government	1	1	1	1	1	1	1	1	1
State government	48	50	50	50	50	50	50	50	50
Local governments	155,067	166,756	102,341	91,186	81,248	78,218	79,862	81,780	83,186
County	3,050	3,052	3,050	3,043	3,049	3,044	3,042	3,041	3,042
Municipal	16,220	16,807	17,215	18,000	18,048	18,517	18,862	19,076	19,200
Township and town	18,919	17,202	17,198	17,142	17,105	16,991	16,822	16,734	16,691
School district	108,579	67,355	50,454	34,678	21,782	15,781	15,174	14,851	14,721
Special district	8,299	12,340	14,424	18,323	21,264	23,885	25,962	28,078	29,532

[1] Adjusted to include units in Alaska and Hawaii which adopted statehood in 1959.

Source: U.S. Bureau of the Census, *Census of Governments*: 1967, vol. 1, No. 1, *Governmental Organization, 1982*, vol. 6, No. 4, *Historical Statistics on Governmental Finances and Employment* (GC82(6)–4), and *Census of Governments*, 1987, vol. 1, No. 1, *Governmental Organization.*

Illustration 8-1a

All Governments—Revenue, Expenditure, and Debt: 1980 to 1990

[For fiscal year ending in year shown; see text, section 9. Local government amounts are estimates subject to sampling variation; see Appendix III and source. See also *Historical Statistics, Colonial Times to 1970*, series Y 505-637 and Y 652-848]

ITEM AND YEAR	All governments (bil. dol.)	FEDERAL [1]		STATE AND LOCAL (bil. dol.)			AVERAGE ANNUAL PERCENT CHANGE[2]			PER CAPITA [3] (dollars)		
		Total (bil. dol.)	Percent of total	Total	State	Local	Federal	State	Local	Total	Federal	State and local
Revenue: [4] 1980	[5]932	565	60.7	[5]452	277	258	10.6	12.0	11.2	[5]4,115	2,496	1,993
1985	[5]1,419	807	56.9	[5]720	439	402	7.4	9.7	9.3	[5]5,943	3,379	3,015
1989	[5]1,917	1,093	57.0	[5]954	587	532	7.9	8.3	7.5	[5]7,724	4,402	3,841
1990	[5]2,047	1,155	56.4	[5]1,032	632	580	5.7	7.8	9.1	[5]8,230	4,642	4,150
Intergovernmental: 1980	(X)	2	(X)	[5]83	64	102	(X)	12.3	13.3	(X)	8	367
1985	(X)	2	(X)	[5]106	90	138	1.6	6.9	6.2	(X)	8	445
1989	(X)	3	(X)	[5]126	116	175	1.5	8.0	7.7	(X)	12	507
1990	(X)	3	(X)	[5]137	126	191	0.3	9.1	8.8	(X)	12	550
General, own sources:												
1980	717	417	58.2	299	169	130	9.8	11.4	9.7	3,163	1,842	1,321
1985	1,050	559	53.2	492	276	216	6.0	10.3	10.7	4,400	2,339	2,059
1989	1,400	740	52.9	660	367	293	7.4	8.4	8.1	5,642	2,983	2,659
1990	1,493	780	52.3	713	391	322	5.4	6.7	9.7	6,004	3,138	2,866
Taxes: [4] 1980	574	351	61.1	223	137	86	9.2	11.1	8.3	2,535	1,548	986
1985	804	454	56.4	350	215	134	5.3	9.5	9.3	3,369	1,902	1,465
1989	1,085	616	56.8	469	284	184	9.5	7.6	7.5	4,369	2,481	1,888
1990	1,134	632	55.8	502	300	201	2.7	5.8	9.0	4,559	2,542	2,017
Property: 1980	68	(X)	(X)	68	3	66	(X)	10.2	7.1	302	(X)	302
1985	104	(X)	(X)	104	4	100	(X)	6.6	8.8	435	(X)	435
1989	143	(X)	(X)	143	5	137	(X)	7.3	7.8	574	(X)	574
1990	156	(X)	(X)	156	6	150	(X)	8.0	9.2	626	(X)	626
Individual income:												
1980	286	244	85.3	42	37	5	10.4	15.0	11.9	1,263	1,077	186
1985	401	331	82.5	70	64	6	6.3	11.5	5.3	1,681	1,386	294
1989	543	446	82.0	98	89	9	11.1	10.8	9.4	2,189	1,795	394
1990	573	467	81.6	106	96	10	4.8	8.2	6.4	2,302	1,877	425
Corporate income:												
1980	78	65	82.9	13	13	-	7.0	13.6	-	344	285	59
1985	80	61	76.2	19	18	2	-1.0	5.8	(X)	337	257	80
1989	129	103	79.9	26	24	2	9.7	10.0	0.2	521	416	104
1990	117	94	79.9	24	22	2	-9.5	-8.9	-11.9	471	376	95
Sales or gross receipts:												
1980	112	[6]32	28.6	80	68	12	5.8	9.6	14.7	494	[6]141	353
1985	176	[6]49	28.0	126	105	21	8.9	9.2	11.7	735	[6]206	529
1989	219	[6]53	24.0	166	139	28	-0.2	6.2	6.3	880	[6]212	669
1990	232	[6]54	23.3	178	147	31	2.8	6.4	11.0	932	[6]217	715
Current charges and miscellaneous: 1980	142	67	46.7	76	32	44	14.3	12.9	13.3	629	294	335
1985	246	104	42.5	142	60	82	9.4	13.3	13.3	1,031	438	594
1989	316	125	39.4	191	83	109	-2.0	11.3	9.2	1,273	502	771
1990	359	148	41.3	211	91	120	19.0	9.8	10.7	1,445	596	849
Expenditures: [4] 1980	[5]959	617	64.4	[5]434	258	261	11.5	11.7	10.9	[5]4,232	2,724	1,916
1985	[5]1,581	1,032	65.3	[5]658	391	391	10.8	8.7	8.4	[5]6,622	4,323	2,756
1989	[5]2,031	1,270	62.6	[5]891	525	533	4.6	8.3	7.4	[5]8,180	5,116	3,589
1990	[5]2,219	1,393	62.8	[5]976	572	581	9.7	9.0	9.0	[5]8,921	5,601	3,924
Intergovernmental: 1980	(X)	91	(X)	[5]2	85	2	14.6	11.3	10.8	(X)	401	8
1985	(X)	107	(X)	[5]2	122	4	3.4	7.6	18.1	(X)	449	8
1989	(X)	127	(X)	3	165	5	7.0	9.1	-5.0	(X)	513	12
1990	(X)	147	(X)	3	175	6	15.5	5.8	19.1	(X)	591	13
Direct: [4] 1980	959	526	54.9	432	173	259	11.0	11.9	10.9	4,232	2,323	1,908
1985	1,581	925	58.5	656	269	387	11.9	9.2	8.4	6,622	3,874	2,748
1989	2,031	1,143	56.3	888	360	528	4.3	7.9	7.6	8,180	4,603	3,577
1990	2,219	1,246	58.5	973	397	575	9.0	10.5	8.9	8,921	5,010	3,911
Current operation: 1980	517	209	40.5	308	108	200	7.8	13.3	11.6	2,282	923	1,359
1985	833	360	43.3	473	172	300	11.5	9.7	8.5	3,488	1,509	1,979
1989	1,073	432	40.3	641	233	408	-0.8	9.3	7.8	4,322	1,741	2,580
1990	1,190	490	41.2	700	258	442	13.4	10.8	8.5	4,785	1,970	2,815
Capital outlay: 1980	99	36	36.7	63	23	40	7.4	5.8	9.2	439	161	278
1985	157	77	49.1	80	31	49	16.1	5.6	4.5	657	323	335
1989	212	100	47.1	112	43	69	6.7	6.0	8.1	853	402	451
1990	221	98	44.3	123	46	78	-1.9	5.6	12.7	888	394	495
Debt outstanding: [7] 1980	1,250	914	73.2	336	122	214	9.4	11.3	7.7	5,517	4,036	1,481
1985	2,396	1,827	76.3	571	212	357	14.9	11.7	10.8	10,036	7,655	2,393
1989	3,679	2,881	78.3	798	296	503	10.2	6.8	5.2	14,822	11,606	3,216
1990	4,127	3,266	79.2	861	318	542	13.4	7.7	7.9	16,592	13,132	3,460

Represents or rounds to zero. X Not applicable. [1] Data adjusted to system for reporting State and local data and therefore differ from figures in section 10 tables. [2] Percent change from prior year, except for 1980, change from 1970 and 1985, change from 1980. For explanation, see Guide to Tabular Presentation. Minus sign (-) indicates decrease. [3] 1980 and 1990 based on enumerated resident population as of April 1; all other years based on estimated resident population as of July 1. Estimates do not reflect revisions based on the 1990 Census of Population. Excludes intergovernmental amounts. [4] Includes amounts, not shown separately. [5] Excludes duplicative transactions between levels of government; see source. [6] Includes customs. [7] End of fiscal year.

Source: U.S. Bureau of the Census, *Historical Statistics on Governmental Finances and Employment (GC 82(6)-4)*; and *Government Finances*, series GF, No. 5, annual.

Illustration 8-2

State and Local Government Finances and Employment

All Governments—Revenue and Expenditure, by Level of Government: 1990

[**For fiscal year ending in year shown,** see text, section 9. Local government amounts are estimates subject to sampling variation; see source and appendix III. See also *Historical Statistics, Colonial Times to 1970,* series Y 505-637 and Y 652-848]

SOURCE OF REVENUE AND TYPE OF EXPENDITURE	All governments (mil. dol.)	Federal (mil. dol.)	State (mil. dol.)	Local (mil. dol.)	PERCENT		PER CAPITA[1] (dol.)	
					Federal	State and local	Federal	State and local
Revenue	**2,046,998**	**1,154,596**	**632,172**	**580,193**	**100.0**	**100.0**	**4,642**	**4,150**
Intergovernment revenue	([2])	2,911	126,329	190,723	0.3	26.2	12	550
Revenue from own sources	2,046,998	1,151,685	505,843	389,470	99.8	73.8	4,631	3,600
General revenue from own sources	1,493,179	780,479	391,101	321,599	67.6	58.8	3,138	2,866
Percent of total revenue	73	68	62	55	(X)	(X)	(X)	(X)
Taxes [3]	1,133,886	632,267	300,489	201,130	54.8	41.4	2,542	2,017
Property	155,613	(X)	5,848	149,765	(X)	12.8	(X)	626
Individual income	572,524	466,884	96,076	9,563	40.4	8.7	1,877	425
Corporation income	117,073	93,507	21,751	1,815	8.1	1.9	376	95
Sales and gross receipts	231,855	53,970	147,069	30,815	4.7	14.7	217	715
Customs duties	16,810	16,810	(X)	(X)	1.5	(X)	68	(X)
General sales and gross receipts	121,287	(X)	99,702	21,585	(X)	10.0	(X)	488
Selective sales and gross receipts [3]	93,758	37,160	47,367	9,231	3.2	4.7	149	228
Motor fuel	33,120	13,077	19,379	664	1.1	1.7	53	81
Alcoholic beverages	9,223	5,753	3,191	279	0.5	0.3	23	14
Tobacco products	10,002	4,268	5,541	193	0.4	0.5	17	23
Public utilities	17,892	6,476	6,514	4,903	0.6	0.9	26	46
Motor vehicle and operators' licenses	11,444	(X)	10,675	769	(X)	0.9	(X)	46
Death and gift	15,355	11,500	3,832	23	1.0	0.3	46	16
Charges and misc. general revenue [3]	359,293	148,212	90,612	120,469	12.8	17.4	596	849
Current charges [3]	204,418	88,877	42,745	72,795	7.7	9.5	357	465
National defense and international relations	8,268	8,268	(X)	(X)	0.7	(X)	33	(X)
Postal service	38,202	38,202	(X)	(X)	3.3	(X)	54	(X)
Education [3]	32,840	-	23,585	9,256	-	2.7	-	132
School lunch sales	3,454	-	13	3,441	-	0.3	-	14
Higher education	26,339	-	23,224	3,115	-	2.2	-	106
Natural resources	29,205	27,385	1,347	473	2.4	0.2	110	7
Hospitals	31,191	77	9,388	21,726	(Z)	2.6	(Z)	125
Sewerage and sanitation	17,647	(X)	224	17,423	(X)	1.5	(X)	71
Parks and recreation	3,456	100	748	2,608	(Z)	0.3	(Z)	13
Housing and community development	5,843	2,997	190	2,656	0.3	0.2	12	11
Air transportation	5,193	20	556	4,617	(Z)	0.4	14	21
Water transport and terminals	2,394	906	355	1,133	0.1	0.1	4	6
Special assessments	2,427	(X)	146	2,281	(X)	0.2	(X)	10
Sale of property	5,270	3,967	246	1,057	0.4	0.1	16	5
Interest earnings	70,037	11,313	27,370	31,353	1.0	4.8	45	236
Utility revenue	55,202	(X)	3,305	51,897	(X)	4.6	(X)	222
Liquor stores	3,441	(X)	2,907	533	(X)	0.3	(X)	14
Insurance trust revenue	495,176	371,206	108,530	15,441	32.2	10.2	1,493	498
Expenditure	**2,218,793**	**1,393,121**	**572,318**	**581,207**	**100.0**	**100.0**	**5,601**	**3,924**
Intergovernment expenditure	([2])	146,990	175,028	5,836	10.6	15.7	591	13
Direct expenditure	2,218,793	1,246,131	397,291	575,371	89.5	84.3	5,010	3,911
General expenditure	1,686,774	855,234	333,256	498,284	61.4	72.1	3,439	3,343
Percent of total expenditure	76	61	58	86	(X)	(X)	(X)	(X)
Education [3]	305,552	17,404	75,497	212,652	1.3	25.0	70	1,159
Elementary and secondary education	202,009	-	1,798	200,211	-	17.5	-	812
Higher education	73,418	-	60,978	12,441	-	6.4	-	295
Public welfare	140,734	33,447	83,336	23,951	2.4	9.3	134	431
Health and hospitals	92,487	17,852	35,543	39,092	1.3	6.5	72	300
Highways	61,913	856	36,464	24,593	0.1	5.3	3	245
Police protection	35,921	5,344	4,487	26,090	0.4	2.7	21	123
Fire protection	13,186	(X)	(X)	13,186	(X)	1.1	(X)	53
Corrections	26,229	1,594	15,898	8,737	0.1	2.1	6	99
Natural resources [4]	96,922	70,266	11,906	14,750	5.1	2.3	283	107
Sewerage and sanitation	28,453	(X)	1,527	26,926	(X)	2.5	(X)	114
Housing and community development	32,430	16,951	1,724	13,756	1.2	1.3	68	62
Governmental administration	57,546	12,710	17,707	27,130	0.9	3.9	51	180
Interest on general debt	237,691	187,952	21,532	28,207	13.5	4.3	756	200
Other	557,710	490,858	27,635	39,214	35.2	5.8	1,974	269
Utility expenditure	74,875	(X)	7,131	67,744	(X)	6.5	(X)	301
Liquor stores expenditure	2,926	(X)	2,452	474	(X)	0.3	(X)	12
Insurance trust expenditure	454,218	390,897	54,452	8,870	28.1	5.5	1,572	255
By character and object:								
Current operation	1,190,147	490,016	258,046	442,084	35.2	60.7	1,970	2,815
Capital outlay	220,960	97,891	45,524	77,545	7.0	10.7	394	495
Construction	98,536	9,422	34,803	54,310	0.7	7.7	38	358
Equip., land and existing structures	122,424	88,469	10,721	23,235	6.4	2.9	356	137
Assistance and subsidies	106,602	79,375	16,902	10,325	5.7	2.4	319	109
Interest on debt (general and utility)	246,866	187,952	22,367	36,547	13.5	5.1	756	237
Insurance benefits and repayments	454,218	390,897	54,452	8,870	28.1	5.5	1,572	255
Expenditure for salaries and wages	*487,594*	*146,436*	*101,338*	*239,820*	*10.5*	*29.6*	*589*	*1,372*

- Represents zero or rounds to zero. X Not applicable. Z Less than .05 percent or $.50. [1] Based on enumerated resident population as of April 1. [2] Aggregates exclude duplicative transactions between levels of government; see source. [3] Includes amounts not shown separately. [4] Includes parks and recreation.

Source: U.S. Bureau of the Census, *Government Finances,* series GF, No. 5, annual.

Illustration 8-3

Expenditures for Capital Outlay

All Governments—Expenditure for Capital Outlay, by Level of Government and by Function: 1970 to 1990

[In millions of dollars, except percent. For fiscal years ending in year shown; see text, section 9. Except for 1982 and 1987, local government data are estimates subject to sampling variation; see Appendix III. See also *Historical Statistics, Colonial Times to 1970,* series Y 523-524, Y 673-674, Y 740-741, and Y 787-788]

LEVEL AND FUNCTION	1970	1975	1980	1984	1985	1986	1987	1988	1989	1990
Total	**47,519**	**66,622**	**99,386**	**143,094**	**156,912**	**176,096**	**195,713**	**197,844**	**211,734**	**220,960**
Federal Government:										
Total	17,869	21,798	36,492	72,456	77,014	85,647	96,871	93,531	99,790	97,891
Annual percent change [1]	-6.0	4.1	10.9	-10.3	6.3	11.2	13.1	-3.4	6.7	-1.9
As percent of direct expenditure	9.7	7.5	6.9	8.7	8.3	8.7	9.3	7.7	8.7	7.9
By function:										
National defense [2]	14,027	14,507	28,161	60,382	64,154	71,995	78,222	74,790	78,891	75,624
Education	9	2	97	58	39	5	13	7	9	41
Highways	9	70	132	187	121	204	173	173	165	181
Health and hospitals	166	311	673	1,016	916	1,160	1,327	1,228	1,403	1,096
Natural resources	1,691	3,416	4,046	4,435	4,092	3,651	4,058	3,581	3,786	4,698
Housing [3]	853	1,059	317	1,471	1,935	2,515	3,642	5,180	5,032	4,343
Air transportation	234	363	151	249	785	391	494	407	658	664
Water transportation [4]	285	251	1,003	482	583	245	315	370	306	385
All other	595	1,819	1,912	4,176	4,389	5,481	8,627	7,792	9,540	10,859
State and local governments:										
Total	29,650	44,824	62,894	70,638	79,898	90,449	98,842	104,313	111,944	123,069
Annual percent change [1]	5.0	8.6	7.0	4.3	13.1	13.2	9.3	5.5	7.3	9.9
As percent of direct expenditure	20.0	16.7	14.5	11.8	12.2	12.6	12.7	12.6	12.6	12.7
By function:										
Education [5]	7,621	9,861	10,737	11,596	13,477	15,490	17,803	18,529	21,854	25,997
Higher education	2,705	2,834	2,972	3,855	4,629	5,217	6,141	6,397	6,851	7,441
Elementary and secondary	4,658	6,532	7,362	7,258	8,358	10,009	11,355	11,789	14,584	18,057
Highways	10,762	13,646	19,133	20,269	23,900	26,807	28,352	31,635	32,754	33,867
Health and hospitals	790	1,781	2,443	2,366	2,709	2,810	3,029	3,436	3,445	3,848
Natural resources	789	1,113	1,052	1,414	1,736	1,803	2,157	1,894	2,019	2,545
Housing [3]	1,319	1,821	2,248	3,104	3,217	3,516	3,394	3,619	3,765	3,997
Air transportation	691	852	1,391	1,814	1,875	2,183	2,632	2,896	2,965	3,434
Water transportation [4]	258	419	623	585	717	911	869	911	943	924
Sewerage	1,385	3,569	6,272	5,664	5,926	6,461	7,483	8,300	8,343	8,356
Parks and recreation [6]	684	1,261	2,023	1,962	2,196	2,554	2,838	3,142	3,350	3,877
Utilities [6]	2,437	4,846	9,933	12,599	13,435	15,340	15,638	14,782	15,371	16,601
Water	1,201	2,111	3,335	3,438	4,160	5,134	6,135	6,052	6,372	6,873
Electric	820	1,485	4,572	5,153	5,247	6,127	5,086	4,473	4,291	3,976
Transit	366	1,203	1,921	3,873	3,830	3,830	4,165	3,998	4,430	5,443
Gas	50	48	105	135	198	250	253	259	279	310
Other	2,915	5,656	7,039	9,265	10,711	12,573	14,645	15,172	17,135	19,623

[1] Change from prior year shown. 1970, change from 1969. For definition of average annual percent change, see Guide to Tabular Presentation. [2] Includes international relations and U.S. service schools. [3] Includes community development. [4] Includes terminals. [5] Includes other education. [6] Beginning 1980, includes outlays by State governments.

Source: U.S. Bureau of the Census, *Census of Governments: 1977, 1982* and *1987,* Vol. 6, No. 4, *Historical Statistics on Governmental Finances and Employment;* and *Government Finances,* series GF No. 5, annual.

Illustration 8-4

Federal, State, and Local Government Spending on Public Works: 1980 to 1990

[In millions of dollars. Public works include expenditures on highways, airports, water transport and terminals, sewerage, solid waste management, water supply, and mass transit systems. Represents direct expenditures excluding intergovernmental grants]

LEVEL AND TYPE OF EXPENDITURE	Total	High-ways	Airport transpor-tation	Water transport and ter-minals	Sew-erage	Solid waste manage-ment	Water supply	Mass transit
1980: Total	72,177	33,745	5,071	3,278	9,892	3,322	9,228	7,641
Federal	5,114	434	2,570	2,110	-	-	-	-
State	22,832	20,661	360	360	334	-	91	1,026
Local	44,231	12,650	2,141	808	9,558	3,322	9,137	6,615
Capital expenditures (percent)	48	57	30	50	63	11	36	25
1985: Total	101,925	45,856	7,153	3,353	12,186	5,212	14,298	13,867
Federal	6,103	834	3,409	1,860	-	-	-	-
State	31,821	27,167	473	534	328	-	69	3,250
Local	64,001	17,854	3,271	959	11,858	5,214	14,228	10,617
Capital expenditures (percent)	42	52	37	39	49	14	29	28
1990: Total	146,762	61,913	10,983	4,524	18,309	10,144	22,101	18,788
Federal	7,911	856	4,499	2,556	-	-	-	-
State	43,787	36,464	635	504	636	891	136	4,521
Local	95,064	24,593	5,848	1,464	17,673	9,253	21,966	14,267
Capital expenditures (percent)	42	55	37	29	46	18	31	29

Represents or rounds to zero.

Source: U.S. Bureau of the Census, *Government Finances,* series GF, No. 5, annual.

Illustration 8-5

LOS ANGELES TIMES

How 'Passive Activity' Rules Affect Investors

BY BENNY L. KASS
SPECIAL TO THE TIMES

Before 1985, investment in real estate was generally considered a "profit-making activity." An investor could buy a rental property, receive rental income and was able to take so-called "paper losses" to obtain a very significant tax shelter.

For example, if you bought a piece of property for $200,000 and the land value was $50,000, the depreciable basis for the building was $150,000. In the good old days, you could take accelerated depreciation, and take large paper loss each year. Indeed, if you decided to elect a straight line depreciation, depending on what year you were in, you might have the option to depreciate the property on a basis of 18 or 19 years. Assuming that you took an 18-year basis, you could take a paper loss of $8,333 each year from your tax return ($150,000 divided by 18).

Thus, after declaring the rental income, you were able to deduct from this income your actual out of pocket expenses–such as mortgage interest payments, real estate taxes, leasing commisions, repairs.

1040A Department of the Treasury
U.S. Individual Income
REAL ESTATE TAX TIPS
Advice for homeowners and investors. Part six of a series

On top of these actual expenses, you were eligible for the paper loss called depreciation.

Congress was quite concerned with the growof the tax-shelter industry. Often, promoters of so-called tax shelters would buy property that would not necessarily be a good investment for the future, but would generate a significant write-off each year.

When Congress enacted the Tax Reform Act of 1986, it established a new concept called "passive activities". Although the primary motivation for the new law as it affected real estate was to curtail the tax-shelter abuse, the net result was was a dramatic impact on the average real estate investor.

Passive activity regulations are very complex. As we have mentioned in other stories in this series, investors must discuss their particular circumstances with their tax advisors.

However, there is a very brief summary of passive activities as they relate to real estate transactions.

For all practical purposes, most real estate transactions fall into the category of "passive activity". Over-simplified, this means that real estate losses may only be used to offset income from other real estate activities.

Before 1986 Tax Reform Act, you were able to deduct your real estate losses from other income sources, such as dividends and wages. However beginning 1987, this situation changed.

To understand this complex law, let us suppose you have two buckets. One bucket is labeled "passive income generators (PIGs)" and the other bucket is labeled "passive activities losses (PALs)."

If you were involved in a real estate investment activity, all of your losses were put in the PAL bucket, and all of your gains were put in PIG bucket. One of the primary objectives of any real estate investor is to make a lot of profit while at the same time not having to pay a lot of tax on that gain.

Under the Tax Reform Act of 1986, real estate gains in the PIG bucket can only be offset by real estate losses in the PAL bucket.

There are provisions, however, for carrying forward the losses. This is referred to as net operating loss (NOL).

You can carry froward these losses indefinitely and can use them as deductions against passive income in later years. Unused losses are allowed in full when the tax payer disposes of the entire interest in the passive activity.

There is one major exclusion from these passive activity rules.

Under certain circumstances, a taxpayer may be able to deduct up to $25,000 of passive rental losses from other (non-passive) activities. This special rule is known as the "$25,000 exemption."

To qualify for this exemption, the tax payer must "activity participate" in the rental activity. To be an active participant, this primarily requires a "bona fide" participation by the owner of the property. For example making management decisions, approving new tenants, approving repairs or writing checks are illustrations of such active participation. A tax payer seeking to use this $25,000 exemption must own at least 10% of the property, or must be a limited partner in a partnership owning the property.

However, the $25,000 exemption is applicable only to tax payers whose adjusted gross income (AGI) is $100,000 or less. Where the taxpayer AGI exceeds 100,000, the $25,000 maximum amount is reduced by 50% of the amount by which the individuals adjusted gross income exceeds $100,000. In other words, if the taxpayer AGI exceeds $150,000, no passive losses can be used for any offset against other income.

For married taxpayers who file separate returns and live apart, up to $12,000 of passive losses may be used to offset income, again with the same phase-out rules.

The Internal Revenue Service is constantly attempting to refine these passive activity regulations. Indeed, there has been significant pressure on Congress to relax–if not appeal–the investor rules.

Benny Kass at Home Fair
Real estate and tax attorney Benny L. Kass of Washington, D.C., a columnist for The Times and The Washington Post, will speak at workshops at the forth annual Time' Home Buyers and Sellers Fair on Saturday at the Anaheim Convention Center.
For times and details on the fair, see the ad in this section.

However, as you are preparing your 1992 tax returns, and if you are involved in real estate investment activities, you have to follow the current rules. You should obtain a copy of IRS Form 8582 entitled "Passive Activity Loss Limitations," which must be filed with your tax return.

It should also be pointed out that under the 1986 tax law, property purchased beginning 1987 is to be depreciated at 31.5 years for non-residential property and 27.5 years for residential property. Property is residential if at least 80% of all gross rental income comes from the rental of dwelling units.

Understanding and using the passive activity rules may give the taxpayer some tax savings, but again you are urged to discuss your individual situation with your own tax advisor.

Kass is a Washington, D.C., attorney who writes on real estate for The Times and The Washington Post.

limited partnership, are taxed based upon income received from the venture, with any portion representing capital gains dividend to treat as a gain from sale or exchange if the asset was held for over six months.

When a corporation acts as a syndicator, individual shareholders are taxed on the basis of dividends received, subject to personal exemptions for same, with special capital gains dividends treated in a similar manner to their partnership and REIT brethren.

IMPACT OF THE TAX REFORM ACT OF 1986 (TRA)

Since investment income is now treated as passive under the TRA, new methods of syndicate arrangement must be considered, particularly in the case of the limited partnership form of syndicate. The idea behind syndication formation then becomes to find a property which will, in effect, provide tax benefits to the investors where the non-cash depreciation deduction available to the investor equates to the income that the investor is likely to receive from the project. Much of the structuring of the transaction will center around allocation of the tax benefits to be derived from the transaction between the general partner(s) and the limited partners. Another consideration is the fact that taxpayers cannot incur losses which are in excess of their investment in the partnership. There are methods which can be used to increase the investment base, thus increase potential loss allocation, such as the use of a non-recourse note given by the limited partner to the partnership and the changing of position of the limited partner by being directly liable in the form of signing a partnership note or guarantying a partnership obligation. Banks and thrifts, particularly the former, frequently look to the personal assets of borrowers over and above the given project to provide them with an additional comfort level in credit transactions. Insurance companies have characteristically focused on equity as protection and only looked to the project in question. In recent years, equity participations have been written into many insurance company notes as a way of increasing investment yield. If the syndication enters into such an arrangement, this would have some bearing on the capital gains derived from the project and preclude the possibility of the use of a 1031 tax deferred exchange as a tax mitigating device upon disposition of the project. It is imperative that the syndicator seek the advice of a competent tax attorney or accountant in creating the required structure of the transaction. Unless investors in a syndication have an active participation in the management of the project (10% interest or more), they are limited to the passive income rules which also state that losses would have to be carried forward if no passive income is available from other investment sources to offset this loss. Those who take an active management role still have the privilege of write-offs up to the $25,000 figure if their taxable income is $100,000 or less, as noted previously.

With these notes of caution, an example of one form of limited partnership structure mindful of the TRA might be this:

The syndicator has identified an office building that has been purchased for $5mm, which generates a NOI of $450,000. Required investment on the part of the limited partners is $1,500,000, while the $500,000 balance was provided by the syndicator-general partner. Interest on the $3,000,000 first lien is $240,000, leaving $210,000 available as a return to the partnership. Considering an allocation of 1/3 to the general partner and 2/3 to the limited partners, a dividend of $140,000 is available for distribution to the limited partners. Considering the fact that the replacement cost of the building is $4.4mm, the annual depreciation allowance, using a 31-1/2 year life, approximately equates the dividend allocated to the investors allowing them a 9.33% return on their investment tax-free. This would equate to a multiple of that number, dependent upon the tax bracket of the individual investor. This is just one example of how the tax consequences of structuring might be addressed by the syndicator as a means of maximizing the tax benefits to the individual investor. Upon filing, the investor would report this on IRS form 8582 entitled Passive Activity Loss Limitations," which is filed with the 1040 long form at tax time.

Another critical area in the tax structuring of a limited partnership vehicle is the allocation of property appreciation. The syndication format should be created in such a fashion to allot the appreciation benefits between the general partner(s) and the limited partners in an equitable fashion. If leverage is obtained that has a provision for equity participation, possibly 25 to 75% of this benefit may be negotiated away in return for favorable financing terms allowing increased cash flow during the holding years of the project.

SELECTION OF THE OWNERSHIP ENTITY

In the previous chapter, the various organizational forms that represent a syndicate were discussed in detail. In addition there was a minor mention of some of the tax implications in pursuing these organizational forms. One aspect that was alluded to earlier in this work was the percentage ownership in a leasehold interest as a form of syndicate. The Empire State Building holding by Larry Wien and Harry Helmsley was on that basis with Wien eventually selling his leasehold interest to Helmsley. A leasehold interest represents probably the maximum form of leverage of any other type of real estate investment, other than 100% financing.

In the annals of syndication history, the Wien-Helmsley syndication of the Empire State Building probably is at the apex of the investment pyramid. When the transaction closed in December, 1961, over three thousand investment units at $10,000 each had been sold to raise the down payment required on the leasehold interest on land acquired from the Crown family of Chicago. The syndicate initially purchased the building from the Crowns for $65 million and the land from Prudential for $17 million. Prudential assisted in the purchase price with a $46 million loan. The syndicate then sold the project back to Prudential for a deflated purchase price of $29 million. Prudential then leased the project back to the Helmsley-Wien syndicate for four successive 21 year terms at an initial rate of $3.2 million for the initial period.

While individual investors were promised $900 annually for each investment unit, the syndicators reaped hundreds of thousands of dollars in annual income due to this favorable lease combined with concentrated management efforts which dramatically reduced operating expenses of this 102 story behemoth. This project served as Harry Helmsley's launching pad as the syndication king pin of Gotham. In the case of the Helmsley syndicate, it would have to be restructured today, since the tax losses incurred by individual investors would far exceed their initial investment. With this thought in mind, the following might represent the structuring of a sale-leaseback transaction negotiated with an insurance company on one of their real estate owned properties. The example is as follows:

Type of structure: 10 story office structure containing net rentable space of 280,000 square feet with a gross building area of 330,000. Off street surface parking is available for 600 cars on the four acre building site. Current replacement cost of subject is $30 million. The building is currently 80% leased with an average monthly rental, including parking privileges, of $1.80 per square foot/month. Annual income of $2,688,000 is reduced by annual expenses of $750,000, leaving NOI of $1,938,000. The syndicator feels that an additional reduction of $338,000 is required for a vacancy factor, thus further reducing the NOI figure for negotiation purposes to $1,600,000. Commercial land prices have been severely depressed in the area for several years, thus the seller now has a land value, based upon current appraisal, of $2 million. Predicated upon that land value, the insurance company was willing to master lease the land on the basis of 9% return and master lease to the developer on a 55-year lease with an annual rental of $180,000. In addition, the insurance company is willing to provide leasehold financing predicated upon 2/3 of the economic value. Considering the fact that NOI from the insurance company's basis was $1,938,000, less their leasehold payments of $180m, leaving a NOI after leasehold of $1,758,000, the company would calculate the value of the leasehold interest at $19,500,000, using a 9% capitalization rate, thus making a $13,000,000 leasehold loan at 9%/30 year terms available to the syndicate. The syndicate, due to their evaluation of the project is able to negotiate a price based upon their view of an added vacancy factor and applying a 10% capitalization rate to the risk of the investment and only offer $1,420,000 for the leasehold (the adjusted NOI of $1.6mm less $180m leasehold payments divided by 10). This leaves a required equity investment on the part of the syndicate of only $1,120,000. Sounds far fetched, doesn't it. Deals almost as crazy as this one have been negotiated in recent years as a means of accommodating to the market place. Due to the considerable depreciation benefits to the partnership ($750,000 annually using an optional 40-year straight line method), it becomes extremely important for the syndicator to allocate these benefits in such a fashion to the partnership that write-offs do not exceed their initial investment. With this thought in mind, the syndicator might assign the greatest portion of the benefits to the general partners in this instance, allowing distribution of the approximate contribution by limited partners to enjoy the benefits of the "real" cash flow of $1,758,000, less annual loan payments of $1,170,000, by distributing $500,000 of that amount to the limited partners to derive a totally tax deferred return. It should be noted by the example that the leverage factor has been stretched to the extreme, thus significantly lowering the rate of return available to the investment group, although the commitment of capital is minimal based upon the size of the project. The Helmsley-Wien Empire State deal would never fly in today's tax atmosphere.

The current tax laws continue to favor projects where taxable income is at the zero or positive ranges. As long as this type of legislation remains in place, the type of investment organization that needs to be chosen that provides the syndicator with the flexibility to arrange distribution of the proceeds in a manner that will attract investors seeking to maximize tax benefits. The flexibility of the limited partnership structure and real estate investment trust organizations provide the best route to follow in that regard.

DOCUMENTATION CONSIDERATIONS

Preparation of the basic agreement which represents the relationship established between the syndicator and the investment group must be done on the basis of thorough consideration of current tax laws. Thus, it is important to address proceeds allocation, rates of return offered, appreciation benefits and all tax impacting provisions of partnership agreements, in particular, with extreme care. Improper language used in a limited partnership agreement could flaw the entire transaction tax-wise, not only on the part of the syndicator, but on the part of the limited partners as well. For this reason alone, professional assistance is required in this most complex of processes. In any prospectus prepared for potential clients, specific admonitions should be provided concerning the tax consequences of the transaction to all investors solicited. Consideration should be given to possibly deeding percentage interests to the limited partners, then having the limited partners deed their interest to the partnership to hold in trust for the balance of the holding as a means of showing active management in the project. Whatever structure is considered, it should be undertaken with advice of competent tax counsel.

TAX TREATMENT OF TRANSACTIONS

As long as the syndicator follows reasonable guidelines in the formation of the syndication vehicle, taxing authorities will not question its structuring. Once formation of the vehicle tries some form of space-age taxation tactics, this is the time that an IRS audit can be assured. Favorable tax treatment of passive income by both federal and state authorities is tempered by reasonable standards used by the taxpayer in reporting passive income derived from these sources. Thus, it is important for investors, in addition to the syndicator to also seek the advice of independent tax counsel prior to devotion of any capital investment in the enterprise to determine the effect on personal finances from a tax standpoint.

OTHER TAXING IMPLICATIONS

With the advent of reduced revenues being available on the federal, state and local level, policy makers within government are in a constant search for sources of additional tax revenues. Obviously one of the more attractive sources of revenue is the ever visible area of real estate, since it is a much more tangible personal asset than personal property, which is more easily sequestered. For this reason, a variety of revenue enhancing projects have been undertaken by the state as a means of increasing funds availability to the citizenry. In California, for example, this type of revenue enhancement has been in the form of an array of real estate related fees and charges imposed, particularly in the development process. Individual governmental units, such as mosquito abatement districts, public schools and the like have found that by creating assessment districts under the provisions of the Mello-Roos Assessment District Act of 1982 provides a means of indirect property taxation which eludes the restrictive clutches of Proposition 13. The latter was designed to limit annual tax increases imposed upon real property. Due to the unclear nature of how government units choose to impose this new tax power, income property ownership becomes a fragile device, since cash flow can be reduced through the imposition of these new, and totally unexpected, taxes. The syndicator must carefully weigh the potential future costs that might incur with respect to a particular project in question based upon the infrastructure needs in a given investment's geographic location. This will be the ultimate challenge for all real estate investors as we approach the 21st century.

Once all the tax implications have been carefully examined, the framework of a partnership structure starts taking shape. Since partnerships, in one fashion or another, continue to be a principal means of syndication, our next chapter will trace the elements which comprise their formation.

9
PARTNERSHIPS — A PRINCIPAL SYNDICATION ENTITY

President Woodrow Wilson had the sage comment: "The highest and best form of efficiency is the spontaneous cooperation of a free people." The partnership form is the quintessential expression of this statement.

Whether the organization is embodied in the general partnership form, or the more popular version of limited partnership, it exemplifies the spirit of cooperation which must be present in order for the enterprise to attain its objective successfully.

Usually there is an individual who serves as the driving force to propel the objectives of the syndicate into a viable investment vehicle to shape the future benefits to be derived from the venture. This person, referred to as the syndicator, needs to be one with foresight, vivid imagination and just plain "horse sense." The syndicator's role might be likened to a tight rope walker whose sheer balancing abilities are the only thing that separates the potential of successfully completing the journey high above a packed arena with only a fragile wire separating success from the grim reaper if sheer bravado has removed the additional comfort of a safety net. In forming a syndicate, not only must the syndicator have the sure-footedness of a tight rope walker, there must also be that safety net of protection provided for the investor in forming the syndicate.

FORMATION CONSIDERATIONS

The key word in forming any sort of an association revolves around the word **confidence with a capital "C."** Without that simple attribute, the syndicate will not even get off the ground. This means, quite simply, that belief in the competence and integrity of the syndicator is a prime ingredient in the determination of how the syndicate is to be formed.

A prime consideration is whether the entity involved should be a general partnership or a limited partnership. From a legal standpoint, in a general partnership, there is an equal sharing of liability on the part of all of the partners. This form of organization is usually used for syndication purposes when each of the parties has something of value in the way of talent as well as money to the project. A typical general partnership would be formed on the basis of a landowner who wants to develop a parcel that is commercially zoned. This person may lack the real estate knowledge or expertise to properly develop the property. In this instance, a partnership might be formed along these lines:

- Land owner
- Legal counsel
- Accountant
- Developer - contractor
- Real estate broker

In this form of partnership, the dollar contribution is in the form of the land owner's parcel. The balance of the monies required for fees, etc. would be contributed by the balance of the partners who each bring their particular talents to bear into the partnership. In the case of the legal counsel, all of the details of forming the partnership and the necessary filings, details of reviewing construction loan documentation and the details of closing the transaction involve this important function. The accountant would be the one who would prepare financial statements and probably be the one who would negotiate the details involving the necessary interim and permanent financing arrangements. The developer-contractor would prepare plans, process them for approvals with the necessary governmental agencies to obtain permits, solicit bidders for subcontracts, supervise overall job progress to completion and receipt of a certificate of occupancy with the objective of a lien-free completion of the project. Once the project is complete or near completion, the real estate broker would then use marketing talents to market the space as well as provide counseling during the acquisition process relative to the highest and best use of the parcel.

In this instance, the land owner would be perceived as the driving force behind the project, since it involves the improvement of a parcel within control of its ownership. The syndicator role is then assumed by the owner who must perform the due diligence necessary to determine that the composition of the general partnership is of the type that will evoke confidence that each member of the partnership will bring something tangible of value to the project.

More importantly, the value of the talents and/or monies to the partnership must be equated in some form of interest distribution. In order to analyze this aspect of the situation, an allocation might be made along these lines:

- The landowner owns an unencumbered C-2 parcel of land valued at $1 million. This is the property that is being placed at risk in the developmental process. It will take approximately another $100,000 for up front costs to develop the proposed office building to be developed on the project. Each of the remaining partners has agreed to contribute $25m toward costs plus the talents that they bring to the enterprise.
- If the syndicator chose to allocate on the basis of dollar contribution alone, the allocation of profits would be 91%, with the remaining four sharing the 9% balance. This, obviously, would not represent a fair allocation of profits.
- If the syndicator were to allocate profit distribution on the basis of proportionate value of monies contributed plus the talents of the individual to the project, another type of allocation might be the result.

For example:

The developer's profit in the project, which carries a development price tag of $4,000,000, would be 15%, or $600,000. This makes the developer's at risk investment $625,000, not $25,000.

The value of the attorney's services is estimated to be $75,000, thus the attorney's contribution is $100,000.

The value of the accountant's services is $25,000, thus the total contribution of this segment is $50,000.

The contribution of lease and/or sales commission on the part of the broker is estimated to be $175,000, making a total contribution of $200,000.

Based upon the information, a new contributory analysis would be performed:

Contributor	**Amount of Contribution**	**Percentage**
Land owner	$1,000,000	50.63
Developer - Contractor	625,000	31.65
Attorney	100,000	5.06
Accountant	50,000	2.53
Real Estate Broker	200,000	10.13
Totals	$1,975,000	100.00

By using this allocative technique, the syndicator has established an objective valuation to the contribution of talents as well as monies by the remainder of the syndicate membership.

In the case of formation of a limited partnership, the process is a bit more complex. Not only must the confidence level on the part of the investors be evident, the means of allocation must be in proportion to the contribution of the investor participants with a clear understanding concerning the composition of the syndicator's share in the enterprise.

When venturing into the limited partnership form, another part of the decision process must take place. This involves whether the syndicate will take the form of a public or private offering to investors. This decision becomes an important one because the volume of paperwork and reporting requirements attendant to a public offering is considerable. The sheaf of documents involved in a public offering is included in the appendix of this text.

If one is contemplating the use of a private offering, it is important to note what differentiates this type of partnership formation from the formal public offering which falls within the aegis of state and federal regulation scrutiny.

In the case of a private offering, this does not preclude the fact that certain disclosures are required for the purposes of investor protection. What it does mean, however, is that the offering is solicited from a few sophisticated investors with a limited number of contacts for purposes of gathering the necessary funds to complete the offering. Whether a public or private offering is involved revolves around many factors: the number of potential investors contacted; the final number that comprises the investment group; accessibility to group sponsors; information access; ability to understand the nature, risk and potential of the investment; financial capability of investors as noted by tests of liquidity and net worth; manner of investor solicitation; and marketing restrictions imposed upon sale of limited partnership units after their initial purchase. This type of offering, in order to qualify for exemption must meet the following tests:

- The partnership securities may be exempt from registration by qualifying as an intrastate issue, thus precluding SEC regulation. This means that the securities may only be offered to residents of that state or territory, and the issuer must also be a person, natural or artificial with residence or business headquartered and incorporated within the state or territory. This is further clarified in Rule 147 of the Securities and Exchange Commission.
- Another form of exemption is that of a "small offering." A small offering is exempted when the offering does not exceed $5 million and when the SEC finds that enforcement of the Securities Act of 1933 with respect to such securities is not necessary in the public interest or for the protection of investors. If there is a claim of exemption under this provision, certain filing requirements are necessary to determine if exemption is applicable.
- The Securities Act of 1933 provides a further exemption from registration to "transactions by an issuer not involving any public offering." The guidelines for whether the transaction involves a public offering are set forth in SEC Regulation D. If the securities are not exempt, sales of such securities must be reported on SEC form D.

On a state level, the state of California test for exemption is outlined in the Corporate Securities Law of 1968. Other states and territories have initiated similar laws regulating the issuance of securities interests, such as a limited partnership offering, as a means of protecting the public. Even though federal exemption may be applicable to a given private offering, this does not preclude the possibility that certain reporting requirements that may be necessary to satisfy particular state securities regulation requirements. Inquiry should be made with the state securities regulator, usually the Department of Corporations, to assure compliance. A typical registration package is shown in the Appendix.

Why opt for private versus a public offering? The question is one of economics, primarily, since the volume of paperwork involved in registration and reporting requirements is considerable. On the other hand, if the syndicator has legal counsel that is familiar with the process, a documentation package can be prepared at a fraction of the cost of hiring counsel that is not familiar with the registration process who must go through the exploration of laws, rules and regulations that apply. It is not a simplistic array. Because of this it requires the experience and professionalism of a specialist. No lesser practitioner will suffice, since the savings made for inexperience will be lost in the entanglements of noncompliance that the resulting paperwork might cause.

One advantage of the public offering is that another set of eyes is available to assure that the offering being prepared is in compliance with the law. This luxury is not afforded in the case of a private offering which will not necessarily have the scrutiny of regulatory authority for assistance.

If one thinks that disclosure is avoided by a private offering, think again. The syndicator must have as a part of the offering package, sufficient disclosure that would allow the prudent man to know the risks as well as the potential rewards of investment in the project. As a practical guideline, the syndicator should follow the dictates of SEC's Guide 5, shown in the Appendix. This outlines in detail how a registration statement for limited partnership interests should be prepared. Additionally, even more restrictive and detailed procedures are outlined in the guidelines prepared by the North American Securities Administrators Association, Inc., the professional group specifically addressing educational and ethical issues involving the syndication process itself.

In order for the formation process to evolve in an orderly manner, the syndicator must either be a legal counsel thoroughly versed in securities matters or must seek one who has those talents. The selection of this key consultant is vital to properly establishing the limited partnership as well as registering these securities for sale to the general public if a public offering is sought. Even in the case of a private offering, a prospectus and other informational data must be prepared with the advice of counsel.

Another item to consider by the syndicator is whether sale of securities requires registration as a broker-dealer in the syndicate in question. Marketing is a significant concern in forming the partnership, since composition of the purchasing group can serve as a weather vane as to the potential success of the offering. Even though one may contrive a situation with an attractive return, if it does not foster investor interest, the offering will fail. There may be other projects due to their nature that may have considerable appeal to an investor with a small initial return. This means that the syndicator must take this into consideration in the project identification stage and match the project to the objectives of the investment group intended to be contacted. The syndicator must decide whether direct offerings are to be made as a principal to the transaction, or opt for registration as a broker-dealer to offer these securities to the general public. An understanding as to when broker-dealers are required in the sale of limited partnership interests is essential. This is another strong argument for knowledgeable securities counsel. State laws also require in certain instances that real estate licensees must have endorsements on their licenses in order to sell real estate securities. This permit is obtained from state regulatory authorities. In California, the Department of Real Estate would be responsible for this activity.

If the syndicator has a cadre of wealthy investors who have communicated their objectives with clarity, the choice of investment vehicle is simplified. Don't try to acquire retail properties when the investment group would be more comfortable with an industrial or office building.

Once all of the aspects of entity formation have been resolved, the question of paperwork rules supreme. By the time this stage of the process is underway, the syndicator will already have the project under control in the form of a closed escrow using temporary financing, like Harry Helmsley, a sales agreement, an open escrow, a lease-option or a straight option might be the devices used in this process.

DOCUMENTATION DRAFTING

When the syndication strategy has been formulated, formal application for permission to sell limited partnership entities occupies the next stage of the documentation trail. As previously noted, if counsel feels that a private offering is possible, there is a considerable savings in processing expense that is entailed in a public offering. However, if a public offering is involved, it also involves an extensive application procedure which strictly adheres to securities regulations that affect the venture in question. Even if there is a private sale involved, application must be made in the state of California for a determination of exemption of a given project.

In any event, the process begins with the filing of an application. The preparation of this document should be the responsibility of competent securities counsel. Some of the items that counsel must consider in applying for permission to sell limited partnership shares in a real estate project are the following:

- The rules and regulations, particularly SEC rules 146, 240 and 243, Regulation D and the guidelines of Guide 5 in combination with applicable statutes at the state level, serve as a regulatory blueprint in the application preparation process.
- Uniform disclosure standards are only applicable to SEC Regulation A and S-11 filings, while each individual state varies with the type of disclosures required for the offering of limited partnership shares.

- Financial statements must be prepared by the syndicator in accordance with state requirements. This is one of the critical areas, since prospective investors are particularly concerned about the financial performance expected from the proposed project. Any improper manipulation of the operating statements supporting a position that bears no likelihood to possibility may create potential syndicator liability to the investor as well as possible fines and incarceration.

- All sales and other forms of promotional material should be examined by counsel to determine that they comply with appropriate disclosure requirements. In this regard, the prospectus, or offering circular, serves as the principal promotional device of the project. In this document all pertinent information relative to the project which includes:

  1) Compensation and profit of the syndicators.

  2) Any assessments that might be required from the limited partners in addition to the initial contribution.

  3) Strict adherence to SEC and state guidelines relative to the drafting of such material. This should apply to private as well as public offerings. In the case of broker-dealers making the offering, the prospectus should also comply with the guidelines established by the National Association of Security Dealers. Some of the areas of disclosure to be addressed are:

     ° Risk factors - These range all the way from the possibility of default or lack of partnership liability to dealing with projects of a highly speculative nature, such as raw land and failure to obtain required zoning.

     ° Escrow Account - A discussion of the handling of initial subscriptions in a holding escrow should be addressed in the plan of distribution section of the prospectus.

     ° Tax Impact - The affect of the project on the tax status of individual investors should be covered in detail.

A suggested checklist for the preparation of a prospectus for an interstate offering in the state of California is shown as Illustration 9-1. Considerable consumer information is required within the scope of the thirty items that represent this comprehensive reminder of the type of information needed to be supplied to the investor in conjunction with the offering. The objective of the prospectus is to provide the potential investor with the vast array of information needed to undertake an informed investment decision weighing risk versus opportunity.

A sample prospectus following the guidelines outline above is shown as Illustration 9-2.

As previously mentioned, nothing of this nature should be undertaken without the advise of securities counsel, thoroughly knowledgeable in this highly specialized form of investment tool. To do anything less would be a foolhardy venture on the part of the syndicator.

This seemingly endless barrage of paperwork will constitute additional focus in the next chapter revealing how the documentation requirements become a function of the project in question and the strategy utilized in finalizing its acquisition by the syndicate.

Illustration 9-1

CHECKLISTS

§ 21:41 Suggested contents for prospectus of real estate limited partnership (intrastate offering)

A. Outside front cover.

1. Name and address of partnership.
2. Number and type of units being offered.
3. Prescribed statement that although securities are offered pursuant to a permit, such permit does not constitute endorsement or recommendation by the responsible agency.
4. Alternate prescribed statements regarding projection for either specified or non-specified program.
5. Statement that securities involve high degree of risk.
6. Price per unit.
7. Number of units required for a minimum purchase.
8. Tabular presentation of price to public, discounts and commissions, and proceeds to partnership.
9. Percentage of the sales price represented by total expenses for marketing.
10. Total of estimated expenses of offering.
11. Indication of extent to which securities are subject to additional assessments, if any.
12. Names and addresses of principal dealers, including issuer if licensed.

13 Maximum acquisition, development and/or construction fee.

---

87. For general discussion of pertinent tax aspects, see § 21:11.

Illustration 9-1 (cont.)

SYNDICATION—LIMITED PARTNERSHIPS § 21:41

c. Disclosure of any construction or development by sponsor of partnership property.

d. Statement of investment objectives and policies, including:
   (1) Indication of whether such policies may be changed by general partner without vote of limited partners.
   (2) Approximate percentage of assets program may invest in any one type of investment.
   (3) For "nonspecified property" programs, include:
      (a) Statement regarding types of properties to be subject of investment.
      (b) Disclosure of ways acquisitions will be financed, including use of wraparound notes and leveraging.
      (c) Indication whether partnership will enter into joint venture arrangements and, if so, extent of arrangements.
      (d) Statement that reinvestment of proceeds resulting from refinancing will not take place after five years from date of effectiveness and unless sufficient cash will be distributed to pay any state or federal income tax liability resulting from such refinancing.

e. Full description of transactions that may be entered into between program and any affiliate of sponsor, including:
   (1) Description of material terms of agreement between affiliate and sponsor.
   (2) Disclosure of services to be performed and compensation therefor.
   (3) Description of equitable principles general partner will apply in resolving conflicts

Illustration 9-1 (cont.)

14. Date of prospectus.
15. Period of offering.

B. Body.

1. Required warning respecting authorization to give information, and information not contained in the prospectus.
2. Table of contents.
3. Required statement of registration.
4. Definitions, to include, where applicable:
   a. Acquisition fee.
   b. Affiliate.
   c. Assessments.
   d. Audited financial statements.
   e. Capital contribution.
   f. Cash flow.
   g. Cash available for distribution.
   h. Deferred payments.
   i. Income property program.
   j. Net worth.
   k. Nonspecified property program.
   l. Organization and offering expenses.
   m. Participant.
   n. Price of property.
   o. Property management fee.
   p. Prospectus.
   q. Sponsor.
   r. Unimproved property program.
5. Description of general and proposed business of issuer, including:
   a. Description of proposed transaction.
   b. Disclosure of maximum rate above prime that may be charged partnership by sponsor on financing made available to program by sponsor.

Illustration 9-1 (cont.)

between program and other programs that will be managed.

6. Description and numbering of risk factors, including:
   a. Speculative nature of raw land investments.
   b. Speculative nature of "interest only" financing.
   c. Effect of inability to obtain proper zoning.
   d. Risks of default for inability to service the debt or failure of investor to pay amounts due in subsequent periods.
   e. Lack of liquidity of limited partnership interests.
   f. Possible disadvantageous tax consequences, such as:
      (1) Potential inability to deduct prepaid interest in year paid.
      (2) Tax liability for potential depreciation recapture.
      (3) Depreciation recapture greater than cash distributions and tax liability in the event of foreclosure.
7. Description of the limited partnership entity, including:
   a. Limited liability feature.
   b. State where partnership was established.
   c. Date of formation.
   d. Business address and phone number.
   e. Rights, powers, and identity of syndicator.
   f. Initial limited partners.
   g. Duration.
   h. Address and telephone number of general partner.
8. Information respecting syndicator (if corporation, respecting officers and directors), to include:
   a. Names and addresses.
   b. Business backgrounds and former occupations.
   c. Company affiliations and dates thereof for the last ten years.

Illustration 9-1 (cont.)

d. If corporate syndicator, audited financial statements (see item 28).

e. If individual syndicator, include:

(1) Statement of net worth (cost basis) at not more than 90 days prior to date of filing application.

(2) If net worth (cost basis) exceeds $1 million, it is sufficient to disclose only that fact in prospectus.

f. If syndicator invests in partnership, disclose amount of investment, number of units purchased, and date of purchase.

g. Disclosure of total number and gross proceeds of syndications with which syndicator may presently have some financial obligation.

h. Disclosure in tabular form of all consideration that may be received directly or indirectly by sponsor, its affiliates and underwriters in connection with offering.

i. Disclosure of fees and other terms of contracts involving self-dealing with affiliates.

j. Language prohibiting rebates or give-ups to be received by sponsor and prohibiting reciprocal business arrangements circumventing such prohibitions.

k. Prominent disclosure of lack of experience or limited experience of sponsor, general partner, principal officer of corporate general partner, or other manager.

l. Disclosure of any transaction within the last five years in which any affiliate had a material interest with sponsor or previously had title to or had a beneficial interest in property to be acquired by the partnership.

9. Discussion of use of proceeds, to include:

a. Specific purposes.

b. Approximate amounts to be used for each purpose.

Illustration 9-1 (cont.)

c. With respect to proceeds for purchase of property, brief description of property disclosing name of grantor.
d. Minimum total amount necessary to initiate program.
e. Disposition of funds raised if insufficient for stated purpose.
f. Schedule for any deferred payments.

10. Discussion of policy on cash available for distribution.
11. Complete description of all compensation to promoters.
12. Discussion of all actual and potential conflicts of interests.
13. Discussion of all prohibitions and restricted activities with respect to syndicator, affiliates and the partnership.
14. Discussion of pending legal proceedings involving partnership property, material legal proceedings between sponsor and participants of prior program, and pending legal proceedings to which program or sponsor is party and which is material to program, including:
    a. Payment of counsel.
    b. Probable extent of liability.
15. Discussion of tax consequences, to include:
    a. Taxability of entity as a partnership rather than an association, basing opinion on ruling of IRS or opinion of counsel.
    b. If IRS ruling based on any continuing conditions, representation to continue to adhere to such conditions.
    c. Tax treatment of the program.
    d. Tax treatment of participants.
    e. Allocation of depreciation, investment credits, construction interest, points, etc.

Illustration 9-1 (cont.)

f. Method of depreciation, useful life, applicable recapture provisions and consequences thereof.

g. Possibility of requirement for filing tax returns with state in which property held.

h. Any other pertinent information.

16. Pictures of the property, to include aerial photos, United States Geological Survey maps, and location maps.

17. Description of property, to include:

a. In general:

(1) Zoning; building codes.

(2) Deed restrictions and covenants.

(3) Easements.

(4) Utilities and water, or their availability.

(5) Leases.

(6) Roads and access.

(7) Frontage.

(8) Title policy, including name of issuing company and brief description of any exceptions.

(9) Type of estate, such as fee simple, leasehold, etc.

(10) Ownership plats.

(11) Mineral and royalty interests outstanding.

(12) Outstanding liens.

(13) Soil condition, drainage, and pollution, if material.

(14) Climate description such as rainfall and temperature, if applicable.

b. Improvements:

(1) Physical description of buildings and units therein.

(2) Parking.

(3) Condition of structure, including:

(a) Roofing and exterior.

(b) Interior.

Illustration 9-1 (cont.)

§ 21:41 REAL PROPERTY

(4) Adequacy of air conditioning.
(5) Termite inspection.
(6) Necessity for replacement of any part of structure.
(7) Furniture, appliances, and carpets.
(8) Rehabilitation, such as painting.
(9) Other deferred maintenance.
(10) Previous occupancy history and rate schedule.
(11) Summary of lease schedule, and description of major tenants, if relevant.
(12) Statement that title insurance and any required construction, permanent or other financing, and performance bonds or other assurances with respect to builders have been or will be obtained on all properties acquired.

c. Prior interests of syndicator.
(1) Either statement that syndicator and affiliates have no previous ownership interests or contractual rights to property in last five years, or description of previous connection, including appropriate dates.
(2) Description of any syndications of property within past three years.

18. Disclosure of financing and related data, including:
a. The terms, such as:
(1) Maturity, rate, amortization, interest only, balloon note, etc.
(2) Personal liability or nonrecourse.
(3) Release clauses—partial or otherwise.
(4) Prepayment penalties or privileges.
(5) Liens.
(6) Name of lender and location.
b. Option, contract of sale or syndicator-owned.
c. Closing date.

Illustration 9-1 (cont.)

d. Insurance (casualty).
e. Earnest money.

19. Description of comparable land sales.

20. Schedule of deferred payments, holding costs, and formal projections.

21. Description of plan of distribution, including:
    a. Plan of distribution of any securities being registered that are offered otherwise than through underwriters, giving names of participants in distribution.
    b. For securities offered through underwriters, include:
        (1) Names and addresses of all underwriters.
        (2) Respective amounts to be underwritten.
        (3) Brief description of underwriters' obligations to take securities.
        (4) Description of any relationship of underwriters to registrant.
    c. Statement of distribution costs, including:
        (1) Cash discounts or commissions to be allowed or paid to dealers.
        (2) Any consideration other than cash to be used in settlement of such costs.
    d. Description of principal provisions of escrow of proceeds of sale until certain minimum units have been sold.
    e. List of expenses of the offering under the following items:
        (1) Attorney fees.
        (2) Accountant fees.
        (3) Printing costs.
        (4) Filing fees.
        (5) Description of other fees and costs of distribution.
        (6) Miscellaneous expenses.

Illustration 9-1 (cont.)

§ 21:41 REAL PROPERTY

f. Commissions to syndicator or its officers or directors for sale of units, including:
   (1) Either statement that such persons will be paid no commissions, or
   (2) Delineation of any commissions to be paid.

22. Description of limited partnership interests, to include:
    a. Amount.
    b. Minimum purchase.
    c. Assessability.
    d. Transferability.
    e. Voting rights.

23. Statement respecting legal opinions and other expert opinions, furnished in substantially the approved form.

24. Description of interests of counsel and experts in sponsor or program, including:
    a. Disclosure of employment by sponsor other than retainer as legal counsel.
    b. Indication of nature and amount of any direct or indirect interest of counsel, other than legal fees to be received, in sponsor.
    c. Description of any interest in the program received or to be received by counsel or counsel's firm in connection with registration or offering of securities.

25. Statement of opinions of counsel, including:
    a. Statement that offered securities are duly authorized or created and validly issued interests in issuer.
    b. Indication that liability of public investors will be limited to their respective total agreed upon investment in issuer.
    c. Indication that issuer will be taxed as a "partnership" and not as an "association" for federal income tax purposes.

Illustration 9-1 (cont.)

26. Statement respecting annual reports, to include:
    a. Representation that annual reports will be furnished annually to security holders and to the Division of Securities.
    b. Indication of whether such reports will contain certified financial statements.
    c. Disclosure of nature and frequency of other reports to be issued by registrant.

27. Financial reports for limited partnership in existence, including:
    a. Audited balance sheet of program as of end of most recent fiscal year.
    b. Unaudited balance sheet as of date not more than 90 days prior to date of filing.
    c. If assets are owned, also include:
        (1) Cash flow statement of program (may be unaudited) for each of the last 3 fiscal years of program (or for life of program, if less).
        (2) Unaudited cash flow statements for any interim period between end of latest fiscal year and date of balance sheet furnished, and for corresponding interim period of preceding years.
        (3) Audited statements of income and statements of changes in financial position for program for each of last 3 fiscal years of program (or for life of program, if less).
        (4) Unaudited statements for any interim period ending not more than 90 days prior to date of filing application.

28. Required financial statements for corporate sponsors, to include:
    a. Audited balance sheet for same periods and in same form required for program itself.
    b. Audited profit and loss statement for last fiscal

Illustration 9-1 (cont.)

year of corporate sponsor (or for life of corporate sponsor, if less).

c. Unaudited profit and loss statements for any interim period ending not more than 90 days prior to day of filing application.

29. Provisions respecting limited partnership agreement.
    a. Attach copy of agreement to prospectus.
    b. Briefly summarize powers of general partner and other material provisions of agreement.

30. Statement of any projections of predicted future results of operations, including, where applicable:
    a. Annual revenue by source.
    b. Annual expenses.
    c. Mortgage obligation—annual payments for principal and interest, points and financing fees shown as dollars, not percentages.
    d. Annual cash flow.
    e. Annual depreciation and amortization with full description of methods to be used.
    f. Annual taxable income or loss and simplified explanation of tax treatment of such results (assumed tax brackets may not be used).
    g. Construction costs, including disclosure regarding contracts.
    h. Accounting policies—e.g., with respect to points, financing costs, and depreciation.
    i. Disclosure of changing economic effects upon limited partners resulting principally from federal income tax consequences over life of partnership property, e.g., substantial tax losses in early years followed by increasing amounts of taxable income in later years.
    j. Adequate disclosure of possible undesirable tax consequences of an early sale of program property (such as depreciation recapture or failure to sell property at a price returning sufficient

Illustration 9-1 (cont.)

cash to meet resulting tax liabilities of participants).

k. Prominent display of a warning notice that projections are based on assumptions that may or may not prove accurate and may not be relied on to indicate actual results that will be obtained.

Illustration 9-2

PROSPECTUS AND RELATED INSTRUMENTS

§ 21:51 Prospectus for intrastate offering—Non-specified property program

[Cover Page]

PROSPECTUS

THE __1______ *[NAME]* LIMITED PARTNERSHIP
__2______ *[ADDRESS]*, IN THE CITY OF __3______,
COUNTY OF __4______, STATE OF CALIFORNIA.

THESE SECURITIES ARE OFFERED FOR SALE TO BONA FIDE RESIDENTS OF CALIFORNIA ONLY UNDER A PERMIT GRANTED BY THE DIVISION OF SECURITIES. THIS PERMIT IS PERMISSIVE ONLY AND DOES NOT CONSTITUTE A RECOMMENDATION OR ENDORSEMENT OF THE SECURITIES PERMITTED TO BE ISSUED.

__5______ *[Number]* Units
__6______ [Limited Partnership Interests]

__7______ *[Name]* and __8______ *[name]*, as general partners of __9______ *[partnership]*, a limited partnership formed for the purpose of investing in real property, hereby offer to California residents meeting the qualifications set forth, an aggregate of __10______ *[number]* units of limited

Illustration 9-2 (cont.)

partnership in the partnership. The minimum subscription price is __11______ Dollars ($____) __12______ (units).

The maximum amount of sales or underwriting commission to be paid by __13______ [sponsor] is __14______ Dollars ($____).

THE USE OF PROJECTIONS IN THIS OFFERING IS PROHIBITED. ANY REPRESENTATION TO THE CONTRARY AND ANY, PREDICTIONS OR PROMISES, WHETHER WRITTEN OR ORAL, AS TO THE AMOUNT OR CERTAINTY OF ANY PRESENT OR FUTURE CASH BENEFIT OR TAX CONSEQUENCE WHICH MAY FLOW FROM AN INVESTMENT IN THIS PROGRAM IS A VIOLATION OF LAW. THE COMMISSIONER OF CORPORATIONS OF THE STATE OF CALIFORNIA DOES NOT RECOMMEND OR ENDORSE THE PURCHASE OF THESE SECURITIES.

The amount of money sought to be raised, the price per unit, and the underwriting discounts and commissions are as follows:

	Price to Public	Underwriting Discounts & Commissions	Proceeds to Partnership
Per Unit	$__15__	$__16__	$__17__
Total Minimum	$__18__	$__19__	$__20__
Total Maximum	$__21__	$__22__	$__23__

__24______ *[If applicable, add:* The maximum amount of acquisition fees that may be received or paid pursuant to this program is __25______ Dollars ($____)].

__26______ *[If applicable add:* The maximum amount of development and/or construction fees to be paid by the program to the general partner or affiliates is __27______ Dollars ($____).]

The estimated amount of organization and offering expenses is __28______ Dollars ($____).

The offering period will extend from __29______ *[date],* to __30______ *[date].*

Illustration 9-2 (cont.)

SYNDICATION—LIMITED PARTNERSHIPS § 21:51

The date of this prospectus is ___31___ *[date]*.

[Inside front cover]

___32___ *[At this point disclose and itemize in tabular form all consideration that may be received from the program directly or indirectly by the sponsor and its affiliates and underwriters, what the consideration is for, and how and when it will be paid].*

Table of Contents

Section	Page
1. The Partnership	___
2. The Offering	___
3. Special Risk Factors	___
4. Plan Distribution	___
5. Qualifications of Investors	___
6. Method of Subscription	___
7. The Impound Condition	___
8. Use of Proceeds	___
9. Investment Objectives and Operating Policies	___
10. Management	___
11. Distributions and Management Compensation	___
12. Redemption of Units	___
13. Transfer of Units	___
14. Term	___
15. Federal Tax Consequences	___
16. Conflicts of Interest	___
17. Annual Reports	___
18. Legal Opinions and Other Experts	___
19. Summary of Additional Terms of the Partnership	___
20. Financial statements of entity	___
21. Financial statements of the corporate sponsor	___

Illustration 9-2 (cont.)

22. Limited partnership agreements .... ____
23. Exhibits .... ____

[Body of Prospectus]

SECTION 1. THE PARTNERSHIP

__33__ *[Name of partnership]* is a real estate investment entity organized as a limited partnership under the laws of the State of California. It was formed on __34__ *[date]*, and will exist until __35__ *[date]*. *[Name]*, a California corporation, the principal place of business of which is located at __36__ *[address]*, telephone number __37__, and __38__ *[name]*, of __39__ *[address]*, whose telephone number is __40__, are general partners. __41__ *[Name]*, is the initial limited partner. The purchasers of units under this offering, and units under any subsequent offering, will also be limited partners.

SECTION 2. THE OFFERING

An aggregate of __42__ *[number]* units of limited partnership interest is being offered, at a price of __43__ Dollars ($____) per unit, to bona fide California residents. Such interests may be purchased only with cash and are nonassessable.

SECTION 3. SPECIAL RISK FACTORS

The purchase of these units involves a high degree of risk, and prospective investors should carefully consider the following factors prior to subscribing for any units:

(a) These units represent the initial financing of the partnership. The price at which they are offered has been arbitrarily determined.

(b) As of the date of this prospectus the partnership has entered into no contracts or understandings with respect to any of the specific properties that will be acquired with the proceeds of this offering. Prospective investors must, therefore, rely on the judgment of general partners with respect

Illustration 9-2 (cont.)

SYNDICATION—LIMITED PARTNERSHIPS § 21:51

to such investments. There can be no assurance as to whether or when the proceeds of this offering will be profitably invested. As properties are acquired, a property supplement will be added to this prospectus.

(c) The general partners are expressly authorized by the partnership agreement to engage in, or possess interests in, other business ventures, including businesses that may be similar to the partnership. The general partners are at the present time extensively involved in other real estate business ventures, and they expect to continue to be so involved in the future. (See Conflicts of Interest, page __[44]__.)

(d) If, for any reason, at least __[45]______ *[number]* units are not sold by __[46]______ *[date],* the offering will terminate and all funds paid by prospective investors will be returned __[47]______ [without interest *or* with interest customarily paid in __[48]______ *(location)* by escrow holders of limited partnership impounded funds]. These units are being sold on a best efforts basis, without prior underwriting commitment, and there can be no assurance that a sufficient number of units will be sold to satisfy this impound condition.

(e) The business in which the partnership will engage is highly competitive and vulnerable to adverse changes in general and local economic conditions and in prevailing interest rates, and to other factors beyond the control of the general partners. Thus, there can be no assurance that the partnership will be a financial success or that investments made in it will be recouped.

(f) The general partners will attempt to make full use of leverage with respect to all real property acquisitions made with the proceeds of this offering. Thus, it is expected that real property will be purchased with cash down payments of between ____% and ____% (or less) of the total purchase price, the balance to be evidenced by purchase-money promissory notes secured by mortgages or trust deeds encumbering the property acquired. Prospective investors should be aware that, while "leveraging" increases the potential for profits and tax shelter, it also increases the exposure to

Illustration 9-2 (cont.)

§ 21:51 REAL PROPERTY

losses, in that a default by the partnership with respect to a purchase-money promissory note could cause the partnership to lose the initial down payment and all payments made prior to default.

(g) The partnership is a limited partnership. While, under existing laws, this form of organization makes possible more favorable income tax consequences for investors than would be permitted with a corporate form of organization, it should be understood that investors in a limited partnership do not have all of the rights, remedies, procedures, protections, and guaranties that are enjoyed by the shareholders of a corporation.

(h) It is not expected that liquidation of an investment in the partnership will be readily possible because of the limited number of units being offered and because a unit can be fully transferred only in accordance with the California Revised Limited Partnership Act, which requires recordation of an amended certificate of limited partnership and other procedures.

The partnership agreement does provide for redemption of units upon demand of any holder, but no unit may be redeemed for ___[49]___ years following the date of its issuance except on the death of a limited partner. There can be no assurance that the liquid assets of the partnership will be adequate to meet redemption demands, and the partnership agreement expressly authorizes the payment of part or all of the redemption price of any unit in the form of promissory notes bearing interest at the rate of _____% per annum and payable over a term of up to ___[50]_______ years from the date of redemption.

(i) Because the units are being offered pursuant to the exemption from registration set forth in Section 3(a)(11) of the Federal Securities Act of 1933 (the intrastate exemption), the following legend will be placed on the documents evidencing ownership of these units, and the partnership will not consent to or recognize any transfer or assignment of units except upon compliance with such regulations:

Illustration 9-2 (cont.)

The limited partnership interest evidenced this prospectus has not been registered with the Securities Act of 1933, as amended. Such interest may not be offered, sold, transferred, pledged, or hypothecated to a person who is not a bona fide resident of the State of California in the absence of registration under that Act or an opinion of counsel for __51______ *[partnership]* that such registration is not required.

(j) There is no guaranty that the Internal Revenue Code or the regulations promulgated under the Code will not be amended during the life of the partnership in such manner as to deprive the partnership and limited partners of any tax benefits they might now be able to receive. (See Federal Income Tax Consequences, page __52__.) In the event the partnership is treated for tax purposes as a corporation in any taxable year, distributions to limited partners would not be deductible in computing the taxable income of the organization and, in addition, net losses of the partnership, which would include depreciation taken on partnership properties, interest paid by the partnership, and operating expenses, would be reflected only on the partnership's tax return rather than being passed through to the partners.

The general partners have not requested a tax ruling on behalf of the partnership, nor do they intend to request such a ruling. In the absence of such a ruling, there can be no assurance from the Internal Revenue Service that the partnership will not constitute an association taxable as a corporation. However, it is the opinion of counsel for the partnership that the partnership will be taxed as a partnership.

Prospective purchasers who are in the lower and middle federal income tax brackets should recognize in addition, that they might not be able to utilize as fully as persons in the higher income tax brackets, the various tax benefits that may be obtained by the partnership for its partners. In addition, the sale of assets may result for all partners in the recapture of accelerated depreciation and hence the taxation of the proceeds of sale. Also, limited partners may not be able to use deductions arising from the prepayment of

Illustration 9-2 (cont.)

interest since such deductions may result in a material distortion of income for the partner. In the event of foreclosure, the partnership may experience greater depreciation that cash distribution and hence incur substantial tax liabilities.

(k) The management and the investment practice and policies of the partnership are not supervised or regulated by any federal or state authority.

(l) The partnership may commence operations on receipt of __53__ Dollars ($__) in the aggregate. (See The Impound Condition, page __54__.) The potential profitability of the partnership could be affected by the amount of funds at its disposal and the application of a smaller sum of money would allow a smaller margin of error than application of a larger sum. It is the intention of the general partners to diversify the investments of the partnership. However, no assurance can be given as to the actual diversification of the partnership investments, since the size of the partnership will be determined by the general partners and/or by the number of units sold. The partnership may have as little as __55__ Dollars ($__) (before expenses) in funds available for investment. If the partnership raises no more than the minimum capital, the degree of diversification will be adversely affected.

SECTION 4. PLAN OF DISTRIBUTION

The units will be sold on a best-efforts basis by __56__ *[name]*, and by other broker-dealers and agents licensed by the California Department of Corporations. No commissions will be paid out of the proceeds of this offering on sale of the first __57__ *[number]* units, but commissions may be paid on sales of the remainder of the units offered in an amount not to exceed ___% of the proceeds of such sales. Such commissions, together with other selling expenses, such as printing and advertising costs, will not exceed ___% of the proceeds of this offering.

Illustration 9-2 (cont.)

SECTION 5. QUALIFICATIONS OF INVESTORS

The units will be offered and sold only to bona fide residents of the State of California. Investors must have either a minimum annual gross income of $30,000 and a net worth of $30,000 or, in the alternative, a minimum net worth of $75,000. Net worth must be determined exclusive of home, furnishings, and automobiles.

The minimum initial cash purchase must be $2,000 per investor (__58__ units at __59______ Dollars ($_____) per unit).

SECTION 6. METHOD OF SUBSCRIPTION

Persons wishing to purchase units should execute one of the duplicate forms of the __60______ [signature page *or* subscription agreement] attached at the end of this prospectus, and deliver such executed __61______ [page *or* agreement] to the general partners or their agent, together with the full purchase price required for the units subscribed for. Subscriptions will be irrevocable for a period of __62__ days. The general partners reserve the right to refuse to accept any subscription.

SECTION 7. THE IMPOUND CONDITION

The initial sale of these units is subject to an impound condition during the term of which all proceeds of the sale of units will be deposited into an interest-bearing trust account. The minimum aggregate amount necessary to initiate the program is __63______ Dollars ($_____), __64______ *[number]* units. Unless such amount is raised on or before __65______ *[date],* the funds on deposit in such account will be returned to the respective investors __66______ [with *or* without] interest and partnership operations will not commence. In the event that the impound condition is satisfied, such funds will be withdrawn from the impound trust account and applied as set forth below. (See Use of Proceeds, page __67__), except that interest earned during the

Illustration 9-2 (cont.)

§ 21:51 REAL PROPERTY

term of the impound condition will be distributed to the respective limited partners.

SECTION 8. USE OF PROCEEDS

The net proceeds of the offering (a minimum of $____ and a maximum of $____ after a deduction of underwriting commissions and estimated expenses) will be held in cash and invested in government securities, certificates of deposit, bank and savings and loan deposits, AAA grade commercial paper, short-term mortgage loans and other short-term obligations that can be readily liquidated or any one or more of the foregoing, all of which may be pledged, hypothecated, or assigned as collateral for loans to the partnership. Proceeds may also be used as compensating balances required by banks or other lenders in connection with loans to the partnership. Thereafter, the partnership will from time to time liquidate not less than ___68___ [88%] of such investments and invest the proceeds as set forth below. The remaining ___69___ [12%] or less will be held as reserves, of which up to ___70___ [10%] will be held to meet carrying costs of properties pending receipt of sufficient income from properties to cover such cost (such as maturing purchase price installments of principal, interest, taxes, insurance, and maintenance) and other obligations and liabilities of the partnership and ___71___ [2%] will be placed in a limited repurchase reserve account for the redemption of units. (See Redemption of Units, page ___72___.)

Not less that ___73___ [88%] of the net proceeds will ultimately be invested as follows on completion of the partnership's investment program:

(1) Not less than ___74___ [70%] of the net proceeds of the offering in improved real estate and real estate with respect to which there is an existing contract with a builder to commence construction of improvements on such real estate soon after acquisition or to complete construction in progress, and in personal property (such as furniture) used in connection with such real estate. Investments will be

Illustration 9-2 (cont.)

made primarily in first-user apartment buildings. If shopping centers, office buildings, warehouses, and mobile home parks appear to present favorable opportunities, such properties may be acquired, providing that at least a majority of the net proceeds of the offering invested in improved real estate and real estate to be improved will be invested in apartment buildings.

(2) Not more that __75____ [18%] of the net proceeds of the offering in other real estate related investments, including certain loans secured by the pledge or hypothecation of mortgages, certain junior mortgage loans, wrap-around mortgage loans, certain first mortgage loans, "gap" mortgage loans, and general partnership interests in other general partnerships and joint ventures primarily in real estate activities, provided that (a) not more than __76____ [10%] of the gross assets of the program may be invested in short-term loans secured by the pledge or hypothecation of mortgages and junior mortgage loans, and (b) not more than __77____ [5%] of the net proceeds may be invested in interests of other partnerships and joint ventures.

To the extent that the partnership does not obtain contributions equal to the maximum amount of the offering ($____) it may be anticipated that the amount of the net proceeds of the offering invested in other real estate related investments will be somewhat less than the maximum permitted under subparagraph (2) above, and that a proportionately greater amount will be invested in real estate and related personal property assets as set forth under subparagraph (1) above.

SECTION 9. INVESTMENT OBJECTIVES AND OPERATING POLICIES

(a) *Principal Investment Objectives.* The principal objective of the partnership in making acquisitions of interests in real estate and in investing in general partnerships and joint ventures is to obtain for investors current tax-deferred income in the first several years, long term capital apprecia-

Illustration 9-2 (cont.)

tion, and partial conversion of ordinary income to capital gain through acquisitions, professional management and ultimate liquidation of a diversified portfolio of income-producing real properties. (See Special Risk Factors, page __78__.)

The principal objective of the partnership in making real estate investments in loans is to obtain maximum possible income yields on funds so invested. No assurance can be given that these objectives will be achieved.

The location of the partnership's properties and investments will be principally in __79______ [Southern and Northern areas of California.] The general partners intend to select properties and investments with reasonable proximity to expanding centers of population having regional shopping centers, industrial parks, and easy access to major freeways, highways, or mass transportation facilities. However, the partnership is not limited as to geographical areas where it may make its investment and conduct operations, and to the extent that the general partners determine that there are other areas in which the partnership may acquire properties and investments consistent with its investment objectives it may do so. To the extent that the partnership makes investments in areas in which substantial overbuilding has occurred and in which there is substantial unemployment, such as the areas in and surrounding __80_______ [Los Angeles, San Francisco, and San Jose, California], revenues from rentals, (and current distributions) could be adversely affected by rising vacancy factors due to such unemployment and oversupply of competitive projects. These named areas are those in the United States with respect to which the general partners believe such conditions now generally exist, but they may not be the only such areas.

Except as set forth under Use of Proceeds (see page __81__), the partnership does not have a policy and there is no limitation as to the amount or percentage of its assets that may be invested in, or the number or amount of mortgages that may be placed on, any one property or group of properties, any specific investment, or any person or

Illustration 9-2 (cont.)

group of persons. The investment objectives and policies contained in this section may not be changed by the general partners without the vote of the limited partners as provided for in Section ___82______ of the limited partnership agreement attached as Appendix ___83___.

It is intended that real estate investments will be made in several properties in various locations in an attempt to achieve diversification and thus minimize the effect of changes in local economic conditions and certain other risks. (See Special Risk Factors, page ___84___.) However, the extent of such diversification depends on the amount of funds available to the partnership from the sale of its units, and if less than the total amount of the offering ___85______ Dollars ($_____) is obtained, the number and type of different properties will be reduced.

The determination as to whether a particular property or investment should be sold or otherwise disposed of will be made after a consideration of relevant factors, including performance of the property and market conditions, with a view toward achieving capital appreciation and a high return or yield from the property or investment. The partnership will generally hold its properties for at least ___86___ years after acquisition. As to its investments other than in real property, the partnership will generally hold such investments until maturity. However, relevant factors may dictate that properties and investments be held for a shorter period. For example, the general partners will consider the sale or liquidation of any real property, the performance of which results in taxable income in later years in excess of that portion of current distributions to the holders of units provided from the operation of such property. Any reinvesting of proceeds realized on disposition or refinancing of partnership properties and investments will not be accomplished unless sufficient cash will be distributed to pay any state or federal income tax liability resulting from such disposition or refinancing. (See Distribution and Management Compensation, page ___87___.) On disposition of such properties there will probably be recapture of a portion of

Illustration 9-2 (cont.)

§ 21:51 REAL PROPERTY

the depreciation taxable at current income tax rates. (See Federal Income Tax Consequences, page __88__.)

(b) *Real Estate Activities.* The partnership's capital will be invested principally in improved income-producing real estate and real estate with respect to which there is an existing contract with a builder to commence construction of improvements on it soon after acquisition, or to complete construction in progress. Interests in real property may include fee as well as leasehold interests, and equitable (such as contracts for purchase of properties on the instalment basis) as well as legal interests. Any combination of these interests may be utilized. For example, a long-term ground lease might be taken on the land and the fee interest might be taken in buildings and other improvements on the land. Properties will be considered for acquisition only if the terms and price are such that, on the basis of projected operating statements and appraisal of the property, the following returns and benefits of holders of units appear possible:

(1) Tax deferred (i.e., free of income tax consequences under then prevailing federal tax laws for the first several years after the property is acquired) cash funds provided from operations available for distribution as current distributions to owner of units. (See Distributions and Management Compensation, page __89__.)

(2) A reasonable tax-deferred mortgage deduction from periodic principal payments on mortgages on the property.

(3) Depreciation in the first several years to supply the tax deferral of (1) and (2), and also to supply some tax shelter for the other income of holders of units.

(4) Appreciation in the property's value.

(c) *Terms of Purchase.* Terms of purchase of properties will vary substantially, depending on the nature of the particular property acquired and requirements of the seller. The purchase price for all types of properties the partnership may acquire will ordinarily vary from __90______ [five] to __91______ [eight] times the anticipated annual gross rental

Illustration 9-2 (cont.)

income, depending on the interest rates available and financing offered. It may be anticipated that the partnership will make a cash downpayment of ____% to ____% of the purchase price and will buy subject to, or assume, deferred obligations for the balance of the purchase price.

Such deferred obligations will generally be represented by interest-bearing promissory notes and other debt instruments in favor of the seller or third-party lender, secured by mortgages, installment land contracts or other liens on purchased property. It may be anticipated that approximately ____% to ____% of the purchase price will be represented by notes secured by junior mortgages on the property. The principal and interest of the notes may be fully amortized by periodic payments over the terms of the notes, or the notes may be of the type payable in installments of interest only or installments of interest with a small amount of principal, with a large payment of principal (balloon payment) due at or near maturity. A balloon payment arrangement will result in lower equity build-up from the mortgage reduction payments of principal that are made over the term of the loan, but to that extent may result in higher cash flow at the beginning of the investment because payments will be smaller. Promissory notes secured by junior mortgages are quite commonly of the interest-only type with a balloon payment due at maturity. The partnership will endeavor to keep to a minimum finance arrangements in which the promissory notes secured by the first mortgage do not require amortization and accordingly do not result in such equity build-up, although there is no assurance it will be successful in doing so.

A form of nonconventional financing that may be used is the secured all-inclusive (sometimes called "wraparound") note made by the partnership to the seller. This is a note in an amount which includes the then existing balance of a mortgage loan owned by the seller to a lender and also includes the additional amount to be paid by the partnership to the seller. The "all-inclusive" mortgage becomes a junior or secondary mortgage to the existing mortgage. The part-

Illustration 9-2 (cont.)

nership would become obligated to pay installments of the "all-inclusive" note to the seller and the seller in turn would be obligated to pay the periodic instalment. In order to eliminate the risk of nonpayment by the seller to the seller's lender, the general partners will require that payments on the first mortgage and tax or other impound payments may be made by the partnership or through a third-party trustee to the lender.

When possible, the partnership will also endeavor to issue only non-recourse promissory notes so that the partnership and the general partners are not personally liable on the obligations, and the lender's rights on default are against the property which secures the obligation and against the seller or some other party. To the extent the partnership is able to do this, it will achieve a desired increase in the tax basis of holders of units. (See Federal Income Tax Consequences, page __92__.) There is no assurance as to whether, or the extent to which, the partnership may enter into non-recourse arrangements. If and to the extent that mortgages are assumed in connection with properties purchased, the desired increase in tax basis will not be achieved, and the limitation as to the amount of depreciation available to be taken by holders of units may be reached at an earlier time than if the foregoing techniques, while providing the partnership with properties having a value possibly 4 to 5 times the capital invested in the property, increases risks of loss to the partnership.

(d) *Loans Secured by Junior Mortgages.* The partnership may invest up to __93______ [10%] of the gross proceeds of the offering in short-term loans secured by junior mortgages maturing in __94______ [6] years.

(e) *Loan by General Partners.* On any loan made by the general partners to the partnership as provided by Section __95______ of the limited partnership agreement (see Appendix __96__), the interest can not be more than the amounts that would be charged by unrelated banks on comparable loans for the same purpose in the locality of the property.

Illustration 9-2 (cont.)

(f) *Interests in General Partnerships and Joint Ventures.* The partnership may invest in not more than ___% of the net proceeds of this offering in interests in either general partnerships or joint ventures, organized to operate a business on a particular property or properties. The partnership may also participate on a joint basis with other programs in the purchase or development of property. The portion of the partnership's capital that may be invested in each type of interest cannot be determined at this time.

These investments present similar elements of risk, or greater risks, than risks associated with the interests in this partnership. To the extent the partnership acquires a general partnership interest or joint venture interest it will be liable for any debts of such entity not paid by that entity. If, as a result of such liabilities, the amount so invested would exceed the foregoing percentage, the general partners will make nonrefundable cash payments to the partnership (which will not be considered capital contributions of the general partners or loans by the general partners) to the extent necessary so that such investments of the partnership will not exceed the foregoing percentage.

(g) *Rebates, Kickback, and Reciprocal Arrangements.* The general partners may neither receive the benefits of, nor participate in reciprocal business arrangements that would circumvent the ban against rebates or give-ups. Furthermore, the general partners may not participate in reciprocal business arrangements that would circumvent the restrictions against dealing with affiliates or promoters as delineated in the rules and regulations promulgated by the California Department of Corporations.

(h) *Requirement for Real Property Appraisal.* All real property acquisitions will be supported by an appraisal prepared by a competent, independent appraisor. The appraisal must be maintained in the general partners' records for at least 5 years and will be available for inspection and duplication by any participant in the program.

Illustration 9-2 (cont.)

§ 21:51 REAL PROPERTY

SECTION 10. MANAGEMENT

The general partners will have general responsibility for supervising partnership operations, including the overseeing of compliance with legal and regulatory requirements, and the preparation and transmittal of periodic and annual reports to the limited partners. The general partners have the ultimate authority in all matters affecting the business and affairs of the partnership and the formulation of guidelines and limitations with respect to the partnership investments.

__97______ *[Set forth brief biographical information and business experience for the past 10 years of sponsors, general partners, principal officers of the corporate general partner (chairperson of the board, president, vice-president, treasurer, secretary, or any other person having similar authority or performing like functions) and other managers of the program. Also indicate the lack of experience of such persons, when applicable. Also add track records concerning previous syndication experience of the sponsor and other relevant parties for all programs during the past 5 years].*

The general partners are not required to secure performance of their duties by bond or otherwise. The partnership agreement absolves the general partners from liability for errors in judgment or any acts or omissions, whether or not disclosed, unless caused by a breach of the fiduciary duty of the general partners to the limited partnership or to the limited partners.

The general partners expect to retain various property management companies to manage specific properties acquired by the partnership. The compensation to be paid such property managers (but not compensation paid resident property managers), will be offset against the management fee to which the general partners are entitled. (See Distributions and Management Compensation, page __98__.)

To preserve the limited liability of investors in the partnership, the limited partners will have no right to participate in the management of the partnership business. However, a

Illustration 9-2 (cont.)

majority-in-interest of the limited partners will at all times have the power to:

(a) Remove the general partners or either of them, and to elect their successors;

(b) Amend the partnership agreement

(c) Terminate the partnership; and

(d) Cause or preclude the sale of all or substantially all of the partnership assets.

SECTION 11. DISTRIBUTIONS AND MANAGEMENT COMPENSATION

As set forth in Section __99__ of the partnership agreement attached as Appendix __100__ [A] to this prospectus, there are two sources of cash distributions to general partners and to limited partners or assignees. These sources are current distributions and disposition proceeds. Current distributions and disposition proceeds, if any, are computed and allocated as of the last day of each calendar quarter and are actually distributed during the following calendar quarter.

(a) *Definitions.* "Current distributions" include (1) lease payments for the period on net leases with builders and sellers (except to the extent they are tenants), and (2) cash funds provided from operations for the period that is determined by the general partners in accordance with generally accepted accounting principles by adding back to the net income (or loss) of the partnership those expenses (primarily depreciation) not requiring current cash outlays and by excluding from net income (or loss) any proceeds from the disposition of partnership properties and investments and any extraordinary non-recurring receipts, but in both cases after deduction of mortgage payments representing reductions in mortgage principal balances, and after deduction (or restoration) of such amounts of lease payments and cash funds provided from operations for the period (or from a prior period) as are determined in the sole discretion of the general partners to be reasonably necessary (or no longer necessary) to be expended or held as reserves for the

Illustration 9-2 (cont.)

conduct of the partnership's business, including future payments of anticipated obligations and contingent liabilities.

"Disposition proceeds" consist of the net cash proceeds, which are not reinvested or used for payment of the charges and expenses or held for the reserves not covered by current distributions, realized by the partnership upon the sale, refinancing, or other disposition of any particular property or investment. The amount of such proceeds is determined on a property-by-property basis. Notes and items other than cash received upon distribution will not be subject to inclusion in disposition proceeds until actually paid or sold, refinanced, or otherwise disposed of for cash.

(b) *Distributions.* As compensation for their services in evaluating and selecting properties and investments, determining and negotiating terms of acquisition and disposition, selecting, retaining, and supervising consultants, contractors, architects, engineers, lenders, borrowers, and others, and otherwise generally managing the day-to-day investment operations of the partnership, the general partners are paid a fee equal to __101____ percent (____%) of the current distributions. The balance of current distributions is distributed to the holders of units (limited partners or their assignees) and allocated on the last day of such calendar month or quarter with respect to which current distributions have been determined in the ratio which the number of units held by each of them bears to the number of units held by all of them.

Disposition proceeds are distributed first to the holders of units, ratably, until they receive a return determined by multiplying the portion of the partnership's initial capital from sale of the units used in making the particular investment by the fraction that results from dividing the gross public offering price of the units sold by the net proceeds of the offering, after payment of sales commissions and other offering expenses. If for example, the gross amount received from sale of units under the terms of this offering is __102____ [$1 million] and the net proceeds after deduction of sales commissions and other offering expenses equal

Illustration 9-2 (cont.)

__103______ [$900,000], the resulting fraction, expressed as a percentage, would be approximately __104______ [111%], so that all holders of units would first receive from the disposition proceeds of any investment a return of __105______ [111%] of the portion of the partnership initial capital used in making that investment. The balance of the disposition proceeds is distributed to the general partners and holders of units in the same proportions as current distributions. The general partners will not make contributions to the partnership to offset any losses on sales of properties. Any loss on one property will not reduce the amounts the general partners or holders of units will receive as disposition proceeds on future dispositions of other properties. Since it is intended that proceeds of any disposition of investments during the first __106______ [five] years of the partnership term will be reinvested, there will be little or no distribution of disposition proceeds, if any, until after that time. In addition, since the disposition proceeds consist primarily of extraordinary nonrecurring cash receipts, distributions of them will be unstable and irregular.

On dissolution of the partnership, all partnership assets are to be sold or otherwise liquidated. The proceeds from the liquidation (after payment of other debts and liabilities of the partnership, deduction of any required reserves, and payment of any current distributions and distributions of disposition proceeds allocated prior to the date of dissolution to holders of units, but not yet paid) are to be distributed in the following order of priority:

First, to holders of units in an amount necessary to return their initial capital investment of $__107__ per unit less all current distributions and distributions of disposition proceeds allocated to such units during the period the units were outstanding;

Second, to repayment of any loans or advances made by any general partners to the partnership;

Third, to the general partners to the extent of current distributions and distributions of disposition proceeds that

Illustration 9-2 (cont.)

have been allocated to them prior to the date of dissolution but have not yet been paid; and

Fourth, of the balance remaining, if any, __109____ percent (____%) ratably to the holders of units and __109____ percent (____%) to the general partners. The partnership will not sell assets to or purchase assets from another partnership controlled or managed by the general partners or their affiliates.

No distributions may be made unless there remains property of the partnership sufficient to pay all liabilities of the partnership, except liabilities to general partners and liabilities to limited partners on account of their capital contributions. There is no assurance that the holders of units will receive such distribution, but the general partners will not receive any such distributions unless holders of units do.

(c) *Communications to Holders of Units.* All communications to holders of units relating to cash distributions will separately identify current distributions and disposition proceeds. With respect to current distributions, such communications will also separately identify the portion of cash distributions attributable to lease payments on net leases with builders and sellers (and will state that distributions of such lease payments represent a return of capital not derived from operations), as distinguished from cash funds provided from operations during the period and from cash funds provided from operations during a prior period that are being distributed because it is no longer necessary that they be expended or held as reserves.

(d) *Losses, Deductions and Credits.* The partnership shall adopt a calendar year as its tax and accounting year. The term "net losses" as used in this agreement means the net losses determined by the partnership for purposes of preparing the partnership's information return for federal income tax purposes.

All of the net losses, deductions, and credits of the partnership will be computed each calendar month until the public offering of units is terminated and after that on a

Illustration 9-2 (cont.)

SYNDICATION—LIMITED PARTNERSHIPS § 21:51

quarterly basis, and will be allocated only to the registered holders of units recorded as of the last day of each such calendar month or quarter in the ratio which the number of units held by each of them bears to the number of units held by all of them, to the extent permitted by law, and such registered holders are entitled to all losses, deductions and credits arising from such losses in computing taxable income or tax liability.

In the case of transfers of partnership interests or the right to income, profits or losses and cash distributions will be allocated between the transferring parties on the basis of the number of days out of 365 that each party has held such units in the ratio which the number of units held by them bears to the number of units held by all the holders of units.

SECTION 12. REDEMPTION OF UNITS.

As already explained (see Use of Proceeds, page __110__), the partnership will maintain a reserve of liquid assets for use in the redemption of units.

Subject to the adequacy of this reserve, the partnership will redeem all units offered for redemption provided that the units have been outstanding for not less than __111__ years. All units will be redeemed at a price that is equal to their initial sales price reduced by the amount of cash distribution previously made on account of such units. It is the intention of the general partners that the redemption price be paid in cash at the time of redemption, but if and to the extent that the general partners determine it to be in the best interests of the partnership to do so, they are authorized to pay part or all of the redemption price in promissory notes of the partnership, bearing interest at the rate of __112______ percent (____%) per annum and payable over a term of not to exceed __113______ years from the date of redemption.

Prospective investors should be aware, however, that there can be no assurance that they will be able to redeem their units. It cannot be certain that the partnership will be able

Illustration 9-2 (cont.)

to maintain the required reserve, because its ability to do so will depend in part on the ratio of redemption demands to proceeds received from sales of additional units.

SECTION 13. TRANSFER OF UNITS.

When a purchaser is admitted to the partnership as a limited partner, he or she is registered on the records of the partnership as the owner of those units he or she purchased. The purchaser continues to be the registered holder until the partnership registers a transfer of such units. The registered holder is entitled to receive all distributions, allocations of losses, and withdrawals or reductions of capital contributions with respect to such units.

Units are transferable only if __114__ or more units are transferred. Transfers of fewer than __115__ units or fractions of units to a new holder will not be registered or recognized unless (a) the general partners agree otherwise and (b) according to the records of the partnership the transferee already is or at some time in the past has been a registered holder of at least __116__ units. Certain documents (which may include the consents of certain governmental authorities) must be delivered to the general partners before a transfer may be effected, although the consent of a general partner is not required for transfer of the units. Transfers will be registered on the __117______ day of the calendar quarter following receipt by the general partners of the required documents unless otherwise agreed by the general partners. The partnership may charge the assigning registered holder of the units a fee not exceeding __118______ Dollars ($_____) to defray the costs of effecting the registration.

The consent of the general partners is required to substitute a new holder as the limited partner with respect to a unit transferred to him or her. A limited partner should understand that unless he or she executes a form setting forth an intention that the transferee become a substituted limited partner with respect to units transferred, the trans-

Illustration 9-2 (cont.)

ferring limited partner will remain a limited partner and will retain voting rights and certain other rights as a limited partner which do not pass with the transfer of such units unless the transferee is made a substituted limited partner. The general partners may elect to substitute a registered holder as a limited partner as to the units transferred to that registered holder if they deem the substitution to be in the best interests of the partnership. Substitutions of new limited partners must be made quarterly and may be made more frequently in the discretion of the general partners.

SECTION 14. TERM

The partnership will last for __119__ years, unless terminated at an earlier date by vote of a majority-in-interest of the limited partners, or unless all of the partnership's real property is sold. The bankruptcy, assignment for the benefit of creditors, death, dissolution, retirement, or incompetency of either or both of the general partners may also cause a termination of the partnership, but on the occurrence of any of such contingencies the remaining general partner, or the limited partners if there is no remaining general partner, may, within __120______ days of the occurrence of the contingency causing termination, form a new partnership to continue on the same terms and conditions.

SECTION 15. FEDERAL INCOME TAX CONSEQUENCES

In the opinion of __121______ *[law firm]*, __122______ *[address]*, City of __123______, County of __124______, counsel for the general partners, the partnership will, for federal income tax purposes, be treated as a partnership, and not as an association taxable as a corporation. However, this opinion is based on applicable tax statutes and regulations and interpretations of the Internal Revenue Service as of the date of this prospectus, and such statutes, regulations, and interpretations are subject to change.

The partnership will file a federal information tax return

Illustration 9-2 (cont.)

each year, reporting its operations on a ___125___ [cash *or* accrual] basis for a calendar fiscal year. Each partner will be required to report his or her share of the partnership's income, gains, losses, deductions, and credits, if any, for the taxable year of the partnership ending within or with the taxable year. Thus, each partner may be taxed on his or her share of the partnership income even though the amount of cash distributed to the partner, if any, may be more or less than the amount subject to income taxes. Each partner may deduct his or her share of the partnership's losses, if any, to the extent of the adjusted basis of his or her interest in the partnership. Under present federal revenue regulations, to the extent that no partner (general or limited) is personally liable for the debts of the partnership, each partner will be permitted to increase the adjusted basis of his or her partnership interest by the pro rata share of such debts, thus allowing each partner to offset against other income his or her share of partnership losses, even though such share may exceed his or her partnership capital contributions. There will be distributed annually to each limited partner a report containing information to be used in the preparation of individual tax returns.

The general partners will, as a policy, attempt to maximize the deductions allowed by federal law in order to minimize the present tax liabilities of the limited partners, and for such purpose they may use accelerated depreciation and prepaid interest. For this reason, the limited partners may be required to pay additional taxes on income in subsequent years, since accelerated depreciation and prepaid interest operate to defer taxable income rather than to eliminate it. Also, the use of accelerated depreciation may require a portion of the income derived from the sale of depreciable assets to be taxed through the recapture of accelerated depreciation when such assets are sold at a profit.

Gain realized on the sale of units by a holder who is not a "dealer" and who has held such units for more than one (1)

Illustration 9-2 (cont.)

year will be a long term capital gain, except that the portion of profits from the sale attributable to such holder's share of the partnership's income for the taxable year of the sale, if any, unrealized receivables, and inventory items that have substantially appreciated in value as defined by the Internal Revenue Code, will be treated as ordinary income,[88] and not allowed to be reduced to the extent of capital losses.[89]

Income realized by the partnership in excess of deductible expenses will either be ordinary income, or in most instances involving the sale of property held in excess of one (1) year, long term capital gain. If it is determined that the partnership is holding any property for sale to customers in the ordinary course of business, gain from the sale of such property will be ordinary income irrespective of the period such property was held, and thus not allowed to offset capital gains.[90] Furthermore, to the extent that the partnership has, for tax purposes, depreciated improved real property at accelerated rates in excess of what would have been allowed under the straight line method of depreciation, gain on sale of such property equal to all or part of such excess depreciation will be taxable as ordinary income. The amount of such excess depreciation that will have to be "recaptured" under these provisions will depend on the total length of time the property is held by the partnership prior to sale of disposition.

The rules and regulations on which the above description of federal income tax consequences is based are subject to change. Each prospective investor is urged to consult a tax adviser with respect to the federal income tax consequences of his or her participation as a limited partner in the partnership. This is particularly important in the light of changes in terms of the new limitation on passive losses embodied in the Internal Revenue Code of 1986.

---

88. See *26 USCS § 1222(3).*

89. See *26 USCS § 1221(b).*

90. See *26 USCS § 1221(b)(2).*

Illustration 9-2 (cont.)

SECTION 16. CONFLICTS OF INTEREST

Prospective investors should be aware that there is a considerable potential for conflict of interest in the proposed plan of operation of the partnership.

The partnership agreement specifically authorizes the general partners to engage in other business ventures, including businesses that may be directly competitive with the business of the partnership. The general partners have been, and presently are, extensively involved in the buying, selling, managing, and syndication of real property, for their own accounts and for the accounts of firms other than the partnership, and it is expected that they will continue to be so involved.

__126______ *[If applicable, disclose total number and gross proceeds of syndications with which each sponsor may presently have some financial obligation].*

Further, the general partners intend to form additional limited partnerships in the future to engage in activities similar to those of the partnership. Such additional partnerships may be in competition with the partnership with respect to the purchase, sale, and rental of real properties, and there may be a conflict of interest on the part of the general partners between the partnership and other similar limited partnerships at such time as the partnership attempts to purchase, sell, or rent real property, or employ resident managers and under other circumstances.

SECTION 17. ANNUAL REPORTS

The general partners will submit annual reports containing annual balance sheets, profit and loss statements, and other information necessary for preparation of income tax returns. The reports will be mailed to the limited partners during the month of __127______.

At least quarterly, the partnership will transmit to participants a "special report" of real property acquisitions within the prior quarter. Such notice will describe the real proper-

Illustration 9-2 (cont.)

ties, and include a description of the geographic locale and of the market upon which the general partners are relying in projecting successful operation of the properties. All facts that reasonably appear to the general partners to materially influence the value of the property will be disclosed. The "special report" will include, by way of illustration and not of limitation, a statement of the actual purchase price including terms of the purchase, a statement of the total amount of the cash expended by the partnership to acquire such property, and a statement regarding the amount of proceeds in the program which remain unexpended or uncommitted. This unexpended or uncommitted amount will be stated in terms of both dollar amount and percentage of the total amount of the offering of the program.

SECTION 18. LEGAL OPINIONS AND OTHER EXPERTS

Legal matters in connection with the limited partnership units offered by this prospectus have been passed upon for the __128__ *[partnership]* by __129__ *[attorney]*, Attorney at Law, of __130__ *[address]*, in the City of __131__, County of __132__, State of California.

The audited financial statements included in the prospectus have been examined by __133__ *[accounting firm]*, independent certified public accountants, of __134__ *[address]*, in the City of __135__, County of __136__, State of California, as indicated in their opinions, attached as Appendix __137__.

SECTION 19. SUMMARY OF ADDITIONAL TERMS OF THE PARTNERSHIP

(a) *Cross References to Summaries Throughout Prospectus.* Certain terms of the partnership agreement are summarized throughout the various sections of this prospectus. Powers of the general partners and the rights and liabilities of participants are summarized in Management (see page __138__). Provisions respecting allocations of distributions are

Illustration 9-2 (cont.)

§ 21:51 REAL PROPERTY

set forth in Distributions and Management Compensation (see page ___139___). Discussion of provisions for replacement and maintenance reserves are set forth in Use of Proceeds (see page ___140___) and Investment Objectives and Polices (see page ___141___).

(b) *Termination and Dissolution.* The partnership may be terminated or dissolved upon the occurrence of any of the following:

(1) The sale, expiration, abandonment, or other disposition of all partnership assets.

(2) Action by limited partners in accordance with the procedure set forth in Section ___142___ of the limited partnership agreement (see Appendix ___143___) approving dissolution of the partnership.

(3) The ___144___ day after the death, adjudication of incompetency, adjudication of bankruptcy, dissolution, withdrawal, or retirement of either general partner pursuant to the provisions of Section ___145___ of the limited partnership agreement (see Appendix ___146___).

(4) The failure to elect a new general partner within ___147___ days after removal of both general partners or of the last remaining general partner in accordance with Section ___148___ of the limited partnership agreement (see Appendix ___149___).

(5) Dissolution of the partnership by judicial decree or operation of law.

(6) Duration of the partnership until the final day of its term.

c. *Meetings.* Meetings of the limited partners to vote on matters as to which limited partners are authorized to take action under Section ___150___ of the limited partnership agreement (See Appendix ___151___) may be called at any time by the general partners, or by one or more limited partners having not less than ____% of the voting power of the limited partners, by delivering written notice of such call to the general partners.

Illustration 9-2 (cont.)

d. *Amendment of Limited Partnership Agreement.* The limited partnership agreement may be amended by adoption of an amendment by action of the limited partners in accordance with Section ___152___ of the limited partnership agreement.

SECTION 20. FINANCIAL STATEMENTS OF ENTITY

___153___ *[At this point attach audited balance sheet of program as of the end of most recent fiscal year, and unaudited balance sheet as of a date not more than* ___154___ *(90) days prior to date of filing].*

SECTION 21. FINANCIAL STATEMENTS OF THE CORPORATE SPONSOR

___155___ *[Set forth three years' profit and loss statements, the most recent fiscal year-end balance sheet, and interim statements for the following entities in the following order:*

(a) *For the corporate sponsor:*

(1) Reproduction of independent accountant's opinion.

(2) Balance sheet.

(3) Statement of income for at least three years.

(4) Analysis of changes in stockholders' equity for at least three years.

(5) Statement of changes in financial position for at least past three years.

(6) Footnotes.

(b) *Financial statements of material, unconsolidated subsidiaries.*

(c) *[If business(es) is/are being acquired concurrently with offering or have been acquired subsequent to balance sheet date, insert formal financial statements].*

Illustration 9-2 (cont.)

§ 21:51 REAL PROPERTY

SECTION 22. LIMITED PARTNERSHIP AGREEMENT

In addition to various pertinent provisions of the limited partnership agreement which have been summarized previously in this prospectus, for a complete reproduction of the limited partnership agreement, see Appendix __156__ [A].

SECTION 23. EXHIBITS

A complete copy of the agreement of limited partnership to be entered into between the general partners and each limited partner individually is attached as Appendix __157__ to this prospectus. __158_____ [A copy of the certificate of limited partnership is attached as Appendix __159__]. Each prospective investor and his or her professional counselors should read the partnership agreement in its entirety.

[Add appendices.]

Tax Notes:

See § 21:11 regarding the possibility of requesting a ruling as to the partnership's tax status.

SECTION 15

For discussion of the federal tax consequences respecting syndicates organized as limited partnerships, see §§ 21:11 et seq., As to drafting the prospectus for discussion of such tax consequences, see § 21:35.

Practice Notes:

This form should be considered as an example of the kinds of disclosures frequently made with respect to "Nonspecified property programs" organized as limited partnerships. It should be noted that each prospectus must be carefully tailored to disclose the particulars of its offering. Such particulars may or may not conform to the disclosures contained in this form.

For convenience, the body of this prospectus is divided into numbered sections. However, the common practice with regard to prospectuses offered to potential investors is to omit the numbering of the sections.

As to preparation of a prospectus generally, see § 21:32. For a comprehensive checklist of suggested contents, depending on the circumstances, see § 21:41.

SECTION 3

For discussion of considerations respecting statements of risk factors, see § 21:33.

SECTION 5

For regulatory provisions respecting suitability of the participants, see *10 Cal C Reg §§ 260.140.112.1, 260.140.112.2.*

Illustration 9-2 (cont.)

SECTION 7

The description of the impound condition reflects current practice among nonspecified property programs and is also intended to satisfy the regulations of the Department of Corporations.

SECTION 9

As drafted, this section presupposes that the general partners are the only principals involved in formation of the partnership. Should other principals be involved, similar information with respect to them should be included.

With respect to appraisals of real property acquisitions, see *10 Cal C Reg § 260.140.114.12* and for requirements regarding the retention of records, see *10 Cal C Reg § 260.140.116.4.*

SECTION 10

This section is designed for the situation where the general partners are the only principals involved in formation of the partnership. Should other principals be involved, similar information with respect to them should be included [see *10 Cal C Reg §§ 260.140.111.1 to 260.140.111.5]*. For information regarding the rights of limited partners, see 10 Cal C Reg § 260.140.116.2 and for reports required to be furnished to limited partners, see *10 Cal C Reg § 260.140.116.3.* The substance of this section will be affected by the types of restrictions placed on the general partners by the succeeding section.

SECTION 11

This section reflects the situation in which only general partners and their affiliates will receive a direct or indirect interest or profit from the promotion and management of the partnership. If any other persons will receive these interests of profits, such persons, and their interest or profit, should be reveal. [See *10 Cal C Reg §§ 260.113.4, 260.140.113.5].*

SECTION 20

This section provides for the inclusion of required financial information. The particular documents are specified with the presumption that the program organized pursuant to this form will not have any assets or have conducted operations prior to the qualification of the program with the Department of Corporations. [See *10 Cal C Reg §§ 260.140.111.2, 260.140.111.3.]*

§ 21:52 Prospectus provision—Alternative statement of investment objectives—Government sponsored programs

The general objective of the partnership is to invest in new and existing low-and moderate-income rental housing projects financially assisted by federal, state, or municipal governments. The investment objective is to provide a return on investment which consists in large part of tax losses available for offset against other taxable income of the limited partners. These losses arise principally from the

Illustration 9-2 (cont.)

large, noncash expense of depreciation and, to a lesser extent, expenses during the period of construction of each project. Under the current provisions of the Internal Revenue Code, subject to provisions governing passive losses and credits, owners of new residential realty are permitted to claim the depreciation deduction calculated on an accelerated basis such as 200% declining balance, 150% declining balance, or sum-of-the-years digits methods. HUD rehabilitation projects may also be written off over a five-year period, using straight line depreciation. In addition, the owners' bases for calculating depreciation will be the cost of acquiring the project, including the amount of the mortgage loan for which none of the owners is personally liable (a "nonrecourse mortgage loan"), and including a "premium" paid to the seller of the project if the cost to the partnership exceeds the cost to the seller-developer. Since it is expected that approximately ________ percent (____%) of the cost of development of each project will be financed with a government insured nonrecourse mortgage loan, the partnership will be able to claim over a period of years depreciation deductions on each project that, together with other expenses, are expected to exceed rental income from such projects. The resulting net losses will pass through to the partners. The amount of such losses allocable to each limited partner's taxable income from other sources can, over a period of years, substantially exceed the amount of the limited partner's investment in the partnership. The amount of losses so available will, however, decrease over a period of years, and will be exhausted within approximately __2__ years. The partnership will also seek, to a lesser extent, to acquire interests in projects best offering the possibility of cash return, or long-term capital gain, so long as such projects provide tax benefits to the limited partners.

The partnership will attempt to make each of its investments at a sufficiently early stage in the project's development to entitle it, as the first user, to utilize accelerated depreciation methods as provided in the Internal Revenue Code.

Illustration 9-2 (cont.)

The following are some of the partnership's investment policies:

1. Except for temporary investments, the partnership's investments will be limited to investments in government-sponsored projects. The partnership may reinvest the proceeds resulting from the refinancing of any mortgages on projects, or from any sale or disposition of projects in other governmental sponsored projects. The partnership intends to seek diversification by investing in projects located in various parts of the State of California.

2. The partnership will probably not develop projects initially, but ultimately, development may be needed in order to secure and finance projects. Any construction will be done at competitive costs if done by the partnership or any of its affiliates.

3. The partnership will not acquire less than a majority interest in any project. Generally, the partnership will advance a portion of its investment on or after the date on which the governmental agency assisting the project has insured the construction loan (initial closing), an additional amount on or after the date such agency has insured the permanent mortgage loan (final closing), and the balance when the developer has met all other conditions of the purchase or construction contract.

4. Projects will be acquired primarily for federal income tax benefits and, to a lesser extent, cash distributions and long-term capital appreciation. Projects will not be acquired with a view to early resale. Government agencies must sanction any sale or refinancing proposal as long as the project remains government financed.

5. The partnership will only make loans to projects in connection with the acquisition or preservation of interests in projects. No loans will be made to the general partners, or any of their affiliates.

6. The partnership will not repurchase or otherwise reacquire the interests after they have been sold. The partnership

Illustration 9-2 (cont.)

§ 21:52 REAL PROPERTY

will invest in income properties financed by government programs that will, in the opinion of the general partners, produce distributable income, tax shelter, and capital appreciation for the limited partners.

Among the techniques to be utilized in attempting to achieve these objectives are the following:

a. The general partners will undertake extensive research and monitoring of potential government-financed real property investments throughout California.

b. Investments will generally not be made in real estate unless there is a projected ____[3]______ percent (____%) tax write-off of the partnership's cash investment in a project.

Government-financed real estate investments necessarily involve certain risks resulting from unforeseeable changes in the economy and in the supply and demand of certain kinds of property in certain areas. The general partners will attempt to minimize these risks through the acquisition of properties located in diverse geographical areas principally within California. To the extent that such diversity is achieved it is reasonable to expect that it will lessen the partnership's exposure to loss resulting from shifting economic conditions.

The general partners will attempt to make full use of leverage with respect to all real property investments. Thus, in most instances, property will be purchased for a cash investment not to exceed ____[4]______ percent (____%) of the total purchase price with the balance to be paid by a government-insured nonrecourse mortgage loan. The holders of such notes and mortgages will be limited to the property itself as security for the debt, and in no event will any of the limited partners be personally liable for any of the obligations of the partnership.

Practice Notes:

For a discussion of applicable depreciations methods generally, see *26 USCS §§ 168 et seq.*

Texts: For discussion of state government programs, see 51 CAL JUR 3d, Public Housing.

For discussion of federal government programs, see 40 AM JUR 2d, Housing Laws and Urban Redevelopment.

10
THE PAPERWORK

With unerring vision and wit, Charles Dickens noted the irony of administrating an office when he noted in *David Copperfield:* "Skewered through and through with office pens and bound hand and foot with red tape. . ." The red tape involved in the syndication process can appear staggering to the would-be investor. Disclosures here, financial data there, partnership agreements, subscriptions, conveyances of property, purchase agreements, escrow instructions - the list seems endless. Such is the life of the syndicator-sponsor of a project. When the cascades of paper start flying around the office, it's time to seek the solitude of wise counsel to sort out all of the nooks and crannies which represent one project and create and artful presentation which will satisfy the letter of the law while seeking some semblance of clarity for investors who become befuddled by all the "red tape."

MEETING LEGAL REQUIREMENTS

Legal requirements, in the final analysis, are a function of the type of entity chosen by the syndicator. The limited partnership form is a frequent choice, since the option exists of going on a private or public basis. In either event, the vicissitudes of the regulatory process must be addressed.

Probably one of the greatest strengths any promotor of a syndication may possess is a background in the securities industry. Secondarily, experience as a real estate licensee, with appropriate endorsement by the Department of Real Estate, who has had experience in the marketing of limited partnership units.

It is important at an early stage of the process to engage counsel to deal with the mountains of paperwork required to comply with all of the legal requirements necessary to form a syndicate. For example, in California, if the syndicate involves 100 or more investors, the Department of

Corporations is involved to the extent that an application must be submitted by the syndicator for permission to sell investment units to the proposed limited partners. Illustrations of some of this paperwork are shown in the Appendix. Other items shown in the Appendix indicate the vast influence that the Securities and Exchange Commission has exerted on the nature and content of limited partnership offerings as securities marketed to the general public.

To provide some order out of chaos, there are check lists available to the syndicator and legal counsel to assist them in the preparation of their documentation. Typical of these check lists is the one shown as Illustration 9-1 in Chapter nine. They become a forced reminder of the types of items that must be addressed in preparing the basic document addressed. In the case of the prospectus, for example, it forces the syndicator to make a variety of decisions about the project at a very early stage in the process. It should be noted that a prospectus form for non-specified uses was shown as an example. **This is not an endorsement to undertake non specified offerings.** There are valid arguments on the side of entertaining an offering for the acquisition of a specific project, since the uses for the funds can be readily identified. In the case of a non specified offering, the monies would be used to undertake certain investment objectives of the partnership which may reduce themselves to specified investments at a later time. For example, a promotor of a non specified syndicate may have the objective of obtaining equity interests in real estate owned from financial institutions and regulatory agencies on the basis of hard-nosed negotiations using a well-balanced plan of equity and leverage to maximize return to the limited partnership. This strategy inherently has the element of risk of the marketplace while balance with the potential rewards of substantial return plus appreciation to lure limited partner investors. The promotor may have several projects under study, but not be sure which will be included within the syndicate. For this reason, the non specified, or "blind pool" approach might be used to attract the needed acquisition capital.

In the latter case noted above, legal counsel is essential in the preparation of promotional material which will comply with the disclosure requirements adhering to SEC Guide 5 and NASAA specifications. Some of the more pertinent matters relevant to the sponsor should be addressed by counsel. Specifically, sponsor background should be covered in detail. NASAA notes that ". . .a Sponsor, the general partner or their chief operating officers should have at least two years relevant real estate or other experience demonstrating the knowledge and experience to acquire and manage the type of assets being acquired, and any of the foregoing or any AFFILIATE proving services to the PROGRAM shall have had not less than four years relevant experience in the kind of service being rendered or otherwise must demonstrate sufficient knowledge and experience to perform the services proposed. . ."

In the experience noted above, the sponsor cannot substitute experience in the residential housing market for office building acquisition, since these markets are separate and distinct from each other requiring quite different management techniques and financial analysis.

In addition, NASAA notes that the sponsor should meet certain minimum levels of financial strength, represented by net worth. In addressing this subject in the guidelines, it states: "The financial condition of the SPONSOR liable for the debts of the PROGRAM must be commensurate with any financial obligations assumed in the offering and in the operation of the PROGRAM. As a minimum, such SPONSOR shall have an aggregate financial NET WORTH, exclusive of home, automobile and home furnishings, or the greater of either $50,000 or an amount at least equal to 5% of the gross amount of all offerings sold within the prior 12 months plus 5% of the gross amount of the current offering, to an aggregate maximum net worth of such sponsor of one million dollars. In determining NET WORTH for this purpose, evaluation will be made of contingent liabilities and the use of promissory notes, to determine the appropriateness of this inclusion in computation of NET WORTH. . ."

The promissory note statement is in reference to the fact that the asset shown on the sponsor's financial statement may be fallacious if the maker of the note does not have the financial ability to repay the obligation.

In studying these guidelines, a typical sponsor financial statement is provided for analysis under the conditions noted.

IRVING SPONSOR
FINANCIAL STATEMENT AS OF 12-31-19__

ASSETS		LIABILITIES	
Cash	$250,000	Accounts payable	$300,000
Notes Rec.	400,000	Notes payable s/t	275,000
Accts. Rec.	250,000	Notes pay- Residence	250,000
Securities- Marketable	750,000	Term note	550,000
Securities- Closely held	500,000	Notes pay. other r.e.	750,000
C.V.L.I.	50,000	Total liabilities	$2,125,000
Real Estate- Residence	350,000	Net Worth	610,000
Real Estate- Other	1,000,000		
Automobiles	50,000		
Personal Prop.	35,000		
Total	$2,735,000	Totals	$2,735,000

After removing the $100,000 equity in the personal residence, plus the $85,000 representing the automobiles and personal property, the net worth that can be used for comparison is $425,000. Based upon the 5% requirement noted above, the sponsor would be limited to the past years offerings plus the current offering totalling $8,500,000. This figure could be reduced even more if the note receivable for $250,000 and the closely held stock of $500,000 were held to be of little or no value. In that case, the sponsor would not qualify financially. Also there is the possibility that the sponsor may lease space with an outstanding remaining obligation on a lease for the next three years totalling another $250,000, which would have to be considered, thus reducing fundraising capabilities accordingly.

Sponsors should candidly discuss their financial affairs with counsel and be advised concerning the disclosure thereof, since this is an item which can instill investor confidence in the sponsorship of any project.

The principal risk taker in any limited partnership project is the general partner-sponsor(s). For this reason there is great temptation to obtain indemnifications from the limited partners vis a vis the general partner's liability. The NASAA has specific guidelines concerning the appropriateness of indemnification. It notes: "The partnership agreement shall not provide for indemnification of the SPONSOR for any liability or loss suffered by the SPONSOR, nor shall it provide that the SPONSOR be held harmless for any loss or liability suffered by the partnership, unless all of the following conditions are met:

1) The SPONSOR has determined, in good faith, that the course of conduct which caused the loss or liability was in the best interests of the partnership, and
2) such liability or loss was not the result of negligence or misconduct by the SPONSOR, and
3) such indemnification or agreement to hold harmless is recoverable only out of the assets of the partnership and not from the limited partners.

Indemnification of the SPONSORS or their affiliates will not be allowed for any liability imposed by judgment, and costs associated therewith, including attorney's fees, arising from or out of a violation of state or federal securities laws associated with the offer and sale of partnership units. Indemnification will be allowed for settlements and related expenses of lawsuits alleging securities law violations, and for expenses incurred in successfully defending such lawsuits, provided that the court either:

1) approves the settlement and finds that indemnification of the settlement and related costs should be made, or

2) approves indemnification of litigation costs if a successful defense is made. . ."

The NASAA guidelines, as previously noted, go beyond the structure of SEC Guide 5. Both of these documents are provided in the Appendix for further investigation.

It can be seen that the assemblage of documentation of even the simplest of limited partnerships containing a handful of sophisticated limited partners provides a challenge to the sharpest of legal minds. This justifies the sponsor seeking competent counsel as a means of meeting both state and federal standards in assemblage of the offering and processing it to acquisition.

SYNDICATION OFFERING CIRCULAR

In noting the checklist outlined in Illustration 9-1 as well as the sample form shown as Illustration 9-2, the attention to the slightest detail by the syndicator in preparing the offering package is critical right down to opinion of counsel relative to tax and legal consequences of the partnership investment on the part of the limited partners. Through careful adherence to the guidelines of the check list, pitfalls of improper disclosure can be reduced to a minimum.

In preparing the offering, other documents are shown as exhibits thereto. The important thing to remember in the preparation of any offering, public or private is to provide the necessary balance to the investors of the upside as well as the downside aspects of the offering itself. For example, when it comes to investment in commercial office buildings, this market is extremely sensitive to shifts in the economy where firms tend to downsize their operations. This, in turn, reduces their need for office space. On the other hand, new construction in office space has subsided in the past few years allowing demand to catch up with supply. This lack of new construction is a positive argument for the potential of future appreciation of this type of property in the future. Naturally, the selection of location for this type of investment is critical, since economic conditions are not uniform throughout the country.

Sponsors must recognize that the offering circular (known in corporate circles with new stock offerings as a "red herring") is one of the key marketing documents in the solicitation of limited partner contribution for purchasing shares in the venture. Extreme care should be taken that it is not perceived by the limited partners that the general partner(s) are taking the lion's share of the profits from the projects leaving scraps of yield not commensurate with the risk of the venture. NASAA provides guidelines along for appropriate allocation of profits as well, further noted in the appendix.

ACQUISITION INSTRUMENTS

The device used for funds acquisition in a limited partnership situation is the subscription form attached to the limited partnership agreement. In order to assure protection for the funds so deposited, a holding escrow is created by the sponsor to collect the funds necessary for investment meeting the project objectives. A check list for the preparation of the syndicate limited partnership agreement along with a sample subscription agreement samples are shown as Illustration 10-1.

In reviewing the aforementioned checklist in preparation for creating the limited partnership agreement, the sponsor must pay particular attention to the financial details of the transaction to be assured that there is adequate capital available for acquisition, consultant fees, closing costs and working capital for the initial months of operating the acquired property to achieve the improvement in cash flow performance required to enhance value. With this thought in mind, the basic structure of the statement of limited partnership will follow the pattern outlined in the sample form shown as Illustration 10-2. The reader will note that this form is prepared along the lines of a public offering. If one is to approach the syndication process in an orderly manner, public offerings will result as the operation takes on projects of larger scope. The form deals with a variety of issues incidental to the acquisition, management and disposition of partnership property as well as reporting requirements, sale of partnership units and dissolution matters. Each area of this form should be examined by potential investors with due regard to their own personal situation. If the nature and thrust of the partnership does not fit into the investors patterned objective, it should not be pursued as a suitable investment vehicle. The optional provisions sections are designed to tailor the limited partnership to the needs of a particular project, since the type and nature of the services provided by the general partner/sponsor may vary due to background and experience.

Illustration 10-1

CHECKLISTS

§ 21:81 Matters to include or consider for inclusion in a real estate syndicate limited partnership agreement[18]

1. Names and addresses of partners.
   a. General partner(s).
   b. Initial limited partner(s).
2. Statement of formation of partnership.
   a. Citation of statute according to which limited partnership formed.
3. Name and principal place of business of partnership.
4. Recordation of certificate of limited partnership.
5. Term of partnership.
   a. Date or occurrence on which partnership commences.
6. Purpose and objectives of partnership.
   a. Acquisition and/or development of specific realty.
      (1) Description, general and legal.
      (2) Type of development.
      (3) Method of holding title.

---

17. For general forms of powers of attorney, and related text, see POWERS OF ATTORNEY (Ch 30A).

18. Items marked with an asterisk (*) are required by the California Code of Regulations *(10 Cal C Reg §§ 260.140.111.5 et seq.)* to be included in the agreement.

Illustration 10-1 (cont.)

b. Restrictions and conditions for nonspecified property programs, including *[10 Cal C Reg §§ 260.140.115.3]*
   (1) Restrictions on acquisition of unimproved or non-income producing property.*
   (2) Restrictions on investments in junior trust deeds and similar obligations.*
   (3) Indications of maximum amount of aggregate indebtedness which may be incurred by program.*
   (4) Manner in which acquisitions are to be financed, including:
      (a) All-inclusive note or wrap around.*
      (b) Leveraging.*
   (5) Indication whether program will enter into joint venture arrangements, and extent of them.* *[10 Cal C Reg § 260.140.115.6]*

c. Restriction on reinvestment of proceeds to effect that proceeds resulting from disposition or refinancing of property may not be reinvested unless sufficient cash will be distributed to pay state or federal income tax created by such disposition or refinancing.* *[10 Cal C Reg § 260.140.118.3]*

7. Capitalization.
   a. Number of authorized units.
      (1) Possibility of increase in authorized number.
      (2) Right of limited partners to first choice of purchase of additional units.
   b. Classes of authorized units.
   c. Minimum number of units required to be purchased.
   d. Value of partnership unit of each class.
   e. General partner's capital contribution, if any.
   f. Allocation of contributed capital.
      (1) Account for purchase of property.

Illustration 10-1 (cont.)

SYNDICATION—LIMITED PARTNERSHIPS § 21:81

(2) Repurchase reserve account.
(3) Operating reserve account.
(4) Disposition of proceeds awaiting investment in real property.* *[10 Cal C Reg § 260.140.115.4]*

g. If allowed, possibility of exchange of limited partnership interests for property.* *[10 Cal C Reg § 260.140.114.2]*

8. Admission of limited partners.
   a. Option of general partners to refuse admission.
   b. Time within which potential partner must be rejected or admitted.* *[10 Cal C Reg § 260.140.116.5(a)]*
   c. Qualifications for admission.

9. Escrow account pending accumulation of initial contributions.
   a. Minimum total contribution prior to release of funds.
   b. Interest on contributions while in escrow.

10. Classification of limited partners.
    a. Registered limited partners.
    b. Substituted limited partners.
    c. Assignees, including time when assignee recognized as such.* *[10 Cal C Reg § 260.140.116.5(b)]*
    d. Distinction between rights of various classes.

11. Substitution of assignee as limited partner.
    a. Prerequisites to substitution.
    b. Required action by general partner.
    c. Time of substitution.

12. Powers and rights of general partners.
    a. Selection and acquisition of real estate, including necessity of appraisal.* *[10 Cal C Reg § 260.140.114.13]*
    b. Expenditures of partnership capital.

Illustration 10-1 (cont.)

§ 21:81 REAL PROPERTY

c. Management of partnership property, including:
   (1) Hiring of personnel management or firms.
   (2) Execution of management agreements.
d. General authority to execute agreements for the partnership.
e. Authority to engage in other business ventures and employment.
f. Authority to sell, lease, trade, exchange, or dispose of partnership property.
   (1) Degree of discretion allowed.
   (2) Restriction on sale of all property.
   (3) Prohibition of exclusive right to sell or exclusive employment to sell property for program property.
   (4) Prohibition of any commissions on reinvestment of proceeds of the resale, exchange, or refinancing of program property.* *[10 Cal C Reg § 260.140.114.4]*
g. Restrictions on pledging of partnership assets.
h. Hypothecation of partnership property.
i. Maintenance of partnership books and records.
j. Purchase of property from and sale of property to partnership.
k. Reimbursement for expenses and fees incurred by general partners.* *[10 Cal C Reg § 260.140.114.5]*
l. Cash loans to partnership.
   (1) Conditions and restrictions for such loans.* *[10 Cal C Reg § 260.140.114.1(c)]*
   (2) Interest rates.
   (3) Manner and source of repayment.
   (4) Characterization of advances as loans rather than capital contribution.
   (5) Provision for repayment on termination and dissolution of partnership.
m. Management of partnership litigation.
n. Prohibition against sponsor's receipt of rebates or

Illustration 10-1 (cont.)

SYNDICATION—LIMITED PARTNERSHIPS § 21:81

give-ups or participation in reciprocal business arrangements circumventing such restrictions.* *[10 Cal C Reg § 260.140.114.7]*

13. Restrictions on liability of general partners; indemnification.
    a. Acts for which general partners not to be liable.
    b. Acts for which general partners to be indemnified by partnership.
    c. Extent of indemnification.
14. Duties of general partners.
    a. Devotion of reasonable time and skill.
    b. Disclaimer as to necessity to devote all time.
    c. Delineation of sponsor's fiduciary responsibility.* *[10 Cal C Reg § 260.140.111.5]*
15. Rights and responsibilities of limited partners.
    a. Liability for assessments.
    b. Extent of liability for partnership losses.
        (1) Capital contribution.
        (2) Capital contribution plus share of undistributed net profits.
    c. Inspection rights.
        (1) Material subject to inspection.
        (2) Time and place of access.
        (3) Requests for information by mail.
    d. Rights to current income and disposition proceeds (see Item 24, below).
    e. Voting rights.
        (1) Majority of outstanding limited partnership interests may, without concurrence of general partner(s)* *[10 Cal C Reg § 260.140.116.2]*
            (a). Amend limited partnership agreement;
            (b). Dissolve program;
            (c). Remove general partner(s) and elect a new one;

Illustration 10-1 (cont.)

(d). Approve or disapprove the sale of all or substantially all program's assets.

16. Reports to limited partners.* *[10 Cal C Reg § 260.140.116.3]*
    a. Annual report and audit.
        (1) Preparation by independent CPA.
        (2) Time for delivery.
        (3) Inclusion of balance sheet; statement of income; cash flow statement.
    b. Semiannual reports and quarterly (special) reports.
    c. Tax return reports.
17. Transfer of units.
    a. Partners capable of transfer.
    b. Registration procedures.
    c. Minimum number of units transferable.
    d. Required instruments.
    e. Transfer fee.
18. Effect of death or incompetence of individual limited partner.
19. Establishment of repurchase reserve account.
    a. Establishment by general partners.
    b. Allocation of funds to account.
    c. Use of reserves to repurchase units.
        (1) Holding period before repurchase of units.
        (2) Minimum number of units subject to repurchase.
        (3) Cash price of repurchased units.
        (4) Resale of repurchased units.
        (5) Prohibition against repurchase if partnership liabilities cannot be satisfied.
        (6) Rights of limited partners after repurchase of their units.

rmination and dissolution.
    Action by limited partners.
        (1) Method.
        (2) Required vote.

Illustration 10-1 (cont.)

- b. Formation of new partnership after dissolution.
- c. Liquidation.
  - (1) Persons to be in charge of liquidation.
  - (2) Order of distribution of assets.
  - (3) Appraisal of assets.

21. Removal of general partner by limited partners.
    - a. Provision for continuation of partnership by other general partner, if any.
    - b. Rights of terminated general partner.
      - (1) Valuation of general partner's interest.
      - (2) Medium of payment for general partner's interest.

22. Compensation of general partners.
    - a. Sale to partnership of assets owned by general partner.
    - b. Broker's commissions.* *[10 Cal C Reg § 260.140.113.6]*
    - c. Contractors' fees.
    - d. Participation interest.* *[10 Cal C Reg § 260.140.113.4]*
      - (1) In partnership income.
      - (2) In profits on sale of partnership assets.
    - e. Management fees.* *[10 Cal C Reg § 260.140.113.5]*
    - f. Interest on loans to partnership.
    - g. Contracts between partnership and affiliate of general partner.

23. Compensation of agents.
    - a. Fees for acquisition of real property.
    - b. Real estate brokerage fees.
    - c. Mortgage servicing fees.
    - d. Distribution fees.
    - e. Sales commissions.
    - f. Reimbursement for certain expenses and fees.

Illustration 10-1 (cont.)

24. Distributions to holders of units.
    a. Definition of all relevant terms.
    b. Partnership income.
    c. Proceeds from the sale of assets.
    d. Cumulative or noncumulative right to return on initial invested capital.
    e. Compliance with regulatory standards respecting distributions.

25. Details concerning losses.
    a. Definition of terms.
    b. Time of computation.
    c. Method of computation.
    d. Method of allocation.

26. Amendment of agreement.
    a. Parties authorized to make amendments.
    b. Required vote.
        (1). Amendment by majority of limited partners [see Item 15a, above].
        (2). Amendments requiring unanimous vote.
            (a) Change from limited to general partnership.
            (b) Authorization to general partners to do acts otherwise prohibited by partnership agreement.
    c. Amendments not requiring approval by limited partners.
        (1) Change of partnership name.
        (2) Change of partnership's principal place of business.
        (3) Change in place of residence of partner.
        (4) Change in amount or character of capital contributions.
        (5) Substitution or withdrawal of limited partner.
    d. Time when amendment takes effect.

Illustration 10-1 (cont.)

27. Meetings of limited partners.
    a. Call.
        (1) By general partners.
        (2) By certain percentage of the voting power of limited partners.
    b. Notice.
        (1) Form.
        (2) Time in which to be given.
    c. Quorum.
    d. Allocation of voting power.
    e. Adjournment procedures.
    f. Action by limited partners without meeting.
28. Power of attorney to general partner from limited partners.
    a. Duplicate power contained in subscription agreement, if such instrument is primary medium for grant of the power.
    b. Scope (special or general).
    c. Duration.
    d. Power to be coupled with an interest.
29. Details concerning notices.
30. Severability of invalid provisions.
31. Governing law.
32. Binding effect of agreement.
33. Waiver of right to action for partition.
34. Interpretation of captions and headings.
35. Date.
36. Signatures.

§ 21:82 Matters to include or consider for inclusion in subscription agreement

1. Name and principal place of business of partnership.
2. Name and address of subscriber.

Illustration 10-1 (cont.)

3. Statement of subscription.
   a. Number of units subscribed for.
   b. Cost per unit.
   c. Total dollar amount.
4. Medium of payment for subscription.
5. Statement respecting impound of proceeds of subscriptions.
   a. Escrow holder.
   b. Minimum amount needed before escrow ended.
   c. Payment of interest on escrow funds.
6. Conditions respecting rejection or acceptance of subscription.
   a. Responsibility for acceptance or rejection.
   b. Time limit for required action.
   c. Effect of inaction.
7. Acknowledgments by subscriber.
   a. Knowledge of contents of prospectus and limited partnership agreement.
   b. Knowledge of degree of risk of the enterprise.
8. Information for intrastate offerings.
   a. Statement of subscriber's residence.
   b. Information respecting subscriber's financial suitability.
   c. Information required by state Security Commissioner.
9. Power of attorney.
   a. Statement of specific powers granted.
   b. Duration of power.
   c. Grant of power coupled with an interest.
   d. Grant of power of substitution.
10. How title to limited partnership interests is to be held.
    a. Separate property.
    b. Community property.
    c. Joint ownership.

Illustration 10-1 (cont.)

11. Date.

12. Signatures.

SUBSCRIPTION AGREEMENTS AND RELATED INSTRUMENTS

§ 21:91 Signature page for limited partnership

SIGNATURE PAGE FOR LIMITED PARTNERS OF

__1_____ *[NAME OF PARTNERSHIP]*

The undersigned, __2_____, applies for the issuance and sale to __3_____ [him *or* her] of __4__ *[number]* units (a minimum of __5__ units) of limited partnership interest in __6_____ *[name of partnership]* (the partnership) at a cost of __7_____ Dollars ($____) per unit. The undersigned delivers with this document a check in the amount of __8_____ Dollars ($____) (a minimum of $____) as __9_____ [his *or* her] capital contribution for such units. By executing this signature page the undersigned acknowledges receipt of the prospectus of __10_____ *[partnership]*; accepts and agrees to be bound by all provisions of the __11_____ [*if applicable,* amended] certificate and agreement of limited partnership (the agreement) and agrees to become a limited partner of __12_____ *[partnership]*; irrevocably makes, constitutes, and appoints __13_____ *[name(s) of the general partner(s)]*, with full power of substitution, __14_____ [his *or* her] true and lawful attorney-in-fact for the purposes and in the manner provided in Section __15__ of the agreement; and confirms __16_____ [his *or* her] understanding that the general partner(s) will have full right to accept or reject this application. Upon acceptance of this application by the general partner(s), the undersigned will receive a confirma-

Illustration 10-1 (cont.)

tion of such acceptance executed by the general partner(s).

Dated __17______.

NAME

RESIDENCE

SIGNATURE

(If units are to be registered in the names of more than one person, all such persons must sign.)

Practice Notes:

As to use and drafting of signature pages and subscription agreements, see § 21:75; for pertinent checklist, see § 21:82.

If partnership interest are to be distributed as intrastate offerings the residence of prospective purchasers should be verified. For information sheet designed to elicit the necessary information for such verification, see § 21:95.

§ 21:92 Subscription agreement

__1______ *[NAME OF PARTNERSHIP]*

SUBSCRIPTION AGREEMENT To: __2______
[Name of limited partner]

The undersigned, __3______, recognizes that the purchase of limited partnership units in __4______ *[partnership]* is a long-term investment and involves a risk. The undersigned also acknowledges that there is no present public market for the units, thus liquidation of my investment in the event of an emergency may not be possible, transferability is recognized as limited, and in the event of a disposition a loss may be sustained.

The undersigned understands that commencing the effective date of the prospectus, all funds received by the general partner(s) from subscriptions for limited partnership units will be placed in an escrow account at __5______ *[bank]*, of __6______ *[address]*. If __7__ *[number]* units have not been subscribed for by __8______ *[date]*, all funds will be released from the escrow account and returned promptly to each subscriber __9______ [without interest *or* with interest as provided in Section __10__ of the limited partnership agreement]. At such time as subscriptions for __11__ *[number]*

Illustration 10-1 (cont.)

SYNDICATION—LIMITED PARTNERSHIPS § 21:92

units have been received (but not later than ___12___ *[date])*, all funds received from the sale of units will be released from escrow and distributed to the general partner(s) on behalf of the limited partnership.

1. The undersigned by this agreement subscribes for ___13___ units consisting of limited partnership interests in ___14___ *[partnership]*, a limited partnership organized under the California Revised Limited Partnership Act, and being offered by ___15___, as general partner(s), pursuant to a prospectus effective ___16___ *[date]*, (the prospectus), at a purchase price of ___17___ Dollars ($____) per unit. The undersigned tenders with this agreement the sum of ___18___ Dollars ($____) per unit in payment for such interests, which payment is made by check or money order. The amount so tendered will be returned promptly if ___19___ [number] units, the required minimum number of units, are not subscribed and paid for pursuant to the terms of the prospectus. The total amount tendered with this agreement is ___20___ Dollars ($____).

2. The undersigned represents and warrants that the units subscribed for are not being purchased for and will not be transferred in such a manner as to cause subdivision or fractionalization of such units, and are purchased solely for the account of the undersigned or for the account of such persons as the undersigned lawfully represents. The undersigned acknowledges receipt of a copy of the prospectus and the limited partnership agreement and represents and warrants that ___21___ [he *or* she] has read and is thoroughly familiar with such documents and is aware of the degree of risk involved in making an investment in the limited partnership. ___22___ [It is understood, however, that this representation does not constitute a waiver of any rights that the undersigned has or may have under the Securities Act of 1933 or rules and regulations promulgated under such Act.]

3. The undersigned understands and agrees that this subscription is made subject to each of the following terms and conditions:

Illustration 10-1 (cont.)

(a) The general partner(s) will have the right to accept or reject this subscription, in whole or in part. Upon receipt of each subscription agreement, the general partner(s) will have __23__ days in which to accept or reject it. If no action is taken by the general partner(s) within such period, the subscription will be deemed to have been accepted. In each case where a subscription is rejected, the general partner(s) will send written notice of such rejection to the subscriber within such period and will direct the escrow holder to return the entire amount submitted by the subscriber, __24__ [without interest *or* with interest as prescribed in the limited partnership agreement]. In each case where the subscription is accepted by the general partner(s) on behalf of the partnership, the general partner(s) on behalf of the partnership will execute the limited partnership agreement on behalf of the subscriber, as provided in the power of attorney provisions of this subscription agreement, and will return an executed copy to the new limited partner as confirmation of acceptance.

(b) The copy of the limited partnership agreement to be delivered if this subscription is accepted by the general partner(s) will be delivered only to the undersigned.

4. The undersigned makes, constitutes, and appoints __25__ [the general partner *or if more than one general partner, give names]* with full power of substitution, the undersigned's true and lawful attorney(s) for the undersigned and in __26__ [his *or* her] name, place, and stead and for the undersigned's use and benefit:

(a) To sign and acknowledge, file, and record all necessary documents, including, but not limited to:

(1) The limited partnership agreement in the form set forth in the prospectus, the certificate of limited partnership and any amendments to it, and any assumed or fictitious name certificates that may be required or appropriate in any jurisdiction in which the partnership intends to conduct business; and

(2) Any documents that may be required to effect a

Illustration 10-1 (cont.)

continuation of the partnership, the admission of any additional or substituted limited partner, or the dissolution and termination of the partnership; as well as

(b) To prepare, execute and file all forms, reports, documents or other instruments which may be required or requested by any agency or commission of the federal government or any state or local government in which the partnership may sell its units, acquire properties or do business; and

(c) To make certain elections contained in the Internal Revenue Code or state law governing taxation of partnerships.

5. The foregoing grant of authority:

(a) Is a special power of attorney coupled with an interest, is irrevocable, and will survive the death of the undersigned;

(b) May be exercised by __27______ [the general partner] for each limited partner by a facsimile signature of one of its officers or, if all limited partners are listed, by executing any instrument with a single signature of one of its officers acting as attorney in fact for all limited partners;

(c) Will survive the delivery of an assignment by a limited partner of the whole or any portion of his or her interest, except that if the assignee of it has been approved by the general partner(s) for admission to the partnership as a substituted limited partner, the power of attorney will survive the delivery of such assignment for the sole purpose of enabling the general partner to execute, acknowledge, and file any instrument necessary to effect such substitution.

In the event of any conflict between the provisions of the limited partnership agreement and any document executed or filed by the general partner(s) pursuant to this power of attorney, the limited partnership agreement will govern.

These limited partnership units are offered and purchased in the State of __28______ [California].

Number of units (at $__29__ per unit) __30__.

Illustration 10-1 (cont.)

§ 21:92 REAL PROPERTY

Total amount enclosed ($__31__ times number of units) __32_____ Dollars ($____).

The units subscribed for are to be owned by and registered in the name or names of __33_____ *[name(s)]* __34_____ [as tenants in common].

In witness of this agreement the undersigned has or have executed the subscription agreement at __35_____ on __36_____ *[date]*.

[Signature]

Accepted:

Dated __37_____.

[Signature]
[Title]

§ 21:93 Subscription agreement—With instructions to purchase

SUBSCRIPTION AGREEMENT

__1_____ *[NAME OF PARTNERSHIP]*
To: __2_____ *[Name of subscriber]*

The undersigned, by signing the Limited Partner Signature Page and Power of Attorney attached, tenders this subscription and applies for the purchase of the number of limited partnership interest (units), set forth below, in __3_____, a limited partnership organized under the California Revised Limited Partnership Act, (the partnership), at a price of __4_____ Dollars ($____) per unit (minimum purchase of __5__ Units), and encloses payment, in cash or certified check payable to __6_____ in the amount set forth below for such units. The undersigned understands that such funds will be held by the Bank of __7_____, as escrow agent, and will be returned promptly, together with any interest earned on them allocable to the undersigned in accordance with the prospectus, to the undersigned in the event that all of the units offered by the prospectus are not subscribed for and the payments for them are not made by

Illustration 10-1 (cont.)

__8______ *[date],* or such subsequent date, not later than __9______ *[date],* as the partnership and __10______, the undersigned may agree upon. The undersigned acknowledges receipt of a copy of the prospectus, as well as the Agreement of Limited Partnership (partnership agreement) of the partnership attached to the prospectus as Exhibit A, and specifically accepts and adopts each and every provision of the partnership agreement and agrees to be bound by it.

The undersigned represents and warrants to you as follows:

1. The undersigned has carefully read the prospectus and has relied solely upon the prospectus and investigations made by the undersigned or his, her, or its representatives in making the decision to invest in the partnership.

2. The undersigned is aware that investment in the units involves certain risk factors and has carefully read and considered the matters set forth under the captions "Management Compensation and Fees," "Conflicts of Interest," "Risk and Other Important Factors," and "Tax Aspects of an Investment in the Partnership" in the prospectus.

3. The undersigned is __11______ [eighteen (18)] years of age or over (if a natural person), has adequate means of providing for his, her, or its current needs and personal contingencies, and has no need for liquidity in this investment.

4. The undersigned, if executing the subscription agreement in a representative or fiduciary capacity, has full power and authority to execute and deliver this subscription agreement on behalf of the subscribing individual, ward, partnership, trust, estate, corporation, or other entity for whom the undersigned is executing this subscription agreement, and such individual, ward, partnership, trust, estate, corporation or other entity has full right and power to perform pursuant to the partnership agreement.

5. The undersigned represents that __12______ [he *or* she] (a) has a net worth (exclusive of home, home furnishings, and personal automobiles) exceeding the greater of (1)

Illustration 10-1 (cont.)

$100,00 in excess of the purchase price of the units subscribed for, or (2) four times the purchase price of the number of units subscribed for, and (b) expects to have during each of the current and the next 3 tax years, taxable income of ___13___ Dollars ($____) or more. The undersigned further represents that the undersigned meets the suitability standards set forth in any sticker to the prospectus to the extent such standards are applicable to the undersigned. The undersigned has net worth, past income, and estimated future income indicated on the Limited Partner Signature Page and Power of Attorney.

If the undersigned is purchasing the units subscribed for in a fiduciary capacity, the above representations and warranties will be deemed to have been made on behalf of the person or persons for whom the undersigned is so purchasing.

The undersigned understands and recognizes that:

1. The subscription may be accepted or rejected in whole or in part by the general partner in its sole and absolute discretion, except that, if this subscription is to be accepted in part only, it will not be reduced to an amount less than ___14___ Dollars ($____).

2. No federal or state agency has made any finding or determination as to the fairness for public investment, nor any recommendation or endorsement, of the units.

3. There are restrictions on the transferability of the units, there will be no public market for the units and, accordingly, it may not be possible for the undersigned readily, if at all, to liquidate his, her, or its investment in the partnership in case of an emergency.

The undersigned acknowledges and agrees that the undersigned is not entitled to cancel, terminate, or revoke this subscription or any agreements of the undersigned and that such subscription and agreements will survive the death or disability of the undersigned.

This subscription agreement and all rights under it are

Illustration 10-1 (cont.)

governed by, and interpreted in accordance with the laws of the State of California.

In witness of this agreement, the undersigned executes and agrees to be bound by this subscription agreement by executing the Limited Partner Signature Page and Power of Attorney attached on the date indicated.

INSTRUCTION TO PURCHASERS OF UNITS

Any person or entity desiring to subscribe for units should carefully read and review the attached prospectus and, if he or she or it desires to subscribe for units in the partnership, complete the following steps.

1. Complete the Limited Partnership Signature Page and Power of Attorney. It is essential that all information be provided and that the purchaser's signature be notarized. In the case where the units will be held in joint ownership, both purchasers must sign and both signatures must be notarized.

2. The purchaser should deliver to his, her, or its __15______ *[selected dealer]* the completed, executed, and notarized Limited Partner Signature Page and Power of Attorney together with payment, in cash or certified check payable to __16______, in the amount of __17______ Dollars ($____) for each unit that the purchaser desires to purchase.

3. The form of acknowledgment on the Limited Partner Signature Page and Power of Attorney attached as Schedule 1 is a form suitable for individuals, partnerships, and individual fiduciaries signing on behalf of trusts, estates, and in other capacities. Persons signing on behalf of corporations and corporate trustees should complete and affix to the Limited Partner Signature Page and Power of Attorney the form of corporate acknowledgment attached as Schedule 1.

4. Corporations, partnerships, and trustees, agents or persons acting in a representative capacity may be required, at the discretion of the general partner, to furnish with the Limited Partner Signature Page and Power of Attorney further evidence that such subscriber has the authority to

Illustration 10-1 (cont.)

become a Limited Partner in this partnership or an opinion of counsel, acceptable to the General Partner, that the subscriber has such authority, such opinion to be attached as Schedule 2.

___18___ *[NAME OF PARTNERSHIP]*

LIMITED PARTNER SIGNATURE PAGE
AND POWER OF ATTORNEY

The undersigned, desiring to become a limited partner of ___19___, a limited partnership organized under The Revised California Limited Partnership Act, pursuant to Paragraphs ___20___ of the Agreement of Limited Partnership (Partnership Agreement) included as Exhibit A to the prospectus of the partnership dated ___21___ (Prospectus), agrees to all of the terms of the Partnership Agreement and the Certificate of Limited Partnership of ___22___ and agrees to be bound by the terms and provisions of them. The undersigned further, by executing this instrument hereby executes, adopts, and agrees to all terms and conditions and representations of the subscription agreement included as Exhibit B to the prospectus. The undersigned further irrevocably constitutes and appoints the general partner of ___23___, with full power of substitution, the true and lawful attorney for the undersigned and in the name, place, and stead of the undersigned to make, execute, sign, acknowledge, swear to, deliver, record, and file any documents or instruments which may be considered necessary or desirable by the general partner to carry out fully the provisions of the Partnership Agreement, including, but not limited to, an amendment or amendments to the Partnership Agreement and the Certificate of Limited Partnership of ___24___ for the purpose of adding the undersigned and others as limited partners in ___25___, as contemplated by Paragraphs ___26___ of the Partnership Agreement (which amendment(s) the undersigned joins in and executes, authorizing this Limited Partner Signature Page and Power of

Illustration 10-1 (cont.)

Attorney to be attached to any such amendment) and of otherwise amending the Partnership Agreement and such certificate, from time to time, or cancelling the same. The Power of Attorney granted will be deemed to be coupled with an interest and will be irrevocable and survive the death, incapacity, insolvency, dissolution, or termination of the undersigned or any delivery by the undersigned or an assignment of the whole or any interest of the undersigned. The place of residence of the undersigned is shown below.

ALL INFORMATION MUST BE COMPLETED

__27__ [Signature of Limited Partner]

__28__ [Number of units—minimum __29__]

__30__ [Dollar amount]

__31__ [Signature of joint owner—if any]

__32__ [Name of Limited Partner(s)—type or print]

__33__ [Residence address]

__34__ [City, State, Zip]

__35__ [Social Security or Taxpayer Identification Number] If Joint Ownership, check one:

__36__ Joint Tenants with Right of Survivorship

__37__ Tenants in Common

__38__ Community Property All parties must sign. If fiduciary or corporation, check one of the following instruction on page __39__:

__40__ Trust

__41__ Power of Attorney

__42__ Estate

__43__ Corporation Indicate capacity of signatory under signature line. If signing as trustee, indicate state whose law governs the trust instruments: __44__

Illustration 10-1 (cont.)

§ 21:93 REAL PROPERTY

CONFIDENTIAL SUITABILITY INFORMATION

Name of Investor ___45___ Account Executive ___46___
Account Number ___47___ Executive's telephone number ___48___
Fax Number ___49___ Branch Office Wire Call ___50___
Office Prefix ___51___

(Include same information separately for each joint owner, if any)

Investor's Net Worth (exclusive of home, home furnishings, and personal automobiles): $___52___

$___53___ *[date]* (est)

$___54___ *[date]* (est)

$___55___ *[date]* (est)

$___56___ *[date]* (est)

§ 21:94 Subscription agreement—Provision—Statement of residence for intrastate offering

The undersigned acknowledges his, her, or its understanding that (1) the limited partnership interest evidenced by this agreement has not been registered with the Securities and Exchange Commission under the Securities Act of 1933, as amended; and (2) such interest may not be offered, sold, transferred, pledged or hypothecated to a person who is not a bona fide resident of the State of California in the absence of registration under that Act or an opinion of counsel for the partnership that such registration is not required. The undersigned warrants that he, she or it is now, and intends to remain, a bona fide resident of the State of California.

§ 21:95 Information Sheet—To elicit information for certification of subscriber's intrastate residence

Limited Partner Information (Please Print)

Name ___1___ Social Security No. ___2___
Occupation ___3___ Birth Date ___4___

Illustration 10-1 (cont.)

Spouse's Name __5______ Social Security No. __6______
Home Address __7______
Telephone No. __8______
Employer's Name __9______
Employer's Address __10______ Telephone __11______
Driver's License Number__12______ State __13______
Where Voted Last __14______
Where Filed Last State Income Tax Return(s), if any __15______
Gross Yearly Salary: $__16______
Net Worth: $__17______
Years of Education __18______ Nature of Degrees __19______
Names of Attorney, Accountant, Tax Advisor, if any: __20______

Practice Notes:

With respect to programs registered with the Department of Corporations, the syndicator and each person selling limited partnership interests on behalf of the partnership or syndicator must make every reasonable effort to assure that those persons being offered or sold the interests are appropriate in light of the suitability standards set forth in the regulations of Department of Corporations and are appropriate to the customers' investment objectives and financial situations. See *10 Cal C Reg § 260.140.112.2.*

§ 21:96 Legend for document evidencing ownership of partnership units—Limitation on transfer of units to nonresidents

The limited partnership interest evidenced by this document has not been registered with the Securities and Exchange Commission under the Securities Act of 1933, as amended. Such interest may not be offered, sold, transferred, pledged or hypothecated to a person who is not a bona fide resident of the State of California in the absence of registration under that Act or an opinion of counsel for __1______ *[limited partnership]* that such registration is not required.

Practice Notes:

This legend is intended to insure that the units will not be transferred to a resident of another state, thereby destroying the intrastate exemption, and to appraise the holder of the limitation on transfers. For discussion of the intrastate exemption, see § 21:22.

Illustration 10-2

§ 21:101 REAL PROPERTY

LIMITED PARTNERSHIP AGREEMENTS

COMPLETE INSTRUMENT

§ 21:101 Limited partnership agreement—To acquire, invest in, manage, operate, own, and lease interest in real estate—Real estate syndicate

__1__ *[NAME OF PARTNERSHIP]*

LIMITED PARTNERSHIP AGREEMENT

This agreement made on __2__ *[date],* between __3__, a __4__ [California] corporation, and __5__, referred to in this instrument as the general partners, and __6__, referred to in this instrument as the initial limited partner.

Table of Contents

§ 1. Formation
§ 2. Name
§ 3. Addresses
3.1. Place of Business of Partnership .... ____
3.2. Residences of General and Limited Partners .... ____
§ 4. Partnership Objectives and Business
§ 5. Units; Limited Partners; Contributions to Capitial
5.1. Authorized Units; Admission of Limited Partners .... ____
5.2. Contributions to Capital.............. ____
5.3. Minimum Contribution; Impound ...... ____
5.4. Investment of Amounts Contributed .... ____
5.5. Change in Number or Value of Units ... ____
5.6. Registered Holders .... ____
5.7. Continuing Rights of Limited Partner After Transfer of Units, but Before Substitution of New Limited Partner .... ____
§ 6. Powers, Rights, and Duties of the General Partners
6.1. Powers and Rights .... ____

Illustration 10-2 (cont.)

SYNDICATION—LIMITED PARTNERSHIPS § 21:101

6.2. Indemnification .... ____
6.3. Duty to Devote Skill and Time .... ____

§ 7. Rights of Limited Partners and Registered Holders of Units
7.1. Limitation of Liability .... ____
7.2. Inspection Rights of Limited Partners ... ____
7.3. Annual Audit and Reports to Limited Partners .... ____
7.4. Voting and Other Rights .... ____

§ 8. Transfer of Units
8.1. Registration of Transfer .... ____
8.2. Substitution of Assignee as Limited Partner—by Assignor .... ____
8.3. Substitution of Assignee as Limited Partner—by General Partners .... ____
8.4. Time of Substitution .... ____
8.5. Death or Incompetency of Limited Partner .... ____

§ 9. Limited Repurchase Reserve Account
9.1. Establishment of Account .... ____
9.2. Repurchase of Units .... ____

§ 10. Term; Dissolution
10.1. Term, Termination, and Dissolution ... ____
10.2. No Dissolution as a Result of Certain Other Events .... ____
10.3. Removal of General Partners .... ____
10.4. Formation of New Partnership .... ____
10.5. Purchase of Interest of Terminated General Partner .... ____
10.6. Winding up Liquidation, Distribution of Assets and Termination .... ____

§ 11. Compensation; Distribution; Losses
11.1. Contracts with and Compensation of Agents .... ____
11.2. Contracts with and Compensation of Principal Distributor .... ____
11.3. Compensation of and Distribution to General Partners and Holders of Units . ____
11.4. Losses, Deductions, and Credits .... ____

Illustration 10-2 (cont.)

§ 12. Amendments
12.1. Adoption Procedures ....
12.2. Unanimous Written Consent for Certain Amendments ....
§ 13. Meetings of and Actions by Limited Partners
13.1. Call and Notice of Meetings ....
13.2. Adjournment of Meetings ....
13.3. Quorum for Meetings ....
13.4. Voting Power........................
13.5. Action by Limited Partners at Meetings
13.6. Action by Limited Partners without a Meeting ....
§ 14. Power of Attorney
14.1. Grant of Power ....
14.2. Irrevocability; Mode of Exercise ....

Section 1. Formation

The parties agree to form a limited partnership (the partnership) under the California Revised Limited Partnership Act, Sections 15611 et seq. of the Corporations Code. Formation of the partnership will take place on recording of the Certificate of Limited Partnership in the office of the Secretary of State. Such recordation will be done by the general partners __7______ *[indicate when recordation will occur]*.

Section 2. Name

The name of partnership will be "__8______", a limited partnership, and the business of the partnership will be conducted under such name.

Section 3. Addresses

3.1. Place of Business of Partnership. The principal place of business of the partnership will be at __9______ *[address]*, in the City of __10______, County of __11______, State of California, or at such other place as the general partners may from time to time designate by giving written notice to

Illustration 10-2 (cont.)

the limited partners. The partnership may also maintain other offices at other places as the general partners deem advisable.

3.2. Residences of General and Limited Partners. The places of residence of the general and limited partners are those addresses set opposite their names at the end of this agreement or in any amendment to this agreement. The general and limited partners may change such places of residence by written notice to the partnership, which notices will become effective on receipt.

Section 4. Partnership Objectives and Business

The primary business of the partnership will be to acquire, invest in, manage, operate, own, and lease interests in real estate. The business and investment objectives and policies of the partnership and restrictions on certain activities, including certain transactions with affiliates, are set forth in its prospectus included in the registration statement filed with the Department of Corporations relating to __12______ *[number]* of its limited partnership units under the captions "INVESTMENT OBJECTIVES AND POLICIES," and "USE OF PROCEEDS," which portions of the prospectus are incorporated by reference and made a part of this agreement. The business and investment objectives and policies of the partnership, as well as the restriction on certain activities, including certain transactions with affiliates, may not be added to or otherwise changed except by amendment to this agreement in accordance with Section 12 of this agreement.

Section 5. Units; Limited Partners; Contributions to Capital

5.1. Authorized Units; Admission of Limited Partners. There are here authorized for issuance and sale __13__ units of limited partnership interests (units). The partnership may, but need not, issue fractional units. The partnership will be formed with capital contributions of __14______ Dollars

Illustration 10-2 (cont.)

§ 21:101 REAL PROPERTY

($____), for __15__ units by the general partners, and __16______ Dollars ($____), for __17__ units, by the initial limited partner. Thereafter the general partners are authorized to admit from time to time as additional limited partners only (1) such persons as apply to become limited partners under a public offering by the partnership of the remaining __18__ of such authorized units, subject to the provisions of Subsection 5.3, and (2) persons who purchase units resold under Subsection 9.2(e). Each such person may apply for admission as an additional limited partner by completing, executing, and delivering to the principal distributor or the partnership a signature page from the prospectus with respect to the public offering (or such other form required by the general partners), which will include and constitute an agreement to be bound by this agreement and to become a limited partner, together with his or her capital contribution. Each such person will be admitted as an additional limited partner not later than the end of the calendar month following the month in which the application is accepted by the general partners. The general partners may in their discretion decline to admit any person or persons as additional limited partners for any reason whatsoever, provided that (1) the general partners accept or reject all applications within __19__ days after they are received by the principal distributor or the partnership (persons whose applications are not rejected during that period will be deemed to be accepted by the general partners and will be admitted as limited partners as set forth above); and (2) rejected contributions of such persons, together with any interest thereon, are returned to them. Limited partners whose applications are accepted will be admitted in priority as to time that their signature pages (or other form required by the general partners) and their contributions are so delivered. Subject to the provisions of Subsection 5.3, the general partners will from time to time execute amendments to this agreement as attorneys-in-fact for such persons, which amendments will also set forth the places of residence and capital contributions of such persons. For all purposes

Illustration 10-2 (cont.)

of this agreement, a person will be deemed admitted as an additional limited partner on the first day of the calendar month in which the general partners record the amendment of the certificate of limited partnership reflecting the admission of such person. General partners and their affiliates may acquire units and may become additional limited partners in the same manner as other persons.

5.2. Contributions to Capital. Each limited partner's capital contribution will be only in cash in the amount of __20____ Dollars ($____) for each unit purchased, and on such contribution each such unit will be fully paid and nonassessable. Each limited partner will purchase a minimum of __21____ units. The general partners will not, as such, be required to contribute to the capital of the partnership.

5.3. Minimum Contributions; Impound. All contributions made by the purchasers of units will be received by the partnership in trust, and such proceeds will be deposited in an escrow account with __22____ *[bank]* or with any other banking institution designated by the general partners. Such bank or banks will act as escrow holder for the proceeds. On receipt of a minimum of __23____ Dollars ($____) in capital contributions from the public offering, the partnership will admit purchasers into the partnership as additional limited partners. At the time a purchaser is made a limited partner, the escrow holder will transfer such person's contribution to the partnership. If the above-specified minimum amount is not obtained within __24____ [365] days from commencement of the public offering, no additional limited partners will be admitted to the partnership and all contributions will be refunded in full to the persons who made them. __25____ *[If desired add:* Any interest earned on the subscriptions will be paid when the funds are released to the partnership or when the subscriptions are returned].

5.4. Investment of Amounts Contributed. The proceeds held by any bank as escrow holder under Subsection 5.3 may be invested in a separate interest-bearing account, bank and savings and loan certificates of deposit, and short-term

Illustration 10-2 (cont.)

government obligations. Additionally, after the minimum capital contribution has been obtained, such funds may be invested both in interest-bearing accounts and other obligations. Any interest earned on such funds after the minimum capital contribution has been obtained will be paid by the escrow holder to __26_____ *[name]* during the month following the month in which the interest is earned, and __27_____ *[name]* will immediately distribute the same to purchasers. Each purchaser will receive that portion of the total interest earned which is attributed to his or her contribution held by escrow holder. The computation of any purchaser's share of the total will be based on the weighted average of the proportion of each purchaser's contribution to the contributions made that month and on the length of time his or her contribution was held in the escrow account. In no event will such interest ever become part of the partnership capital.

5.5. Change in Number or Value of Units. By amendment to this agreement, the number and value of authorized but unissued units, or of authorized but unissued units and all outstanding units, or of all outstanding units, may be altered by dividing such units into a greater number of units of lesser value or combined into a smaller number of units of greater value, provided the proportionate interests of the limited partners or other holders of units will not be changed thereby. The general partners may also sell additional units at such price and on such terms as are determined by the general partners, thereby altering the proportionate interest of current limited partners or other holders of units, provided that limited partners or other holders of units have the first option to purchase additional units to the extent necessary to preserve their proportionate interests.

5.6. Registered Holders. On the admission of a person as a limited partner or as an additional or substituted limited partner, the person will be registered on the records of the partnership as the holder of the units in respect to the capital contribution of the person. The person will continue to be the registered holder of such units until due registra-

Illustration 10-2 (cont.)

tion of the transfer to a new holder in accordance with Subsection 8.1. The holder in whose name the ownership of a unit is registered on the records of the partnership will be deemed the registered holder of such unit for purposes of this agreement, and whether or not such person has been substituted or admitted as a limited partner, such person will be entitled to all distributions, allocations of losses, and withdrawal or reduction of capital contributions with respect to such unit and to all other rights of a holder of a unit specified in this agreement so long as he or she is the registered holder. The partnership will not be affected by any notice or knowledge of transfer of any interest in any unit, either actual or constructive, except as expressly provided in this agreement. The receipt, by the registered holder of any unit, of any distribution with respect to such unit will be a sufficient discharge of the unit.

5.7. Continuing Rights of Limited Partner after Transfer of Units, but Before Substitution of New Limited Partner. Once a person has been admitted to the partnership as a limited partner as to any unit, that person will continue to be the limited partner as to such unit for all purposes until admission of a substituted limited partner with respect to such unit. However, if the limited partner assigns the unit to another person, such other person will become a limited partner when he or she becomes a registered holder of such unit; the limited partner will continue to have all other rights of a limited partner with respect to such unit until the new registered holder becomes a substituted limited partner pursuant to Subsections 8.2, 8.3, or 8.5, or until the unit is repurchased from the registered holder as provided in Subsection 9.2.

Section 6. Powers, Rights, and Duties of General Partners

6.1. Powers and Rights. The general partners will have full, exclusive, and complete authority and discretion in the management and control of the business of the partnership for the purposes stated in this agreement and will make all

Illustration 10-2 (cont.)

decisions affecting the business of the partnership. The general partners will manage and control the affairs of the partnership to the best of their ability and will use their best efforts to carry out the business of the partnership set forth in Section 4, and with the powers and rights that include, but are not limited to, the power and right to:

(a) Evaluate, select, and acquire interests in real estate through agents retained and paid on terms set forth in Subsection 11.1, and evaluate, select, and make investments, all to the extent permitted by Section 4;

(b) Expend the capital and revenues of the partnership in furtherance of the partnership business;

(c) Manage, operate, service, improve, and develop any partnership property or investment, retain persons and firms, and enter into agreements on behalf of the partnership with respect to the operation, management, and development of all or any portion of the properties and investments acquired by the partnership, such agreements to contain terms, provisions, and conditions (including fees and expenses to be paid therefor by the partnership) as the general partners approve, provided that agreements with agents for the services set forth in Subsection 11.1, contain the terms and limitations as to fees and expenses and as to termination of the agreements as set forth in such section; and provided further that any of such agreements entered into with any persons or firms who are affiliated with general partners will be terminable immediately on written notice by any new general partner elected after removal of a general partner under Subsection 10.3;

(d) Negotiate and execute in the name and on behalf of the partnership such agreements, commitments, and any and all documents, instruments, receipts, releases, and discharges as are deemed by the general partners to be necessary or appropriate to carry on the business of the partnership or to exercise the powers and rights, and perform the duties, of the general partners hereunder (including but not limited to the registration, qualification, sale, and distribution of units);

Illustration 10-2 (cont.)

(e) Sell, lease, trade, exchange, or otherwise dispose of all or any portions of partnership property on such terms and conditions and for such consideration as the general partners deem appropriate through agents paid on the terms set forth in Subsection 11.1; provided that whenever the general partners (1) propose to pledge substantially all of the partnership assets, or (2) propose to sell or have an offer from a third party to purchase any property that comprises ten percent or more of the total value (at cost) of the property owned by the partnership, limited partners holding a majority of the limited partnership interests will have the right to reject or reverse the decision of the general partners as to such matters. The general partners may pledge assets on and in connection with the acquisition of such assets or pledge assets in connection with the refinancing of substantially all of the assets to obtain more favorable terms on obligiations secured by the assets, and do such other things as provided for in any amendment to this agreement adopted in accordance with Section 12;

(f) Borrow money from banks, other lending institutions, and other lenders for any partnership business or purpose, and in connection therewith, issue notes, debentures, and other debt securities and hypothecate all or any part of the assets of the partnership to secure repayment of the borrowed sums and to prepay, obtain replacement of, refinance, increase, modify, consolidate, or extend, in whole or in part, any obligation for borrowed money or any other obligation, mortgage, encumbrance, pledge, hypothecation, or other security device of the partnership or affecting its properties or investments;

(g) At the expense of the partnership (including payment of salaries), maintain or cause to be maintained the books and records required by Subsection 7.2, and be reimbursed for such expense, and at the expense of the partnership cause the books and records to be examined and reports to be furnished to limited partners and registered holders of units as required by Subsection 7.3;

Illustration 10-2 (cont.)

(h) Admit additional and substituted limited partners, hold meetings of limited partners, obtain action by limited partners without a meeting, and amend this agreement as provided for in this agreement, and register, qualify, and cause to be sold and distributed units of the partnership;

(i) Make such elections under the tax laws of the United States, the State of California and other individual states, and other relevant jurisdictions as to the treatment of items of partnership income, gain, loss, deduction, and credit, and as to all other relevant matters, as they believe necessary or desirable, including, without limitation of the preceding, the power to make an election to adjust the basis of partnership property under the circumstances and in the manner provided in Sections 734, 743 and 754 of the Internal Revenue Code of 1986, as amended, and the regulations under such Code;

(j) Place and hold title to properties and investments in the name of a nominee; permit the general partners or any of their officers, directors, agents, or affiliates to purchase properties and investments in their own names (and assume loans in connection therewith) and temporarily hold title to the purchases for the purpose of facilitating the acquisition of the properties and investments or the borrowing of money or obtaining financing for the partnership or any other purpose related to the business of the partnership, provided that the properties and investments are purchased by the partnership from the general partners, their officers, directors, or affiliates for a price no greater than the cost of the properties and investments to such persons plus any commission payable to an agent as set forth in Subsection 11.1 (such persons may, however, continue to be liable on such loans), and provided there is no difference in interest rates of the loans secured by the properties at the time acquired by such persons and at the time acquired by the partnership, nor any other benefit arising out of the transaction to such persons apart from their interest as general or limited partners or agents or as lenders as permitted under Subsection 6.1(1);

Illustration 10-2 (cont.)

(k) Pay and be reimbursed by the partnership for expenses and fees incurred by the general partners and their affiliates in connection with the organization and formation of the partnership, and the legal, accounting, and escrow holder fees and expenses, printing costs (for prospectuses, sales literature and selling agreements) and filing and qualification fees and disbursements incurred in connection with sale and distribution of the units;

(*l*) In their discretion, advance monies to the partnership for use by the partnership in its operations, provided that such loans may be made only when the partnership cannot obtain funds from local lending institutions at interest rates lower than the interest rate to be charged by the general partners. The total amount of such advances will become an obligation of the partnership to the general partners, and subject to the provisions of Subsection 10.6, will be repaid to the general partners out of the gross receipts of the partnership with interest at not in excess of __28__ percent (____%) above the prime commercial rate as quoted by __29__ Bank, City of __30__, State of California, at the time the respective loan is made, but not to exceed the maximum legal rate of interest. Such advances will be deemed a loan by the general partners to the partnership and will not be deemed a capital contribution; any and all unpaid advances will become immediately due and payable on the termination and dissolution of the partnership, but payment will be subject to the provisions of Subsection 10.6;

(m) Arrange at the expense of the partnership to prosecute, defend, settle, or compromise such actions at law or in equity as may appear necessary to enforce or protect partnership interests, and satisfy any judgment, decree, decision, or settlement in connection with such actions, subject to the limitation on confession of judgments set forth in Subsection 12.2;

(n) Perform any and all other acts or activities customary or incident to (1) acquisition, ownership, management, operation, improvement, development, leasing, and disposition of interests in real estate, and (2) investment in mortgage loans and conduct of other real estate financing activities;

Illustration 10-2 (cont.)

(o) Exercise other rights and powers of general partners of limited partnerships authorized or permitted under the laws of the State of California, except to the extent any of such rights or powers may be limited or restricted by the express provisions of this agreement including, without limitation, Subsection 12.2.

6.2. Indemnification. The general partners (including any of their directors, officers, or employees) will not be liable for, and to the extent of its assets the partnership will indemnify such firms and persons against, liability arising out of their activities as or for general partners resulting from errors in judgment or any acts or omissions, whether or not disclosed, unless caused by misconduct, bad faith, or negligence.

6.3. Duty to Devote Skill and Time. General partners will devote such of their time (or time of their officers and employees) to the business of the partnership as may be reasonably necessary to conduct its business. The general partners (or their officers and employees) will not be bound to devote all of their business time to the affairs of the partnership, and they and their affiliates may engage for their own account and for the account of others in any business ventures and employment, including ventures and employment having a business similar or identical to or competitive with the business of partnership.

Section 7. Rights of limited partners and registered holders of units

7.1. Limitation of Liability. No limited partner or registered holder will be subject to assessment, nor will any limited partner or registered holder be personally liable for any debts or obligations of the partnership or any losses beyond the amount contributed by him or her to the capital of the partnership and his or her share of undistributed net profits of the partnership. To protect and preserve such limitation of liability, no limited partner or registered holder will, as such, take part in the management of the business,

Illustration 10-2 (cont.)

transact any business for the partnership, or have the power to sign for or, except with respect to this agreement and as set forth in this agreement, to bind the partnership to any agreement or document.

7.2. Inspection Rights of Limited Partners. The general partners will maintain or cause to be maintained at the principal place of business of the partnership adequate books and records setting forth a true and accurate account of all business transactions of the partnership, a complete list of names, addresses, and interests of the limited partners and the registered holders of units, and executed copies of this agreement and any amendments to it. Limited partners will at all times have the right of access to and the right to inspect and copy such books, records, and documents at the principal place of business of the partnership. Any limited partner will, on written request therefor and a showing that the request is for a proper purpose related to an interest as a limited partner, be sent a list of names and addresses of all limited partners.

7.3. Annual Audit and Reports to Limited Partners. The general partners will cause books and records of the partnership to be examined at least annually by independent certified public accountants and will cause an annual report to be sent to the limited partners not later than 90 days after the close of each calendar year. Such annual report will include (1) a balance sheet as of the end of the partnership's fiscal year, statements of income, partner's equity, and changes in financial position and a cash flow statement, for the year then ended, all of which, except the cash flow statement, will be audited; and (2) a report of the activities of the program during the period covered by the report. Such report will set forth distributions to limited partners for the period covered by such distributions and will separately identify distributions from (a) cash flow from operations during the period, (b) cash flow from operations during a prior period which had been held as reserves, (c) proceeds from disposition of property and investments, (d) lease payments on net leases

Illustration 10-2 (cont.)

with builders and sellers, and (e) reserves from the gross proceeds of the offering originally obtained from the limited partners.

The general partners will also cause to be sent, within 90 days after the partnership's fiscal year, to the registered holders of units accounting information regarding the partnership as is necessary to enable such persons to prepare their income tax returns.

To the extent permitted by regulatory authorities, the general partners will, within __31__ *[60]* days of the end of each quarter, also distribute reports to the limited partners and registered holders of units setting forth an informational summary of the properties and investments of the partnership and a detailed statement setting forth the services rendered, or to be rendered by the general partners and the amount of fees received for services by the general partners.

The partnership will furnish to the limited partners, within __32__ *[60]* days after the end of the partnership's first six-month period, a semiannual report containing a balance sheet, which may be unaudited, a statement of income for the semiannual period then ended, which may be unaudited, a cash flow statement for the semiannual period then ended, which may be unaudited, and other pertinent information regarding the partnership and its activities during the semiannual period covered by the report.

7.4. Voting and Other Rights. Limited partners will have the right (a) to remove one or more general partners and elect one or more general partners and to dissolve and terminate the partnership, as provided in Section 10, (b) to amend this agreement as set forth in Section 12, (c) to hold meetings as set forth in Section 13, and (d) to vote on decisions of the general partners as to certain pledges or sales of partnership assets, as set forth in Subsection 6.1(e).

Illustration 10-2 (cont.)

SYNDICATION—LIMITED PARTNERSHIPS § 21:101

The registered holders of units will have the right (a) to receive the distributions, losses, tax deductions, and credits against tax as provided in Section 11 by reason and on account of their registered ownership of units, (b) to withdraw or reduce the capital with respect to such units as provided for in this agreement, (c) to have their units repurchased out of the limited repurchase reserve account as provided in Section 9, and (d) to transfer their units as set forth in Section 8.

Section 8. Transfer of Units

8.1. Registration of Transfer. Units will be transferable on the records of the partnership to a new holder only

(a) when the partnership's counsel advises that such assignment is not a violation of the limited partnership laws in effect in California, and that the program should be taxable as a limited partnership rather than as a corporation or an association under any federal tax laws;

(b) By the registered holder of such units, or in appropriate cases by his or her personal representative;

(c) As part of a transfer of __33______ or more whole units to the new holder; and

(d) After delivery to the general partners of the holder's units (represented by the holder's copy of the amended certificate and agreement of limited partnership executed by the general partners and evidencing the holder's units) together with a written assignment of such units in a form satisfactory to the general partners, duly endorsed by the registered holder or his or her personal representative or authorized agent, and accompanied by such assurance of the genuineness and effectiveness of each endorsement and of the obtaining of any required consents or authorizations of any governmental or other authorities as may reasonably be required by the general partners.

Transfers of fewer than __34__ units to a new holder or of fractions of units will not be registered or recognized for any

Illustration 10-2 (cont.)

purpose by the partnership, unless (1) the general partners in their discretion agree otherwise and (2) according to the records of the partnership the transferee already is or at some time in the past has been a registered holder of at least __35__ units.

Permissible transfers will be registered by the partnership and will become effective for purposes of allocation of distributions and losses and the withdrawal or reduction of capital contributions on the first day of the calendar quarter following receipt by the general partners of the required documents referred to above, unless the general partners agree otherwise. The partnership may charge the assigning registered holder of units presented for registration of transfer a fee not exceeding __36______ Dollars ($____) to defray the costs of effecting the registration.

8.2. Substitution of Assignee as Limited Partner—By Assignor. In connection with assignment by a limited partner of the ownership of any unit, the limited partner of such unit will have the power and the right to substitute the assignee of such unit as the limited partner of such unit if all the following conditions are satisfied:

(a) A duly executed and acknowledged written instrument in a form satisfactory to the general partners is submitted to the partnership setting forth the intention of the limited partner that the assignee become a substituted limited partner in his or her place as to such unit;

(b) The limited partner and assignee execute and acknowledge such other instruments as the general partners may deem necessary or desirable to effect such admission, including the written acceptance and adoption by the assignee of all provisions of this agreement including, without limitation, the power of attorney provisions in Section 14; and

(c) The general partners have consented to substitution of such assignee as the limited partner as to such unit; such substitution will become effective as provided in Subsection 8.4.

8.3. Substitution of Assignee as Limited Partner—By

Illustration 10-2 (cont.)

General Partners. The general partners, in their sole discretion, may at any time elect to substitute the registered holder of any unit as the limited partner of such unit if they deem that such substitution is in the best interest of the partnership. The limited partners hereby expressly consent to any such substitution.

8.4. Time of Substitution. The general partners will be required to amend this agreement at least once each calendar quarter to effect the substitution of substituted limited partners, although the general partners may elect to do so more frequently. A person will become a substituted limited partner as to any unit only upon such amendment.

8.5. Death or Incompetence of Limited Partner. Subject to the provisions of Subsection 10.3, upon the death or legal incompetence of an individual limited partner, the personal representative of his or her estate will have all rights of a limited partner for the purpose of settling or managing the estate of the decedent or incompetent, as well as such power as the deceased or incompetent possessed to constitute a successor as an assignee of his or her interest in the partnership and to join with such assignee in making application to substitute such assignee as a limited partner. The limited partners hereby expressly consent to the substitution of such personal representative as a limited partner.

Section 9. Limited Repurchase Reserve Account

9.1. Establishment of Account. The general partners will establish on behalf of the partnership a special account to be known as the "limited repurchase reserve account" (account). Of the net proceeds of the partnership derived from the public offering of its units (after deduction of underwriting commissions and estimated expenses of the offering) __37______ percent (____%) will be deposited in this account. The funds in the account will be invested and may be hypothecated in the same manner as funds held on reserve as set forth under the caption "USE OF PROCEEDS" in the prospectus, referred to in Subsection 4.1. Any income

Illustration 10-2 (cont.)

earned by investment of funds from the account may be retained in the account or transferred to the general account of the partnership, at the discretion of the general partners. The general partners may, in their sole discretion, deposit additional monies from the general account of the partnership into the limited repurchase reserve account, either as an outright grant or on an interest-free loan basis.

9.2. Repurchase of Units. Funds in the limited repurchase reserve account will be expended by the general partners from time to time to repurchase units (except units owned by the general partners and their affiliates, which will not be repurchased out of the account so long as such units are owned by them or their affiliates), for cash, from the registered holders of such units, desiring to resell their units to the partnership on the following terms and conditions:

(a) No registered holder may require the partnership to repurchase (i) any unit out of funds in the account during the first ___38___ months after the date the original owner of such unit was admitted to the partnership as a limited partner, or (ii) less than ___39________ units.

(b) The registered holder of any units may require not less than ___40___ *[number]* of such units to be repurchased out of the account by delivering to the partnership a written request therefor, together with a written assignment of such units to the partnership, and accompanied by such other documents as the general partners may require pursuant to Subsection 8.1. Repurchases will be made effective as of the last day of the calendar quarter in which such requests and other documents are received by the partnership. Payment of the purchase price will be made as promptly as possible thereafter, subject to compliance with the other conditions set forth in this agreement.

(c) The partnership will repurchase each unit out of funds in the account for a price that is equal to the unit's initial sales price reduced by the amount of cash distributions allocated to such unit during the period the unit has been outstanding in the hands of the original and all subsequent

Illustration 10-2 (cont.)

holders of such unit. Each unit will be repurchased for cash unless the general partners determine that it is in the best interest of the partnership to pay part or all of the redemption price in promissory notes of the partnership, bearing interest at the rate of __41______ percent (_____%) per annum and payable over a term of not to exceed __42______ years from the date of redemption.

(d) If, in any year, the partnership receives more requests for repurchase than can be honored due to limitations of funds in the account, the excess units will be repurchased in the following year and in the order in which the requests are received. When there are no assets in the account no repurchases need be made.

(e) Subject to compliance with applicable laws, and notwithstanding the provisions of subsections 5.1 and 5.2, units that are repurchased by the partnership may, at the discretion of the general partners, be offered for resale at a price and on terms to be determined by the general partners.

(f) Upon commencement of proceedings looking toward dissolution of the partnership, no further repurchases out of the account need be made by the partnership, and upon dissolution the account will terminate, and all assets therein will be transferred to the general accounts of the partnership.

(g) No repurchases may be made unless all liabilities of the partnership, except liabilities to the general partners and to limited partners on account of their capital contributions, have been paid or there remains property of the partnership sufficient to pay them.

(h) Prior to payment of the repurchase price the general partners will amend this agreement in accordance with Section 12 to set forth the withdrawal or reduction of the capital contribution evidenced by such unit and the withdrawal of the limited partner as to such unit.

All limited partners here consent to the withdrawal or reduction of the capital contributions under this Section 9 and Subsection 11.3(f). Upon the repurchase of any units,

Illustration 10-2 (cont.)

they will cease to be outstanding units for all purposes of this agreement, and the limited partner as to such units will not be entitled to exercise any rights with respect to such units. Upon reissuance of such units, the purchaser will be substituted by the general partners as the limited partner as to such units in accordance with Section 8 and the purchase price will be treated as a capital contribution.

Section 10. Term; dissolution

10.1. Term; Termination and Dissolution. The partnership will commence on the date of formation as specified in Section 1 and will continue to exist for a term ending on the date of occurrence of the earliest of the following, on which date the partnership will be dissolved:

(a) The sale, expiration, abandonment or other disposition of all partnership assets.

(b) Action is taken by limited partners in accordance with the procedures set forth in Section 13 approving dissolution of the partnership;

(c) The ___[43]___ day after the death, judgment of incompetence, judgment of bankruptcy, dissolution (except in connection with or by way of a merger, consolidation, sale of substantially all the assets followed by dissolution, or other corporate reorganization), withdrawal, or retirement of either general partner or removal of one general partner without removal of the other (last remaining) general partner (any of such events are referred to here as the dissolving event and the partner affected the terminated partner); provided, however, the last remaining general partner, if any, will have the right to continue the business of the partnership by sending to all limited partners prior to the ___[44]___ day after the dissolving event a written notice of his or her agreement to continue to act as general partner of the partnership, together with an opinion of counsel to the effect that under the law and regulations then in effect the partnership will not thereafter be taxed as an association taxable as a corporation, and provided further, the last

Illustration 10-2 (cont.)

remaining general partner purchases the interest of the terminated partner in accordance with Subsection 10.5.

(d) The failure to elect a new general partner within __45______ days after removal of both general partners or the last remaining general partner in accordance with Subsection 10.4.

(e) Dissolution of the partnership by judicial decree or operation of law.

10.2. No Dissolution as a Result of Certain Other Events. The partnership will not be terminated or dissolved by the death, incompetence, bankruptcy, insolvency, dissolution, or any other reason which might affect its existence as a legal entity, withdrawal, or expulsion of any limited partner; by the assignment by any limited partner of his or her units; or by the admission of a new limited partner. None of these events will entitle a limited partner or registered holder of any unit to the return of the capital contribution in respect to such unit.

10.3. Removal of General Partners. Either or both general partners may be removed by action of limited partners having a majority of the voting power of the limited partners. The limited partners will have the right to elect one or more new general partners in place of the removed general partner(s) within __46______ days following the effective date of such removal, by the action of limited partners having majority of the voting power of the limited partners; provided, that if both general partners are so removed and replaced, upon request of the former general partners, the partnership will be required to change its name in such a way as to eliminate all reference to __47______ *[name]* and any variation or combination of such name.

10.4. Formation of New Partnership. In the event of dissolution of the partnership as a result of a dissolving event specified in clause (c) of Subsection 10.1, a meeting of limited partners will be held at the principal place of business of the partnership without notice (notwithstanding Subsection 13.1) on the __48______ day after such dissolu-

Illustration 10-2 (cont.)

tion, or if such day is a legal holiday, on the first day immediately following such __49______ day which is not a legal holiday, to consider whether to form a new partnership on the same terms and conditions as are contained in this agreement (except that the general partner or general partners may be different) and to select a general partner or general partners for the new partnership or whether to wind up the affairs of the partnership, liquidate its assets, and distribute the proceeds in accordance with Subsection 10.6; provided, that this Subsection 10.4 will be of no force and effect if the former general partners exercise their option to purchase the assets for cash as set forth in Subsection 10.6(a). If limited partners having at least a majority of the voting power of the limited partners vote in person or by written consent to form such a new partnership, then the second order of business at the meeting will be to select a general partner or general partners for the new partnership. If limited partners having at least a majority of the voting power of the limited partners vote in person or by written consent in favor of selection of a certain general partner or general partners for such new partnership, then all of the limited partners by their execution of the signature page (or other form) with respect to the original partnership, will be deemed to have entered into and executed a new limited partnership agreement having the same terms and conditions as are contained in this agreement (except that the general partner or general partners may be different), and the assets and liabilities of the partnership will be assigned to and assumed by the new limited partnership, all provided that the general partner or general partners of the new partnership purchase the interests of the terminated partner(s) in accordance with Subsection 10.5. Any registered holder of a unit of the limited partnership who does not vote in favor of forming a new partnership will have the right to require the former partnership to pay such holder the fair market value of his or her units or the amount that would have been received under Subsection 10.6(b)(4), whichever is greater, by giving notice, within __50______ days after such holder is

Illustration 10-2 (cont.)

SYNDICATION—LIMITED PARTNERSHIPS § 21:101

sent notice of the election to form a new partnership, to the partnership of his or her election not to contribute capital to the new partnership, stating in such notice the value of his or her units. Such value will be paid by the former partnership to such holder within ___[51]___ days after it receives such notice unless it disagrees with the value set forth in the notice in which case it will offer to pay the estimate of the value of the units, which offer, if not accepted within ___[52]___ days after it is sent, will be deemed rejected by such holder, and the value will be determined by arbitration in accordance with the rules of the American Arbitration Association; for this purpose the new general partners will act on behalf of the former partnership.

10.5. Purchase of Interest of Terminated General Partner. For purposes of Subsections 10.1(c) and 10.4, the terminated partner will receive from the last remaining general partner or new general partner or partners (acquiring partner), as the case may be, the fair market value of his or her interest in the partnership, determined by agreement between the terminated partner and the acquiring partner, or if they cannot agree, by arbitration in accordance with the then current rules of the American Arbitration Association. For this purpose, the fair market value of the interest of the terminated partner will be deemed to be the amount the terminated partner would receive upon dissolution and termination of the partnership under Subsection 10.6, assuming such dissolution or termination occurred on the date of the dissolving event, and assuming the assets of the partnership were sold for their then fair market value without compulsion of the partnership to sell such assets. Payment will be made by a promissory note bearing ___[53]___ percent (____%) simple interest per annum in the principal amount of the fair market value, secured by assignment by the acquiring partner to the terminated partner of the future distributions by the partnership or new partnership to the acquiring partner, which principal amount together with accrued interest will be payable at the times and in amounts equal to ___[54]___ percent (____%) of such distributions

Illustration 10-2 (cont.)

until such time as the principal amount, together with accrued interest, is paid in full. However, payment will become due and payable in full by the acquiring partner at such time as the partnership or a new partnership, as the case may be, is finally wound up and liquidated; provided, that if the terminated partner requests, the sale and payment will, to the extent required, be made on terms and conditions that will allow such sale to qualify for the installment method as provided in Section 453 of the Internal Revenue Code. The terminated partner will be required to sell and the acquiring partner will be required to purchase the terminated partner's interest in the partnership no later than the __55_____ day after the dissolving event or immediately prior to formation of the new partnership, whichever occurs later.

10.6. Winding Up; Liquidation; Distribution of Assets and Termination. The following will apply in the event of dissolution of the partnership, provided that this Subsection 10.6 will not be applicable if a new partnership is formed under Subsection 10.4, except to the extent set forth in that subsection:

(a) The remaining general partner, or if none is remaining, the former general partners, or such partners' representatives or successors, will wind up the affairs and sell or otherwise liquidate, dispose of, or abandon all the partnership assets as promptly as is consistent with attempting to obtain the fair value thereof and will terminate the partnership; provided that if the partnership is dissolved for any reason without the approval of the former general partners or their successors, the former general partners will have an option to purchase all the assets at their fair market value for cash as determined by the report of an independent appraiser retained by the partnership.

(b) The proceeds from disposition or purchase of the assets will be applied and distributed in the following order:

(i) All debts and liabilities of the partnership, in the order of priority as provided by law, except debts and liabilities described below;

Illustration 10-2 (cont.)

(ii) Deduction of any reserves that the general partners may deem reasonably necessary for contingent or unforeseen liabilities of the partnership, which reserves will be held in escrow;

(iii) Distributions to the registered holders of units provided for in Subsection 11.3 that have been allocated prior to the date of dissolution, but have not yet been paid;

(iv) Payment to the registered holders of units of record on the date of dissolution of such amounts as are necessary to return to them an amount equal to ___56___ Dollars ($____) for each unit held by them, less all cash distributions allocated to such units during the period the units were outstanding in the hands of the original and all subsequent registered holders of such units, to be allocated among such holders on the same basis as set forth in Subsection 11.3(e);

(v) Repayment of any loans or advances made by the general partners to the partnership;

(vi) Payments and distributions to general partners provided for in Subsection 11.3 which have been allocated prior to the date of dissolution, but have not yet been paid;

(vii) Payment of ___57___ percent (____%) of the balance remaining, if any, to the registered holders of units of record on the date of dissolution to be allocated among them on the same basis as set forth in Subsection 11.3(e), and ___58___ percent (____%) of such balance to the general partners, to be allocated between them on the same basis as set forth in Subsection 11.3(g).

(c) Each registered holder of units will look solely to the assets of the partnership for the return of the capital contribution with respect to the units registered in his or her name. If the partnership property remaining after payment or discharge of the prior debts, liabilities, and distributions of the partnership is insufficient to return the capital contributions with respect to such units, such registered holders will have no recourse against the general partners or any other limited partner or registered holder.

Illustration 10-2 (cont.)

(d) The winding up of the affairs of the partnership and the liquidation and distribution of its assets will be conducted exclusively by the general partners, who are hereby authorized to do any and all acts and things authorized by law for these purposes.

Section 11. Compensation; distribution; losses

11.1. Contracts with and Compensation of Agents.

(a) The partnership may enter into a written contract with __59______, a __60______ [California] corporation __61______ [and affiliate of the general partners], and, if necessary, may enter into additional written contracts with other persons or firms, such corporation and other persons or firms being collectively referred to in this agreement as agents, for services as follows:

(i) Such acquisition services as locating interests in real property for purchase by partnership, and, if the general partners determine that the partnership will make such purchase, assisting in negotiating and closing the acquisition of such properties and the financing for them;

(ii) Continuing such real property management services with respect to real properties owned by the partnership as renting, leasing, and inspecting the premises and collecting rentals with respect to such properties, and, on behalf of the partnership, making contracts with or employing third parties, and supervising the activities of such parties, with respect to the operation, maintenance, and repair and alterations of the premises by such parties at the expense of the partnership and paying all other expenses with respect to the properties;

(iii) Such real estate brokerage services with respect to the disposition of real properties by the partnership as locating potential purchasers when the general partners determine that the partnership should dispose of partnership real property and assisting in negotiating and closing the sale;

(iv) Such mortgage servicing with respect to mortgages held by the partnership as collecting payments from mortga-

Illustration 10-2 (cont.)

SYNDICATION—LIMITED PARTNERSHIPS § 21:101

gors and paying taxes, special assessments, insurance premiums, and other payments required under a mortgage. All such services will be subject to the review and ultimate control and authority of the general partners. Any contract with an agent will be subject to termination without penalty by the partnership or the agent thereunder on not more than __62__ days' written notice, or sooner as provided in Subsection 6.1(c).

(b) As compensation for services, agents will be paid fees by the partnership as follows:

(i) For acquisition services in connection with the purchase of real properties, __63__ percent (____%) of the full purchase or contract price to the partnership (which may include all payments made and to be made, all debts assumed and to be assumed and incurred and to be incurred, and the commissions paid to agents and others) of each property purchased through the services of the agent. Such fee will be paid only as to properties actually acquired by the partnership or contracted to be constructed or completed for the partnership, and only at the time of the first closing of each purchase or, in the case of a property to be constructed or completed, at the time of the first closing or payment of the first portion of the purchase price under the contract. If, to the knowledge of the general partners, there is a selling broker, finder, or other agent receiving a commission in connection with the purchase of a property by the partnership, or in the event the agent receives or is to receive a commission from some party other than the partnership, the general partners will obtain written assurances from the seller, broker, finder or agent as to the amount of the commission, and based on and assuming the validity of such assurances, the total combined acquisition services fee and real estate and other commissions in the transaction will not exceed __64__ percent (____%) of the purchase price.

(ii) For continuing real property management services, __65__ percent (____%) of the gross rentals and other receipts (before payment of expenses and costs with respect

Illustration 10-2 (cont.)

to the property) from the operations of each property managed by the agent, which fee will be payable on the __66__ day of the month following the month in which such rentals and other receipts are actually received;

(iii) For real estate brokerage services in connection with the disposition of real properties, brokerage fees customarily charged by independent real estate brokers for the type of service performed for each property in the area where each property is located. As to any agents affiliated with the general partners, the fee will in no event be more than __67__ percent (__%) of the sale price (which may include all debts assumed or incurred and the commissions paid to agents and others). Such fee will be paid for each property sold through the services of the agent, but it will be paid only as to properties actually sold by the partnership and only on the closing of each sale. No brokerage fees will be paid to any affiliate of the general partners or the general partners on the sale of real property by the partnership with respect to any portion of the proceeds derived from such sale which are reinvested in other real properties.

(iv) For mortgage servicing activities, __68__ percent (__%) per month of the principal amount of each obligation secured by a mortgage serviced by the agent as of the first day of each month, which fee is payable on the first day of the following month. Fees may be paid to more than one agent, but the combined total of such fees will not exceed the fees set forth above.

11.2. Contract with and Compensation of Principal Distributor. The partnership will enter into a written contract with __69__, a __70__ [California] corporation __71__ [and an affiliate of the general partners] or, if such corporation is unable to serve, with such other person or firm as the general partners select, such corporation, person, or firm being referred to as the principal distributor. Under the contract the principal distributor will use its best efforts to sell and distribute to the public, primarily through registered broker-dealers, up to __72__ *[number]* of units of the partnership. As compensation for its services, the

Illustration 10-2 (cont.)

principal distributor will be paid by the partnership out of gross proceeds of the offering a sales commission at the rate of ___[73]______ percent (____%) of the capital contribution for each unit sold by it; provided, that payment will be made after and only if units in the minimum amount of ___[74]______ Dollars ($____) are sold. Any other compensation may be paid by the general partners or their affiliates to the principal distributor in such amounts as may be agreed on between them, but such amounts will not be paid by or charged to the partnership or deducted from the proceeds of the offering of the units. The principal distributor may be reimbursed by the partnership only for the printing expenses and fees described in Subsection 6.1(k) to the extent paid by the principal distributor.

11.3. Compensation of and Distributions to General Partners and Holders of Units.

(a) Current distributions will include (1) lease payments for the period on net leases with builders and sellers (except to the extent the builder or seller is a tenant), and (2) cash funds provided from operations for the period determined by the general partners in accordance with generally accepted accounting principles, by adding back to the net income (or loss) of the partnership those expenses not requiring current cash outlays, and by excluding from the net income (or loss) any proceeds from the sale, refinancing, or other disposition of partnership properties and investments, but in both cases after deducting mortgage payments representing reductions in mortgage principal balances and after deducting (or restoring) such amounts of lease payments and cash funds provided from operations for the period (or from a prior period) as are determined in the sole discretion of the general partners to be reasonably necessary (or no longer necessary) to be expended or held as reserves for the conduct of the partnership business, including future payment of anticipated obligations and contingent liabilities of the partnership.

(b) The term "disposition proceeds" will mean the net cash proceeds that are not expended or held to defray

Illustration 10-2 (cont.)

charges and expenses and to provide reserves in the same manner as set forth in Subsection 11.3a and that are not reinvested, realized by the partnership on the sale, refinancing, or other disposition of any particular partnership property or investment, and will be determined on a property-by-property or investment-by-investment basis. Notes will not be included as net cash proceeds until and except to the extent actually paid, and property other than cash received on any sale, refinancing, or disposition will not be so included until and except to the extent actually sold, refinanced, or otherwise disposed of for cash. Cash payments of principal on investments described under the caption "INVESTMENT OBJECTIVES AND POLICIES" in the prospectus referred to in Section 4 are to be regarded as a "disposition" of a portion of the investment represented by such payment, and accordingly will be subject to inclusion in disposition proceeds. Disposition proceeds will also include distribution from funds originally held by the partnership as reserves to meet carrying costs of properties pending receipt of sufficient income from such properties to cover such costs, but which are no longer required to be so held.

(c) The current distributions and disposition proceeds will be (1) computed each calendar month and allocated as of the last day of each month until the public offering of the units is terminated, and will thereafter be computed each calendar quarter and allocated as of the last day of each quarter; and (2) paid or distributed during the calendar quarter following the calendar month or quarter in which the allocation was made.

(d) As compensation for their services rendered during the calendar quarter prior to receipt of the distribution in evaluating and selecting properties and investments for the partnership, making decisions as to the nature and terms of the acquisition and disposition of the properties and investments, selecting, retaining, and supervising consultants, contractors, architects, engineers, lenders, borrowers, agents, and others, and otherwise generally managing the day-to-day investment operations of the partnership, and as compensa-

Illustration 10-2 (cont.)

tion for lending their names, contributing their credit and contributing a portion of their good will and know-how to the partnership, the general partners will be paid a fee of __75______ percent (____%) of the current distributions.

(e) The balance of the current distributions will be allocated to the registered holders of units of record on the last day of the calendar month or quarter that the current distributions have been determined. Allocation will be in the ratio that the number of units held by each holder bears to the number of all units held.

(f) Disposition proceeds will be allocated in the following order of priority:

(i) To the registered holders of units of record on the last day of the calendar month or quarter with respect to which the disposition proceeds have been determined in the ratio that the number of units held by each holder bears to the number of all units held until such time as they, as a group, receive from such proceeds a return determined by multiplying the portion of the partnership's capital from sale of units used in making the particular investment by the fraction that results from dividing the gross public offering price of the units sold by the net proceeds of such offering after payment of sales commissions and other offering expenses.

(ii) The balance will be apportioned __76______ percent (____%) to the general partners and __77______ percent (____%) to registered holders of units. Notwithstanding the preceding, original reserves will be distributed in their entirety to registered holders of units of record at the time and in the ratio set forth in Subsection 11.3(f)(i) above, and in no event will the general partners share in distributions of original reserves, if any.

(g) The general partners will agree between themselves as to the portion of the current distributions and disposition proceeds and other items to be allocated to and received by each of them, provided that unless otherwise agreed by them __78______ *[fraction]* of the amount of each such cash distribution or item allocated to the general partners will be

Illustration 10-2 (cont.)

allocated to and received by ___79___ *[name]*, and ___80___ *[fraction]* of it will be allocated to and received by ___81___ *[name]*.

(h) No registered holder of any units will receive any distribution which constitutes a return of the capital contribution in respect to the units until the same conditions as for a repurchase set forth in Subsections 9.2(g) and (h) are met with respect to the return.

(i) All communications to holders of units that relate to cash distributions will separately identify current distributions and distributions of disposition proceeds. With respect to current distributions, communications will also separately identify the portion of distributions from lease payments on net leases with builders and sellers, except to the extent the builder or seller is a tenant (and will state that distributions of such lease payments represent a return of capital not derived from operations), from cash funds provided from operations during the period, and from cash funds provided from operations during a prior period that are being distributed because it is no longer necessary that they be expended or held as reserves. With respect to disposition proceeds, communications will separately identify distributions from original reserves.

11.4. Losses, Deductions, and Credits.

(a) The partnership will adopt a calendar year as its taxable year and accounting period.

(b) The term "net losses" as used in this agreement will mean the net losses determined by the partnership for purposes of preparing the partnership's information return for federal income tax purposes.

(c) All net losses, deductions, and credits of the partnership will be computed each calendar month until the public offering of units is terminated. Thereafter they will be computed each calendar quarter and (without limiting and subject to the provisions of Subsection 8.1 as to the effective date of assignments of units) will be allocated only to the registered holders of units of record as of the last day of

Illustration 10-2 (cont.)

each such calendar month or quarter, as the case may be, in the ratio that the number of units held by each holder bears to the number of all units held. To the extent permitted by law, such registered holders will be entitled to all losses, deductions, or credits arising from such losses in computing taxable income or tax liability.

Section 12. Amendments

12.1. Adoption Procedures. This agreement may be amended in any respect whatsoever by adding to, omitting from, removing, or otherwise altering all or any portion of any of the provisions hereof (including provisions incorporated by reference from other documents) by adoption of an amendment to this agreement by action of the limited partners in accordance with Section 13, and subject to the provisions of Subsection 12.2, except that an amendment to Section 11 will require the consent of the general partners.

12.2. Unanimous Written Consent for Certain Amendments. Notwithstanding Subsection 12.1, without approval by the vote or written consent of all limited partners and the general partners, no amendment will:

(a) Change the partnership to a general partnership or change the limited liability of the limited partners (this provision will not apply to incorporation of this partnership or sale of all of the assets of this partnership for securities of a corporation or other entity, but such actions will require amendments to this agreement pursuant to Subsection 12.1); or

(b) Authorize the general partners to do any of the following acts unless the amendment requires each specific act to be approved or ratified by the written consent of all limited partners: (i) Do any act in violation of this agreement, (ii) do any act that would make it impossible to carry on the ordinary business of the partnership, (iii) confess a judgment against the partnership, (iv) possess partnership property, or assign a general partner's rights in specific partnership property, other than for a partnership purpose, or (v) admit a person as a general partner.

Illustration 10-2 (cont.)

§ 21:101 REAL PROPERTY

Section 13. Meetings Of and Action by Limited Partners

13.1. Call and Notice of Meetings. Meetings of the limited partners to vote on any matters as to which the limited partners are authorized to take action under this agreement may be called at any time by the general partners, or by one or more limited partners having not less than ________[82] [ten percent (10%)] of the voting power of the limited partners, by delivering either in person or by registered mail written notice of such call to the general partners. Upon the call of a meeting, the general partners immediately will within ________[83] [10] days after receipt of such request, cause notice to be given to the limited partners entitled to vote on such matters that a meeting will be held at a time and place fixed by the general partners, which time is not less than ________[84] [15] nor more than ________[85] [60] days after the date of the notice. If such a notice is not given by the general partners within ________[86] days after the date of call of a meeting by limited partners, the limited partners calling the meeting may fix the time and place for the meeting and give the notice of it.

Meetings of limited partners may be held at any place within or without the State of California, which place may be designated by the persons calling the meeting. In the absence of any such designation, meetings will be held at the principal place of business of the partnership. Notice of meetings will be in writing, will set forth the place, day, and hour of the meeting, will indicate the voting power of each limited partner to whom it is given, and will be given to each person who is a limited partner entitled to vote on the date of giving of the notice, either personally or by registered mail addressed to such person at his or her address appearing on the records of the partnership. Included with the notice of a meeting will be a detailed statement of the action proposed, including a verbatim statement of the wording of any resolution proposed for adoption by the limited partners and of any proposed amendment to this agreement and, in the case of proposals for amendment of

Illustration 10-2 (cont.)

SYNDICATION—LIMITED PARTNERSHIPS § 21:101

this agreement, an opinion of counsel as to the legality of such amendment. In addition, if such notice is given by the general partners, they will include a statement of their recommendations as to the action proposed. A person giving such notice may also include a form on which the limited partners may indicate their written consent to any action proposed to be taken at the meeting.

13.2. Adjournment of Meetings. Any meetings of limited partners may, whether or not a quorum is present, be adjourned from time to time by a vote of limited partners having a majority of the voting power of the limited partners attending the meeting, but in the absence of a quorum no other business may be transacted. When a meeting is adjourned for less than ___[87]___ days it will not be necessary to give any notice of the time and place of the adjourned meeting or of the business to be transacted thereat, other than by announcement at the meeting at which the adjournment is taken. When a meeting is adjourned for ___[88]_______ days or more, notice of adjourned meeting will be given as in the case of an original meeting.

13.3. Quorum for Meetings. There will be deemed to be a quorum at any meeting of the limited partners if the voting power of the limited partners attending such meeting, plus the voting power exercised by limited partners who have submitted to the general partners effective written consent to action at such meeting, constitutes a majority of the voting power of the limited partners entitled to vote at such meeting.

13.4. Voting Power. The voting power of a limited partner on any matter will be equal to the number of units as to which the limited partner is entitled to vote. The voting power of all the limited partners on any matter will be the sum of the voting powers of each of the limited partners on such matter. The voting power of the limited partners for all purposes of this agreement will be determined as of the date of giving of notice of meeting or of proposed action without a meeting, as the case may be.

Illustration 10-2 (cont.)

13.5. Action by Limited Partners at Meetings. Subject to the requirements of Subsection 12.2, any action that may be taken by the limited partners under this agreement may be taken at a meeting by the affirmative vote or written consent of limited partners comprising or having a majority of the voting power of the limited partners entitled to vote on such matter. A limited partner, attending any meeting and voting in person, will revoke any written consents of such limited partner submitted with respect to action proposed to be taken at such meeting. Submission of a later written consent as to any action will revoke an earlier one as to such action.

13.6. Action by Limited Partners Without a Meeting. Any matter as to which the limited partners are authorized to take action under this agreement or under law, including but not limited to amending this agreement as provided in Section 12, may be acted on by the limited partners without a meeting, and will be as valid and effective as action by the limited partners at a meeting assembled, in accordance with the following procedure:

(a) Proposals for action by the limited partners without a meeting on any matters as to which limited partners are entitled to act hereunder may be made by general partners, or by limited partners having not less than __89______ [ten percent (10%)] of the voting power of the limited partners, by delivering to the general partners a detailed statement of the action proposed and a verbatim statement of the wording of any resolution proposed for adoption by the limited partners and of any proposed amendment to this agreement. Upon receipt of any such proposal from limited partners, the general partners will send by registered mail the notice and other documents referred to in subparagraph (b) below to the limited partners entitled to vote thereon within __90______ days.

(b) The general partners will give to the limited partners notice of a proposal for action without a meeting of the limited partners made pursuant to subparagraph (a) above. Included with the notice will be a detailed statement of the

Illustration 10-2 (cont.)

action proposed, including a verbatim statement of the wording of any resolution proposed for adoption and of any proposed amendment to this agreement and, in the case of proposals for amendment of this agreement, an opinion of counsel as to the legality of such amendment. Such notice will be in writing, will indicate the voting power of each limited partner to whom it is given and the recommendations of the general partners as to the action proposed, and will be given to each person who is a limited partner entitled to vote on such matters on the date of giving of such notice, either personally or by mail or other means of written communication, charges prepaid, addressed to such person at his or her address appearing on the records of partnership. Action may be taken by the limited partners on any matter without a meeting by the written consent of limited partners having a majority of the voting power of the limited partners entitled to vote on such matter (subject to the requirements of Subsection 12.2);

(c) If at any given time there are no general partners, the limited partners may take action without a meeting by the written consent of limited partners having a majority of the voting power of the limited partners entitled to vote.

Section 14. Power of attorney

14.1. Grant of Power. __91_____ *[Name of one general partner]* is hereby appointed, and with respect to future limited partners will be appointed by specific language contained in the __92_____ [signature page *or* subscription agreement] for this agreement, with full power of substitution, the true and lawful attorney-in-fact for the limited partners (including substituted limited partners), and each of them, with full power and authority for them, and in their names, to make and execute and, where required or permitted, acknowledge, file, and publish:

(a) This agreement, as well as any authorized or required amendments to it, under the laws of the State of California, or the laws of any other jurisdiction in which this agreement is required to be filed;

Illustration 10-2 (cont.)

(b) Any certificates, instruments, and documents, including any assumed or fictitious name certificates, that may be required by or appropriate under the laws of any jurisdiction in which the partnership intends to do business;

(c) Any other instrument that may be required to be filed by the partnership under the laws of any jurisdiction or by any governmental agency, or that the general partners deem advisable to file to effectuate the terms and provisions of this agreement;

(d) Any documents that may be required to effect the continuation of the partnership, the admission of an additional or substituted limited partner, the withdrawal or reduction of capital contributions, or the dissolution and termination of the partnership in accordance with this agreement.

14.2. Irrevocability; Mode of Exercise. Such grant of authority

(a) Is a special power of attorney coupled with an interest, is irrevocable, and will survive the death or dissolution of any limited partner;

(b) May, as to any corporate general partner exercising it, be exercised by such general partner for each limited partner by a facsimile signature of one of its officers or by listing all of the limited partners executing any instrument with a single signature of one of its officers acting as attorney in fact for all of them.

The undersigned general partners and initial limited partner have executed this agreement at __93__ on the date first set forth above.

General Partners:

Name	Place of Residence	Capital Contribution (Limited Partners)
__94__	__95__	$__96__

__97__
(Signature)

Illustration 10-2 (cont.)

SYNDICATION—LIMITED PARTNERSHIPS § 21:101

__98__ __99__ $__100__

__101__

(Signature)

Initial Limited Partner:

__102__ __103__ $__104__

__105__

(Signature)

Additional Limited Partners:

__106__ __107__ $__108__

__109__ __110__ $__111__

__112__ __113__ $__114__

By __115__, dated __116__, 19_117_

OPTIONAL PROVISIONS

1. PURPOSE CLAUSES

§ 21:111 General purpose clause

The business of the partnership is to invest in, acquire, hold, maintain, operate, improve, develop, sell, exchange, lease, and otherwise use real property and interests therein, including buildings and improvements on land owned by others, and to engage in any and all activities related or incidental to it. Partnership may make its investments and otherwise conduct its operations in such areas as may be selected by general partner.

§ 21:112 Development of agricultural land and production, distribution, and sale of agricultural products

The business of partnership will be the development of agricultural land and the production, distribution, and sale

Illustration 10-2 (cont.)

of agricultural products. The initial and principal business will be the development of lands for the production of ___1___ *[agricultural product]* and other products that can be grown or produced in connection with ___2___ *[agricultural product]* and to dispose of such products or otherwise turn the same to account; the leasing, acquisition, development, ownership, and disposition or other turning to account of property, real, personal, and mixed, that is necessary or convenient for the production, disposal, or turning to account of such products; the acquisition and ownership of water supplies and facilities for irrigating the land owned or leased by the partnership and, to the extent the supply of water is surplus to the needs of the partnership, to dispose of or otherwise turn such surplus to account; and other activities related either directly or indirectly to the foregoing as may be necessary, advisable, or convenient in the promotion or conduct of the business of the partnership.

§ 21:113 Development and management of government assisted housing

The purposes of this limited partnership will be:

(a) To acquire real or personal property (including debt and equity interests in any partnership, or joint venture that is a limited distribution entity as defined by Federal Housing Administration Rules and Regulations), for the purpose of

(1) Acquiring, financing, constructing, improving, managing, and/or operating government assisted housing (the Projects);

(2) Any other purpose authorized by this agreement.

(b) To hold, own, maintain, manage, improve, develop, operate, sell, transfer, convey, lease, mortgage, exchange, or otherwise dispose of or deal in or with such property.

(c) To perform any acts to accomplish the preceding purposes.

Tax Notes:

A limited partnership devoted to the acquisition and development of residen-

Illustration 10-2 (cont.)

tial rental property or low-income rental housing may take advantage of one of the accelerated methods of depreciation for federal income tax purposes. See *26 USCS § 167(j), § 167(k).*

§ 21:114 Development and management of multi-unit apartment projects

The business of the limited partnership will be to invest in, acquire, operate, own, lease, and improve interests in real estate that is developed or in the process of being developed into multi-unit apartment projects. Pending initial investment or future reinvestment of its funds, or to provide a source from which to meet contingencies, the limited partnership may invest in government obligations, bank certificates of deposit, short-term debt securities, and short-term commercial paper.

§ 21:115 Development and operation of specific property

The purpose, nature, and character of the business of the partnership is to acquire, own, improve, maintain, operate, lease, sell, and hold for investment a parcel of real property consisting of __1______ acres, located at __2______, County of __3______, State of California, referred to as the property, which is more particularly described in Exhibit __4__, attached to this agreement and incorporated by reference, and to engage in any and all general activities related to such activities or in any way incidental to them and to do all things necessary for the operation of such activities.

2. CLASSES OF LIMITED PARTNERS

§ 21:121 Classification into two groups—Different cash amounts for units of each class

The limited partners will be divided into two classes as follows:

(1) Class A limited partners will consist of those who subscribe to become and who may from time to time be admitted as Class A limited partners in the partnership and who contribute as their capital contribution cash in an amount equal to __1______ Dollars ($_____) per Class A unit subscribed for.

Illustration 10-2 (cont.)

(2) Class B limited partners will consist of those who subscribe to become and who may from time to time be admitted as Class B limited partners and who contribute as their capital contribution cash in an amount equal to __2__ Dollars ($____) per Class B unit subscribed for.

The general partner(s) may admit additional limited partners who subscribe for such interests, on such terms and conditions and in such class as the general partner(s) deem reasonable; provided, that Class A limited partners and Class B limited partners will be admitted in such number that the Class A units and Class B units held by them are held in a ratio of not less than __3__ [one] Class A unit for every __4__ [two] Class B units and not more than [three] Class A units for every __5__ [two] Class B units; and provided further, that the total capital to be contributed by all limited partners will not exceed __6__ Dollars ($____). No action or consent by limited partners of any class will be required in connection with such admission of additional limited partners. An amendment of the certificate of limited partnership, reflecting such admissions, will be filed.

Practice Notes:

This provision is meant to be combined with other provisions [see §§ 21:111 et seq.] providing for differing rights and preferences for the respective classes. For discussion as to classification, see § 21:121.

§ 21:122 Classification into two groups—Equal cash amount for units of each class

Class A and Class B limited partners will contribute to the capital of the partnership cash in an amount equal to __1__ Dollars ($____) for each Class A or Class B unit subscribed for, to a total of __2__ Dollars ($____). Additional capital may be contributed on the same basis to a total capitalization of __3__ Dollars ($____) at the sole election of the general partner(s).

All funds of initial subscribers will be placed in a separate interest-bearing account in a bank or savings and loan association, and if not more than __4__ Dollars ($____)

Illustration 10-2 (cont.)

is subscribed and contributed on or before ___5___ *[date]*, the partnership will not be formed and each subscriber will promptly receive his or her original investment together with interest actually received.

Practice Notes:

(See Practice Notes following § 21:121)

3. COMPENSATION OF GENERAL PARTNER

§ 21:131 Fees for management services plus percentage of distribution

A. Compensation. The general partner will receive fees and similar compensation from the partnership only as follows:

(1) The general partner will have the right to designate itself or any affiliated entity as listing broker for the partnership for the sale of any real property owned from time to time by the partnership at the time such property is offered for sale, provided that the commissions charged the partnership on sale will not exceed a flat ___1___ percent (____%) of the sale price. The general partner will not obligate the partnership to pay a real estate brokerage commission on the purchase of real property, and except as provided in subsection (a) below, neither the general partner nor any affiliated entity will be entitled to commissions on the purchase of real properties for the partnership from the partnership, from sellers of real properties, or from listing brokers.

(2) The general partner or any other entity controlled by it will be entitled to a property manager's fee for management services rendered to the partnership, to include the following:

(a) Undertaking a program of continuing management of partnership property to establish that the overall business objectives of the partnership are being fulfilled.

(b) Assuming and discharging its obligation to manage and conduct the partnership business with respect to real

Illustration 10-2 (cont.)

property owned by the partnership to insure that all such property is being professionally and capably managed and properly maintained, that major remodeling and property replacement programs are implemented when necessary, that after the initial rental schedules for partnership properties have been established they are periodically adjusted to reflect current market conditions, and that properties are sold at times justified by economic conditions at prices and terms advantageous to the partnership.

(c) Assuming overall responsibility for operating and managing real estate projects owned by the partnership, including employment and supervision of resident apartment house managers, preparation of operational manuals for guidance of resident managers, and establishment of procedures in connection with collection and deposit of rentals, rental of vacant apartment units, eviction procedures, maintenance requests by tenants, and preparation of records and reports.

The amount of compensation payable to the general partner or the controlled entity acting as property manager will not exceed ____2____ percent (____%) of gross rentals or the customary fees of property managers which prevail in the community from time to time, whichever is greater.

(3) The general partner will have the right to render maintenance and repair service to the partnership for its properties, or to employ any other entity controlled by it for such purpose, provided the cost to the partnership for such service does not exceed the customary charges for such services which prevail in the community from time to time.

(4) The general partner or any other entity controlled by it will have the right to enter into fixed-cost construction contracts with the partnership, provided that the contract price established thereby is competitive with the charges prevailing in the community of other general contractors similarly situated.

(5) The general partner or any affiliated entity will have the right to sell new furniture and furnishings and other

Illustration 10-2 (cont.)

SYNDICATION—LIMITED PARTNERSHIPS § 21:132

articles of a tangible or intangible nature to the partnership, provided the cost to the partnership for such service does not exceed the customary charges for such services and supplies which prevail in the community from time to time.

Practice Notes:

For discussion of compensation of general partner, see § 21:73.

☑ **Comment:** In the interest of simplification, the form set forth above and subsequent forms in this subdivision [§§ 21:131 et seq.] are drafted in terms of compensation of a single general partner. However, appropriate changes can easily be made if more than one general partner is involved.

§ 21:132 Single management fee

For its services in providing management and investment advice to the partners, the general partner will be entitled to an investment management fee, to be paid quarterly based on the real estate assets of the partnership. The term "real estate assets" as used in this section will mean those real property assets, and the personal property assets related to them, that appear on the quarterly balance sheet of the partnership prepared on the basis of accounting used for federal income tax purposes. The investment management fee will consist of the following:

(1) With respect to those real estate assets reflected on the quarterly balance sheet of the partnership that were not acquired during the calendar year in which the computation is made, a fee equal to ___1___ percent (____%) of so much of the total value of such assets as does not exceed ___2___ Dollars ($____), plus ___3___ percent (____%) of the balance of such value.

(2) With respect to those real estate assets reflected on the quarterly balance sheet of the partnership that were acquired during the calendar quarter for which the computation is being made, a fee equal to ___4___ percent (____%) of the value of that portion of the assets acquired during such calendar quarter which, together with the value of the other real estate related assets of the partnership shown on such balance sheet, have a total value of up to ___5___ Dollars ($____), plus ___6___ percent (____%) of the value of

Illustration 10-2 (cont.)

such assets acquired during the calendar quarter having a total value in excess of __7______ Dollars ($____). This portion of the investment management fee will be payable in equal installments following the end of each calendar quarter remaining in such year, including the quarter in which such property is acquired by the partnership.

The appropriate investment management fee will be paid within __8______ days after the end of each calendar quarter.

Practice Notes:

(See Practice Notes following § 21:131)

§ 21:133 Performance incentive fee

The general partner will be entitled to a performance incentive fee in addition to __1______ *[other fee]* in the event of a net gain realized by the partnership on the sale of capital assets during the fiscal year of the partnership. The performance incentive fee will be an amount equal to __2______ percent (____%) of the net gain. For purposes of this section, the term "net gain" is defined as the sales price, including __3______ [brokers' fees], less the original cost, including __4______ *[description of items],* but excluding __5______ [depreciation]. The performance incentive fee will be paid by the partnership to the general partner within __6______ days after the end of the fiscal year of the partnership. The obligation to pay the performance incentive fee will become absolute when the transaction for the sale of the asset is closed and will not thereafter be conditioned in any way on completion of the sale transaction or receipt of the proceeds by the partnership.

Practice Notes:

(See Practice Notes following § 21:131)

4. DISTRIBUTION OF ASSETS

§ 21:141 Allocation of profits and losses between classes

A. Definitions. For the purpose of this agreement, the

Illustration 10-2 (cont.)

following terms and phrases will have the meanings set forth below:

(1) "Invested Capital" will mean the original investment in the partnership less any amount received from proceeds from the resale or refinancing of partnership investment properties.

(2) "Net profits from operations" and "net losses from operations" will mean the profits or losses of the partnership from the operation and management of partnership property after all expenses incurred in connection with the partnership business have been paid or provided for, exclusive of prepaid interest, points and investment advisory fees, and any gain or loss realized by the partnership on the sale, refinancing, or other disposition of the partnership assets or any part of such assets, but including deductions for the depreciation of partnership property. Consistent with the definition, net profits from operations and net losses from operations will be determined in accordance with generally accepted accounting principles as determined for federal income tax purposes. All books and records of the partnership will be kept on the cash basis and on the basis of an annual accounting period ending __1__ [December 31 *or as the case may be],* except that the final accounting period will end on dissolution or termination of the partnership without reconstitution. All references to a "year of the partnership" are to such an annual accounting period. Accelerated methods of depreciation __2__ [will *or* will not] be elected by the partnership for purposes of reporting federal or state income taxes.

B. Profits From Sale of Partnership Assets. The net profits of the partnership for each year of the partnership, if any, from the sale of partnership assets will be credited to the accounts of the partners as follows and in the following order of priority:

(1) First, an amount equal to the amount, if any, of any deductions previously allocated to the Class B limited partners as a result of expenses for prepaid interest, points, and

Illustration 10-2 (cont.)

§ 21:141 REAL PROPERTY

advisory fees pursuant to ________ [subsection D (1) of this section] will be credited ratably to the account of the Class B limited partners.

(2) Then, the balance of the net profits from the sale of partnership assets will be credited ratably in the ratio of ___4___ [twenty percent (20%)] to the accounts of the Class A limited partners and ___5___ [eighty percent (80%)] to the accounts of the Class B limited partners.

C. Profits from Operations. The net profits from operations, if any, as defined above will, for each year of the partnership, be credited to the accounts of the partners as follows: ___6___ [Twenty percent (20%)] to the Class A limited partners and ___7___ [eighty percent (80%)] to the Class B limited partners.

D. Allocation of Certain Expenses and Losses. Certain expenses incurred by the partnership, as well as losses from partnership operations, will be charged among the partners as follows:

(1) First, all prepaid interest, points, and advisory fees, to the extent such expenses are not paid from operating income, will be charged to the Class B limited partners making a capital contribution to the partnership in the calendar year in which such prepayments and payments are actually made by the partnership, in proportion to the capital investment actually made by such Class B limited partners in such year.

(2) Second, losses in an amount equal to the First Priority Payments actually paid to the Class A limited partners in such year pursuant to Section ___8___ hereof will be charged ratably to the Class A limited partners.

(3) Third, losses in an amount equal to the Second Priority Payments actually paid to Class B limited partners in such year pursuant to Section ___9___ hereof will be charged ratably to the Class B limited partners.

(4) Thereafter, except as provided in Section 179 of the Internal Revenue Code, the balance of all losses will be

Illustration 10-2 (cont.)

charged to the Class B limited partners (a) during __10_____ *[current year]* and __11_____ *[next year]*, proportionately to the amount of their total capital investments and the number of weeks of investment in the partnership, and (b) thereafter, proportionately to the amounts of their total capital investments; provided, that for __12_____ *[current year]* all partners will, in addition to the weeks actually invested in the partnership, be deemed to have been invested in the partnership for each week of __13_____ *[year]* up to the date on which the first partner was admitted to the partnership.

Tax Notes:

SUBSECTION D(4)

In the case of Internal Revenue Code § 179 property, i.e., tangible personal property, new or used, of a character subject to the allowance for depreciation under *26 USCS § 167* [see *26 CFR § 1.179-3]*, a taxpayer may, for the first taxable year for which a depreciation deduction with respect to such property is allowable, elect to include as part of the "reasonable allowance" allowed by *26 USCS § 167* an additional allowance of 20 percent of the cost or of a portion of the cost of such property *[26 CFR § 1.179-1]*. There is, however, a dollar limitation on such allowance [see *26 CFR § 1.179-2]*.

Practice Notes:

This form, intended to be used with the forms set forth in §§ 21:121 and 21:141, provides generally for allocation of profits and losses among partners when a partnership is formed with two classes of limited partnership interests. Corresponding provisions in the form of a complete partnership agreement [§ 21:101], which provides for only one class of such interests, appear in sections 11.3 and 11.4 of that form.

§ 21:142 Distribution of proceeds from operations

A. Definitions. As used in this agreement, the term "gross spendable funds" will, for any year of the partnership, mean the excess, if any, of (1) the funds that the partnership will receive from operations and any other source (other than the sale of assets and from borrowing or refinancing) for such year over (2) the sum of (a) all expenses, plus (b) all amounts paid or accrued by or on behalf of the partnership in such year on account of the amortization of any debts or liabilities of the partnership, other than debts to partners. The term "spendable funds" will, for any year of the partnership, mean the excess, if any, of (1) gross spendable

Illustration 10-2 (cont.)

§ 21:142 REAL PROPERTY

funds over (2) the sum of (a) all amounts retained as reserves, plus (b) priority payments to the limited partners as provided in this agreement.

B. Reserves and Priority Payments. For each year of the partnership, the gross spendable funds will be used as follows and in the following order:

(1) First, for retention as reserves to the extent that the general partner(s) will, in the exercise of reasonable business judgment, believe necessary to meet the needs of the partnership business.

(2) Second, for first priority payments, which are payments made ratably to the Class A limited partners, each year, in an amount equal to a __1______ [ten percent (10%)] per annum cumulative return on their invested capital.

(3) Third, for second priority payments, which are payments made ratably to the Class B limited partners, each year, in an amount equal to a __2______ [five percent (5%)] per annum cumulative return on their invested capital.

(4) The amounts payable to Class A limited partners and Class B limited partners pursuant to subsections b(2) and b(3) above will constitute guaranteed payments within the meaning of Section 707c of the Internal Revenue Code, as amended, and will be treated as expenses in determining the net income or net loss of the partnership.

C. Distribution of Spendable Funds. For each year of the partnership spendable funds, if any, will be distributed ratably __3______ [twenty percent (20%)] to the Class A limited partners and __4______ [eighty percent (80%)] to the Class B limited partners.

Tax Notes:

SUBSECTION B(4)

To the extent determined without regard to the income of the partnership, payments to a partner for services or the use of capital are considered as being made to one who is not a member of the partnership, but only for the purposes of *26 USCS § 61(a)* (relating to gross income) and *26 USCS § 162(a)* (relating to trade or business expenses). *26 USCS § 707(c)*.

Practice Notes:

(See Practice Notes following § 21:121)

Illustration 10-2 (cont.)

§ 21:143 Distribution of surplus funds

A. Definition. Surplus funds will mean the net proceeds from the sale or refinancing of partnership assets other than as part of the process of liquidating the partnership.

B. Method of distribution. Surplus funds, giving cumulative effect to all prior distributions, will be distributed at the end of the next succeeding quarter following their accrual as follows:

(1) First, there will be distributed to the Class A limited partners an amount which, when added to all priority payments and other distributions of spendable funds and surplus funds up to that time received by such partners, equals one hundred percent (100%) of their capital contributions together with a sum equal to a __1__ [ten percent (10%)] per annum cumulative return on the invested capital of such partners.

(2) Second, there will be distributed to the Class B partners an amount which, when added to all distributions of spendable funds and surplus funds up to that time received by such partners, equals __2__ [one hundred percent (100%)] of the invested capital of such partners.

(3) Third, of the amount remaining, __3__ [eighty percent (80%)] will be distributed ratably to the Class B limited partners and __4__ [twenty percent (20%)] will be distributed ratably to the Class A limited partners, provided that such payments will continue only until, as a result of all priority payments and distributions of spendable funds and surplus funds, the Class B limited partners have received an additional amount equal to a cumulative return on their invested capital of __5__ [ten percent (10%)] per annum and the Class A limited partners have received an additional amount, added to that provided for in subsection A(1) above, equal to a cumulative return on their invested capital of __6__ [two and one-half percent (2½%)] per annum.

(4) Finally, any balance will be distributed __7__ [seventy-two percent (72%)] to the Class B limited partners,

Illustration 10-2 (cont.)

__8__ [eighteen percent (18%)] to the Class A limited partners, and __9__ [ten percent (10%)] to the general partner(s).

C. Withholding of Distributions to Certain Class B Limited Partners. Notwithstanding the provisions of Subsection B(2) above, if the funds available for distribution to the Class B limited partners are, when added to all prior distributions to the Class B limited partners, insufficient to return to all Class B limited partners the amount of their capital contributions, then and in such event there will be withheld from the funds otherwise distributed to Class B limited partners who contributed capital in __10__ *[year]* (the __11__ *(year)* Class B limited partners) a sum equal to the amount of deductions charged to the __12__ *[year]* Class B limited partners pursuant to Section __13__ of this agreement. Such withheld amounts will be distributed to the Class B limited partners who contributed capital to the partnership in __14__ *[year]* (the __15__ *(year)* Class B limited partners) to the extent necessary to effect a return to such partners of an amount that, including all prior distributions to such partners, equals __16__ [one hundred percent (100%)] of their capital contributions. The balance of such withheld amounts not so distributed to the __17__ *[year]* Class B limited partners will then be distributed to the __18__ *[year]* Class B limited partners.

Practice Notes:

(See Practice Notes following § 21:121)

§ 21:144 Redemption of units

Class A units may be redeemed, but Class B units may not be redeemed through the reserve account as provided in Section __1__ *[refer to section concerning redemption reserve account].*

Practice Notes:

(See Practice Notes following § 21:121)

PROMOTIONAL DEVICES

A variety of sales techniques are undertaken by the sponsor of a syndicate as a means of accumulating the necessary capital to undertake a given project. Obviously the techniques will vary dependent upon whether the offering is a nationwide public offering done through a NASD member firm, as opposed to a smaller localized operation. In the case of the former, name recognition of the syndicator, such as Harry Helmsley, would have more attraction than Joe Schmoe from Kokomo. Additionally, an underwriter, such as Shearson Lehman, or some other nationwide brokerage would be utilized for the sale of investment units. Additionally, pictures of prior successful operations with a complete biographical breakdown of the staff would be provided as further means of investor assurance.

Localized syndication efforts would probably be a little more low key with the sponsor stressing reputation for honesty and competence; business involvement in the community, and an avowed determination to act in the best interests of the investment group.

As previously noted, when no specified property is involved, emphasis on the investment concept combined with the goals and objectives to be attained in property acquisition to fulfill this conceptualization serve to appoint the general partner as the limited partner's representative to "make it happen."

In effect, all syndications, whether specified or not, deal with concept. The persuasive techniques involved must deal with selling the concept to the investment group as a means of meeting their own personal strategies.

ENTITY FORMATION

The limited partnership itself is formed under the provisions of the Uniform Limited Partnership Act, as previously noted. Each step in the process of filing the limited partnership agreement, advertising requirements and the recordation of the partnership agreement itself in the country recorder's office where the syndicate anticipates conducting business with respect to real property in that area, should be carefully planned and orchestrated by counsel. Many of the securities laws involving limited partnership are similarly in place with respect to joint ventures, corporations and real estate investment trusts who deal in similar areas of real estate investments. The entity formed is strictly a function of what organizational form that the syndicator/sponsor feels will provide and effective device for capital accumulation combined with potential yield and equity enhancement potential. Again, this is an area where legal and tax counsel can be of incomparable assistance to the syndicator.

SETTING SYNDICATION GUIDELINES

Instruments of entity formation serve as the blueprint pointing out how the structure of the syndicate will evolve. In the case of real estate investment trusts, this form of syndication has a certain appeal to investors who desire a maximum distribution of income. On the other hand, limited partnerships have the advantage of being able to build up adequate reserves for replacement in income property investments while still providing a satisfactory return to investors, if properly managed. In addition, by doing those preventative maintenance items the general partner adds value to the investment. This gives the investor a double barreled advantage of yield plus appreciation in the bargain.

For investors to gain a better insight into the process of syndication in a limited partnership mode, it becomes incumbent upon this text to explore the duties and responsibilities of the general partner to the maximum extent possible. The final chapters will follow down that well-traveled path.

11
THE GENERAL PARTNER'S ROLE

Sir Charles Spencer (Charlie) Chaplin, in his description of the quintessential character he played on the screen, seemed to capture the essence of what it takes to be a sponsor/syndicator. He described the tramp role as: ". . .a gentleman, a poet, a dreamer, a lonely fellow, always hopeful of romance and adventure. . ."

To some extent the syndicator is an island surrounded by the thousand and one details needed to amalgamate a very complex process. He has to combine that poetic dreamy style of the right brain into the left brain realities that will tickle the imagination of his investment group. He has to stretch the imagination of those who would share this dream in order to bring the group objective into fruition. The greatest challenge is in the undertaking of 1) finding the proper money source, and 2) persuading this source that the devotion of capital to the project or the concept is worthy of investor consideration.

CREATING EQUITY

The stage is set. Documentation has been created. The type of entity to use in the project in question has been decided. Now comes the acid test. How does one identify the proper marketplace for a given project? The answer to this question involves several approaches to the situation.

If the syndicator intends to undertake a fairly small project ($1 million or less in equity requirements), the possible solution is an intrastate private offering, as opposed to a public offering and the mountains of documentation required. In this case the investment units might be greater than in a public offering as well. For example, the syndicator might need $1 million to acquire a $5 million dollar project. In this private offering, the syndicator might contribute $200,000 requiring another $800,000 to complete the offering. With this thought in mind, investment units might be $40,000 a piece. The sale of 20 units at $40,000 a piece to individuals of financial substance is less difficult than trying to find one limited partner with $800,000.

The key question in this matter is how do you find investors in the first place. Sales, no matter what the product or service involves identifying the marketplace and then contacting those who represent the market. In the case of wealthy individuals, its a question of what type of media do they read. If one resides in California and desires to form a partnership of Californians, a quick method of reaching a majority of the population who have at least the means to read the newspaper is through placing ads in three metropolitan daily newspapers, namely, The *Los Angeles Times:* The San Francisco combined *Chronicle* and *Examiner;* and the *San Diego Union.* Sunday is probably a better (and more expensive) day to advertise than during the week, because your potential investors take more time to read the newspaper than during the week, where a quick glance at the summary of articles is the order of the day with concentration on specifics only if it appears of interest. The reason that the San Francisco suggestion is made for the Sunday edition is because the two papers publish independently for the balance of the week.

A note of caution: If one plans to form a syndication, it is important to review your ad copy carefully, since the Securities and Exchange Commission has very strict guidelines concerning how prospective investors can be solicited. It is incumbent upon the promotor to pre screen ad copy with the commission prior to placement.

In the event that a larger more geographically representative cross-section involving a large number of investors is required, such as the purchase of a major office structure where $10 million in equity capital is required, the strategy might change dramatically. In the initial case, advertising may not even be required if the syndicator has gained a reputation locally, possibly a few phone calls to friends will complete the syndicate. When it comes to serious money, the approach takes on a massive exposure to the general public, such as the three publications noted which will reach several million readers at one printing. When one gets to that stage where large dollar amounts are required for a single project, serious consideration has to be given to a SEC registration and the attentive paperwork. Some samples of the extent of paperwork involved are included in the appendix.

There are several advantages to public offerings, since the newspapers become an open forum for promoting the project. In addition, public meetings can be arranged to offer information to interested investors and the very fact that a registration has been made will tend to lure the investing public. Another advantage of a public offering is that limited partnership shares can be offered in smaller investment units, similar to shares of stock in a corporation. Limited partnership shares might be offered through broker-dealers in $1,000 or $5,000 increments, thus broadening the marketplace for partnership units considerably. If the marketplace for the units is expanded, then potential investors will see a clearer light relative to one of their investment objectives, i. e., liquidity. In review, the three basic goals of any investment are:

- Yield - Adequate return relative to the risk undertaken. In the case of real estate, the return should be multiples of what a treasury bill would bring.
- Safety - Here is where real estate has its greatest weakness. There is no definite guaranty in **any** real estate investment that the investor's capital has found a safe haven. There is not only the possibility of no interest return on principal, but loss of principal as well. This should be carefully explained to all potential limited partner/investors in the prospectus.
- Liquidity - In the case of a private offering, the investor has to stick it out to the end, since there is little possibility that the interest is marketable, unless there is some form of buy back agreement from the syndicator. In the case of registered partnership interests, there may be a market created by broker dealers who specialize in this form of investment where the shares may be readily traded.

Still, the syndicator has to look at the private offering as a more acceptable route to acquire the needed equity capital, since the disclosure requirements are not as stringent and the offering circular (prospectus) does not normally get regulatory scrutiny, unless problems occur with the project in question. This tends to fortify the argument that promoters should only handle private offerings where the potential for success is definitely within the realm of possibility. The alternative is the potential of civil and criminal penalties for the improper handling of syndicate formation.

In the acquisition of equity phase, the syndicator really is in a mode of self-selling. If the investment group is not convinced of the integrity and professionalism of the project promotor, all marketing efforts will be of no avail. Thus, in promotional material the syndicator must indicate sufficient background professionally to handle this enormous task as well as show that past performances have produced the results promised.

The strategy will also change in soliciting equity dollars dependent upon whether money is being solicited for a specific project, or a shelf registration of partnership shares with no specified project indicated. The strategy involved in the second area varies considerably from the first. In the initial situation, at least the investors have something that they can touch, see, feel, etc. In the latter, the only thing that is offered is a **concept**. It is much easier to sell **substance** than **idea**. When marketing is in the area of abstract, some form of concrete reference must be given.

If the syndicator intends to arrange for a non-specified offering, it is incumbent to stress that this **abstract** idea is intended to be devoted to a **concrete** investment. As an example, a syndicator might decide to have a shelf registration of 5,000 limited partnership shares at $5,000 each to raise $25 million in capital. This is a substantial sum of money, but, as one can see from the Harry Helmsley investment in the Empire State Building, there are projects which might take that amount - and more!

When one deals with this large amount of capital, some form of investor blueprint must be drawn in order that a certain degree of confidence can be elicited. To do this the promotor/syndicator must draw on a past performance record that shows a unerring degree of success in that area. Syndicators should never offer a shelf registration such as this with the intent to branch out into new areas of investment. Stick to what has provided success in the past, at least for the initial effort. If the syndicator has office building investment as an area of expertise, a venture into housing development would not be a wise move. Today, lender's misery is investor's delight when it comes to office structures, since they can be acquired at a fraction of replacement cost with little fear of competitive buildings being erected in the near future. This is probably the case for retail stores, but it requires some one with management expertise in that area to deal with the specialized problems that retail is encountering in today's markets. Even more specialized is the investment arena of industrial properties where lost tenancies could result in almost permanent vacancy, in certain instances. In the case of any real estate investment, the vulnerability of the property to cyclical change is of utmost importance to the investing public. Thus, economic factors and the criteria for investment spelled out by the syndicator in the prospectus is of prime importance.

With these thoughts in mind, what if the syndicator wants to shelf register these $25 million in limited partnership interests with the intent of acquiring well located office structures at less than 100% occupancy from real estate owned portfolios of institutional investors or their regulatory authorities, based on prices that will still provide positive cash flow at the lower occupancy. This being the case, that provides the great investor motivational device of **yield** in a two-fold manner. Initially, there is a return on invested capital from the cash flow of the project. The major pay day, however, can be elicited from appreciation that can occur through the implementation of efficient and affective property management strategies to increase occupancy and add value to the structure accordingly. Let's take an example:

The syndicator, after registering the securities, locates a building in an area where there is considerably growth potential economically, such as Orlando, Florida where Epcot, Universal Studios and other travel and entertainment related industries have located in recent years. The building contains a total of 200,000 net rentable square feet and is currently 75% occupied at a rent level of $1.25 per square foot/month. The project analysis becomes:

Total current annual gross rents = 150,000 x $1.25 x 12 =	$2,250,000
Vacancy allowance 7 and 1/2% =	168,750
Effective rent - according to syndication analysis	$2,081,250
Expenses - 32%	666,000
Net Operation Income (NOI)	$1,415,250
Offering Price, based upon a 9-1/2% capitalization rate =	$15,000,000
Down payment required from shelf registration -	$5,000,000
Remainder financed by lender/seller at 8-1/2%, 30 year fixed terms with a 10 year call =	$10,000,000
Annual Debt Service requirement =	857,610
Cash flow available to limited partners*	$557,640

Return on partnership investment =
557,640 divided by 5 million, or 11.15%

*Considering a very conservative $22 million dollar replacement value for the building and using the optional 40 year life, depreciation write-off would be $550,000, leaving a high degree of investment capital totally sheltered from taxes with advantages of equity build-up and appreciation possible. The amount used in the analysis for vacancy allowance is a fudge factor to be used for replacement reserves, particularly if the occupancy is on a long-term lease basis.

Through the use of hypotheticals such as this, which represent existing project performance, the syndicator can provide the concrete investment structure required to persuade investment in the registration. In registrations of this nature, the caveats required by the SEC would be considerable, since there is no specific project involved and investment is at the sole discretion of the promoter. This is still another reason that the syndicator should stick to the type of investment where success has been derived, rather than branching out into new areas.

If the syndicator decides to use seminars or some form of presentation format, it then becomes a question of whether one uses a rifle to take aim at an identified segment of the market, like talking to local chambers of commerce, or an open forum to present the program to the general public. The most exposure for liability on the part of a project promoter is to go the public forum route, since members of the audience tend to be less sophisticated in this form of investment vehicle. The main consideration in making presentations is to encourage those **eligible** investors to pick up the offering materials. This is the principal objective of using any forum to expose investors to the offerings. Once the decision to pick up the offering materials is made, the basic decision to invest then falls in the investors' hands.

Another popular method of getting investor interest in a public offering is to hire a public relations firm whose sole objective is to get the name of the syndicator in the media. Media consultants perform this task and are well paid in the effort if they perform their duties professionally. They can provide assistance in locating your target market and using the proper media source to reach it. They also know the type of copy to expose the syndicator to the public that is acceptable by the media source felt most suitable to reach the target market. In the case of public offerings, the use of a media consultant is critical. Even more so, their assistance can enhance the limited scope of private offerings.

In addition to the use of broker-dealers, a popular device for large public offerings, the private sale to investors can be enhanced by finders who have contact with the investment community and will refer its members to the syndicator in return for a referral fee. They should be differentiated from sales personnel, since the finders merely refer clients, they don't close the deal. This differentiation should be made perfectly clear.

Probably the safest route to follow is the securities brokerage one in the long run, since they already have an established sophisticated client list which does not require the extensive pre-selling tactics involved in other securities marketing approaches.

Before leaving this critical area of marketing, it is also incumbent upon the promoter not only to promote the sale of equity in a real estate venture, but the geographic location where the equity dollars will be placed. For this reason alone, considerable economic data relative to the feasibility of real estate investment in the area should have extensive coverage. Data such as population, income, demographic mix, employment and business opportunities should be explored in detail. As an addenda to this coverage, occupancy levels, median home prices and the general real estate sales and leasing environment should be explored in detail. Just being a nice place to live does not fit the suitability bill for deploying hard earned investment dollars.

BALANCING RISK AND REWARDS

In order that the syndicator continue to gradually develop the structure of the organization, it is important that a comprehensive examination of any proposed investment as well as alternative choices in the selected target area be considered.

One example is the city of Tucson, Arizona. In recent years major national concerns, such as International Business Machines and Hughes Aircraft have chosen this area as a location for major business facilities. Hughes announced in March of 1993 that they intended to relocate their missile systems division located in Canoga Park, California to their already existing facility. This means that some 1,900 workers will be involved in a relocation, lay off, retirement or other mode. Each of these employees would be considered in the middle or upper middle class income category. How the decision is made concerning how many will relocate, how many will lose jobs, etc., has a definite bearing on California and Arizona's economy. These are core employment positions that will be lost to California and new core positions to be introduced to Arizona. The story doesn't stop there, though. For each core job, 1-1/2 to 2-1/2 service jobs are created in the service industries that support core employment. Any time jobs of this magnitude are lost in one area and gained in another, there's a geometric effect.

That doesn't mean that investors should give up on California, even Southern California, for that matter. Northern California seems to have weathered the economic scythe a bit better than their Southern counterparts. There still remains one bright star on the business horizon which deals with the free trade pact between Mexico and the United States. In the Otay Mesa area of San Diego, a free trade zone has been created causing a boom in demand for warehouse space for goods being shipped from Mexican manufacturers into the United States from American firms that have relocated manufacturing facilities south of the border. These goods still have to be warehoused and shipped to various customer destinations. Industrial activity in the Otay Mesa area has been speeding up at an accelerated pace as a result.

The ideal syndicator either has the personal tools necessary to notice these marketplace nuances to be able to take advantage of the situation or have the staff available who are on top of such situations.

The syndicator has to be half Svengali and half miracle worker with that touch of miraculous "real estate sense" to identify the proper location for investment real estate opportunities. The key is the ability to foretell. We're all familiar with the expression "cutting edge." When the real syndicator is there, the knife hasn't even arrived by UPS yet. That's the time that money can be made through appreciation. Once the parade of lookie loos comes along, the bloom is off the real estate rose. The profits have been made and the syndicate goes riding down another avenue of opportunity.

Nobody's riding anywhere in the syndication conveyance unless the driver of the vehicle is in control. Some of the methods used to steer a straight course keeping the goals in sight will be covered in the next chapter.

12
MANAGEMENT AND CONTROL

Friederich August von Hayek observed in *The Use of Knowledge in Society in Individualism and Economic Order,* published in 1948, that, "Many of the greatest things man has achieved are not the result of consciously directed thought, and still less the product of a deliberately coordinated effort of many individuals, but of a process in which the individual plays a part which he (sic) can never fully understand. . ." This trite statement probably represents one of the most pessimistic reflections upon management's role ever written. One has to go beyond von Hayek to understand the role of the syndicator/promoter as one who manages the entire process. Management plays a key role in the **value preservation and enhancement process** of the properties acquired by the syndicate.

MINDING THE STORE

Webster's describes manage in its simplest form ". . .to conduct or direct affairs; carry on business. . ." Within that terse statement lies a plethora of duties necessary to properly conduct the affairs of a syndicate. Syndicates range from the simple structure of a single project to a vast array of holdings nationwide with variations of the theme in between. The management style necessary to perform the tasks at hand vary with the duties and responsibilities undertaken by the syndicator.

In any event, there is a need to coordinate, direct and control the effort of a variety of resources in order to initiate and bring a given syndication to fruition. Once acquired, the property then needs megadoses of operating statement massage together with application of remedial actions related to the property management function. All of these responsibilities lie directly on the shoulders of the syndicator. Proper allocation of assigned duties, preparation of job descriptions, job specifications, management goals and objectives, budget preparation, investor reporting, interface with regulators and consultants, ad infinitum all fall within the aegis of management's responsibility. Much of the success of the enterprise depends upon how each of these matters is addressed.

Management of any enterprise starts out with the formulation of a basic business plan. Foundational to the plan is a **mission statement** for the enterprise which, quite simply, just tells the public what management feels is the direction and thrust of the organization. A mission statement for a syndicate who has as its objective the creation of yield plus appreciation for its investors might be something like this:

"The objective of Foresight Investors is to identify real estate investment opportunities throughout this country which will provide maximum return combined with future appreciation potential. Within this objective our efforts will be tempered with prudent investigative efforts to minimize risk, application of modern property management technology, accurate reporting of financial results, and employment of skill professional employees and consultants to properly fulfill the mission of this enterprise. . ."

The hidden asset of **any** enterprise's balance sheet is probably the most valuable of all - human resources. In the budget-paring, facility-closing, debt-ridden enterprises glutted by the leveraged buy out fever of corporate America in the 1980s, the human element has been shoved to the wayside. Current management mentality is geared to staff reduction, reliance on part-timers with no benefits and other cost-cutting devices to provide short-term solutions. Organization charts do not make the enterprise - people do! Once this concept is firmly implanted in management, the business of the organization can once again be conducted by a staff that is totally dedicated to its mission.

How many times have you personally observed persons who seem more like automatons than animated with joy over the job that they're performing? This observation is being repeated all too often these days. Part of this stems from the fact that diffidence on the part of their superiors leads to sub par job performance.

Management has the responsibility of assuring its clients (in this case, the investors) that the staff is not only well trained and competent, but that their efforts are appreciated and they will be aptly compensated for their contribution to the goals of the enterprise. This means that syndicators must have personnel, either on staff or on a consultancy basis, that are thoroughly familiar with their systems and procedures with the skills necessary to perform their assigned duties. With this in mind, some form of an orientation process is required of all new staff members in order that they feel comfortable with their assigned tasks. This means that job specifications and job descriptions are the order of the day. Job specifications are required in order that the personnel function (probably the syndicator in a small operation) outline what skills are needed for the candidate to perform the assigned task outlined in the job description properly. Just as in any business decision, there may be compromises. Organization charts may be attractive as a display on the office wall, but they not only must reflect the mission statement of the enterprise, they must be **functional**. This implies that the following regimen must be in place:

- A means of communicating policy matters to new hires
- Training and indoctrination
- Performance evaluation.

The third step in this human resources regimen is probably the most critical. If a person is unaware where he/she stands with his/her employer, this feeling of insecurity will be communicated formally or informally with clients. This tends to erode confidence with a capital "C" in the process. This implies that the manager must also have attributes essential to perform or delegate the tasks needed for human resource development. These aptitudes center around the following areas of concern:

- Dedication to efficiency and profit
- Tact - Impatience is an employee turn-off
- Proficiency in communication and learning skills
- Marketing expertise - The native ability to smell a prospect
- Assuming the mantle of leadership.

How effective is a rudderless boat? In the same way, if the syndicator does not develop the leadership qualities essential to commanding loyalty and support of the staff and any consultants required, the organization will fail by inertia. A leader is a decision maker. Good or bad, the decisions need to be made in order for the organization to function in an efficient manner. Management should also opt up to their mistakes - not trying to shift the blame. Harry Truman said it all with the trite "the buck stops here." It serves as a humble reminder to all who are in the management mode.

PROBLEM SOLVING

The greatest challenge facing any management entity, whether it be syndicating income properties or manufacturing widgets, lies in the area of problem solving. In syndication the problem can be quite complex, since one has to define the problem before addressing it. The principal problem faced by all syndicators is finding the product in the form of an income-producing property that is a worthy candidate for the syndication process. The approach required entails a variety of procedures to reach a satisfactory solution.

The initial step in this process involves the macroeconomic approach, or the "big picture" analysis of what is happening economically throughout our country. The 1980s were a sort of macroeconomic nightmare waiting to happen due to various abuses imposed upon our system by the financial community, in particular the securities institutions through merger mania and marketing of junk bonds combined with the out of control credit extensions by certain financial institutions to literally deal a fatal blow to the exuberance of our economic health. This caused a stumbling, bumbling, barely breathing economy to venture its tentacles into the untamed business waters of the 1990s. Of all of the 48 contiguous states, California was probably delivered the most painful blow, economically, of any state. One of the reasons for this major impact was the fact that a large part of the economy in that state was slavishly tied to the defense industry. When peace broke out, the defense community had not developed a plan B, C or D as an alternative. They figured that the government, as usual, would bail them out of their predicament with some new program which would keep their engineers occupied. Surprise. No bail out. In fact, the situation has now been exacerbated by the Clinton administration's plan for military base closings, which will again tend to erode business activity in the state. The syndicator must sift all this economic information and make some sense out of it.

The solution to this problem coming out of management's logic system (in this case syndicators who have opted to form the bottom fishing vulture funds) in determining that the lender's malaise of the 1980s have become the investor's resuscitation in the 1990s. Income producing properties subject to loans based upon inflated appraisals combined with overestimated projections of future performance in the prior decade become an easy investment prey today. Buildings having a $9 million dollar lien on them may be purchased for $4 or $5 million today. Today's reality forces the financial institutions to deal with the matter based upon the current economic productivity of their buildings, far below earlier expectations. This provides a partial solution to the basic problem for the syndicator concerning what area to concentrate an investment strategy. The second, and probably most crucial, segment to consider involves the region of the country which offers the most promise for the future. This involves a delicate matter of timing. The syndicator doesn't want to get on the bandwagon that is already full. In contrast, the search entails identifying those certain economic events, such as the maquiladora program in Mexico, which have implications in this country.

Another matter to address is the fact that some areas are losing jobs through business relocation. What areas, in turn, become major beneficiaries of the relocation move. When General Motors decided on a truly unique location for manufacture of the Saturn automobile, they didn't choose Detroit. Rather, they chose Tennessee. There seems to be a tendency of corporate America to seek headquarters locations away from the urban hustle and bustle of major metropolitan centers possibly choosing a midwest location as an alternate. These subtle shifts in attitudes are based, somewhat, on the aggressiveness of state governments in seeking industry within their borders. Examples of this phenomena are the efforts of the states of Kentucky and Florida who have experienced more than a modicum of success in attracting new business within their borders.

Once the syndicator has identified the geographic location which offers the most promise, then it becomes a matter of identifying the proper property which **meets the investment objectives spelled out in the syndicate's mission statement.** If the syndicate has a minimum before tax return yield criteria for its investment group of 12% or more, then properties have to be identified that, through negotiation, have the reasonable expectation of providing that minimum return. In addition, there has to be some potential upward mobility, value-wise, as the additional financial "carrot" for the investment group. This is what sells partnership shares quickly. If the limited partner investor can perceive the opportunities, very little persuasion to purchase is needed.

Problem solving is not just exclusive to identifying the economic factors essential to potential success of a project to be acquired, the mechanics of acquisition, the documentation process, establishment of investor reporting following acquisition, property management and the thousand niggling details of running a business all fall on the very burdened shoulders of the syndicator. Without the full-fledged support of staff and consultants - it's never going to happen. One of the principal concerns of the syndicator involves the fact that we all live in a regulatory environment. How one conducts business within this arena separates the champions from the contenders.

REGULATOR CONCERNS

One of the problems facing all syndicators in the 1990s is the abuses of limited partnerships created during the 1980s. One could invest in anything from railroad tank cars to cattle feeding partnerships to partnerships marketing bogus computer programs. The list was continuous and exhaustive. Yes, there were a lot of turkey real estate limited partnerships formed where the general partners sucked the projects dry and left the limited partners holding empty pocket books.

The Tax Reform Act of 1986 took a lot of these seedy players out of the game. In their place are real estate partnerships based upon the simple premise that income-producing property is supposed to do just that - produce income. It may seem a startling revelation to those who used negative cash flow in the 1980s being churned out by a limited partnership to offset high personal employment income. That little loophole was neatly closed by the TRA.

The net result of this nefarious activity of the previous decade has caused a resurgence of consumer awareness that is reflected in the regulatory process. Between the Securities and Exchange Commission, whose stringent rules are noted in the appendix, and the Department of Corporations of the state of domicile, limited partnerships, real estate investment trusts, corporations and the like have gone through more serious regulatory scrutiny than in the past.

Due to the high profile approach that regulators have taken in the syndication area, syndicators must be acutely aware of their documentation procedures when forming the syndicate. The two hypersensitive areas of concern that get the most regulatory attention revolve around the following:

- Solicitation of investors through newspaper ads and informatory seminars.
- The actual content of the prospectus.

In the former, it is important that the syndicator share ad copy and seminar material with the regulatory process as a matter of courtesy. It could avoid harsh enforcement actions at a later date. In the case of the latter, it is important that the prospectus fairly depict the project and its prospects without misleading the reader. In following this regimen the syndicator will hopefully avoid the entanglement of costly litigation involved when a prospective investor has been led down the garden path by a prospectus which slickly avoided pitfalls known by the syndicator but not indicated by this powerful sales tool.

Within this management problem solving regimen is the toughest decision of all. This also revolves around the project offering. The choice of a specified offering versus a nonspecified offering and whether the offering is a private or public one. These critical decisions may also limit the involvement of regulators in the process as well. In the case of a private offering, only the adherence to regulator guidelines controls. In a public offering, regulators get involved with both feet from the start.

The more difficult decision of specified versus unspecified offerings requires considerable study. The latter should never be undertaken by a novice. It is better for the initial offering to be done on the basis of a private offering by the syndicator to individuals known to the syndicator on a specific property capable of personal identification by the investment group. Only then, after successful acquisition, management and disposition of the initial project should the syndicator think in terms of the more involve process of public offerings for unspecified property acquisition.

Management of the property itself may also involve interface with local governmental regulators running the gamut from tax assessors and collectors to local planning commissions. Management expertise in government relations becomes essential in dealing with all levels of governmental authority. It is also vital in the establishment of appropriate investor reporting systems and the distribution of profits in accordance with the provisions of the agreement under which the syndicate operates. In a majority of cases, this is the limited partnership agreement.

The management process provides the essential elements of organizing, coordinating, directing, and controlling the efforts of others in a meaningful and professional fashion. To do anything less would be a disservice to syndicate clients.

Even though consultants are not formally staff members, they perform an important staff function. The syndicator must be aware of this relationship. The interface of staff and consultants should always be open and direct. Any form of evasive behavior on the part of the syndicator/boss that is perceived by the employees as undercutting their authority can cause irreparable harm to the overall morale level. Syndicators should attempt to be open and communicative keeping the staff fully informed of development, so they are not blind-sided by a decision that is not communicated to them by the boss, but the consultant. All decisions relative to consultant matters that involve internal procedures should be communicated by the syndicator either directly or by delegation to some other responsible staff member.

Management can possibly be one of the most vexing areas of syndication. The only way that the syndicate can survive is on the basis of doing business. How the business is created will serve as the centerpiece of the next chapter.

13
CREATING THE MARKET

Economist John Kenneth Galbraith in *The New Industrial State* observed: "The enemy of the market is not ideology but the engineer..." This subtle phrasing indicates the importance of a syndicator in the scheme of things. It almost takes a person possessing financial and marketing omniscience uplifting efforts above that harried crowd that is constantly wooing the investor's dollars. In order for any investment engine to purr smoothly through its assigned task, the purifying lubricant of money is needed in order for it to reach its assigned destination. In order to launch any syndication effort, the syndicator must be a person of some means in order for the engine to even get on the tracks.

FINANCING CONCERNS

In our prior description of the Harry Helmsley involvement in the Empire State Building acquisition from the Jacob family and Prudential Insurance, hopefully the reader did not overlook the fact that Mr. Helmsley was able to borrow several million dollars on the swipe of a pen. Anyone who has a modicum of knowledge about banking will come to the conclusion that Mr. Helmsley must have had a very impressive financial statement to warrant that much unsecured credit.

If one is about to embark on the entrepreneurial adventure of starting a syndicate, there are a few ground rules that need to be observed financially. If one has sufficient financial and real estate expertise to identify an appropriate investment, this is only part of the process. It will take some financial wherewithal to tie up the property in the first place to allow time to form the limited partnership or whatever other form of entity desired in order to attain the balance of capital required to close the deal. One of the steps that might be taken in the process is the formation of a limited partnership where the syndicator takes the initial role of general and limited partner just to get things going.

Usually the hiring of consultants or the engagement of staff also requires devotion of capital. There are usually no free lunches in the investment world. Everybody expects payment in some form. Sometime this payment may be in the form of a limited partnership interest. This is one way that the syndicator can conserve capital. Practically every approach used to tie up property requires some form of consideration as assurance to the seller that the deal is binding. If one observes the ways that parcels can be controlled, each has its own form of consideration. Each is examined in detail:

- Development property - Sellers may agree to a combination of a cash down payment with a purchase money lien for the balance to be subordinated to a future construction loan for the intended improvements. Another method is to take the seller into the partnership with the land as the partnership contribution. In some cases additional capital will still be required for the preparation of plans, the permitting process and closing costs, some of which may be reimbursable. Another method which has been used is for the seller to take cash and **an unsecured note** for the balance of the land cost. This is not a recommended procedure, since it offers little or no protection for sellers in case of some adverse situation.

- Identified improved income property - There are several methods used by syndicators to control present or future use of the property:

  1) Lease with option to purchase - In this case, working capital is required to pay the lease payments and for ordinary maintenance and repair of the property in an ownership mode. Also the costs of forming the syndicate will be borne by the syndicator as well.

  2) Straight option to purchase - For a monetary consideration the syndicator has the price of the parcel frozen in place. For example, an office building containing 100,000 square feet of net rentable space is tied up by the syndicator through the use of an option to purchase. Based upon a NOI of $810,000, the syndicator has negotiated an option price of $8,000,000. To obtain assurance of this purchase price, the syndicator is required to pay $200,000 for a one year option. This provides the syndicator adequate time to form a limited partnership and sell the shares sufficient to make a down payment of $2,000,000 on the property while arranging permanent financing for the

balance of the purchase price. Again, this requires seed capital to be provided by the syndicator.

3) The least satisfactory method of tying up property is through the use of a long term escrow with contingencies. This device is merely a method of supplanting the option, which is a more appropriate device. The syndicator with limited funds may choose this route, since possibly a $50,000 deposit can be used in place of the option monies described above.

Just tying up the property doesn't get the property acquired. This takes the engagement of several consultants in order for the next stage to come about. Some of the more important participants in this area would be:

- Media consultant - Engagement of a professional in this area allows the syndicator the means of exploring the appropriate advertising vehicle or marketing approach to use in order to attract funds for the syndicate. If advertising is used, the advertising cost, which can be considerable, plus the commission paid to the consultant for its placement in addition to consultation fees are all expenses to be borne by the syndicator.
- Legal and accounting expenses - In this area the processing of entity formation, interface with regulators, structuring tax advantages, paperwork preparation and the like all contain a price tag to be borne initially by the syndicator.
- Real Estate Brokerage - Buyer's agencies are becoming more and more popular as real estate professionals are used to scout for properties either locally or nationwide, depending upon the scope of syndication, in the ever frantic search for the appropriate property. Any expenses incurred by brokerage also have to be initially borne by the syndicator.
- Underwriting expenses - If the offering is to be made through a broker-dealer, expenses of underwriting the issue must be borne by the syndicator, subject to future reimbursement by the entity.
- Staff expenses - It normally takes clerical and administrative support to undertake investments that comprise any magnitude. The syndicator must have sufficient funds to remunerate the staff in their activities.

Depending upon the individual qualifications of a particular syndicator, these expenses may vary. For example, if the syndicator has a securities background combined with legal and accounting expertise, considerable expense reduction may occur in these areas. The bottom line is, **the syndicator must have sufficient seed capital to see the project through the sale of investment units to the investment group.** How the syndicator moves from tying up the property to energizing the syndication in this ever evolving market place is another move in this fascinating financial chess game where the next move may be checkmate.

MARKETING CONCERNS

In any form of sales presentation, there must be some form of persuasive approach needed to convince the investor that this is an appropriate commitment of funds. In the case of syndication, marketing does not stop at the preparation of a prospectus, obtaining finders to locate investors, hiring broker-dealers to sell securities, advertising the opportunity through target marketing publications and the like. Marketing is a continuous activity throughout the life of the syndicate. Marketing represents the difference between a successful venture and one that falls flat on its heels. It has been previously noted that the three investor objectives in any investment deal with yield, safety and liquidity. The most compelling of these forces is the first one - yield. This is the grabber that salivates investor appetite coupled with any tax benefits that might be derived in the process. The marketing effort of the syndicate **after** the capital has been obtained, the deal closed and operation of the partnership property is underway, can prove the true mettle of the syndicator.

Property management plays a key role in the syndication process. If this duty is not performed in a professional and efficient manner, the investment can be eroded through management inertia. In order to entice investors to entertain the next project, syndicators must pay particular attention to property management. In order to illustrate how property management plays a role in syndication success, let's take that 100,000 square foot net rentable office building and see how management can enhance value. Let's consider that at the time of purchase, the building was less than 100% occupied with an average rental of $1.60 per square foot month on 80% of the space with an average of seven years left on the existing leases.

Our analysis for management purposes would look something like this:

80,000 x $1.60 x 12 =	$1,536,000
Vacancy factor allowance 7-1/2%	115,200
Effective income	$1,420,000
Expenses 32%	454,656
Net operating income	$ 965,344

Upon analyzing competitive properties with the use of a rental survey, the syndicator noted that the average lease rate was $1.45 per square foot. This caused considerable unrest with the existing tenancy, since they felt that the market had changed and their rental rates adjusted accordingly. With this in mind, the $8,000,000 price had been negotiated with the seller based upon current market conditions, not what was being collected contractually. Upon acquisition of the property, the syndicator immediately adjusted the rents of the existing tenants down to $1.45 per square foot and started an aggressive marketing effort to lease the balance of the space for $1.40 per square foot. At the same time through the use of preventive maintenance devices and operating efficiencies, the expense ratio was lowered to 28% on the building. Within six months another 12,000 feet had been rented at $1.40 per square foot. The net benefits to the syndicate through this unique marketing device are shown as follows:

80,000 x $1.45 x 12 =	$1,392,000
12,000 x $1.40 x 12 =	201,600
Total gross rent	$1,593,600
Vacancy allowance 7-1/2%	119,520
Effective rent	$1,474,080
Expenses - 28%	412,740
NOI	$1,061,340

Using a 9-1/2% capitalization rate, the new NOI has caused an increase in economic value from the original purchase price of $8,000,000 to $11,200,000 (rounded). A very impressive $3.2 million increase in value! This is the type of marketing analysis and application that indicates the true worth of the syndicator to the investment group. It doesn't take too many of these examples to make true believers out of loyal investors who continue to come back with more of the same. All syndicates do not necessarily end up with happy endings. With the litigious nature of our society today, the syndicator must be sensitive to the consumer involved in the transaction. In this case the consumer is the investor. For this reason, legal concerns are high on the market place agenda. In order to address this, adequate counsel must be available.

LEGAL CONSIDERATIONS

Risk is the inevitable partner in any syndicate venture. Risk of location, the economy, Acts of God, security concerns, adverse publicity - the list goes on. Real estate is right at the height of risk investments since there are so many risk items totally out of the syndicator's control. One of the risks is that there is not enough product to go around for the investment public that wants it. One might label this the prosperity factor. There was a case of a loan broker quite a few years ago that guaranteed a 10% return to all of his trust deed investors. The money started pouring in to the point that the broker ran out of product to sell to his clients. Undaunted, he forged ahead by manufacturing trust deeds to place in clients names on properties that were either overburdened with debt or totally inaccessible. The scam worked something like this. A salesman from his firm would show a prospective client a nice little bungalow located on the west side of Los Angeles with a small matured first trust deed that they had placed a well margined second lien on the same property. It looked like a solid investment to the prospective client. Not so. In the fine print of the investment agreement signed with the loan broker, the loan broker had the right to substitute **any other trust deed in the portfolio for the initial investment**. It doesn't take a space scientist to realize what happened next. As soon as the initial investment was made, the investor's monies were then transferred to one of the worthless phony non-performing trust deeds. The eventual result of this fiasco was one of the largest bankruptcy proceedings ever held in the District Court in Los Angeles leaving the investors' group holding the proverbial "bag."

Obviously a lot of consumer oriented legislation has been placed on the books on a federal and state level as well in order to avoid investment scams such as this. If for this reason and this reason alone, the syndicator must carefully prepare all promotional materials with the objective of **full** disclosure concerning all aspects of a given investment offering. The most difficult of these disclosures to prepare is the non-specified offering which sells a concept, as opposed to a specific income property location. In this case the objective becomes the marketing device. In any prospectus the past record of the syndicator is shown with the admonition that the current investment **may not experience the success that past performance indicates.** One must still remember that, unlike personal property, real property is not portable. You can't just pick up an income property site and move it someplace else. It is fixed by location. Thus the location and its environment become a paramount issue in its acquisition. The environment economically, physically, socially and politically must be explored in detail as well as the impact it may play upon the investment itself. Since real estate investments appeal to that silent messenger of greed that lurks within, any adverse performance with the investment will usually incur the wrath of an investor.

Another area where care must be taken involves how much profit the syndicator takes from the project. There are a variety of income sources other than the stated participation as an investor where income is derived by the syndicator. This income could be derived in the form of commissions, finder's fees, management fees, consulting fees and the like in addition to return on personal investment in the project. Sometimes the balance of the investment group thinks that the return to the syndicator may be egregious. There should be **full** disclosure of the nature and extent of compensation to the syndicator spelled out with clarity on the prospectus as well as other entity formation documentation. This is where legal counsel plays an important role. Not only is legal counsel required to assure proper entity formation, but to serve as an overseer to assure that the offering meets all the regulatory tests for the investment vehicle.

Money does not just pour in automatically into any syndicate. The acquisition of the needed capital is the result of the combined effort of many. Our next chapter will discuss how it's done.

development [illegible] that intent [illegible] works within any adverse [illegible] In this investment will [illegible] wealth [illegible]

[illegible] involved [illegible] syndication [illegible] property. [illegible] all of the [illegible] by [illegible] controls [illegible] In addition to [illegible] the project [illegible] the balance of the investors [illegible] more [illegible] program. There should [illegible] nature of the amount of compensation [illegible] prospectus, as well as other [illegible] information [illegible] where legal counsel plays an important role. [illegible] to [illegible] proper entity for [illegible] the [illegible] all the [illegible]

Money [illegible] money. Our next chapter will discuss [illegible]

14
MONEY — THE GREASE THAT MAKES IT ALL WORK

In *La Question d'Argent,* Alexandre Dumas the Younger summed up the rational for the syndication process when he wrote: "Business. It's quite simple. It's other people's money. . ." Money provides the fodder for a syndicator's stable of projects by using collective bargaining power to extract the business competitive edge. Capital acquisition in a country where the annual rate of savings is at an anemic rate languishing between three and six percent in recent years becomes a bit of a feat. In essence, much of the capital obtained by the syndicator may be the result of leverage from the contributing source.

ACQUIRING CAPITAL

The syndicator to undertake any project requires seed capital to defray the necessary expenses of due diligence in aN effort to locate the appropriate investment. Once the investment has passed the rigorous testing of feasibility, running the numbers, etc., the second stage of getting the property under the syndicator's control requires still more capital. As noted in the previous chapter, one should not entertain the role of syndicator unless he/she has adequate capital to get the investment to the point that it is under the syndicator's control. This means that either 1) The syndicator has been able to acquire considerable personal wealth through inheritance or other business activities, or 2) The syndicator has sufficient equity in assets that can be leveraged to acquire the capital needed with the expectation of reimbursement upon formation of the syndicate. Another alternative is a wealthy friend who may assist the syndicator by providing the necessary capital.

In this regard, a strong argument can be made for the inclusion of a co-general partner or partners in the syndicate. This is particularly true if the promoter/syndicator feels that there may be some element in the structure of the syndicate which could be fortified by the inclusion of an associate with particular talents or capital to provide an extra element of dimension to the organization which was lacking.

Capital acquisition in any venture requires a certain degree of adroitness in order to assure success. Syndication is no different from any other form of investment vehicle. There has to be motivation not only on the part of the general partners in a limited partnership form, but incentive to the limited partner investors as well. The strongest persuasive tool on each side of the partnership pendulum is tax benefits which will maximize the return on invested capital.

With the advent of the Tax Reform Act of 1986, the allocation of tax benefits is centered around projects which will provide either break-even or some semblance of after tax income. It is important for the syndicator to determine the structure of income allocation from the project to the general partner(s), representing the promotion side and the limited partners, representing invested capital. Some limited partners have need for additional after tax income in order to shelter passive losses in some other venture. Contrarily, there may be instances where investors have a large degree of passive income that requires sheltering. Depending upon the group that the syndicator desires to attract to a given project, the allocation of benefits could change accordingly. Specialized syndications, such as the restoration of historical building sites which provide some unique tax benefits may be of interest to a select few investors, but today the focus is on reportable after tax income. Usually investors already have sufficient tax losses resulting from passive investments that need some passive income protection. In certain instances the general partner might be viewed as an opponent by the limited partners, since the suspicion on the part of the latter is that the general partner will take all the benefits leaving what few scraps of income and appreciation that are left for the limited partners to divide. If this suspicion persists, the general partner/syndicator has failed in the assigned task of properly forming the syndicate.

In analyzing the various types of real estate investments suitable for a syndication venture, the developmental/rehabilitation form of project has the least appeal from an investment standpoint. The reason for this is very simple. Income-producing property, on the main, in this country has been the victim of 1980s oversupply creating a vast inventory of high vacancy levels in its wake. Higher building costs, fueled by a rash of regulatory charges, environmental concerns, plan rejections by local building officials, etc., which add appreciably to the cost of developmental projects create unrealistic rental levels not reflective of marketplace demand. For this reason alone, existing buildings hold a greater appeal than any form of developmental project. Even more appealing is the availability of existing structures which comprise part of the real estate owned portfolios of financial institutions or their regulatory liquidators, such as the F.D.I.C. and the Resolution Trust Corporation. Within these portfolios are billions of dollars worth of commercial/industrial structures scattered throughout the land. Identification of specific geographic areas of opportunity, negotiation of a proper price reflective of current cash flow and getting control of the property is essential to the syndicator in order to acquire capital to complete the acquisition.

Even if the syndicator finds the ideal location, has properly negotiated the price, and tied up the property, this isn't assurance that the balance of the capital can be acquired to complete the purchase. Several elements must be present in order that the syndicate works:

- Prior track record - The investors will want to know how successful the syndicator has been on past projects.
- Reputation - Is there a proverbial "skeleton in the closet" of the syndicator that will serve to drive away investors? Integrity is not a dirty word in the business of syndication. Investors not only want it - they demand it!
- Background and experience - It's a tough world out there for a tyro syndicator. Investors want to know that the promoter has sufficient aptitude involving the type of property in question, whether it be retail, industrial, office space, residential income or whatever, before they plunk hard earned dollars into the subject project. Inexperience is a hard sell.
- Marketing expertise - If the project is not properly packaged, it is an investor turn-off. The proper use of media, finders, broker-dealers and the like is essential to capital acquisition.
- Being an effective communicator - Don't leave investors out in the dark after the acquisition capital arrives. By keeping the investment group fully apprised of syndicate activities, the syndicator has a method of assuring possible future investment by the limited partnership group in future ventures. Of extreme importance is accurate reporting of the financial results of the investment. This is not only important for tax reporting purposes, but to indicate to the investor how effective was the utilization of this capital in meeting personal investment objectives. Since communication is a two-way street, the syndicator should be fully

aware of these investment objectives in order to properly structure the tax benefits of cash flow, appreciation or, in some cases, tax losses.

Fully convinced of the appropriateness of the project, investors create the limited partnership. Now it's up to the syndicator to apply the capital in such a fashion as to not only meet personal reward expectations, but to also meet or exceed the investment expectations of the limited partnership group. To this objective, the problem of proper capital allocation needs to be addressed.

ALLOCATING CAPITAL

In dealing with a specific project, the allocation of capital is fairly spelled out in the prospectus and limited partnership document. It is somewhat different in the case of the non-specific project or "blind pool." Here the question of capital allocation is high on the agenda of investor priorities. When selling a concept, capital accumulation takes on a higher degree of difficulty. This is normally the province of a seasoned syndicator who has undertaken a number of specific projects with a modicum of success in the past. The novice will fall by the wayside if the initial syndication device used is a blind pool. It's like betting a horse to win in its first race. The odds are not in the favor of the syndicator or the investor. One has to prove that the area of investment is one where the syndicator has a certain degree of familiarity **with proven success.**

Today the office building market is replete with vacancies throughout the major urban areas of our country ranging from the concrete canyons of New York to midwest's Chicago to the groaning economy of Los Angeles. Even in this seemingly dismal world there is a ray of investment opportunity. Income property with reduced occupancy levels when purchased at price levels based upon existing occupancy can provide a win-win situation for both the syndicator and the investor as well. The key to this success, albeit fraught with potential risk, is the proper identification of economic opportunity in special situations. Several specific areas of the country offer this type of opportunity. These are the areas that syndicators study to determine if there are buildings which meet an exacting criteria of return not only to the promoters, but the investors as well. In order to illustrate, let's take an example of an area of opportunity where there is future potential. Take, for example, the city of Houston, Texas, once referred to as the "foreclosure capital of the United States." In the early 1990s, Houston has emerged as an area of new economic opportunity. Upon completion of a feasibility study, the syndicator is convinced that a well located office structure in Houston can prove to be a mutually rewarding investment from a promotional aspect as well as for the investment group to be formed for acquisition purposes. Furthermore, a financial institution has an office building in its portfolio which has 75% occupancy in its 250,000 square feet of net rentable space. The average rental rate based upon leases which average a remaining term of 7 years, is $1.75 per square foot/month. The syndicator desires to structure a project which can provide a double digit yield to the investment group in addition to appreciation potential made possible through aggressive space marketing using proven property management expertise. The project acquisition might be structured like this:

Property Analysis:

187,500 square feet x $1.75 x 12 =	
Annual rents of	$3,937,500
Vacancy allowance = 10%	393,750
Effective income	$3,543,750
Expenses - 35% (rounded) -	
Includes property mgmt.	1,243,750
Net Operating Income	$2,300,000

Through the negotiating process with the lender, the syndicator by posing the argument that some of the tenants may not have the financial ability to complete the terms of their lease obligations, has negotiated purchase combined with financing terms as follows:

Acquisition price	$20,000,000
Equity Requirement	4,000,000
Purchase Money Lien	16,000,000

The lender/seller is willing to take 8% interest only for the first year, converting to a 29 year amortization and a ten year call for the purchase money obligation. The one year interest only period will allow the syndicator to effect certain upgrades to the building with an estimated cost of $1 million and to attract additional tenants. This means that the syndicate needs to provide $5 million consisting of equity dollars plus rehabilitation monies. The syndicator is providing professional building management services, is acting as the broker in the transaction and will cover all costs of due diligence, consultancy services and closing expense. For the subject services, the syndicator will be taking a 20% participation in profits with the investment group sharing the balance. An analysis of the first year's earnings on the project would be as follows:

Note: the replacement value of the 295,000 gross square foot structure is $25 million.

NOI	$2,300,000
Debt service 1st year	1,280,000
Cash flow available to partnership	$1,020,000
Share to general partner = 20%, or	$ 204,000
Share to limited partners = 80%, or	$ 816,000

Return on limited partner capital =
$816,000 divided by $5,000,000, or 16.32%!

Other tax benefits based upon 31.5 years depreciation of the $25 million replacement value is $793,650, sheltering a majority of the NOI, thus significantly enhancing investor return from a tax standpoint. Considering that the due diligence, closing expense on the part of the syndicator to be $500,000, the return on risk is slightly in excess of 40%. The syndicator return does not take into account the various charges for services made to the partnership. This type of capital allocation would represent a win-win situation. By the time that the first year is over, hopefully property management efforts will have reached the point that the increase in annual debt service to $1,327,680 (rounded) will be more than offset by additional tenancy. At that point the syndicate would then have the additional advantage of equity build-up from amortization.

A note of caution: In certain instances, especially where additional working capital may be required **after** acquisition, there may be some partnerships where limited partners can be liable for additional assessments, based upon their percentage contribution, for supplemental capital contributions. Syndication documentation should be examined carefully by prospective investors in these cases in order to properly assess their investment strategy and the risk attendant thereto.

MAXIMIZING RETURN TO THE SYNDICATE

As the above sample indicates, investment rewards can be substantial just based upon cash flow alone. The real bang from the investment buck comes in the area of appreciation if the syndicate has "bought right." Take the case of our 75% occupied office building noted above. It is now year three of the partnership ownership of the property. The nature of the project has changed considerably. Through the use of judicious property management techniques, the yield to the investment group has improved substantially. Not only has the rehabilitation expense enhanced the appearance of the building and built up tenant morale which had suffered considerably under institutional ownership, the occupancy percentage has improved dramatically. Although the average rent level of $1.75 per square foot has not been maintained due to market conditions, 90% of the building is now leased at an average monthly rental of $1.55 per square foot. Conversely, the expenses, including management fees, have been reduced to 31% of effective income. The analysis of value at that time, which represents a potential acquisition price thus becomes:

225,000 square feet rented @$1.55 p.s.f./month x 12 =	$4,185,000
10% vacancy allowance - purchaser fudge factor =	418,500
Effective income	$3,766,500
Expenses = 31%	1,167,615
NOI	$2,598,885

Using a 9-1/2% capitalization rate, the buyer would be willing to pay $27,400,000 (rounded) for the property. A fifteen percent increase in occupancy is equivalent to appreciation in value over $7 million in the three year period.

In order to see if this analysis is fair, how would the approximate $12 million down payment on the part of the buyer fare as far as return on equity is concerned? By subtracting the annual debt service requirement of $1,327,680 from the NOI, a net after debt service cash flow of $1,271,205 is available leaving a respectable 10.59% return on equity.

It can clearly seen by example that proper utilization of effective property management techniques by the syndicator can provide a significant contribution to the value of the investment. Property management is vital to maximizing both yield in the form of cash flow plus additions to capital in the form of appreciation upon disposition of the investment.

The selection of the property management team is probably one of the most critical decisions that the syndicator makes in the overall supervision of the syndicate. Ultimate rewards to all participants hinge on this critical decision. In the selection of a property manager it must be borne in mind that the property manager must be one who is totally familiar with the nuances of the market. Don't hire a Los Angeles property management firm to oversee a Houston property. Local people know the territory better. In the same way feasibility studies are performed better by personnel closer and more connected to the subject property area than personnel coming in from another area.

It's been a long journey in our pursuit of the syndication process. Our final chapter will serve to summarize the lessons provided in the prior text.

15
MAKING THE DREAM HAPPEN

One has to return to Coleridge to grasp the essence of syndication which lies in the recesses of imagination as quoted from an 1817 publication of *Biographia Literia,* when he noted: "[Imagination] reveals itself in the balance of reconciliation of opposite or discordant qualities; of sameness, with difference; of the general, with the concrete; the idea, with the image; the individual, with the representative; the sense of novelty and freshness, with the old and familiar objects; a more than usual state of emotion, with more than usual order; judgment ever to awake and steady self-possession, with enthusiasm and feeling profound or vehement; and while it blends and harmonizes the natural and artificial, still subordinates art to nature; the manner to the matter; and our admiration of the poet to our sympathy with poetry. . ." Powerful words. In many ways the fuel of imagination sparks the everyday activities of the syndicator. Within imaginations' profound scanning of the scene, foresight beyond that of others holds rewards to be shared with others through the resulting syndicate. No person is a self-contained island. Intradependence is a pragmatic fact of our every day existence. We have to rely on others to complete the assigned task.

THE IMPORTANCE OF COORDINATION

How many recall the story of the blindfolded men who were asked to touch different parts of an elephant and describe what they perceived? The answers to the question posed were as varied as the number of participants. The syndicator cannot operate with the same sort of blindfolded tactics. His goals and objectives must be clearly stated and understood by all parties involved in the process. Whether these goals are spelled out formally in a mission statement or within the prospectus of an offering, somewhere they must be aired and fully understood by all involved. It is not a simple process to identify investment opportunities that will attract the capital essential to fulfill imagination's dreamscape. The syndicator must deal with a variety of entities in the quest for adequate information upon which to base an objective decision. Some of the attributes that must exist within the syndicator to make this happen are:

- Being a good reader - Numerous magazines and government publications provide clues as to the economic well being either locally or throughout the nation. Being an avid reader, the syndicator will identify these clues and act upon them.

- Being a good listener - Rather than looking at the false echo of personal preference, the syndicator should keep an open mind with respect to others who may have a different perspective on the project. The cadre of consultants required on a given project are:

  1. Real estate brokers - Local brokers have a better handle on San Diego, California; Houston, Texas; Orlando, Florida; San Francisco, California; Seattle, Washington; ad infinitum than a syndicator that just got off the plane from New York or Los Angeles. Listen to the local people sifting out the real estate puffery to ascertain the real estate opportunity that may be lingering underneath all the fluff.

  2. Appraisers and feasibility study preparers - Sometimes feasibility may be undertaken as part of the appraisal process going beyond the usual rent surveys for in-depth analysis of economical aspects of a given project. If a study is required of a given area, many Big 6 accounting firms have established special consultancys for the purpose of feasibility studies taking on geographic areas, as opposed to a given project location. The more independent and objective the feasibility source, the more reliable the information tends to be. Syndicators should try to avoid feasibility studies undertaken by those who might have a vested interest in producing a favorable opinion concerning an area.

  3. Attorneys - Lawyers with S.E.C. and documentation experience are preferable over general practitioners who will only bill the syndicator on the basis of using this assignment as a learning experience. You need specialists, so deal with specialists.

4. Accountants - Since financial reporting, regulatory reporting requirements and tax aspects comprise a large portion of syndicate activity, it is important that financial results be accurately depicted. Don't foist this duty off on the local public accountant who does bookkeeping and tax work for small businesses. The syndicate requires accounting assistance that is totally familiar with the particular nuances that real estate investment represents including the specific tax laws that impact the process.

5. Media consultants - If the syndicator ever expects to get the project off the ground, there is a definite requirement that a consultant be engaged who can identify the target market, get the message to potential investors within this market, and provide the effective exposure the project needs to enable a successful partnership formation to acquire the desired project.

6. Broker-dealers - If the project is to be a registered security and a market is being established through the brokerage community, don't select a broker-dealer who is not familiar with this process or does not have sufficient contact with clients interested in this type of investment. It will cause a mutual waste of time and frustration on the part of both parties.

7. Printers - The placement of a partnership offering requires not only careful preparation of the paperwork involved from its inception, it also requires the use of printers to replicate the paperwork to get it into the hands of regulatory authorities and potential clients as well. Proof reading skills and absolute accuracy in content far outweigh the advantage of speed. Any mis-wording in a prospectus could create problems with regulatory authorities.

8. Regulatory authorities - Syndicators have to deal on both the federal and state level with registered securities for a public offering. The process can be a smooth one if the proper consultants have been engaged to process the paperwork with these agencies. In the case of a private offering, exemption from the necessity of registration still has to be ascertained. Again, the use of expert consultants if the syndicator does not have this background can eliminate any potential enforcement actions resulting from non-compliance with regulatory matters.

9. Sellers - Syndicators must be adroit in negotiation skills. Failure to have the alternative approaches needed during the heat of negotiation can lose a particularly favorable transaction.

The syndicator must have the flexibility to be able to adapt during the give and take of the process. To conduct activities otherwise would result in not project available at all.

10. Closing personnel - All the negotiation in the world is meaningless unless the transaction is consummated. In the case of a syndication, two types of closing are required. The initial step is to serve as a holding escrow for the accumulation of the funds necessary to form the limited partnership followed by the second step of transferring these monies into the purchase escrow for the identified project. Close supervision of this process by the syndicator is extremely important, since the subject matter of the offering represents the result.

11. Property management - Upon acquisition, this phase represents the blossoming of limited partnership investment into a full blown success or a withered failure. It is therefore necessary to pick the type of property management personnel who can deliver results through proper attention to service with the objective of maximizing yield and investment appreciation available to the partnership.

Through the process of coordinating the efforts of all of these various elements requiring interface, the syndicator earns the expected return from a given process. This is exactly the regimen which must be undertaken to assure any modicum of success. Coupled with the realization that coordinative efforts are important, management skills of the syndicator immediately come under scrutiny by the investment group. If the management skills are evident by a course record, this does not become an issue. In a new syndication venture, the syndicator must show that the necessary management expertise has been attained through efforts in another area. Typical of this would be one who has previous experience in related fields, such as the securities industry where a successful career had been previously established. If, however, the syndicator cannot prove the business acumen to effect proper interface with all of the elements that might exist in a given situation, investor confidence level would be minimal.

When dealing in a developmental partnership, the syndicator takes on a whole new set of relationships to coordinate ranging from planning departments to architects to contractors as well as all of the other parties needed to consummate the transaction. In the final analysis, the investor makes the ultimate decision as to whether the transaction moves forward or collapses from lack of support.

CONCERN FOR DUE DILIGENCE

If the syndicator has not taken the precaution of due diligence, the potential for success in a given venture ebbs considerably. Not only must the potential of a given investment be adequate to whet the syndicator's appetite, there is also a group, possibly not yet identified, which serves to provide the necessary capital to acquire the project that needs to know that the homework lesson needed to serve as a means of risk reduction has been performed. In the case of real estate, a very heterogeneous type of commodity, this means that proper studies have been performed regionally with due regard for national and international economically impacting activities. An example of how international events can impact domestic investment is the maquiladora program in Mexico that could impact cities in the United States that are adjacent to Mexican counterparts where American manufacturers have located their facilities. Another international situation which can affect domestic economies is a difference in currency exchange rates which might give this country a trade advantage over competing countries, thus stimulating manufacturing.

The heart of due diligence lies in the study of a particular region which has been identified as an area of economic opportunity. Opportunity is only as good as the inventory of available real estate investments in the area. If no income property is for sale, occupancy levels are hovering around 100% and rent levels are high, no investment opportunity exists, since, cyclically, the only way for value to go is down. In order for an investment to make sense, the syndicator has to look for something with upward mobility, such as an office, retail, residential or industrial income investment where occupancy level is not at its maximum allowing upward mobility in future rent income. Due diligence would then center around this type of property search. Location of the subject property is critical. Office building investments should be centered around locations which offer long term potential as ideal for office use. Secondary neighborhood office investments have a certain degree of vulnerability.

The syndicator must be true to the overall plan or mission statement for the enterprise. If one specializes in office buildings, don't go venturing into the retail world without having someone on staff who is familiar with this particular type of property. That's why Ernie Hahn stuck to regional shopping centers all of his life. That's why the Tishman family stuck with office structure development and ownership. Each figures out their own particular niche in the investment pecking order. It's a matter of personal choice. When the syndicator finds the right niche, it's probably a good policy to stick with what you know. That doesn't mean that one still doesn't need a little help along the way. Proper investigation and seeking of competent counsel is a form of investment insurance not available from the Hartford, Connecticut denizens.

CONCLUDING REMARKS

As the reader can observe, there is a considerable body of knowledge required for placement of any syndicate. It is not something to be undertaken by the tender hearted. The syndicator has to have turtle shell determination combined with blind faith about the potential of any project undertaken. To do anything less would be a foolhardy venture. Real estate syndication is the ultimate adventure in risk taking. The sting of headlines that screamed during the 1980s of the hapless ventures undertaken by syndicators still leaves a bitter taste in the mouths of investors. The confusion of The Tax Reform Act of 1986 has dissuaded many investors of sticking their capital toe into the icy waters of income-property investment as a result. Syndication now has the additional role of building up the confidence level of the investing public.

The tragedy of the 1980s, however, has produced an interesting opportunity for the 1990s investing public. With the vast array of unsafe and unsound lending practices that were rife during the prior decade, many well located, but over leveraged properties were unceremoniously dropped in the laps of financial institutions for disposition as real estate owned. One has to surmise that if the lender ends up with the property, it was probably overburdened with debt. In a majority of cases, that was exactly what happened.

Regulatory pressure is then exerted on the financial institution to dispose of this unwanted real estate owned. Because of this pressure, institutions are forced to cut deals that they would not normally expect in order to cut their losses, lick their wounds, and go on. For this reason there are investment vehicles available which can prove to be most attractive to investors. Several examples of negotiations which are possible have been used throughout this text.

As an assistance to the reader, considerable documentation and examples are included in the Appendix with regard to formation, particularly of the limited partnership device. These examples are provided as a means of illustration and should not be considered as a means of advice with reference to addressing the formulation of a partnership to address a particular syndication situation. The distribution of profits and the percentage share between the syndicator and the limited partners will vary by the situation and the needs of the various parties in the transaction.

If this text inspires the reader to participate as a promoter/syndicator or as an investor in a limited partnership, such participation should be tempered with the application of the three "P's" in dealing with any syndication problem:

- **Preparation** - Do the homework necessary to reach an acceptable comfort level.

- **Prudence** - Deal with risks that are acceptable — not outlandish.

- **Pragmatism** - Always get your feet down to ground level after your head's been up in the clouds when dealing with a particular investment opportunity. Sometimes the wings of imagination need to be clipped with the sheer starkness of reality. One has to deal with real world issues in a real world setting. Alchemy in real estate investments is not a satisfactory approach in the eyes of a real estate investor. Don't undertake a project which doesn't have the income potential to make it worth while.

Whatever your quest for the elusive butterfly of profit — may you have unsurpassed joy in its pursuit.

[illegible]

[illegible]

- [illegible]

- [illegible]

- [illegible]

[illegible]

INDEX

A

A. G. Edwards & Sons 136
accountant 63
accounting, 78
acquisition instruments 258
Acts of God 358
affordability index 75
amortization 66
appreciation 59, 66, 346

B

Beverly Hills, City of 6
Black's Law Dictionary 143
broker, real estate 61

C

Cal FIRPTA 63
Cal-Vet 137
California 85, 145, 177, 179, 194, 201, 202, 338, 343
"Canadian Rollover" 134
Canoga Park, California 343
capital efficiency 58
capital,
accumulation of 43, 89, 336
acquisition of 362
Chaplin, Charlie 337
Chapter 7 proceedings 79
Chicago 85, 180
Chrysler Tower 84
Clinton administration 348
Clinton, President 75
Coleridge, Samuel Taylor 53, 369
commercial banks 133, 138
commercial finance companies 136
consultants, 65, 351
hiring of 354
types 355
consultation services 67
Corporate Securities Law of 1968, California 199
corporation,
by-laws 149
defined 143
types 144
corporations 143
Corporations Code 175
California 145, 177
Crown family of Chicago 191

D

de facto corporation 145
de jure corporation 145
Delaware 145
Department of Corporations 199, 1-350
Department of Housing and Urban Development 137
Department of Real Estate, California 201
Des Moines 180
Detroit 349
development property 354
Dickens, Charles 253
documentation,
considerations 193

due diligence 373
Dumas, Alexander 361

E

economic factors 72
Empire State Building 84, 180, 191, 340, 353
environmental legislation 76
environmental review 68
escrow, 62, 355
account 202
holding 89
loan 89

F

F.D.I.C. 363
financial analysis 79
financing, 137
seller-based 136
FIRREA 48, 134
flagship 85
flagship property 84
Florida 73, 341, 349
Friedman, Milton 61
future use review 68

G

Galbraith, John Kenneth 143, 353
General Motors 349

H

Helmsley, Harry 84, 180, 191, 335, 340, 353
Hippocrates 46
hucksterism 56
Hughes Aircraft 343

I

Illustrations
5-1, 90
5-2, 117
7-1, 146
7-2, 150
8-1, 184
8-2, 185
8-3, 186
8-4, 187
8-5, 188
9-1, 204
9-2, 217
10-1, 259
improved income property 354
income 66
industrial buildings 49
insurance companies 138, 189
integrity 139
Internal Revenue Service 69, 183
International Business Machines 343
investment goals 54
IRS 193

J

Japanese corporations 88
joint ventures 177

K

Kennedy, John Fitzgerald 83, 88
Kentucky 349
King, Larry 87

L

legal considerations 358
Legal requirements 253
legal restraints 56
legal review 67

leverage 81, 83, 89, 133
life insurance companies 134
liquidity 54, 60, 339
locational factors 84
Los Angeles 180, 368
Los Angeles Times 338

M

magnification, principle of 50
manage, defined 345
management 346
maquiladora program 373
Marshall, Alfred 71
Maslow, Abraham Harold 74
Maugham, Somerset 133
mission statement, 346, 349, 373
  example 57
money, 133
  sources of 133
mortgage bankers 136
mortgage brokers and "hard money" lenders 137
mutual savings banks 134

N

NASAA, 254, 256
  guidelines 257
NASD 335
National Association of Securities Dealers 202
negotiation, 57, 68, 81, 88
  techniques 87
New Jersey 135
New York 85, 135, 180
Newark 180
North American Securities Admin. Assoc, Inc. 200

O

offering 257, 351
offerings,
  public 258, 338
office buildings 48
Orlando, Florida 73, 341
Otay Mesa 343

P

Panell, Kerr, Foerster & Co. 78
partnership, 195
  certificate 175
  defined 175
  general 175
  limited 139, 176, 200, 354, 364, 374
  limited, defined 176
  limited, shares 339
  limited. tax structure 190
partnership offerings,
  limited 254
partnerships 44, 183
  general 44
  limited 44, 350
passive income 190
past performance 358
Philadelphia 85
planning and zoning 76
political atmosphere 77
political factors 75
political interface 77
population statistics 73
pragmatism 375
preparation 375
price 80, 81
private offering 200
project analysts 63
property management 356
Proposition 13 194
prudence 375
Prudential 191
public offering 199-200
public relations firm 342
purchase,

lease with option to 354
straight option to 354
purchase contract 88
purchasing power 73

R

Real Estate Invesment Trust 183
Real Estate Investment Trusts 45, 178, 336
real estate owned 134
regulators 69
regulatory concerns 69
regulatory pressure 374
REIT, 139, 178
defined 178
rent control 75
residential income property 47
Resolution Trust Corporation 363
risk 86, 358
risk factors 202

S

safety 54, 60, 339
San Diego 343
San Diego Union 338
San Francisco Chronicle and Examiner 338
Saturn 349
Schine, J. Myer 180
Schumpeter, John Alois 43
SEC 199, 341, 370
Guide 5 200, 254, 257
Regulation A, 201
Regulation D 199, 201
Rules 201
Securities Act of 1933 199
Securities and Exchange Commission, 254, 350
Rule 147 199
See also SEC
securitization 135
service industries 74
shelf register 340
shopping centers 47
social factors 78
Society of Industrial Realtors 62, 84
special purpose properties 49
sponsor,
financial statement 255
indemnification of 256
"sun belt" 72
syndicate, 85, 141, 190, 352-353, 362, 374
definition 43
exposure of 139
forming 195
maximizing return 366
necessary elements for success 363
syndicates 180, 345
syndication, 51, 84, 177, 196, 369
arguments for 58
developmental 86
documentation 366
group 87
guidelines 336
negative factors 59
offering circular 257
process 253
Wien-Helmsley 191
syndications 180
syndication 69, 71-72, 77, 79, 81, 83, 85, 87, 183, 189-190, 197, 201, 203, 339-340, 342, 344, 349, 351, 369
acquiring capital 361
analytical sense 56
background 53
compensation 359
documentation 193
econometrics 55
integrity 60
investment team 61

leadership qualities 347
management acumen 57
necessary attributes 370
opportunities 59
organizational acumen 54
problem solving 348
project feasibility 55
property management strategies 341
real estate sense 55
role 196
seed capital 356
straight option to purchase 354
syndicators,
documentation procedures 350

T

1031 tax deferred exhange 180
tax impact 202
Tax Reform Act of 1986 46, 183, 350, 362, 374
tax shelter 66
taxes, 183
accounting and 56
implications of 194
Tenancy in Common 45, 136
Tenessee 349
thrifts 134, 138
time management 58
Tishman family 83
TRA 189-190, 350
See also, Tax Reform Act of 1986
transaction, sample, 50-51, 64-65, 79, 81-82, 367
effective property management 341
equity buy down interest rate 139
loan to value advance 135
project acquisition 365
property management 357
sale-leaseback 191
straight option to purchase 354
Trump, Donald 84
Tucson, Arizona 343

U

Uniform General Partnership Act 175
Uniform Limited Partnership Act 177, 335
UPS 344

V

value added 84
von Hayek, Friederich August 345

W

Webster 78, 345
Wien, Larry 180, 191
Wilson, Woodrow 195
Woolf, Bob 87
World Trade Towers 84

Y

yield 54, 59, 133, 339-340, 346, 365